B&T
$4.95

W9-ADS-113

BEING and DOING

MARCUS G. RASKIN

BEING
and
DOING

Beacon Press   Boston

Wingate College Library

Copyright © 1971 by Marcus G. Raskin
First published as a Beacon paperback in 1973
by arrangement with the author
Beacon Press books are published under the auspices
of the Unitarian Universalist Association
Published simultaneously in Canada by Saunders of Toronto, Ltd.
All rights reserved under International and Pan-American
Copyright Conventions
Printed in the United States of America

9 8 7 6 5 4 3 2 1

Library of Congress Cataloging in Publication Data

Raskin, Marcus G
    Being and doing.
    Based on the Campbell lectures in Christian faith and morality
at Michigan State University in 1967, sponsored by the Dept. of
Higher Education of the National Council of Churches and the National
Campus Ministry Association.
    Includes bibliographical references.
    1. Political participation — United States. 2. United States —
Politics and government — 1945. 3. United States — Social conditions —
1945– I. Title
[JK271.R25 1973] 320.9′73′092 72–8654
ISBN 0–8070–4385–0

To My Wife,
BARBARA RASKIN

069226

Acknowledgments

My colleagues and friends engaged me in continuous dialogue and criticism on the questions raised in *Being and Doing* without knowing it. Each one sustained me intellectually and emotionally during a difficult time in my life. Each contributed to my understanding. Each in his own way is a master scholar-craftsman and activist.

I want to thank especially the Fellows of the Institute for Policy Studies: Gar Alperovitz, master builder, who understood my intention and meaning; Richard Barnet, savant who opened up the national security state for all of us to see and shared the vision of radical reconstruction; Jeremy Brecher, whose wisdom goes far beyond his age; Robb Burlage, a master of policy analysis and policy action; Ivanhoe Donaldson, whose courage and analysis strengthened the purpose of my work; Paul Goodman, Cherif Guellal, who quietly taught all of us the ironies and potentialities of revolution; Marv Holloway, whose masterful analysis invariably instilled doubts in us; Walter Hopps, leading cultural historian and modern art critic; Christopher Jencks, master social scientist who helps us to see things as they are; Milton Kotler, master scholar and rhetorician, who reminded us of other traditions and our own roots; Michael Maccoby, master psychoanalyst, who came and taught us that there was an inside to people; Leonard Rodberg, whose humane commitment and supreme knowledge of technology helped me to know the limits of it; Frank Smith, who instinctively knew what the rest of us had to learn; Ralph Stavins, master political scientist; Sue Thrasher, who came to learn, stayed to administer, and left to build; Joe Turner, a master of education and social philosophy; and Arthur Waskow, keeper of the prophetic tradition, who insists on demanding from us the best that is in us.

Each book is a cooperative effort. It requires the work of people who assist in the most specific ways; they help in the research, in typing and secretarial matters. I had special help from Michael Athay, Mark Sommer, and Barry Weisberg, students of mine in the beginning years of the Institute. My assistants during this period were Jacqueline Lushin, whose memory I cherish; and Janice Hackman. Her insight, resourcefulness, and understanding made the final completion of the manuscript possible. I also wish to thank Tina Smith and, especially, Bethany Weidner, who assisted me in the last stage of the manuscript.

My thanks to Daniel Bernstein, Michael Gellert, Phil Stern, Leni Stern, Ed Janss, the Janss Foundation, Sam Rubin, Fiona Rust, Peter Weiss, Cora Weiss for their support, insight, friendship and participation in reconstruction.

In the spring of 1967, I gave the Campbell Lectures in Christian faith and morality to national campus ministers and chaplains, out of which *Being and Doing* grew. I thank Messrs. Lovell, Noble, and McNeur for their patience in waiting for the manuscript. From time to time I have lectured at various universities and political groups on questions raised in *Being and Doing.* This experience has been invaluable to me. I also wish to thank John J. Simon, Jean Pohoryles and Beryl Levitsky, editors at Random House; and finally, my children, Erika Raskin, Jamin Raskin, and Noah Raskin.

It is the old who stand on the shoulders of the young to see what is happening.

Contents

Introduction

When a body politic can no longer deal with the simple, the human and the obvious; when its structure is beyond human scale and dimension, and people believe that there is no human or natural necessity that causes things and relationships to be ordered or authorized as they are, the body politic and the institutions within it first wobble and then collapse.

The process of collapse is Promethean. It forces new modes of thought and action upon those of us who want to do more than dodge the falling bricks or live in the rubble of a deteriorating political structure. It forces those who do not identify themselves with the collapse to rummage through the ash-heap of history to seek ideas and projects which have been needlessly discarded after power struggles in which the better ideas, and the groups who were humane in their analysis and action, were destroyed or submerged.

The collapse of the body politic forces us to think theoretically and act practically on the openings that are thus created. We are obliged to ask what is the nature of the body politic that is collapsing and to inquire into the type of body politic that it can become, within the limits of human nature and the present development of our politics and technology. I have chosen to call such an investigation an attempt to develop a "philosophy of reconstruction" in politics and public policy. The task of such a philosophy is to break the bounds of absurdity—an absurdity created by institutions, expressed in official ideologies and reflected in much of man's inner life. The reconstructive aspect of a philosophy that overcomes absurdity concerns itself with questions of shared associative authority and a politics beyond violence and magic.

The words and ideas that I use will at first seem strange, but I hope that through my explanation, and the reader's own intuitive senses where my explanation fails, he will see their utility and applicability. This may require a somewhat different use of language. I am attempting to engage the reader in a dialogue that goes beyond the mere presenting of conceptions. It is intended to promote what the Chinese call the "attitude of civilizing actions." It is my view that at this stage in the philosophy of reconstruction, our projects and our language are meant to create and deepen that mood and direction. In this process our plans and attempts to see things in new ways mean the development of a kind of language which creates an emblematic mood. C. W. Mills, in commenting on this use of language, states that "This language does not furnish an instrument for analysis, but rather channels all thought into a sort of organ of conduct."[1]

We are not relieved of the tasks of analysis and planning that are to prove themselves in practice. Instead, a new analysis can begin only when we develop a *mood* of thought which sees things in new ways and expects actions to flow from seeing things in those new ways.

An example: Ideas appear first as metaphors and exaggerations because they may break the "objective" view that we have of ourselves. During the cold war it would have seemed shockingly impertinent to think of America as a colony. When I suggested that the Vietnam war and the civil rights struggle were related because white "citizens" were powerless in such public matters as foreign policy, and black "citizens" were also powerless, thus showing evidence of Americans as colonized, the notion was put down as a metaphor. Now it appears that the idea of America as a colonized society is neither impertinent nor metaphorical. It is closer to a realistic description of what the

American body politic is than can otherwise be imagined. This is no surprise.

Once Americans lift their ideological, linguistic mask, they see that they are living in a pyramidal political, social and economic structure. It does not differ—except in potentiality—from the way nations have been governed since their emergence as a political form. When it is said that nations operate so that power rests in the hands of the few acting in institutionally defined roles who decide for the many, some very harsh judgments are being made about the way people "spend," "rent" or "live" their lives. The implication is that the many live their lives for the few, and political and economic institutions operate in such a way as to make this situation either bearable (liberal authoritarian) or painful (totalitarian). Whether the institutions are socialist or capitalist, the pyramidal structure operates to reinforce the pyramid and the sense of living the life of the hierarchic other.

But as in all things, besides the dynamic there is the contradiction. There are real needs and desires which are not met in the colonized situation. People look for a way out. We might imagine sleepwalkers who wake up because they bump into physical objects which cause them pain and sensation. In turn, they discover that they are hungry, their bladder is filled, or nobody listens to them as they cry out in pain. So it is that the led, tortured and commanded are finding that the commanders, torturers and leaders are empirically unable to fill anyone's needs, desires and impulses, either in the material sense or in the sense of politics and spirituality.

This failure is now recognized, and the pyramidal authority is collapsing. What role-respecting pope would cry in order to get people to accept the magic of his authority on the issue of birth control? As Simone Weil has pointed out, ". . . every new development for the last three centuries has brought men closer to a state of affairs in which absolutely nothing would be recognized in the whole world as possessing a claim to obedience except the authority of the State."² As I suggest in the Violence Colony, even that claim to obedience is now falling away, giving man the chance to redefine authority and legitimacy. Each year we find more people who have been living their lives as part of the pyramidal structure discovering the nasty fact that their human needs are not being met. But discovery that one is on the wrong road does not tell the one who is lost what the right road is. On the other hand, such personal discovery by large enough "groups" enables us to describe the collapsing body politic in a language and analytic style that would not have been acceptable when the individual was totally lost or when most elements of the society were totally in a sleepwalking trance. It now becomes possible to analyze and suggest a series of decolonizing activities and reconstructions which allow for the reconstruction of the American political structure.

Pyramidal authority in the American body politic can be seen in four overlapping colonies. Each colony, through its dynamics and processes, hollows out man and objectifies him for the purpose of running the colony. Each colony enforces the others and is reciprocally dependent on them. Conversely, change in each one has a powerful ripping effect on the other three. While such colonies are physically and spiritually destroying, there are now long-term forces which emerge from the colonies individually and in relation to each other which contradict their debilitating effects.

The most crucial and dangerous colony is the Violence Colony, where specialists in the techniques of violence are given power by those at the top of the pyramid. Ultimately, the violence specialists tear all mediating influence away and the nation-state stands exposed for all to see, its rulers using the rest of the society as their hostage. Such a situation cannot last because the hostage sees no advantage to himself once he is aware of what is going on. He will see no reason to accept his transformation to hostage or prisoner, where he might have thought he was a citizen. In America the Violence Colony grew out of technology, anticommunist paranoia and a subsidized socialist system of corporate entities (a crackpot Keynesianism). Although hardly visible, the operation of the Violence Colony is the central fact of human relations in American society. It dictates the contours of the political structure and announces that no social contract exists.

In the Plantation Colony, people find that they work at meaningless and unreal jobs to obtain things that they are led to want. Yet their work does not help them satisfy human needs. This same colony—reflected in its supply and demand of work as well as its supply and demand of "goods"—sustains a pool of unemployed or underpaid with a surfeit of consumptionist goals. As Veblen pointed out, what it is that people work at has little or nothing to do with their needs or the needs of the community, or the instincts for creativity and artisanship. It has to do with profit and totem status. The long-term effect of such a structure of economics is to force people to recognize the meaninglessness of their work. Whether for reasons of surplus or meaninglessness in work, the employed find it a *necessity* to control their *work* time. They choose their own work groups and insist that they intend to control their lives in the work situation. The corporate structure and its values are forced to change through the process of workers' participation and control in a reconstituted social contract as applied to the work situation.

The third is the Channeling Colony which establishes, through the schools, achievement standards and orders of privilege and merit for young people. The most signif-

icant short-term purpose of the school is to break people
in to accepting authority structures. Its inmates learn to
become bored, user-used and hollowed out. If anything
is actually learned in the schools it is the specialization
which buttresses pyramidal authority. On the other hand,
because the American ideology of education assumes the
right—indeed the obligation—of an individual to shape
reality in terms other than those in which it is presented,
the school's long-term effect is to create a consciousness
among many students and professors which stimulates the
need for decolonization and reconstruction.

The fourth colony, the Dream Colony—specifically
television—provides a surrogate of action and passion for
the colonized, replacing their own actions and passions,
which could stem from human feeling. Its purpose
is to buttress the Plantation and Violence Colonies.
Yet the media, in its output, can provide the basis for
empathetic extension of self with undiscovered others
pointing up the relationship and universality of human
feelings.

The collapse of liberal authoritarianism is not a bad
thing in itself. Indeed, it is all to the good if we understand the profound changes that are occurring and that
can occur. On the other hand, the collapse of liberal authoritarian structures where people are colonized tender-
ly can result in a final and active totalitarianism in which
violence and magic are no longer mediated through education, consumer goods and dreams, but are stated as goals
and the basis of life. To stop the dreary dynamic of totalitarianism it is necessary to develop a sophisticated politics which will include the initiation of projects, social
inventions, analysis and a new political party that will
reconstruct the body politic in a nonhierarchic direction
with shared authority.

The sense of such a possibility is present since those

young people, black people and dropouts from their class who are now confronting the colonial structure are revolted by Pharaohistic enterprises and do, when they know how, attempt projects that stem from a new meaning of politics. It seems to me that this meaning asserts that a reconstructed form, method of communication, technology and education have to stem from human feeling, which begins even while the liberal authoritarian structures are in wobbly existence.

In America, meaning and human feeling are now rekindled by the deep personal dissonance between the objective reality within which one is supposed to live — what Fromm calls his "social character" — and the fact of what one subjectively feels about his life. The pyramid's psychological "skin" over the individual — the beside-himself — is feeling. The dissonance gives rise to the search for "project." If a project of mine is to have political meaning, it will emerge from the sense of dissonance that I feel and the sense of empathy that comes to me about others. It is more than the immediacy of thrashing out. Dissonance and empathy cause me to join with others in *continuous* action and potentiality. The project, which stems from human feeling, will result in a political structure that is associative and cooperative. It will appear as egalitarian-in or egalitarian-toward. If the project begins with feeling toward others, it will assert values which create trust, good will and cooperation, rather than hierarchy and command. Relatedness will result.

In our projects, the development of new knowledge has a central analytic and organizing place. Without its development, we will find that the activities we undertake will either buttress colonization, avoid necessary confrontation or allow the appearance of change merely to mask the psychoexotic. In the latter circumstance, we find that the psychoexotic will revert to the variant forms of totalitarianism, so well known in the twentieth century, where destruction is thought about in aesthetic terms and action is preached as liberation from reason. Consequently, one assumption of a new politics of reconstruction is that knowledge in practice will be relevant to the actions of people. New knowledge based on empathy and verification replaces the meaningless facts of unshared authority and hierarchy as the means for guiding and judging action.

In the university and among those who have taken seriously the idea that knowledge can improve the lot of people, there is a search for a direction and mode of thought that will help make sense out of problems that people create by their political, social and economic organization. Some philosophers hoped and believed that the modern revolution in science would carry over into politics and fill this role. The American pragmatist philosophers William James and John Dewey hoped that pyramidal authority in the political sphere could be broken by the facts and method of science. Their hope was not to be. Science and technology seem to have left hierarchy and command untouched in the political, social and economic spheres.

The human examples of this fact are touching. In 1961, the scientist Von Karman received a medal from the United States for his work on ballistic missiles. He thanked those present, the generals and the heads of corporations, saying that he was honored to be in their presence and to serve their needs. While science and technology are revolutionary, they have not changed the social and political framework of authority. The logic and method of science did not attack those political and social assumptions that nurtured the practices of hierarchy, threat and the use of violence as a method of deriving authority. These assumptions became part of the pyramidal structure—until now.

As Simone Weil has pointed out,[3] science turned out to be terribly limited and with limited applications:

> Our science is like a store filled with the most subtle intellectual devices for solving the most complex problems, and yet we are almost incapable of applying the elementary principles of rational thought. In every sphere we seem to have lost the very elements of intelligence: the ideas of limits, measure, degree, proportion, relation, comparison, contingency, interdependence, interrelation of means and ends.

After the Second World War, John Dewey again tried to show the applicability of scientific methodology to social problems. Criticizing his fellow philosophers, Dewey, in 1946, feared that a philosophy would be fatal if it failed to analyze critically the relationship of knowledge to the question of who organizes political and economic power and how. Dewey rightly feared that people would act as if there were no difference between the use of atomic power for "destruction of mankind and its use in peaceful industry to make life more secure and more abundant."[4] Dewey learned from his World War I experience. He had been an apologist for the war, having thought at that time that knowledge did not have to be analyzed in terms of whom or what it served. The writer Randolph Bourne understood Dewey's mistake, and after the First World War, so did Dewey. But Dewey failed in his attempt to persuade philosophers—or almost anybody—about means, intent and purpose. Instead, other views dominated.

American intellectuals developed, as Mills pointed out, a form of crackpot pragmatism. This ideology served the powerful and the foolish in their empty quest for empire and superiority in all things, whether more nuclear weapons, more chemical-biological-radiological warfare, more police, more schools, higher body counts, higher growth rates or whatever. To excel meant to be better than other people in all areas, and then if we so chose, to dominate them.

In the academy, the encroachments of science on philosophy steered philosophic thought in the United States to the linguistic form of philosophy, which feared abstraction and empty meanings. In turn, that mode itself fell victim to its own form of abstraction. No doubt political reasons can be found for the retreat of American philosophic and intellectual thought. Pragmatist thought, which has been the basis of American philosophic thought, is predicated on commitment and involvement. However, paranoia and its social corollary, the need for dominion in all things because of fear of all things, gave birth to a threatening political and social climate typified by McCarthyism and the cold war. In retrospect, the threats and punishments appeared greater than they were. Among intellectuals there was a streak of cowardice which was supported by the fear of economic ruin plus the blandishments of public reward for playing it safe. In the nineteen-fifties many of the Marxists of the thirties now stood on *their* heads to support America as the great empire. The cold war ideology was so pervasive that the political scientist and sociologist came to serve the status quo—no matter who or what established the "givens." Of course, historically this has always been true. Clerks, monks, and astrologers have always served the powerful.

But now political and social problems are getting worse; the stubborn facts that we know and serve won't go away, and people are getting braver. Perhaps we are more desperate. Where do we turn for guidelines? Linguistic philosophy seems irrelevant; nor are its devotees in Academia concerned particularly that their methods and interests appear occult and without very much appeal to the humble outsider.

Other ways of thought are picking up the slack. Such positive social philosophies as Marxism are beginning to have a larger following in an underground way. We are all Marxists—either by using that analysis or playing out, as actors, the tragic role Marx foresaw. Yet, in America, but for a few books in recent years which were Marxist in analysis—C. W. Mills, Herbert Marcuse, P. M. Sweezy, Erich Fromm, Gabriel Kolko and P. A. Baran—there has not been very much written in that mode of analysis either.

William Appleman Williams has pointed out that the Academy has evaded Marxist thought for the last generation.[5] This is one important and profound reason that the mass of the student movement hugs phrases of Marx, Mao and Che uncritically and without sufficient understanding of their relevance to American life. This forbidden fruit now seems very tasty, even though the forms and rhetoric used are more in the nature of wax fruit samples.

One Leninist argument has been that the intellectual revolutionary was politically necessary to the worker. Without the intellectual it was not possible for the worker to determine what was to be done. The argument of both Marx and Lenin was that the worker could not differentiate between piecemeal advances which might be brought to him at the expense of other workers through the trade unions and real advances which manifested themselves through changes in structure and the emergence of worker-class-consciousness. The revolutionary philosophers were the ones who showed a not-quite-conscious class which overall changes were necessary and which piecemeal changes were chimerical.

The role of the revolutionary philosopher was that of teacher, prod and conscious organizer for a class that was not conscious of itself. Ironically, such philosophers were bourgeois; their roots were in a tradition that based its

very being on the class structure which nominated the
workers to be an underclass. In existential pragmatism
this contradiction is not present because *we start from the
fact of the situation which assumes the humanness of all
within the situation and the pain of all within it.* The
situation is created through the roles and functions which
inhere in the pyramidal structure. So long as the hierarchic, pyramidal structure exists, we will find unshared
authority, space-hogging and role-dictation as the values
that are passed on. People are unable to escape characterization.

The reconstructive philosopher does not stand in
judgment as the vanguard of another class. He sees himself within the same situation—as one who must, through
his actions and thought, lay bare the colonized relationships and change them. Thus, he cannot stay enamored of
the Soviet system or other socialisms which assert that a
revolution of social relationships has occurred, when all
that has happened is that those within one country assign
themselves the name of commissar and those in another
call themselves manager. The feudal and bourgeois
values of hierarchy based on privilege have remained.

In its own way the anarcho-pragmatism of my friend
and colleague Paul Goodman, whose philosophic roots
are in Kropotkin and Dewey, has had a more salutary
influence. He sees the way existing structures dictate
man's unfreedom and unbeing. He has seen the importance of immediacy and affect, as has Lewis Mumford,
who pointed to the grotesque effects of the megamachine
and the importance of the reaffirmation of the human
personality. Both men noted that American society
enclosed itself in a nuclear pyramid, thus systematically
destroying the promise of human fulfillment.

I have chosen to view their work as subjective because
it relates to a sense of immediacy from which structures
derive. This modern subjective view is a new and halting

scientific method. The approach stems fron an inductive-immanent approach *in which the proof is in the action.* What was once the task of the scientist alone now becomes the experimental task of those who want to bring about profound change in the society. In more than a metaphorical sense, the "new scientists" are the insurgents and dropouts who try to break the hierarchic structure as well as comprehend and resolve the contradictions in American life; for the portion of recent history that has embodied freedom has been the history of their new experimental method.

This historical spirit has spread to intellectuals who identify their cause with the spirit of radical change and reconstruction which has emerged in the American empire. There is an attempt to cut through the ideology which taught false rationality and pseudo-excellence.

In America there is a mood among many which is not different from the one that pervaded France after the Second World War. Sartre and Merleau-Ponty, Camus and De Beauvoir created around their intellectual work a deepened meaning of the importance and ironies of freedom. The solidarity of commitment tempered in the French underground helped them in understanding the meaning of relevance and purpose of any attempt to apply reason/ethics to the real world. And now at universities like Harvard, the Philosophy Department again attempts to give living meanings to philosophy and theology by re-examining the basis of the university and what knowledge has become in practice. In the 1969 confrontations at Harvard the Philosophy Department became the center from which change emanated on the nature of the university and the definition of student demands.

In the United States there is now a new dimension of bravery adopted by individuals and groups when they speak and act. Taking personal risk is the way of maintaining relevance to one's intellectual work. I think of my brethren in Resist and the Resistance who see themselves as unable to function as men of ideas without commitment, which taxes them and their ideas, in action in the present. I cannot talk against the irrationality and immorality of the Vietnam war or of the colonized structure of American life without letting the colonizers know that what I say and do has meaning and purpose. Just because we live in a situation where the limits are undefined, we have to act and confront the colonizer to define our own limits, to define our intellectual work and our freedom. Each has come to know this in his own way—to sense his limits and his capacity for involvement and resistance.

Each of us has attempted to act openly and directly as a citizen, knowing the penalties and not being unaware of the pleasure of reaching out toward one's own depth of political existence. Yet, if one's forays in decolonization and reconstruction are to be meaningful beyond the immediate event, he must be joined with others who relate themselves to a general mode of thought and political action that builds beyond isolated acts of heroism and insight. This new feeling of identity, which has come and gone in the decade of the 1960's and may come again, presents us with those potentialities and virtues upon which to build a new foundation. It is important that we comprehend that without such a foundation there can be no profound cumulative changes.

What is the basis of that foundation? As Wolfgang Köhler pointed out, human civilization rests, in the last analysis, "on the conviction that ultimately certain things are intrinsically sensible and ought to be pursued, whereas others are against sense and must be prevented. Obvious experiences cannot be ignored. If they are, the very fundament of human culture is threatened."[6] This point may be extended to include the limits of the human condition. As one old man told me, "You must remember that no matter which way you turn, your ass is always in back of you."

The needed foundation for a new public philosophy can stem from an existential pragmatism rooted in experience and experiment. Support for the development of this mode of thought can be found among insurgents in the churches, the young, the dispossessed and those who see how the institutions to which they have devoted their lives are colonizing instruments. Intellectual and political comradeship and mutual sustenance will be found in those groups which sense the American crisis most immediately in their own lives. They can aid mightily in the decolonizing reconstruction of American society either through rational analysis or through confrontation, by joining with individuals or groups who objectively have or do not have "power."

Consequently, my hope is that what I have to say has immediate relevance in action. Since the final test of knowledge, religion and politics can only be known in practice, and the final test of man is what he does in the world, I am directing my remarks not only to those in the university and in the church but to those whose emerging consciousness demands an end to the colonization of themselves. What I have to say does not exclude the colonizers who, formerly submerged by absolutes and trapped by their function, may now see themselves as beyond their assigned function and role. This book is aimed neither at the free nor at those who see themselves as slaves.

Those who are already free need only relate their being to Being. Even though they may be young and in no danger of immediate death, save what the body politic may bring, the free may view their lives as complete and whole, with judgments, changes and patterns set so that their lives—the business of seeking ultimate relationships and personal well being—can go on. We should not interfere in what they do, because theirs is the final work of people.

Where there is no freedom or search for it, and people accept the characterization of who they are through the *hierarchic other,* there is no need to make moral judgments on what people do because they are not free to choose what they do. It is only when they act freely that we can ask whether they acted responsibly or irresponsibly. To their lives we may speak without wrath or danger of violating the business of being.

If we are neither so fortunate as to be free nor so unfortunate as to accept characterization, thinking that we are free or not caring about such matters, we are forced into finding our being with the searchlight of what we do. I am concerned with being and doing in the sense of becoming and attempting to come to oneself. Consequently, where we talk about finding being through what we do, we necessarily are talking about changing and directing the nature of the body politic in quite different ways than we accept as characterized people.

We are attempting to find ways of moving from colonization to decolonization and reconstruction. I am not concerned with final judgments, final accounts, and continuous dialogues to relate being with Being. As characterized or even as free men, such concerns are always present. They wait to terrorize us in our loneliness, on our deathbeds, in the middle of the night when we wake up with sweaty palms from fears of unrelatedness to either the past or the future, our own or others, Nature or Man. But now we are too busy discovering and fencing with the immediate and the now as it is presented to us through a body politic that insists on finding ways of structuring man's destruction and making hollow his individual death through his own choices, because of the way the pyramid visits or intends to visit this destruction on him collectively.

A word about the academy is in order. Many in the

academy are threatened by the notion of man performing outside of assigned roles and functions. The academy —properly ensconced as the state's partner rather than its challenger—fears the return to sense impression and active participation toward something beyond rationalization. It fears a comprehension which stems from the subjective and builds to the subjective. Some academicians may hold that such a movement is anti-intellectual. They neither perceive nor conceive the need for a knowledge which starts from human existence as a series of problems which are capable of confrontation, resolution and reconstruction. Too often, they hide behind the rhetoric of quantitative measurement in foolish emulation of the bad natural scientist. They assume that the method of quantitative measurement is superior to a subjective feeling predicated on primary sense perception.

The academy fears an experimental, subjective social science since, in science as in art, in order to perceive "a beholder must create his own experience."[7] Creating one's own experience is necessarily a moral statement of how one acts and lives. It designates and defines personal responsibility in action. The academician in this sense is not that easily distinguished from the civil servant who uses the veil of bureaucratic authority to hide personal responsibility.

Just as the academician is threatened by the sense impression and action experiment, and by the battle on the doorstep of his classroom, so those responsible for these great institutions are threatened. The basis of these hierarchic structures—the unions, the corporations, governments and universities—is under attack because these structures defined themselves in terms of function and role, and lost sight of what the function and role meant. They, too, now fear the fact of the end of role and function which assumed an objective pose.

To begin with feeling and sense impression as the

starting point for analysis is to reconstruct our present relationships to people, institutions and things. Such a reconstruction will lead to radically different social and political structures as well as different educational institutions. Their principal way of operating on a day-to-day basis will be primarily egalitarian and associational. Their success will depend on the ability of those who form such institutions to confront the colonies of American life and to fill the spaces with institutions that are not predicated on the old conceptions of authority. The outbreak of feeling transcends old conceptions of power. It is a new principle of action and understanding. As Bob Dylan says, "[something] is blowing in the wind."

PART ONE

THE COLONIZED REALITY

The Psychology of the Pyramidal State and the Beginnings of an Alternative

> The citizens should be molded to suit the form of government under which they live. For each government has a peculiar character which originally formed and which continues to preserve it. The character of democracy creates democracy, and the character of oligarchy creates oligarchy; and always the better the character the better the government.
>
> —Aristotle

Beside-Himself

Each body politic has a political psychology. The most common political psychology in the pyramidal state is one where all people seem ordered and feel ordered and situations are ordered for the people to *be* ordered. Such a body politic builds a social character for the individual of the *beside-himself*. The beside-himself becomes the outer layer by which the individual is *characterized* in the pyramidal state. It is the skin that he wears to get ahead or keep his head. It is developed through a series of situations in which the individual finds himself as a result of the economic, communicating, educational system of sanctioned violence and common ideologies of the body politic.

For the person, the beside-himself becomes his profile of performance and behavior in given situations over which he has no control. The beside-himself enables the authentic person to sleep in his waking moments. The sleeping person lives programmed objective experiences where the situations are "given" and where the individual relationships are based on being told and tolled.

The political psychology of colonization attempts to use authentic subjective experience solely for the purpose of strengthening the ordered relationship of the state. The psychology of the pyramidal relationship denies the personal subjective experience which might threaten the ordered relationship of the given situation or of characterization. It is necessary to deny such experiences, since they include a variety of feelings and reasonings that, if acted on, would cause people to live purposefully in their ordered way.

In the pyramid, personal experience becomes repressed into inaction. Individual feelings are denied. We see each other through assigned roles. The operational result is that people become hostages or prisoners to anonymous authority. Where people find themselves in this condition it is academic to talk about an individual psychology, since their uniqueness is lost and their freedom is reduced to the "freedom" that is allowed to them within the character created for them by the colony. They share a solution to life—that of being part of the game.

One's ability to deduce correctly his obligations and relations to others is severely hampered because all associations are mediated through a colonized structure that distorts feeling and the meaning/actions derived from those feelings.*

---

* In *Roads to Freedom*, Bertrand Russell divides the "evils" in our lives into three parts: (a) those due to physical nature, for example, "death, pain and difficulty of making the soil yield a subsistence"; (b) defects in the character of the

We may, for oedipal reasons, seek to prop up Authority in order to feel protected and Ordered. Once we accept being hostages, our tools—language, abstraction and conceptualization, technology and social organization—limit our primary sensory perceptions.† We invent things

---

sufferer such as ignorance, lack of will, and violent passions; (c) those that depend upon "the power of one individual or group over another." He points out that "A social system may be judged by its bearing upon these three kinds of evils." The change from one social system to another depends on whether it reflects human feeling in the way it confronts the three classes of evils which Russell details.

†Whole industries, armed forces, communications media, political science institutions and factories are given over to meaningless and senseless questions about the problem of quantitative power to destroy each other now presented to us by the pyramidal state. On August 6, 1967, the 22nd anniversary of the atom bomb dropping on Hiroshima, Grumman Aircraft Engineering Corporation ran the following full-page advertisement in *The New York Times:*

EXTENDING MAN'S CENTRAL NERVOUS SYSTEM IS THE
CHALLENGE AT GRUMMAN

Under the pressure of military combat and improved science which demanded and provided greater and greater aircraft performance, man became aware of his own missile, sensor and computer limitations and turned to the development of mechanical and electronic devices to augment them. . . . to extend his central nervous system to the outmost perimeter, as it were. In doing so, he remained in control of events.

Operating at the outer fringe for the U.S. Naval forces at sea, the Grumman E2A Hawkeye is a case in point. The "nerve center" of Hawkeye is a system called ATDS—Airborne Tactical Data System. The automation in this system is far in excess of human capabilities in the collection, storage, collation and relaying of information. But . . . the crew monitoring this automation can interrupt its judgment to alter the information being sent back to major surface units.

Grumman has always recognized that Man is the heart of the system . . . not only for his ability to make "moment of truth" decisions in case of equipment failure, but also for the "bring-back" capability which only he has. Man is economic. Engineering at Grumman (the man behind the man) takes on deeper significance because of this outlook. Grumman is vitally interested in the welfare of the man who joins our company. Engineers and scientists who can [sic] distinct advantages in such an atmosphere are warmly invited to contact us regarding the following immediately-available positions in advanced aerospace programs.

(This advertisement superimposed a picture of a Navy aircraft plane against a man's central nervous system.)

that hear or see better than we can, we assume that they
supersede our personal need to sharpen, or have, sense
perception. The most immediate sense of experience is
robbed of its meaning because no attention is paid to
our experience that would matter. Instead, the experience
is quantitatively felt for the *beside-himself* by the *hierarchic other*. The sense of perception from which man's
understanding and consciousness must begin is distorted
and rendered useless. Our senses are dulled by a lan-
guage/thought process which stems from the social structures that create our problems.

Descriptions in the pyramidal state are given in numerical or calculative language which emphasizes human
extensions but denies human existence of others except as
things to be dominated. Modes of thought are invented to
protect and justify abstractions or institutions that need
not be. We hope, as Marx did, that from our sense perception, we can develop empathy. Instead, we continue as the
people of the beside-himself—as partial people.

Where purpose and primary feeling are divided so that
man is either forced or teased into becoming beside-himself, disastrous consequences can ensue. For example,
those trained to press buttons against Soviet missiles or
cities are encouraged to train and specialize, even obtain
university master's degrees of science or arts, while they
man the missiles. But they are not to ask *why* questions
about the work they perform. Specialized education is
used as a mask against thought about one's work task. At
Grumman Aircraft, engineers are not hired to relate
purpose and intent to their task; in the American ideology
this is *someone else's* job that itself is viewed as a professional task. Thus the question, "What is the purpose and
consequence of what you are doing if what you do or make
comes into being?" never gets asked. Such a question
would begin to destroy the carefully constructed beside-

himself which is predicated on the part and particular, never the relationship.

In the pyramidal system of authority, political and moral questions remain an abstract inquiry determined by technological judgments which are quantified in a non-referential and non-emotive language. The result is that our ability to judge the beginning, middle and end of man's work projects—what he *pro-jects* through his institutions—is lost. The *homo faber* (the economic part upon which the state depends), by creating specialized extensions (machines or bureaucracies) either to his fellow workers or for himself, has lost the harmony and creative tension of a man working within and as part of a natural environment. The *homo faber* has created jobs and social organizations which limit awareness, and has attempted unsuccessfully to commit future generations to rely on those same institutions and functions. It is not because the engineer is a bad man that he thinks nothing of working and training for the institution of mass destruction. Through the mechanism of organization, he has become a function of the hierarchic other.

Emphasis on process destroys purpose and intent. The mode of presentation of the organizational form becomes everything. In this context R. D. Laing's analysis is pertinent. He notes in *The Politics of Experience* how Freud both sees and demonstrates that the "ordinary person is a shriveled, desiccated fragment of what a person can be."[1] He is such a desiccated fragment because of the nature of pyramidal economic and political structures. These structures give people the profiles they need to appear normal, successful and contented (for themselves) or the reverse. The pyramidal structure manufactures false experience which the individual comes to believe is the only experience he can have. It is the experience, action and biography of the beside-himself which creates and demands regulated, impotent or alienating actions.

The envelope of man, his profile, is molded through the hierarchic other. Riesman, Glazer and Denney in *The Lonely Crowd* point out how "social institutions can harness a gamut of different motivations, springing from different character types, to perform very much the same kinds of socially demanded jobs. Thus we are forced to take account of the possibility that people may be compelled to behave in one way although their character structure presses them to behave in the opposite way."[2] In *Individualism Reconsidered,* Riesman says that "many of the motives which were in earlier decades built into the character structure of individuals are now built into the institutional structure of corporate life."[3]

However, man begins to bridle at the beside-himself when it does not meet desires or human needs, or when situations created for him are untenable. His own self may begin to emerge because the individual becomes aware of his need for survival and change. At the point where people neither understand nor accept pyramidal authority new *social characters* emerge in which different purposes, styles and needs are expressed. These in turn intimidate or change the political structure of the society. On an individual basis, people begin to break out of the *beside-himself.* People act *injectively* and in surprising ways to *seek* a new social character. Attempts are then made by pyramidal authority to coopt the new character, in order to make them modish and cosmetic, so that the authority appears to adjust to meet those desires or needs which are in revolt against the beside-himself. (Note comment on the television program, *Mod Squad,* Chapter Five, page 152.)

The individual's search for his personal psychology can only go forward after we have peeled back the pyramidal structure's suit of social character which the self wears.

What the individual looks like without that suit is beyond the scope of this book. My concern is with characterization and the hierarchic other which gives the colonized and pyramidal structure the glue necessary to keep going without continuous turmoil. As the reader will see from the definition of project, my argument is that the discovery of the self cannot occur except through the process of being *within* activity which is joint and self-defined against or outside of the pyramidal structure. So long as the pyramidal structure remains unchallenged, the self can only wear the clothes of that structure. In pyschological terms we must ask two questions: How is the beside-himself created and molded? What are the characterizing situations which the person lives within to create the beside-himself?

Hierarchic Other

Just as an individual has a personal psychology, the system of a body politic develops motivational patterns which can be described as institutional psychology. The psychology of the body politic is more important in shaping an individual's action than the individual's psychology. We see this most clearly when noting the way the psychological professions describe abnormal or aberrant behavior. In a jingoist state I am ordered to fire on an enemy. I refuse and state my reasons and individual biography. I am considered a malingerer or passive-aggressive by psychologists, who judge me from institutional perspectives laid down by the state. On the other hand, where authority is shared or collapsing, and the psychologist's ties to the political authority structure are weakened, my activity may now be described as autonomous, humane, integrated, and my personality may be described in similar terms. From each of these judgments a series of institutional and personal consequences will flow to reinforce the original designation that was made of me. I may be jailed and begin to think criminally and act accordingly, or I may be praised and my sense of esteem and fullness will be reflected in future activity.

In the pyramidal state the psychology of the hierarchic other is central to organizing relationships among roles and functions. That is to say, the self has no affect on others: it can only be effected, like dead matter. The *hierarchic other* asserts that authority is removed from the self to another who is known only as a process or function in the social pyramid. It does not credit the cooperative instinct of man in which the self attempts to share with others but remains in-self (shared authority*). The hierarchic other depends on the herd-follower instinct, which turns out to be basic to two kinds of overlapping bodies politic. One is the society of scarcity, where for economic reasons it appears necessary for the few to control the many for the good of the group. The rationale for this type of society is related to the idea of scarcity of resources, such as food or shelter. The second is the society of political authority where decision-making is no longer shared within the group, but is vested instead in a series of hierarchic relationships in which people are told what to do and, because of habit, act according to what they are told. Thus the hierarchic other grows out of the notion that a group or another individual knows better than the individual himself *how he should relate* and what he should do. And, by the nature of the structure of functional and role relationships in the society, he will act within a situation of being told.

In their earliest stage of life, Piaget and Schachtel have pointed out, children make indefatigable attempts to manipulate their emotions and immediate environ-

* This will be referred to as the cooperative other.

ment (crawling, looking, walking, talking, sitting up, etc.). In this process, the child learns (or thinks he learns) from his expectations and experimentations what he can and cannot do. As the child grows older, the hierarchic other defines psychologically the moveable objects and those that are "fixed" and appear to be unchanging and unmanipulable. That part of the individual—his uniqueness—which is reserved to himself and which attempts to discover the reality of what can be done with others from a sense of self, either remains inert or is fixed in infantile fantasy and magic in the pyramidal state. The hierarchic other now fits this perverted definition of the superego, since *in practice* the superego *now* reflects the worst in individual man.

It is useful to note Freud's meaning in this regard. He points out that the ego-ideal (part of the superego) retains the character of authority and acts to repress the individual through such processes as religious teaching, schooling, laws of the group applied to other groups, etc. In one sense, Freud suggests that the ego-ideal reflects "the higher nature of man," even though the superego forms itself out of the desires of the id which has repressive characteristics. Repression becomes the tool of the hierarchic other (the perverted and collective superego) as it wields its authority upon individuals to create the *beside-himself* in the pyramidal structure. Operationally, authority is built out of the collective id wishes, which are then mediated through the hierarchic other in the relationships which are presented to him in his daily life. He is repressed, and his repression turns out to be the *mock* integration of self in the pyramidal social system. His acceptance, even though it is mock, allows the pyramidal social system to act in infantile regressive ways, which the individual comes to applaud and accept— in real and mock ways. Thus, we allow mass destruction and murderous rage (Are these our collective id desires or are they the self-hatred generated as betrayal of self that could have been?) to be played out by the hierarchic other in the political sphere through "legitimate" institutional structures while individual rage (and creativity) is repressed by group and institutional authority. Authority structures such as schools, nation-states and corporations, act out the id wishes as mediated through the semiconscious. Economic needs are also fulfilled for those who perform according to their role in the pyramid. This process is acknowledged through ratificatory politics, where we are given the chance to vest the collective murderous rage in the hands of a particular few who hold certain functions and roles.

In this sense the hierarchic other takes on the id's purposes. Individuals turn themselves over to the hierarchic institutions which then make the basic choices for them. They play out their lives according to the hierarchic other which they are psychologically attuned to internalize. By accepting the authority structure of the pyramid, they limit their scope to the space of their hierarchically or economically defined function. The result is that their uniqueness goes untested and individual creativity atrophies or is deadened. This deadening is central to the operation of pyramidal power. It fosters the idea of expertise on basic political and moral matters so that only the few get to share in judgments of everyone's concern. In one way or another everyone becomes "officialized" (to use John Dickinson's phrase) and then, because of his official position, seeks to accept the judgment and decision of the few.

McGeorge Bundy, in his book, *Strength of Government,* uses the idea of greater power accruing to smaller groups in government as the way to resolve public problems. (It is also, supposedly, a way of keeping the pyramid intact.) According to this view, there is no other psychology or politics on basic issues but that of the hierarchic other and its characterization. Yet, such issues are profoundly personal. Bundy says that one's own particular interests may obscure the public interest. No quarrel there. But the example he uses clarifies his meaning. ". . . In questions of limited war [the public interest] may not be best discerned by those who are most directly affected, either by the rewards of battle or by its dangers."[4] Baldly stated, those most directly involved in situations which could reflect the fundamental disintegration of relationships on a public and private scale (war) the people who are the hosts to war are not the best ones to decide whether or not the war should be fought. The manipulator can best decide whether war should be fought. This means that the few in America decide whether there should be a limited war in Vietnam, Thailand, Latin America, irrespective of the views of the people who live there. Foreign populations are pawns in the hands of "disinterested" chess players who are expert in deciding for others how and whether they will or will not live. This principle of authority is the essence of colonization and the pyramidal state.

We have understood things or known each other through hierarchically organized social mediations and explanations. We do not see each other in terms that would allow us to know our human relationship outside of the one which is either set for us by the marketplace or the feudal pyramidal structure. Where I do encounter you in my organized experience, I know you only in terms of function, role and value. Knowing you in this way also includes price. The typical market personality, as Erich Fromm has pointed out, defines his relation to the other as commodity. It should be noted that in the capitalist system of economics once people see themselves as renting themselves they can hardly escape seeing one another except in the context of a buyer-seller commodity.

Where the market system gives way to the hierarchic

Wingate College Library

structure, our definitions of each other remain in the terms of the hierarchic other. The other is reduced to the function he performs, either as master or slave. Suppose someone comes to your house. He introduces himself as the "gas man" or the "mail man." You see him as performing that function and he comes to see himself in that way in relation to you as "consumer." We have our uniforms which describe you to me or me to you. Whether it is the army, the police or an anthropological convention, each member is known by assigned rank and appropriate colonial badge. Thus, obligations and actions are not freely deduced from self-initiated projects. They are assigned by the hierarchic other. Until now, it has only been in the accidental that I see you and me outside of function. But now, because the roles themselves don't enclose our identities and the functions we perform are not meaningful, we reach out beyond them.

In a pyramidal society with great social mobility there is a reluctance to believe in the role that the individual performs or finds himself in. The individual is taught to look for the next opportunity. The result is that there is a permanent dissatisfaction with the jobs that an individual has to perform. This situation is intensified where there is no material reason for the individual to perform a particular job since he won't go hungry if he does not. In such situations, the basis for profound transformation is present where the contradictions between the picture of self as potentiality and feeling is no longer met in any way through the pyramidally defined profile of the individual.

Part of the reason for such a transformation is economic and psychological. The market no longer matters to the lives of many people. In other cases, large numbers of young people intuit that their existence is predicated on feeling because they do not have a role. Conversely, the hierarchic structure reduces the meaning of a person, increases the preeminence of role, but does not provide existentially over time for the symbolic translation of the importance of that role so that a young person can believe in what he is doing. He may perceive his role as mad or dysfunctional. Suppose he is a systems manager for a nuclear weapons factory. If the society doesn't need nuclear weapons, and he comes to realize over time that such weapons are a reflection of madness, how can he believe in what he does? He smothers his humane-ness (good faith) as a prerequisite for fulfilling his role. If a person is a garage mechanic, to use Paul Goodman's example, and he knows that the car he is to fix is made to wear out quickly, that it is badly made with no chance of "righting" it, how can he believe in his role as garage mechanic? Operationally, we find that role and function disappear or disintegrate because they no longer matter. Role and function no longer have materiality, substance or weight.

The organization of modern society and its things, be they physical or abstract, habits of mind, social systems or automobiles, block the I-Thou and pervert the I-It relationships. We do not see each other through naïveté and openness, only through destructive mediations. Consequently, we cannot see each other except as mediated through characterization and the hierarchic other. Without understanding the finitude of man that is found in his experience and inner life (his personal felt experience), man becomes the slave to his detached abstract forms, extensions and systems. He does not know how or why to reach out to another nor does he know how or why to receive another.* He becomes prey to a leadership class

---

* It is for this reason that those who yearn for the simple must be heard and understood. In his memoirs Carl Jung said: "I have done without electricity, and tend the fireplace and stove myself. Evenings I light the oil lamps. There is no running water and I pump the water from the well. I chop the wood and cook the food. These simple acts make man simple; and how difficult it is to be simple.

which tries desperately to save itself through memorialization, great undertakings and pyramidal adventures.

This manner of enslavement has had profound political implications. Historically, it has meant the subjugation of the masses to the great undertakings of an insecurity-ridden leadership attempting to become either the Godhead or His representative through feats that included massive armed invasions and the erection of awesome material structures to God or to themselves. The intent of the great revolutions of the eighteenth century was to end the historic form of kingship and pyramid building by constituting a new form of political community which enabled the individual to create new definitions of himself and thus, his relation to the body politic. That is why there was such a great emphasis in France, England and the United States on constitution and re-constitution by the revolutionary groups. In this sense, the eighteenth-century revolution in America was an attempt to break the hierarchic other and characterization.

For example, Jefferson's image of the farmer was of a political-ethical man who maintained control of his judgment and lived in that harmony and tension with his fellows and the nonhuman environment which necessarily sharpened his sense-impressions and, as a result, his political faculties in the direction of freedom. Jefferson objected to the European political society organized around particular cities because the citizens of the cities were deracinate, controlled by others, and at the mercy of the whims of others. He believed cities merely expanded the serf system. The democratic society was to be formed

---

In Bollingen, silence surrounds me almost audibly, and I live in modest harmony with nature. Thoughts rise to the surface which reach back into the centuries, and accordingly a remote future. Here the torment of creation is lessened; creativity and play are close together."[5] Jung's view should not be dismissed as the romanticism of an old man who lived in a time which passed him by.

in such a way that the colonizer-colonized classes would not come into being.

In the United States, a primary concern of at least one strain of political thought was how to avoid the colonizer-colonized relationship so that humanness could obtain. One answer was constant expansion so that the colonized relationship could be imposed across national borders, but not at home for the United States, except if you happened to be black or Indian. Another was the idea of Opportunity. The ideology of Opportunity in America is the continuous attempt to amalgamate elitism with democracy. The reformist goal is that everyone starts the race up the pyramid equally. Indeed, opportunity and expansion are integrally combined in the American ethos. One's psychological opportunities to expand self (when it is really only the beside-himself which is expanded) are an important personal ingredient of the social character which puts forward the political notion of new frontiers.

The ironic part is that in history those who feared most the ideology of opportunity and expansion have ended up serving that view which could only be maintained in the pyramidal context. When Jefferson undertook the Louisiana Purchase he gave up his own hope for America.

Unfortunately, the Jeffersonian fear has come to fruition in the present organization of American society. In psychological categories, the sense of generalized other gave way to the easiness of the hierarchic other. The colonized structure gave rise to a series of hierarchic relations in which people lost the craft to do anything or to see purpose or feeling in their work or in their play. Instead of meaning in the present, the people were to be given easy access toward becoming a colonizer through the route of opportunity. The present in which the person found himself was only important as an instrument to another future. The common ideology that the people shared assumed and asserted that each individual has nothing outside of opportunity—opportunity for jobs, equality, power, ease, omnipotence and education. Since each person now has only opportunity, the aura which surrounds American man is that of infinite possibility and the overwhelming sense of going nowhere.

The industrial and over-developed society creates and reflects the predicament of nowhere man whether rich, poor, stupid or brilliant, human or inhuman, who seeks opportunity in every activity. When the body politic is organized according to such purposes, the most aggressive groups undertake the exploitation of all units of life. In imperialist terms, it is the discovery of areas of the world which could be exploited or brought into exploitation for the leading pyramidal state. Finally, it means the exploitation of land, air, space, the sea, the earth's inner core, American Indians, Vietnamese, as opportunities that will not escape the challenge of the will to dominance and profit. (In part, such activity has been undertaken to stem the power of the military by the scientific and business elite to keep a balance on top of the pyramid with the military.)

In psychological terms the will to dominance becomes a shared obsession in the society. The hierarchic other exploits the human suspicion that life, sexuality, and attractiveness are inextricably intertwined with force and dominance. Not to attempt to dominate or be forceful may indicate weakness, impotence and ultimately castration. Consequently, rather than face or accept this possibility, the individual will play out the role of the higher interest as perceived in his official capacity or as an extension of the pyramidal structure where he is given status as both asexual tough guy and missionary. In General Westmoreland's report on the operations of American troops in Vietnam this sense of dominance, tough guy and missionary role which attaches to the nowhere man in the American pyramid is very clear. Westmoreland, the nowhere man, believes in the war as magic against a group of people who are unclean, impure and deserving of punishment. The American zealots of the late fifties and early sixties, in their official capacity, first began by thinking of the war as an act of purifying those who were defiled with communism. But the day-to-day activity of the war made it clear that it was an opportunity to test weapons, advance careers, make profits, see Asia and escape boredom!

Characterization

I have suggested that in the individual's personality there is the creative impulse which attempts to propel man into working toward self-discovery and self-with-others freedom. This creative impulse is that part of the life instinct *beyond need* which creates new things, structures and art, focuses its understanding of the past to life purposes, and sees human potentiality as outside of the terrors of anxiety and need. In the development of the child we see this sense of creativity and spontaneity most clearly, although adults are more likely to see the child as frightened, in need or anxious. The tenderness of the individual's creative and spontaneous impulse is most open to being "blotted" out through a series of authoritarian and colonizing relationships which emphasize the individual sense of anxiety, need and powerlessness, in contrast with pyramidal institutions that appear focused, well-heeled and powerful. The individual self's view of potentiality, and impulsive but necessary quest for liberation and space, are channeled through the colonized relationships in school, work, media and the state.

By this means the attempt is made to characterize the individual as without the creative impulse.

Operationally, characterization is the a priori conception which the pyramidal structure has of social situations which the individual comes to accept in his relations with the world. The idea of self-with-other-in-equality relationships is submerged or destroyed. By the time the individual is through the various sorts of handling in the pyramidal structure he is not prepared to see himself in any other way than the way he is seen or made by the hierarchic other. Sartre's idea of being-for-itself, in *Being and Nothingness* (and rejected in his later work) is not a useful distinction because in the context of politics it emphasizes individual choice outside of self-with-other.

A slight digression should be made. Self-with-other is not self in hierarchic other, which denies the individual's being. Self-with-other is the democratic process of creating, choosing and evaluating structures of the world that are brought into being by others from a past and by the individual himself with others outside of the lived or officialized situation, where the individual plays out the hierarchic or pyramidal role. In the law of agency, the master is responsible for the servant because the servant is lived. In this context a political and economic reality is recognized. Ironically, in the law of states the leaders are exempted from such responsibilities because of the illusion of democracy and citizenship. Yet reality is that the people are lived by the pyramid.

The process of being "lived" is characterization. One is lived through colonized relationships, which the colonized are constantly prodded to internalize. The process of characterizing blots out the public meaning and importance of the individual. Thus, the individual comes to be seen by others only in object terms. The individual also sees himself only in those terms. He understands his own life in terms of anxiety and need and in no other terms. When a person is so reduced, he is easily manipulated by authority.

In the pyramidal structure, even if the individual has great latitude in his life style and the appearance of choice (freedom for lust), he lives according to forces external to the relationships which he might otherwise freely seek. As the individual grows older, he comes to represent those forces in his own life relationships. The psychoanalyst Georg Groddeck put it the following way: "Our ego behaves essentially passively in life," and we are "'lived' by unknown and uncontrollable forces."[6] Thus, most people allow the structure of the society to force them to live an external existence as characterized by the hierarchic other without reaching their unique selves or finding a way to reach others cooperatively.

In this formulation, the matter of characterization and colonization is circular. Colonization is based on the individual finding himself in situations in which he accepts the characterization of himself (school, work) and characterization is strengthened within the colonized relationship. The type of characterization may vary according to the colony, since each has its own footprint on the face and actions of the individual. Each makes up a portion of that part of man's consciousness which is most in tune with the acceptance of someone else's authority, preferably the unnamed "they." In its most general form, characterization may be seen symbolically in terms of master and slave, in which the master sets self-fulfilling terms for the slave. The master trains the slave so that he accepts all relationships as being mediated through the opaque wall of function, role, and station. In a stable, traditional, feudal society, characterization requires that the master must be right and the slave must be wrong. Over the generations, each internalizes his role. Objectively, the master and slave see themselves in this mirror.

The kinds of characterization made by the colonizer over the colonized is predicated on the needs of the colonizing institution. The preconceptions and material needs of those occupying the colonizer's function dictate the model of the slave who must then fit the pattern and reasoning of the colonizer. The colonizer's need is the colonized's anxiety to know whether he can produce satisfactorily the colonizer's need. The result is that a very specific system of punishments and rewards is set up. Once custody is proclaimed or taken by the colonizer, he is free to do anything with the colonized that he cares to.

Let us assume that I take on the role of the colonizer. I take on the double function of making the colonized work and taking care of him according to the fashion that I choose (that is, of course, historically the way upper classes, whether industrial or landed, have acted toward the poor). The black man is lazy, so he can't learn anything. Which means I teach him what I want him to know, which invariably means that he earns his keep by doing my bidding. The colonizer constructs the model for the colonized, which the colonized is then expected to fit into. As Michael Athay pointed out to me, "Since the colonist controls the society, his actions and behavior constitute the colonial's condition of existence." Once the slave loses any chance for self-definition and accepts the colonizer's role for himself, he loses touch with his own being and sees himself only as a series of externalized happenings. He now believes that that is who he is, and the horror of self-hate and self-destruction takes over. Those in the same position now believe this series of relationships. Frantz Fanon talks about the self-hate and fighting which go on in the ghetto community as an example of the self-fulfilling prophecy of the master who then uses his objective and analytical method as the way to show just how irresponsible and terrible "these people" are.[7]

Characterizing

Characterizing of others comes in many forms, through many masks and mediations. The characterizations which I describe are the basic psychological and political parts of our individual identities as they are played out in relation to each other in a colonized reality. While the most blatant manifestations of the colonized relationships exist in other parts of the world, and may have disappeared or changed costumes in America, the psychological presuppositions which created and sustained such relationships remain.

We do not have to belabor the obvious by saying that a pyramidal economic system, one predicated on the authority of the other and the primacy of the goods made, requires a very particular sort of individual to operate within it. This individual accepts the structure of "being told" which allows no compromises. We may term this situation total characterization. It goes a long way toward keeping the creative impulse blotted out, but not far enough. The same economic organization which deprives work of meaning also causes new impulses for self-controlled time. In itself the psychological result of self-controlled time may be either madness or liberation against the beside-himself. In partial characterization, the individual may be teased into doing what he wants to in order to find himself as a creative individual, while formally learning the methods of staying in line. Educational institutions find themselves fulfilling this contradictory function. In casual characterization, the individual may be blotted out by the make-believe reality which is created for him to aspire to, or to imagine he has attained. The media offer themselves to the individual for this purpose. Finally, in latent characterization, the individual who does not operate in the context of knowledge of what is going on or control over what is going on, now finds that he turns over to the pyramidal structure the right of committing suicide for him. That right becomes the state's purpose. His death is not only in the hands of himself and his own deterioration. It is in the hands of the state. This is latent characterization which permits only minimal creativity in the political sphere outside of ringing denunciations and confrontations with the state.

Total Characterizing

The slavery and plantation system historically was predicated on total subjugation. (The factory may be viewed historically as part of this pattern.) The master attempted to exclude the slave from human existence, reinstate him as a property and commodity, and treat him as the total function of the master. There are ironies. The master also became the reciprocal function of the slave, being characterized in turn into a role which he could not easily escape, either through force or pressure. Both ceased to be people and became functional relationships.

The master in the context of total characterizing attempts to use the system but not be bound by it. Ultimately, the group of people who dominate the relationship find that they are bound by the colonized who, either out of pain, accident, or surplus, are no longer able to live in that condition.

Characterization changes, and hence political realities are transformed when the worker-slave acquires skills beyond the function of a particular task and addresses himself through the prism of what he knows to ask questions beyond technique. Skills of workers become necessary for the operation of the factory. They then ask questions about the plant and governing outside the plant.

Political realities also change when those who traditionally live off the production of others are uninterested in technique and skill. They lose their ability to judge profit and value as defined in the colonized relationship. The stock-clipping families which made great fortunes have lost touch with knowing about the control of production, what makes production, and what the source of their economic power is. The absentee owner gives control to the mandarin bookkeeper. The young rich attempt to break with being characterized as the colonizer by living in ways that first appear as having nothing to do with being the colonizer. Thus, rich individuals may live as artists or philanthropists, hoping in this way to escape their situation as colonizers.

Partial Characterizing

An institution such as the school emerges as legitimate because its apparent task is to make the individual whole through education. Unlike the system of total characterizing, where the plantation colonizer makes no pretense at using the servant exploitatively, the Channeling Colony is defined in terms of its service function. The ideology of the Channeling Colony, of which the school is its central part, attempts to take a person beyond his present situation and make him better than he is. He is to be transformed as a person.

Since the process of partial characterizing allows space to the individual, dissonance and possibility are more likely to occur within people in the school. They are usually young and not totally captured. The school becomes a battleground because its tenets of freedom and "self-fulfillment" are not followed, or cannot be followed. A contradiction exists between the organization of the school and its pretension or rhetorical promise.

It should be noted that since the process of partial characterization remakes people, either in preparation for the Plantation Colony or away from it, the Channeling Colony creates a new class of colonizer who develops or reflects exploitative knowledge used to train people for colonizing roles.

Casual Characterizing

Play and leisure establish a manipulative relationship under the guise of giving entertainment. The television, drug, movie and advertising industries treat you as an individual thing, sell you a surrogate reality or soften you for the continuous colonization of the society. The casual characterizing is the most subtle mediation which comes in the form of dreams and circuses. It seems to open up the world to you, but it helps to deny the self's individual space. It gives a false sense of community. As R. D. Laing has pointed out, "It is not enough to destroy one's own and other people's experience. One must overlay this devastation by a false consciousness turned, as Marcuse puts it, to its own falsity."[8]

Latent Characterizing

The most complete and politically totalizing of all is latent characterization. The process of latent characterization replaces and distorts political being-in-the-world into passivity and control by leadership. The ability of people to act outside of the characterization placed upon them in the American empire is not possible once there is acceptance of the nuclear weapon as the basis of the state, and of the right of intervention all over the world as a way to "protect" people at home. Their beings-in-the-world are controlled by social structures and technical inventions that appear to be uncontrollable except by the few at the top of the pyramid. The nature of citizenship—let alone the meaning of one's being or building a community—is now dictated by the ancient leadership rite of survivorship.

In *Crowds and Power,* Elias Canetti suggests that the basis of leadership is survivorship; that the whole purpose of being on top is to have everyone die before you. The issue is immortality.[9] Swearing oaths of allegiance to protect the life of the leader is generally the way this psychological and political phenomenon operates. There are poignant examples of the way the right of leadership survivorship presents itself. During his administration, President Eisenhower did not have any special civil defense shelters and programs to protect the President and his staff. The Kennedy administration felt that special protections should be built for the President and his staff so that if nuclear war should come "the war could continue to be prosecuted." Robert Kennedy told John Kennedy that he has no choice but to endanger everyone's life through the Cuban missile crisis. Otherwise he might be impeached and lose his personal political position. Clark C. Abt and Ithiel de Sola Pool in *The Constraint of Public Attitudes* stated: "That conclusion [that Americans probably would not tolerate limited thermonuclear exchanges] does not automatically rule out a limited-retaliation strategy (use of missiles on selective targets in a continuous and controlled way over a period of time beyond a first nuclear strike and the opponent's retaliation). It is at least conceivable that such a strategy could be so designed as to assure its being carried out regardless of the eventuality of extreme public opposition. The retaliatory forces and their commanders, including the President, might be located inside completely isolated and heavily defended areas. They might be given advance instructions and training to cut themselves off completely from external influences and to go ahead at all costs with the retaliatory strategy."[10]

And yet the horrible deaths of Robert and Jack Kennedy seem to prove the reverse point. Jacob Bronowski in his essay on "The Face of Violence" points out that the leader accepts the role of king knowing that he will have his throat cut in a riotous saturnalia of the mob once it has used him up. He sees leaders as sacrificial goats who must either give the mob themselves or a mock leader. Bronowski believes that the society's attack on leaders is a hatred for the rule of law.

> The rule of law: that is our scapegoat; into this image we gather all the impersonal forces of society which keep us in our place. The conditions of civilized living do much to sap our lives of adventure and risk. We take our revenge by equating spirit with lawlessness, and adventure with the criminal.[11]

It is hard to comprehend that the activity may be in the way the society is organized. What does it mean to talk of the rule of law where the powerful see no law as in the case of Vietnam, or nuclear bomb dropping, or the fact that a society is more easily able to drop three million tons of bombs a year on innocent peasants than it is to allocate funds to build thirty schools; and where leaders can now risk everyone's life according to their whim. Dostoyevski's point is not to be avoided. The question remains—whose law and whose rules?

The criminality of a Napoleon is accepted and praised.

The beggar is imprisoned and reviled. In a system of the social contract, controls were to be exercised over leadership through the law and the right of recall. The leaders (really, the *representatives*) were to be held to stricter account than the citizen who merely participated. The underlying assumption was surely that the greater the power to act, the more it was important to act legally. What can it conceivably mean to enforce vagrancy laws and property laws when the structure of American life is predicated on opportunity, exploitation and risk of others?

The colonizers and colonized in the other categories are all latently characterized by the infinitesimal few who operate the Violence Colony. The Violence Colony may seem the most remote from influencing individual action. Yet the manner in which the state operates mediated through nuclear weapons, military power and the theory of dominance is the most important shaper of the individual. It is total in intent and result. The monopolists of violence have achieved their position of preeminence through accretion, the inertia of others, technology as the handmaiden of the powerful, and even the citizens' encouragement and acquiescence. In this process, people have internalized and accepted the argument and values of hierarchic organization, with its dependence on unquestioned authority and cultist knowledge, and its political assumption of violence. They wait to be sacrificed.

Breaking the Hierarchic Other

The psychological dialectic between impotence and domination as the motive force of American man in his official capacity has led to the description of American power as one which suffers from certain "gaps." The basic gap which is felt by those officialized at the top of the pyramidal system is the void that nothing matters in our actions and that we have no choice but to seek the next opportunity. Yet, this choice turns out to be increasingly unsatisfactory.

Since mattering and meaning are intertwined, and many people do not see either meaning or mattering in their colonized role, the ground is laid for great, perhaps convulsive changes. Fewer people can live in bad faith where there is no economic reason to do so and where the "opportunities" are patently empty and dangerous. In this context "bad faith" has a specific meaning: it is the act of becoming the function which is assigned to me by another and eventually not believing that function as being me although I do not act to change my situation or attempt to humanly reach and change the one who assigns me to becoming a function.

Because of the economic changes in post-industrial society, bad faith is not a condition that an individual has to accept. The result of no longer having to accept bad faith is that there are now social movements looking for politics based on feeling (matter and meaning as well as empathy and intuition). They intuit bad faith as the recognition and acceptance of the colonized role.

Rebels in institutions like the churches rally against the bad faith of contradicting basic human purposes within institutions. Consequently, churches are now changing their theological perspective to accommodate a mode of doing that presumes a breakthrough from the abstract or the quantitative to events and selves, from the mediate to the felt. This accommodation has meant that the organized churches are beginning to pull out their support from the state. The church and the army, both of which have been thought of as the twin supports of the bourgeois and feudal state, are now beginning to be at odds with each other. Ministers offer sanctuary for conscriptees against the state. Debates proceed on whether chaplains should be in the armed forces. Priests form unions to seek shared authority, brotherhood and sisterhood. The church is pressed by insurgents to reform and even to be revolutionary and reconstructive in its purposes. The state, meanwhile, becomes subservient to the military. Besides the insurgency within the church, the black liberation movement, the civil rights movement, the peace movement, the brightest and most articulate young people indicate that they can no longer, nor do they intend to, live with the droning blah, blah, blah. They intend to break through to the tear. After all, it is with the tear that clarity may begin. (There may be unclarity about whether I mean tear as in cry or tear as in rip. I mean both.) Politically and intellectually, their meanings are now related as we attempt to decolonize and reconstruct.

These groups see American man as the essential Western man. They reject him. And it is understandable. He feels very little; consequently, he can *do* very little. They see our ability to comprehend, to feel and to create (to adapt what we do to what we need) as limited and perhaps atrophying. Indeed, on an individual level, few of us know what we are doing and what we, as human beings, need. After all, the task of the hierarchic other is to capture that part of the individual's consciousness which says that he can be otherwise than what is assigned and direct it to the social mobility and opportunity route; while the task of the individual is to create situations out of his dissonance which keep alive his lust for freedom with others. Those are his projects, which stem from his feeling. Feeling becomes the psychological and political basis of breaking the hierarchic other when it is transformed into doing. That is, activity for specific ends that are potential realities. But what is feeling? We are informed by Suzanne Langer that the status of "'feeling'

. . . has been an asses' bridge to philosophers ever since Descartes treated *res extensa* and *res cogitans* as irreducible and incommensurable substances."[13] But we know that serious political philosophy, that is, thought which concerns itself with the analysis of new forms of human relationship, *begins* from the interaction of physical phenomena and the consciousness by the person of his total experience. Jefferson is a case in point.*

In a letter to John Adams, Thomas Jefferson provided the starting point for decolonization and reconstruction. Jefferson said, "I feel, therefore I exist." This letter to Adams, written by Jefferson, August 15, 1820, at the end of both of their lives is an extraordinary one. Jefferson said that he "feels bodies which are not myself." For him this is proof that there are other existences who share his being and his sense impression of what is. Jefferson, like all good rationalists, however, was afraid of seeking more than sensation. He feared talk of immaterialism because when we seek that world, "all is in the wind." He does not care to admit the fact of feeling in fantasy and dreams. Nor does he want to torment himself with these matters about that "which indeed may be, but of which I have no evidence." The close of the letter, however, shows the meaning of feeling in its most powerful, loving and empathetic sense. In what must surely be the most unusual statement of feeling of one President (of a different political party) to another, Jefferson announces that there is no distance—institutional, psychological or otherwise— between him and Adams. "I am sure that I really know many, many things and none more surely than that I love you with all my heart, and pray for the continuance

---

*I do not believe that Jefferson was an unalloyed character. Imbued with the revolutionary spirit, he also foresaw a great American racist empire—for "freedom." Yet in his work, we still see the alternative, the non-imperialist alternative, the alternative of non-domination.[12]

of your life until you shall tire of it yourself."[14] I am reminded of Buber's saying in *I and Thou,* "The relation to the Thou is direct. No system of ideas, no foreknowledge, and no fancy intervene between I and Thou . . . No aim, no lust and no anticipation intervene between I and Thou."[15]

Feeling is the composite of impressions that we receive from our senses. Our sense impressions also create feeling for another, a plant or a thing. In the colonized world it is mediated through the ideas and instructions of the powerful. However, feeling is also that raw and immediate response that may be termed our intuitive/empathetic sensibility. And as Jefferson suggests, the rediscovery of feeling teaches me that I exist and then explains my identification, my relatedness with another. This tells me what needs changing around me and enables me to understand why others change what is around them. Suppose, for example, that you and I are in the same overheated room together. Without saying anything, you walk to the window. I know that you are going to open it, because I am also warm. I have felt the heat with you. Consequently, I am also glad that you opened the window.*

As the example suggests, by adopting the Jeffersonian dictum, we may discover each other, because we will be able to step outside of our institutional house of cards in which the more role-oriented we become, the less we use our senses. Since my senses give me my consciousness, I need them to reach another. From these senses, which grant me a response to physical matters, I must also build a political understanding of need. Thus, from the fact of feeling I deduce the probability of the action to be undertaken, and the obligation to be derived from my

---

* Note Sartre's discussion in *Being and Nothingness,* pp. 225 ff.

action. The quest of knowledge about such actions becomes an attempt to develop the social and political structure which is most relevant to the definition and resolution of obligation to human feeling rather than to function. We are required to ascertain what obligations we feel for another, and whether certain political structures are more able than others to realize human feeling.

Hazel E. Barnes has pointed out in her important book, *An Existentialist Ethics,* "that there are millions of experiences of reality where we needlessly create trouble if we refuse to accept a practical certainty. These are the areas where disagreement is rarely or never found. Where individual rational conclusions do not agree, the appeal cannot be to something beyond Reason or to Reason and Truth as if they were tangible entities. One must choose between various beliefs or propositions, each one of which claims to be Reason or Truth."[16] The question of disagreement becomes a political and epistemological one. It is sufficient to say here that differences exist on perception of action and its consequences. The problem is that those who operate with power use it for the purpose of setting the terms of reality to their view of what is rational. The result is that disagreement about experience is not expressed in ways which *matter,* have insight and can be compared scientifically and objectively. The pyramidal institutions enforce their definition of mattering so that intersubjective perception is unobtainable. Historically, philosophers believed that the way around differences of perception, requirements and human obligations were resolved through the social contract. We may now add to that view the notion of space of creation. Politics becomes the art of guaranteeing such spaces *and* reasserting the social contract. One without the other is a hobbled system, which continues to produce the social character of the nowhere man with infinite dreams and potentialities which appear achievable through technology.

Breaking the Beside-Himself

As I have implied, the contradiction between the creative impulse in the self and our hierarchically assigned role is one important motive force for change. Our subjective sense creates in us a double sensitivity. First, it allows us to do what seems to be our necessary task of being in a world where we are contingent and colonized. Second, we retain our private feeling about our personal/social situation. We become dimly aware that we live in a world where what is does not have to be, where the external situation is constantly or invariably contradictory to our personal feelings. The subjective tension and dissonance create an impulse which has profound external political and social consequences. No matter how expert the colonizer becomes, no matter how powerful the colony is, no matter how he makes it appear that the social fact of my condition is not his doing, I remain independent of his will and my personal impulse for freedom remains. Because of that impulse, I wish to confront the ersatz, inauthentic freedom as it is given to me in order to build real freedom with others. At a time of profound social transformation, we are left in a continuous state of dissonance (anxiety, wonderment, boredom, and meaninglessness), between the colonized systems into which we are born and which we are expected to reinforce, and the felt sense that things don't have to be as they are. This state of dissonance (individually or collectively) is the psychic precondition necessary to change the "objective" situation. One individual's motive for wanting change may be quite different from that of another. We may conjecture that the same motives causing dissonance operate in all of us, except that they manifest themselves in varying ways depending on our class, stage of life, sex and work. The mask may be different, but there are basic drives beneath the mask.

. . . As soon as a freedom other than mine arises confronting me, I begin to exist in a new dimension of being; and this time it is not a question of my conferring a meaning on brute existents or of accepting responsibility on my own account for the meaning which Others have conferred on certain objects. It is I myself who see a meaning conferred upon me, and I do not have the recourse of accepting the responsibility for this meaning which I have since it cannot be given to me except in the form of an empty indication. Thus something of myself—according to this new dimension—exists in the manner of the given; at least for me, since this being which I am is suffered, it is without being existed. I learn of it and suffer it in and through relations which I enter into with others, in and through their conduct with regard to me. I encounter this being at the origin of a thousand prohibitions and a thousand resistances which I bump up against at each instant: Because I am a *minor* I shall not have this or that privilege. Because I am a Jew I shall be deprived—in certain societies—of certain possibilities, etc. Yet I am unable in any way to feel myself as a Jew or as a minor or as a Pariah. It is at this point that I can react against these interdictions by declaring that race, for example, is purely and simply a collective fiction, that only individuals exist. Thus here I suddenly encounter the total alienation of my person: I am something which I have not chosen to be. What is going to be the result of this for the situation?[17]

Once we act persistently from our dissonance, whatever the motive, we will change the "objective" situation of the locale in which we dare to operate. Because the situation is changed in which the injectors live, the potentialities of freedom become real through the project.

Such political and psychological attempts to establish one's own identity,* his freedom, are found through test-

---

* Where identities are held together by mythical constructions or material need, the analysis of the individual finding his identity will also apply to a group or nation. In the decolonization process of nations, we find that once the period

ing the limits of boundary and separation which defined our being. At one time or another, a person finds himself dependent upon parents, friends, groups, churches, charismatic figures and powerful myths. At one moment or another an event will occur that calls into question the entire relationship of dependence. Where opposition and separation result and the person separates himself, he will feel alone and without external referent, since the individual's meaning was given to him through the reference group and through those persons or myths which dominated him. He is lonely and confused. The reason for his loneliness and confusion is that he has no standards for judging what he is doing and how to act. In most cases, he must either revert to the pyramidal structure's method of judging worth and "freedom" or to his former experiences which he may only be able to recognize through the description of his experiences as described "objectively" by others — a psychiatrist, a policeman, a friend. The individual finds that the only way he can burst through the objective experience of who he is as described through the pyramidal structure is by undertaking the project.

It is through this process that he begins to form his identity. At that moment, the person pro-jects a future condition that he defines and for which he is responsible. After this initial crisis, he is left with attempting to define his identity through choice-making in the present, which then shapes his contingent choices for the future. It is at such a moment that a new and more healthy relation-

---

of the establishment of a new identity occurs, that identity now allows for active and practical association with those who formerly colonized them. We also find, as for example in the case of France and Algeria, close relations are again restored. But now these relations are based, more or less, on equality and respect. These relations now turn out to be even more advantageous for France than at the time when it tyrannized Algeria. As Fanon has said, the process of decolonizing is important not only for those who suffer under it but for those who caused it.

ship to the environment may develop. Through the projects which he chooses, either alone or as part of a group or movement, he is able to define himself as a subject, as an equal who is not an instrument serving as the tool of a person or a group which colonized him. But note that the individual must choose with, and not be swept up— act with, and not be acted upon.

The situation in which consciousness for change occurs results in an individual standing aside or moving in ways different from the expectations which the hierarchic other places and creates by its own action. As I have said, there is not merely the Other. It is a cooperative or hierarchic other. In the cooperative other, one's own definition of freedom and potentiality is included in what will socially result. In the hierarchic other, my projects and definitions of freedom are obliterated. To leave the situation of the hierarchic other, the essential ingredient necessary is the injective sense; that is, where the individual or group asserts itself in ways different from those predicted by the colonizers or thought possible by those who objectify reality. Take oneself as a case in point. My hard fight for space is still limited by the fact that I exist within a group. Since I am born dependent on others, I learn that my existence can only be in association with others. Whether I or others think of me as an artist, scholar, farmer or politician, I remain dependent. Because I am a human being, I seek cooperation, since perpetuation and fulfillment of self is achieved through cooperation. Yet my free actions with others now determine the kind of association which will result. It is easy to return to a colonized state either as colonizer or colonized. But where cooperation and association is an important part of decolonization, a different basis might be laid.

Relations can be found among people after they are separate in their equality-toward or equality-in, when they find their boundaries through reaching out for others. We know that such relationships cannot exist in a colonized situation where limits and boundaries are set by totally different means. In the decolonized situation, a person can begin to reason and risk. It is only through the project and the experiment that we are able to ascertain which limits and which boundaries are the negation of man. Mistakes will be made. There is no simple test of experiments *not* to perform, although those which deny the space of another, where there is no feeling for another, are dubious enterprises, since they have the effect of reinforcing colonized relationships and the psychology of the hierarchic other. They repeat the structure of the pyramid. We can see this process in terms of authority, dominance and narcissism, the integral parts of the "fountainhead complex."

Those who suffer from the fountainhead complex are usually creative in ability and see themselves as beyond the hierarchic other and have broken through the *besidehimself.* That is to say, they believe that there are no rules for them which require that they act in restricted ways of the pyramid. They sit on top of the pyramid or are outside of it, having a social character which plays the system as an instrument for personal opportunity.

The Fountainhead Complex—and Reinstating Colonization

The fountainhead complex can most clearly be seen in children at play. After building a sand castle or stacking building blocks, they will test their dominance over what they make by knocking down their creation. As a general rule no child will accept the situation in which, after he creates something, another child or adult knocks down the work of the young builder. The builder will cry and fight against the "destroyer." In most cases, the child will destroy what he has made if another child attempts to change the originator's creation. In part, the child is demanding to rule.

The architect, Howard Roark, in Ayn Rand's novel, *The Fountainhead,* viewed himself as an "artist" who was to be put in total control of that structure which he created. He identified his self with what he created, believing that that which he created was for self. For him, project was for self at the expense of others even though others have their lives tied to the project. The creators of organizations and the initiators of projects invariably determine to have "things" their own way. And where they don't, they are prepared to risk the destruction of their creation because of their insistence on seeing themselves as self in the work that they think they have produced alone. They search for self and end up the colonizer, risking everyone in their attempt to find self in terms of opportunities and options either made or grasped. In the fountainhead framework, there is no room for communication and cooperation which asserts the creative experience and impulse of others. Instead, self merely becomes more expansive toward colonizing others in the pyramidal state so that more people are collected to do the individual's bidding, or entrapped to hold the expansive colonizer's views and interests. The colonizing self asserts authority against others by their internalizing the values of the fountainhead. The worker wears the badges of the employer who is branded as an instrument of the hierarchic other's expanded power. The fountainhead complex destroys the social contract of consent, equality and space.

The political society which begins from the assumption of equality toward and association in, can be destroyed through the energy of a group or one person who initiates an idea in practice and who, through power, is able to blot out the space of another. One's originating action may have stemmed from personal need or from the technological possibilities of any given moment—the power and profit motive which causes powerful groups to seek more power. Indeed, his reason might have been to be the independent man uncontrolled and unrelated to others. Whatever the primary motivation, those afflicted with the fountainhead complex either blot out those who previously resided in the physical or social space, or exploit them for their own purposes. This occurs in classic cases of taking, which whites may express as drive, talent or creativity. The subjugation of the white man and his colonization of non-European areas of the world over the blacks, browns and yellows is an example of expanded white self through the pyramidal state. The land and bodies become subservient to the hard-driving Social Darwinist who assumes that the winners are the creators and, by definition, the betters. In the United States, the space of the Indian and the land which was thought by the Indian to be, like freedom, indivisible, turned out to be eminently divisible. The colonizer (with his sense of expansive self) occupies spaces which were unoccupied, invents technological systems which create new spaces that others must live within. They have no choice.

In the Violence Colony, for example, the technologists and the military were able to create a perpetual situation of nuclear Armageddon in which the people had no choice but to live voiceless. In the Plantation Colony, the colonizer created a situation in which by the risk which he took, a risk for profit, or the profit which was really theft, he forced a relationship in which the tenant farmer, or the worker, or later the person on welfare, was dependent for his material existence on the frame of

reference which the colonizer created. There was no escape. They characterize the lives of the many in ways which leave the colonized to be "free" because he does not know how to be "free"; that is, to act in freedom.*
He is bedazzled by formal rights and "opportunities" which have little to do with the programs of inauthentic self presented on the television screen; that is, the structure in which he is engulfed . . . the school, the corporation, the military.

Inherent in the project which builds non-hierarchic relationships is the principle that those who enter into the project choose to participate freely and understand that those who choose belatedly are no less part of the project than those who first initiated it. If the individual has found himself in situations where he had no choice but to curb his competitive drive, it is possible that the projects or social inventions which he undertakes will be approached in openness with others, naïveté and self-examination. He will control the tendencies toward the fountainhead complex. In this framework what happens is that the inventor himself will be changed. His freedom is based on openness and relatedness. Yet he does not escape the potentiality of new needs and further dissonances. After all, once the project and the freedom that he feels within or through is limited by the definition set through the other, the dialectical process continues. The difference is that the project awakens the other to find himself. (Political organizers, if they are skillful, awaken others to find their selves, which will force the organizer to confront whether his roots are in fact in the project he initiated. If they are he now will find himself limited by the others.) If the *zone of dissonance* enlarges between the inventor and others, he is forced to leave the project, drop out and begin again. The psychological as

---

* Note definition of freedom, pp. 77–81.

well as political meaning to the project is that it is the part of the individual that is freely chosen. Where the individual cannot leave and the choices are nonexistent or summarily assigned, the individual reverts to someone else's instrumental object. I leave the political arena of reconstruction and am returned to the old pyramid or the revolutionary pyramid.

The Left Fountainhead Complex

Most of the literature of the left continues to assert authority in the old way. Even if we were to take the most eloquent of the Marxist, existentialist thinkers, we would find the problem of authority (which in my view contradicts the nature of the project as the instrument for the decolonizer) unresolved. The right asserts authority for elites, whether they are creators, kings, the military or capitalists. They all share the winner-take-all mentality, thus assuring Roark's problems of *self-against* or *self-as-user* of others. The question remains whether the left, either in theory or practice, has found a more satisfactory answer to the nature of authority.

In *Being and Nothingness,* Jean-Paul Sartre attempts to distinguish between the intentional action, the conscious project and the negligent action. "The careless smoker who has, through negligence, caused the explosion of a powder magazine, has not acted. On the other hand, the worker who is charged with dynamiting a quarry and who obeys the given orders has acted when he has produced the expected explosion; he knew what he was doing, or if you prefer, he intentionally realized a conscious project." Sartre points out that one does not have to foresee all the consequences of his act for the action to be viewed as a project.[18]

As I study this example, I cannot help but conclude that what Sartre is describing is not a project which is chosen by the worker. Instead, the event he describes is one in which the worker is ordered, through Authority, to undertake an act which is not his, but someone else's. The fact that he is aware of the consequences of his blowing up the quarry does not make him a free man, freely determining what is to come; nor does it mean that he participated in the determination of what he is doing. Sartre's worker is no different from the SAC bombardier who knows that if he presses a button on his plane it could release a nuclear weapon which would destroy a city. In both cases, the project continues to belong to someone else. The hierarchic other chooses the future consequences, even though the individual man thinks he is choosing. This process works through officializing the individual; that is, giving him a social character which makes him responsive in the framework of the hierarchic other and the pyramidal state. Unless the bombardier chooses to disregard authority and vest the choice only in himself, his methods, goals, and ends are predestined. However, where he vests the choice in himself by disregarding authority, he breaks his role relationship to the rest of the world. Sartre's analysis of the social condition of freedom does not distinguish the problem of authority, whether it be the party or the capitalist, from the performance of the freely chosen act with another. Sartre's worker remains under the thumb of another.

It appears that we are left with bitter choices in the right or left existential mode of freedom. We can accept either the gratuitous/selfish will of a Caligula or Roark, or we can opt for the discipline, will and authority of another, of the party. In both cases, the colonization remains. The colonized society attempts to repress the fountainhead complex of anyone but the colonizer through orders and controls. Just in that way, the colonized society accepts the revolutionary position of freedom as defined in Sartre's example. It is one which continues to assert that the worker cannot be free, is someone else's object, and not an end in himself. The worker remains a servant whose choices are pre-determined through authority. It does not see, nor does the Sartrian method see another way to relate to individual or group creativity and freedom except through the dialectic between absoluteness and absolution on one side, with coercion and control from the hierarchic other.

These are not casuistic distinctions. Whether a project is something which I am ordered to do and therefore it is a project because I do it and "understand" it, or whether a project is an intentional action whose meaning I understand and whose shape I help create, including awareness of its consequences, is the difference between coercion or freedom in action. Whether it is a part of me and remains so is the continuous struggle of relatedness which I feel toward my work and with others.

The projects which I conceive and in which I involve myself are my strokes in reality. Even where it is my project, if it does not engage my subjective feelings, there is no possibility for authenticity or meaning. The work itself becomes inauthentic and I become merely an extension of the machine or process which now captures me. I become a functionary of the committee room, the subsistence farm, the research project or the assembly line. Those activities, hierarchically organized, and standardizing thousands into the same process, result in the colonized form which causes madcap decisions and choices that I have to abide, neither consenting or dissenting, but being lived. In that context we do not know what is authentic, that is, what we cause to be experienced, what to feel and how to act. Our needs are unknown or remain undetermined because they are mediated through a hierarchic system of authority which has its own agenda of our needs. We are lost in knowing what to offer others which will relate us to them.

2

The Violence Colony Authority and the Social Contract

A tacit contract! That is to say, a wordless and consequently a thoughtless and will-less contract: a revolting nonsense! An absurd fiction! An unworthy hoax! For it assumes that while I was in a state of not being able to will, to think, to speak, I bound myself and all my descendants—only by virtue of having let myself be victimized without raising any protest—into perpetual slavery.

—Mikhail Bakunin[1]

No generation can bind the next generation to commit suicide.

—Benjamin V. Cohen[2]

Since the eighteenth century political thought has attempted two difficult tasks. One task was to justify the importance of the nation state to the individual. The other was to show what obligations a citizen owed to the nation state and what services he could expect from the state. Because a new class emerged in the eighteenth century which intended to redefine its rights and obligations, the philosophers of that new class needed to investigate the basic question of authority and allegiance. Until that time, there had been very little reason for the peasant, the worker or the bourgeois to pledge allegiance to the nation state. They had few rights and many obligations. The people internalized the rights of kings and palace courts to operate as they pleased with the people's money and their lives. They accepted the idea of a be-

wildering system of privileges which they could not begin
to understand let alone control. In many cases this view
of government was accepted as the divine right of kings
to keep Order. The new classes, on the other hand, began
to see governing, with its ornaments of power—the military and the idea that protection was being provided to
the people—as a hustle. Once people doubted the symbols
of authority and saw themselves as awakening to their
rights and to their beings, new definitions of allegiance
and authority were needed to reflect those groups which
did not think that the further they were away from the
king's court the less useful or valuable they were as
citizens.

The rationalization of obedience to the nation state was
accomplished by these philosophers through logic and
myth, not through the historical description of how states
in fact formed. While in America, some pamphleteers
like Thomas Paine or Puritans like John Winthrop might
have believed in the literalness of men coming together
to form a society through the social contract, in Europe
the way states formed was not through the method of
individuals freely consenting together. The new philosophers outlined ways that power, conquest and authority
could be mediated through the concepts of law and shared
sovereignty by the people. It was philosophically fashionable to argue that a government would be predicated on
the idea that the people could judge their governors and
their administration, choose others and where necessary
rebel against tyrants or authoritarians. While such ideas
of limited authority served a new bourgeois class coming
to power in the West, they set new limits of authority
which allowed for greater space for *all* individuals. John
Locke in England, the philosophes in France, Thomas
Jefferson, James Madison and Alexander Hamilton in the
United States spelled out the new meanings of the social
contract.

Yet conservative thinkers of the eighteenth and nineteenth centuries feared the revolutionary flames of such conclusions. Some argued that without leaders who wielded the powers of hierarchy and authority of the state, man could not be steadied in a group. He would be reduced to a natural condition, that is, a state of nature, which was usually described as a situation in which the individual lived at continuous war on a personal level with others. According to the reactionary Joseph de Maistre, anything was better than a society in which men returned to their animal nature. If society had to be held together by the guillotine in which a king and/or an elite set the order, so be it. For De Maistre, all organized society rested on the subordination of the people to fear of the executioner.* While the violence of the guillotine and the whip were (and are) very much in evidence for all to see, the first line of defense for the ordered society in De Maistre's time (and now) is respect for authority. The grandeur and power of the kingly class, the whipholders,

---

*This principle of governing later came to be applied by Europe and the United States in the poor countries of Asia, Africa, and Latin America — children to be spanked and intimidated, or women to be bought, towns to be destroyed which had to be taught a lesson, or to comprehend that stability-making subordination to the grandeur of the civilizers, set the terms of reference for the world. I am reminded of Simone Weil's discussion of the Roman Empire and her quotation from Polybius on the destruction of Carthage:

> Some people killed themselves without motive; others fled from their towns through deserted parts of the country, with no definite aim in their wanderings, from the panic prevailing in the towns. People denounced one another as having been hostile to the Romans; they arrested and accused their neighbors, although as yet, no one was being called to account for anything. Others went to meet the Romans with suppliants' branches, confessing their political transgressions and asking what penance they were to pay, although no one as yet had made any inquiries about them. Everywhere there was a fetid smell, because so many people had thrown themselves down wells or over precipices. So dreadful was the situation that, as the proverb says, "even an enemy would have pitied" the state of Greece. . . . The Thebans fled from their city in a body and left it entirely empty.[3]

had to be respected and followed. If obeisance were paid by the individual to the king or elite class as an ordinary matter of psychological need or physical fear, using the whip would not be necessary; the hierarchic other, or characterization, would do the job of brute force.

De Maistre's view fitted well with the Prussian idea of the State. There was law in the idea of the Prussian state. Indeed, its existence was identical with what law was. There was no law outside of the state and outside of the hierarchic structure of the state. Those who needed the notions of social contract to justify the existence of the state came to understand that the individual gave up all rights once he became part of the social contract. The state, therefore, was the highest authority and those who ran the state through the armed forces, the churches and the landed gentry were the highest authorities. The forces of the state were to be represented in governing through acceptance of the law of authority and order. This was a Lutheran view of the state.

On the other hand, political thinkers of disparate views held certain conceptions in common in the Age of Enlightenment that contradicted the authoritarian mode of statecraft. The power of the state was not absolute, nor was the power of those who ruled it. The views of Machiavelli, in which the State was concerned merely with power and its extension, were challenged by the more democratic-minded philosophers who were concerned with the question of how the state was to be controlled and how the citizen would still live with authority as defined in practice by the bourgeois class. Thus, while Machiavelli was correct in his static description of the operation of states and men who administered states in that the power wielders could dictate the external actions of men, by the eighteenth and nineteenth centuries, the views of Locke, Rousseau and Jefferson had changed the frame of reference of concern to aspirations of justice and the self-governing community. Laws and obligations gave new meaning to the idea that people were *within* a community, not objects of the few who ruled it. Even in the Hobbesian scheme of the state, the individual citizen could act in his own behalf if the sovereign coveted the life of the citizen. The citizen was protected through the social contract which, in the eighteenth century, had an extraordinary effect on governing. For example, the social contract was a widely accepted way of the Puritans in seventeenth-century New England. As J. W. Gough has pointed out, contract theory was enshrined in the American state constitutions.[4] Consent of the governed as spelled out by Locke and Paine, found its way into the constitutions of Delaware (1776), Pennsylvania (1776), Vermont (1777), Maryland (1776), Massachusetts (1780) and Tennessee (1796).

The themes of social contract and limited control over the individual were primary in the preparation of the American Constitution. H. St. George Tucker, a prominent constitutionalist, stated in his commentaries on Blackstone that the Constitution "is an original, written federal and social compact, freely, voluntarily and solemnly entered into by the several states, and ratified by the people thereof respectively; whereby the several states have bound themselves to each other, and to the Federal government of the United States, and by which the Federal government is bound to the several states and to every citizen of the United States." Jefferson supported this view. He believed that the states entered into a constitutional compact by which they agreed to become a single government.

While less idealistic motives can be found and indeed were present in the choices which were made by the handful who accepted the invitation to write an American constitution, certain important general assumptions applied. The constitution-doubters feared that governors

would emerge as a separate and despotic class representing only their own whims and wishes. According to
Charles Beard, some influential revolutionaries like
Patrick Henry, who refused to attend the Constitutional
Convention, argued that any "strong government might
end in a monarchy or that it would mean, in any case,
big armies, big navies, heavy taxes, mountainous debts,
and interference with personal liberty. . . ."[5] The people
feared a government which might, either by its form or
through its actions, transform itself into an unquenchable
militaristic despotism or become enamored of abstract
concepts which would be Prussian in outlook and purpose,
to the point where a man was paying obeisance to the state
for his life and livelihood. These fears were generally held
and Constitution-drafter Alexander Hamilton found that
it was politically necessary to address himself to the fears
of the "extremist anti-authoritarians" if the Constitution
was to be ratified by the states. Hamilton pointed out that
the power of the Congress was to provide for a military
force in times of peace was absolutely essential because the
United States was encircled by British settlements, "sav-
age tribes on our Western Frontier," and shared interests
between Spain and Britain which posed a threat to the
United States.[6] But his argument for the right of armed
forces during peacetime was based on the idea of control
over the armed forces and the actual operational working
of constitutional control by Congress. He rejected the
argument that "we must expose our property and liberty
to the mercy of foreign invaders and invite them by our
weakness to seize the naked and defenseless prey, because
we are afraid that rulers, created by our choice, dependent
on our will, might endanger that liberty by an abuse of
the means necessary to its preservation."[7]

In his analysis Hamilton assured the doubters that there
was no time in the foreseeable future in which the "federal government can raise and maintain an army capable

of erecting a despotism over the great body of the people of an immense empire. . . . "[8] As we shall see, that situation, the apprehension of which Hamilton thought to be a "disease, for which there can be found no cure in the resources of argument and reasoning . . . " has now come to pass.

In any case, whether one favored the Constitution or was opposed to it, the primary concern which occupied the minds of its proponents and opponents was the fear of the absolute power of a ruler or a military class which could engage in war without the consent of the people, in which case the people would be reduced to objects. The solution which such men as Hamilton found to provide for the common defense (but not to build a military class) was through two methods of governance. One was that sovereignty rested with the people and not with the state; the second, that a system of continuous control would operate over the governors and the military. Administrative control over the military would be exercised through a system of fractionated and dual power measures shared by the President and the Congress. On the other hand, the gratuitous use of power was to be controlled by splitting authority between the several branches of government. During the period of Constitution-making, revolutionaries and their supporters argued the question of the Constitution on the basis of how much sovereignty would remain with all of the people or the more "responsible" property holders. Those who favored the kingly or military form per se fled to Canada, the Indies or England.

In the eighteenth century the idea of sovereignty residing in "the people" was an exciting provocation which seemed to sum up the revolutions in England, the United States, and later, in France. Although each had different roots and purposes, as Hannah Arendt points out, the fact is that they all assumed as the minimum purpose of revolution the ideological need for sovereignty of people over monarch. As Ranke has pointed out, "there is no political idea which has had so profound an influence in the course of the last few centuries as that of the sovereignty of the people. At times repressed and acting on opinion, then breaking out again, openly confessed, never realized and perpetually intervening, it is the eternal ferment of the modern world."[9]

But sovereignty of the people and by the people, while it had the political effect of removing legitimacy from one particular class or person which could call on that legitimacy as a way to keep the people as objects, did not operationally have the effect of controlling the powers of those chosen by the people, who might act from avarice and usurpation. Once a group began to think that it had unlimited power the government, or one man, or some of his appointees could use the people any way it or he cared to. The method of control to be exercised by the people was similar to a contract in which the obligation of support for the government was given by the citizen in exchange for the provision and guarantee of his protection and peaceful existence. These latter assurances were to be buttressed by the continuous right of choice for those officers of the government who would be responsible for upholding such obligations. But the seeds of contradiction were set as to the power of such a government in Hamilton's version of the comprehensive power of the government. Enemies could invariably be found to justify necessity and the extension of state power. "And as I know nothing to exempt this portion of the globe from the common calamities that have befallen other parts of it, *I acknowledge my aversion to every project that is calculated to disarm the government of a single weapon, which in any possible contingency might be usefully employed for the general defense and security.*"[10] [Emphasis added] Although in this context Hamilton's view relates to the particular embattled situation of the proposed United States, there is sufficient evidence to note that already the definition of security, general defense, threat and other such concepts would result in very different interpretations, and hence, in very different sorts of adventures and governmental purposes. It seemed that threats of the moment would be used as the pretext for expansion and bellicosity. Such interpretations could only result in the derogation of the social contract since some group or class would have to act for everyone on interpreting when to risk the life of the society. For a long while, this risk was run without adverse consequences. Americans thrived on wars and expansion.

The activists who administered the United States intended that the imperialist impulse of an aggressive people was to be satisfied. Parts of the *Federalist Papers* make clear that the United States was to be an empire with imperial designs, weak now but not for long. The imperial design took on its most immediate and brutal meaning through the decimation of the American Indian and his continued removal from place to place, much in the manner that the United States is now using the Vietnamese peasant and removing him. Of course, the other brutal meaning of the American empire was to be found in the system of slavery and its attempts to "liberate" the slaves. The most important and immediate contradiction to the social contract in America was slavery. From our ·constitutional beginning it was clear that the "pox of slavery" would force a redrafting of the compact if the idea of humanity as basic to the compact was to exist in the life of the country. Beyond these instances of imperial action there have been the approximately 125 conflicts in which the United States has engaged.* All of them have been

* See Senator Everett Dirksen's listing of U.S. interventions in 91 Cong. Rec., 1 Sess., June 23, 1969, pp. S6955-6958.

imperial conflicts in which the leadership class has grown richer, more aggressive and more truculent.

What we see, therefore, is a people who began an ideology of liberty with great energy, and with the idea of becoming an important imperial power. Its leaders would be clever and, when necessary, bellicose. The leadership class would decide when to buy, when to be politic, and when to make war. This stance of statecraft operated on two assumptions: that military power was merely a tool for the political-economic leadership class because the military man could always be controlled, and that technology did not bring with it either another group of challengers or a system of knowledge and things which would alter political control over the military who would try to acquire political leadership. Beginning as an instrument for the leadership class, by mid-twentieth century the military became the system upon which the leadership class depended to uphold its power and the "order" of the society. Power and military action were no longer mediated through law. They were rationalized through self-deceiving rhetoric and propaganda. Thus, we see two important conditions which pervade the Violence Colony. One strain is that of militarism per se. The national security bureaucracy, as Richard Barnet has shown, is an important rationalizing organization within which militarism fits. The violence colonizer who controls or works within that bureaucracy enjoys the fact of excellence of his military organization. He views the military organization as efficient, privileged and with powerful instruments for use. It appears to be precise, efficient and paramount. No doubt as the democracy and the ideology of the society reduce all questions to function, efficiency, and violence, militarism grows in all areas of life because it stands for such qualities.

In a government the mode of efficiency through militarism shows itself as a function of command. For example, if the President wants ten thousand troops sent to Thailand tomorrow, or if he wants a staff paper today on options for use of weapons on American cities tomorrow, he knows that the necessary papers will be presented on time, and if he requests military actions, they will occur. Yet it does not follow that the President has the power to stop covert and military actions once they have begun. In comparison, the civilian side of the government, as President Kennedy was fond of pointing out, seemed lumbering and inefficient. Because of its apparent initiating efficiency, militarism is rewarded with a greater number of assignments and tasks. Its ideology and adherents begin to pervade more of the society as the assumptions of militarism engulf other activities.

The other strain is bellicosity, the heroic warlike stance. This strain is generally supplied by civilian leaders who want to see themselves remembered in history as great leaders. They are prepared to risk and court war as an instrument of personal and state aggrandizement. For example, President Roosevelt risked war prior to World War II; President Johnson made war in Southeast Asia; President Kennedy chanced war in Asia and during the Cuban missile crisis; President Truman made war in Korea; and yet, President Eisenhower, the militarist, avoided war. Finally, the civilian leadership, because of its own glory or foolish sense of purpose and efficiency, is swallowed by the militarist tradition of efficiency. This tradition is related to the modern economic organization of the industrial state.

The average "citizen" has accepted the military system and the judgments of the leadership class because he believes that his security and well-being are protected by the military and provided for through the judgments made by an elite. In the last generation, for example, this average citizen accepted the establishment of a Department of Defense which has spent over $1,400 billion since World War II, while allowing incursions on himself through military conscription and an extraordinarily high tax for the idea of common defense. Given the historical ethos of "protection" which the military class sells and citizens have been in the habit of internalizing, it has been difficult for Americans to see that the defense they were offered was merely a new version of the old empire builders and pharaohs who used the defenseless for their greater glory, whether they were part of one's own state, or had yet to be conquered or absorbed.

The difference between the use of force externally (*in* other nations) on those yet to be absorbed or subjugated, as against those who are already absorbed and thought of as citizens, generally washes away when a nation's internal economic and political instabilities make clear that there is no legitimacy of action except force. The technology used externally, as well as the people who use such technology, are then called upon to perform domestically in the same way they performed in the imperial wars or in imperial administration. For example, the use of the same techniques in Saigon, Berkeley, and Chicago has had the effect of internationalizing the confrontation of the colonizer and colonized, especially because the American imperium is so powerful. It is now viewed as the world's primary enemy by the poor and the young. The hierarchic, pharaohistic relationship is under attack in the twentieth century as a result of a world egalitarian and democratic rhetoric in which the socialists and capitalists, the Maoists and the liberals, vie with one another in showing the importance of the people's rights and the people's power. Such rhetoric is used by leadership for the purpose of keeping and extending power. It is, of course, self-delusive, and has the effect of causing delusion among the citizens as to the purpose of their leaders. In the United States it is the democratic ideal which people fight for and believe in.

However, when they realize that the rhetoric no longer reflects anything near the reality—this contradiction is presented to them through television, or in deprivations and depredations which they suffer—it is only a matter of time before the people realize they are not citizens, but are instead colonized. They then begin to examine the value of imperialist adventures in which young men are called upon to pay the price of protecting the colonizing class. The conservatives doubt the state structure because they begin to see that those who run the state do so according to whims and fancies. They see legislative control eroded into a non-deliberative, rubber-stamp body on major issues over which the legislature should have power. The conservative sees this result in the growth of an imperial bureaucracy and commitments which the legislature ratifies virtually without question. Such ventures as the American war in Vietnam and virtually unlimited commitments are advanced, even though they destroy the monetary system which the conservative covets. The young men—the colonized—see the military from a different perspective than the pomp and efficiency the colonizer sees in his military organization. The young men in the service of the militarist see inefficiency, the doing and re-doing of the same activities for no purpose while waiting to be called upon to fight for unexplained purposes. People wonder but are silent. As Georges Bernanos wrote in *Tradition of Freedom:*

> I have thought for a long time now that if, some day the increasing efficiency of the technique of destruction finally causes our species to disappear from the earth, it will not be cruelty that will be responsible for our extinction and still less, of course, the indignation that cruelty awakens and the reprisals and vengeance that it brings upon itself—but the docility, the lack of responsibility of the modern man, his base subservient acceptance of every common decree. The horrors which we have seen, the still greater

horrors we shall presently see, are not signs that devils insubordinate, rather that there is a constant increase, a stupendously rapid increase, in the number of obedient, docile men.[11]

Bernanos' fears were not misplaced, but the mask is now lifted. What is the face?

The national security state emerged from conditions of the economic depression. The first contracts awarded in 1938 were to Navy yards as a means of getting into the world imperial game and employing workers. Ideologically, the New Deal had run out of ideas and therefore blamed the organization of the Congress. Liberals believed that the legislative branch of the government could not perform those functions necessary to right the economy or move quickly enough to deal with crises and opportunities which leadership could react to. Furthermore, liberals saw themselves as collaborators with the more decent and empty-headed of the corporate establishment. Their power plus that of the bureaucracy under executive leadership could provide the necessary active force to deal with depressions and capture world leadership. In this process, the Keynesians espoused the theory that the economy could operate to the "general" benefit with some state guidelines, but it would remain under private control and direction except where it was necessary to get together through the Federal Reserve system or through Business Advisory Councils to act in concert for their interests. The state itself would expand its activities. First there would be a strong bureaucracy which would operate as a force that had to be bargained with because it would be staffed with people who had new sorts of knowledge and could assess information. Second there would be a strong emphasis on force and control to fight authoritarianism and totalitarianism.

To the authoritarians the national security state would

see internal threats to itself which it would control through an internal security network. It would chip away at pluralism while praising its existence, and it would build the internal power of the military and economic groupings which appeared to reflect the stability and growth of the state. The cosmetic elements of pluralism which the liberals had thought were necessary for their security—free speech, for example—would be guaranteed so long as free speech had no effect on the political life of the country; that is to say, on how it was ruled and who ruled it. Where free speech became a threat to the pyramidal structure, to those at the top of the structure who made deals with each other and brokered huge interests within the national security state, then free speech would be eliminated, curtailed or flooded by other information until people had no choice but to tune out.

Nuclear weapons took the national security state system outside of a more classic analysis of an authoritarian-totalitarian state which was held together by rhetoric and national guardsmen who were called to defend property of industrialists. (As one of the violence commission reports points out, the guard was established to deal with labor at the insistence of the capitalist class.) Military technology changed the nature of the authoritarian-totalitarian state. Whereas in communism, Nazism and fascism, the state planned its genocide and destroyed a class or race over a period of time, the advent of military technology has meant that huge military and technological bureaucracies prepare as a way of institutional being for a nuclear genocide which could occur in one moment of Gotterdämmerung.

By this I do not mean to depreciate an important aspect of the Vietnam genocide. In that adventure the military and civilian bureaucrats attempted to find out if they could fight a brushfire genocidal war by quickly moving communications networks, bombs, whole administrative teams across the world in an imperial show of force and organization. This methodology, of course, is the more classic method of the modern security state with imperialist designs. The report of General Westmoreland and Admiral Sharp showed the imperial war as a colossal success for such forms of organizational "rationality." The new difference is in the nuclear weapons, which demand arms in being and a whole social system committed to genocide.

To put this matter another way, the history of the cold war and Great Power politics has been an exercise in using millions of people as hostage. Stripped of pretense and rhetoric, the cold war has been nothing more than a situation in which a group of people who have the keys to nuclear destruction brandish nuclear weapons because their views of interest or ego say that that is what must be done. They offer others for slaughter on their own authority, self-inspired and self-initiated, in order to assert their power or personal prestige. Thus in a rich, technologically advanced mass society, politics is reduced to the ability of small groups of people to dictate suicide for the rest. In the summer of 1961, I was a member of the special staff of the National Security Council. The nation was caught up in the Berlin crisis and the cry for civil defense. The latter notion was initiated by those who saw the possibilities of using nuclear weapons as first-strike threats to be carried out against the other side, provided we had some civil defense. The "policy-maker" and the President were to be armed with what was called "will stiffeners," i.e., more missiles and shelters. During the Berlin crisis, the President asked that a paper be written on how to perform a first strike against the Soviet Union. Five people were privy to the war-plans paper, which outlined the methods of attack, how many would be killed if we hit them first, how we would use S.A.C., etc. I was given a copy of the paper by one of the five and after reading it I went to see him. The paper was, to my way of thinking, quite mad and morally bankrupt. I came into the office and said that the paper was morally bankrupt, foolish, etc. We yelled at each other and screamed, *and cried*. I said that we were no different than the planners who worked out the train schedules and the movements of Jews into concentration camps. Who were we to "tear up" the Russian people, or East European people, or any people at all?

In 1962, fifteen men in the entire world at the time of the Cuban missile crisis played out their nuclear poker hands while 500 million people waited to find out whether they themselves would live or die. In 1967, the ruling junta in the United States bombed on the border of China while the world waited to see whether it would be plunged into nuclear war. In 1967, an unctuous Undersecretary of State, Nicholas Katzenbach, announced that the Congress has no power to stop unauthorized wars, and the Senators were flabbergasted. Aren't these examples of the end of one politics and the need for another? They are the stark illumination of how hierarchic structures, coupled with a massive war technology, turn people into things and objects, if those at the tops of the pyramids so decide.

What we see here is a double reality, one political, the other technological. The political structure has broken down, since operationally there is no control which the Congress or the people is able to exercise over the bellicose and the militaristic. Second, the nation-state cannot protect its "citizens" because of runaway technology and an unaccountable corporate-defense structure. In this situation, we will find the military-political leadership expecting and demanding total obeisance to its will. To command such obeisance it will become even more arrogant and take more risks in order to bring about a populace which will bend to its needs and purposes. Consonant with this demand will be greater reliance on force and violence in the American society. The Dream Colony will serve the purpose of bringing forward an immobile mass who fantasize about personal violence as an heroic act.

The violence colonizers who control the state (and those whom they have given the keys to) have now arrogated to themselves the right to commit suicide for everyone in the society. Their ability to foster a political situation in which the power of suicide is given to the violence colonizer stems from the belief on the part of the colonized that the hierarchic structure acts according to the interests of the colonized. Accepting the idea of function, role and specialized knowledge, the people are easy prey for the argument of superior information and intelligence. The colonized assume that the choices of the colonizer are based on superior information and intelligence which the colonizers have in their possession. Existentially, people give their allegiance or accept their passive situation because they are led to believe that they are secure and protected by the colonizer.

But the roots are now exposed. The national security state system can no longer keep the social and political pieces in place. All people in American society tremble at the possibilities of revolt in their cities, and they cannot imagine any apparent way to handle such revolts. They are stunned by a war in Southeast Asia in which the average soldier is befuddled and demoralized by what he is doing, and they are beginning to sense the probability of continued imperialist wars in non-white countries as a result of American commitments and games of nuclear chicken. Furthermore, controls over the armed forces are loosened as each internal military grouping gets its own nuclear weapons to control. For example, once MIRV is in place, each submarine and crew will be able to destroy 180 cities, and there is no way to know whether the submarine commander can or cannot, will or will not, once he undertakes his threat. It is virtually impossible for people to internalize the idea that the state technology and bureaucracy knows what it is doing. The "facts" which seep to the top of the pyramid through the bureaucracy appear as mass delusion when exposed. Historically, the colonizers of violence play the kingly game of superior "intelligence" and information to justify their wars, mistakes, and power. The colonized in this view are like children who are not expected to understand the sorts of choices leaders have to make. Furthermore, they are not expected to have the information, technical knowledge or intelligence to pass judgment or comprehend decision-making. The leaders use locked doors, guards, electric fences, and quantities of hearsay and other forms of make-believe in order to help them think and encourage others to think that they have important intelligence and objectively found information which cannot be shared. "If only you knew what we in power know," says the colonizer. In a statement before the House Armed Services Committee, the madness of this situation was unfolded. The Secretary of the Air Force was testifying on the Vietnam war budget with specific reference to the Air Force bombings and their "success" . . .

MR. LEGGETT. Yes. Thank you, Mr. Chairman.

[Deleted.] I wonder if you could just give us a thumb-nail sketch of how that aircraft is doing, what additional capability does it give us out there, and what are the nature of the missions that are being run?

SECRETARY BROWN. We are using a variety of [deleted] aircraft [deleted] out there, Mr. Leggett. I would like to go off the record and then put as much of it as I can back into the record, because I know you will want some of it in the record.

MR. PRICE. Yes.

SECRETARY BROWN. May I go off the record?

MR. PRICE. Yes, off the record, Sam.

(Further statement of Secretary Brown off the record.)

SECRETARY BROWN. I wanted to go off the record on that because it is a quite sensitive subject.

MR. PRICE. We are off the record, Mr. Secretary.

(Further statement of Secretary Brown off the record.)

SECRETARY BROWN. Maybe I should now go back to the record.

[Deleted.]

SECRETARY BROWN. Yes.

MR. BATES. It says that. These things are not very closely held at this point in time.

SECRETARY BROWN. It is one thing for him to say it and it is another thing for me to say it.

MR. BATES. Yes, you will confirm it, I think is your point.

SECRETARY BROWN. That is right. I think Mr. Bray made that point very, very well. And I would like that statement off the record.

MR. BATES. We all have that same problem. Every time you have information, people ask you, even though it might be common knowledge. There is a question of confirmation.

SECRETARY BROWN. Let me see what I can do about determining how much of this information can be legitimately declassified. It will so appear in the record and can be so used.

(The following information was received for the record:)

Additional information, which could expand the subject under discussion, cannot be provided in unclassified form.

MR. LEGGETT. [Deleted.]

SECRETARY BROWN. Well, I definitely want this off the record. [Deleted.]

THE CHAIRMAN. Yes.

(Further statement of Secretary Brown off the record.)[12]

But now those who subjectively feel their dissonance between what is told to them and what is obvious, answer the colonizer by announcing that it is he who is imprisoned in the temples of power. An extraordinary dialectical trick is played: the colonizer who profiles others ends up as the profile because his ways of living and obtaining knowledge are so abstracted.

The fact of knowing only the profile of the body politic does not mean that the colonizer has no power to destroy. The power of destruction has been deeded to him by technology, hierarchy and the mandarin intellectual. As I have suggested, the pyramidal structure is buttressed by the rationalizers of colonized knowledge, see pp. 48–49. During the administration of President John Kennedy, leading professors from Harvard, MIT, the RAND Corporation and other institutions spent their time computing ways to destroy the Soviet Union and other communist countries through a series of nuclear strikes. The same habit of mind, and in some cases the same people, developed our stance for brush-fire wars. They are also developing technological methods and economic controls to work with the military and the police in putting down revolts in the slums. The nation-state structure (and now the universities) finds itself reduced to an arm of the Violence Colony, specifically the militarized caste, in its attempt to put down internal rebellion, not only in the form of research input but also of methods of dealing with dissenters in the university who object to its research for war on the campus. The People's Park at Berkeley, where the university president sent in 2500 guardsmen, armed and shooting, is an example. To keep power the militarized civilian caste will protect itself by giving more power to the police and military to deal with internal rebellion. Consequently, they will lose power to the military-police group as well as any independent controlling authority over them.

In its foreign relations, the nation-state becomes an anomaly because of technology:

The physical security of its citizens can no longer be provided by it. Each nation-state at best mythically protects its citizens. In the present nuclear arms race world, the national security of the United States is dependent on the Soviet Union, while the national security of the Soviet Union is dependent on the United States. And further, both societies are dependent on the whims and rationalities of military and civilian strategists; that these specialists in violence will not use the nuclear weapon to threaten or blackmail their own societies.[13]

The nation-state has reduced itself to an arm of military power, and its leadership ends up as destroyers of community. The habits of mind are bellicose and military.

Some time ago my wife and I had dinner with an American ambassador, a man who had thought often of becoming Secretary of State. In our discussion about nuclear war and weapons he said that such a war was absurd and impossible. No one wanted to use such weapons in Vietnam, or anywhere else. "Quite so," I responded, "and I am sure that no rational man such as yourself, if you were Secretary of State, would use nuclear weapons." "That isn't what I said," he replied. "If I were Secretary of State, perhaps there would be instances in which I would have to use them."

By allowing the leadership every option, including the ultimate one, we have allowed ourselves no option at all. Where everything is permitted, in Dostoyevski's phrase, nothing is possible. By allowing a leader the right to destroy us if he ever gets the technical and political power to do so, we have put ourselves in the position of the exploited and oppressed. The people are instruments who are dependent on the leader's wish to keep open options of our destruction. Our existence is dependent upon someone's mask of rationality. In the elementary, secondary and university schools the mandarins develop the attitudes and knowledge which give leaders violent options. The case of civil defense is pertinent in this regard. While it was sold as a measure to protect people, the mandarins viewed civil defense as a necessary instrument to strengthen the will of the people so that they would be more willing to allow the leaders to take risks in their name. Herman Kahn and others talked about the evacuation of cities to strengthen the policy maker's hand at the bargaining table.

While submission to this perverted view of Hobbesianism might be thought of as a way for a state to operate which explicitly started from the assumption that there was no social contract between the people and their government, the American experiment assumes and acts on the basis of a social contract. This social contract rejects the idea that man can give up his uniqueness or his own personality in such a way as to become a plaything in the hands of others.

> This fundamental right, the right to personality, includes in a sense all the others. To maintain and to develop his personality. It is not subject to freaks and fancies of single individuals and cannot, therefore, be transferred from one individual to another. *The contract of rulership which is the legal basis* of all civil power has, therefore, its inherent limits. There is no *pactum subjectionis,* no act of submission by which man can *give up the state* of a free agent and enslave himself. For by such an act of renunciation he would give up that very character which constitutes his nature and essence: he would lose his humanity.[14]

It may appear surprising to think of the social contract in merely negative terms. After all, the social contract was not merely a political contract. By the eighteenth century it was a primary instrument for the individual to seek his humanity. One hope was that it could be found through community. But the tragedy and the hope of the moment is that the positive aspects of the contract cannot

be fulfilled through a hierarchic and authoritarian structure of society.

The social contract historically has had two separate
meanings. On the one hand, its terms may be viewed as
those of a community which binds itself together, based
on reciprocity and the presupposition of equality. It is
an agreement of equals who associate themselves together
in a relationship of equality. The Greeks referred to such
a relationship as that of non-rule or no ruler (isonomy).
The second meaning of social contract emerged from the
most minimal notion of relationship to sovereign. It was
of course the idea of obeisance in exchange for protection.

It is obvious that the latter definition of the contract
was most easily opened to a non-consensual view of relationship. In both cases, however, once one leaves the
framework of face-to-face communities, the daily operation of the state and large organizations on the lives of
individuals invariably favors the idea of obeisance for
protection as the way people come to live. The contradiction is manifest when the governors are no longer able
to give protection. In that case, the question remains
whether obeisance is still required. The answer to this
question is profoundly practical. People will attempt
to find ways in their own lives of achieving protection
or security for themselves. If they do, the objects and
institutions which they once accepted as the means for
those protections will go unsupported as new modes of
institutional arrangements will come into being to supply
protection. This is especially true in the case where the
stronger presupposition of the social contract as it is
understood in America—at least theoretically—is that it
reflects the coming together of an association of equals.
Consequently, demands and practice will require that
people find ways of fulfilling that definition of the social
contract, once it is clear that the idea of obeisance for

protection no longer operates in practice. The redefinition of the social contract will most likely emerge from the seeming inability of the present Constitution to deal with either national defense or face-to-face relationships.

There are some who hold to the uniqueness of the individual as the basic promise of the social contract, and therefore individuals must be protected against majorities. We find, however, that given the present structure of technology and authority, the question we seek to answer is much more mundane. How do we protect ourselves from elites who use us, the majority, as hostage for their whims and purposes?

Because the terms of allegiance for protection are shattered, the contract between the individual and those who arrogate sovereignty to themselves ceases to exist. The *de facto* termination of the contractual obligation forces people to define different contractual relationships which assert new legitimate objects of authority *in themselves.* (In Part Three we shall deal with the search for new legitimate objects of authority.) However, it should be noted that the replacement of the social contract with a theory of elitism and hostage holding, as mediated through the national security state, is not a stable mode of governing, although this theory has been an important counter theme in American history. The problem of hostage holding and elite control has been consistently attacked by a vocal minority in the United States since its inception. For example, in the Midwest the prospect of war has never been taken lightly. Led by Senator Robert La Follette, the Progressive Movement had as one of its cardinal principles the idea that war should not be declared either by the President or the Congress. War was a matter of such basic interest to each of the citizens according to the Progressives that it should only be declared through popular referendum. Whether or not the method which the Progressives put forward was the perfect way of deciding the question of war or peace for the body politic, it assumed the rights of citizens to know and make known their will on basic questions of their existence. It is difficult to comprehend the importance, for example, of Senator Borah's resolution on December 12, 1927, in the United States Senate as a way to protect the people against the follies of government, thus protecting the power of lawful government. His resolution stated that as war had been a lawful institution among states, he wanted the Senate to resolve "that it is the view of the Senate of the United States that war between nations should be outlawed as an *institution or means for the settlement of international controversies by making it a public crime under the law of nations,* and that every nation should be encouraged by solemn agreement or treaty to bind itself to indict and punish its own international war-breeders or instigators and war profiteers under powers similar to those conferred upon our Congress under Article I, Section 8 of our Federal Constitution, which clothes the Congress with the power to define and punish offenses against the law of nations. . . . "[15]

Such ideas do not die easily. At first they may be used rhetorically, and then worn as the clothes of vengeance. The United States pressed Borah's argument in the allied case against Japanese leaders who were successfully tried for war crimes after the second world war. In the latter part of the twentieth century it is likely that many people in the name of a national community will insist that the people, *as a community,* should decide questions of war and peace, not the rulers, and punish those who arrogate authority over others. Such a position taken by dissenters and resisters who believe that the social contract has ended unless leadership can be held to account, may have produced for themselves a generation of grave personal risk.

Such people will find themselves in confrontation with a military class which views war as the basic activity of the state.

Attempts by the students and faculty of the academic community to resist the military conscription system suggest a first step in challenging part of the structural foundation of the national security state. How this confrontation will resolve itself and what the results of such a confrontation will be cannot be predicted. While the confrontation will continue through an entire generation, that is, through the last part of the twentieth century, as one person after another and one institution after another discover how they have become hostage and are totally characterized, positive alternatives will be tried which will attempt, in a pragmatic way, to redraft the social contract in all life areas which are interdependent and shared. New places of authority outside of the state will emerge.

There are certain necessary requirements to the redrafting of the social contract. One primary requisite is to find the way in which the participation of the individual citizen and the corporate unit of which he is a part may be democratized so that he will not feel himself to be part of the powerless and alienated masses. The project in reconstructing the social contract requires new attention to boundaries between the individual and the community, note pp. 51–52. Not only are there constraints which the individual accepts in the community and vice versa, so it is the case that the leadership of the community will have to deny itself certain tools and sanctions which by their use will destroy the community. The hubris of the leader who reserves to himself the right to destroy whole cities for his good and sufficient reasons is an example of one who can be controlled only through the horizontal group which specifically reserves rights of uniqueness to individuals and the right of finding ways to join their uniqueness with others. We are required to change leadership and the function known as leadership. This view now requires a new politics of participation and control.

I suggest one mode hesitantly and only in the hope that we may begin to find ways of reasserting control over the fundamental political parts of our unique existences. There is a stubborn and irremediable fact. The national government now collects resources, men and wealth, which are used to make the fundamental human problems of our society greater. These irrational choices by the colonizer force those in politics to suggest the necessity of returning to first principles, to principles of definition about such matters as the social contract. No doubt they present themselves in ways which at first appear to be disrespect for "law and order"; this phrase becomes the way for many in the society to insist on protecting the colonizer by whatever means or cost. But protection of the state or of its colonizing power is not the concern of the young. They refuse to fight in colonial wars. Others flee. Within the society those who accept its pyramidal structure cannot abide expenditures on military intervention abroad. Those who are elected to public political office on a local level begin to see the contradiction of huge expenditure for irrelevant and mad items while their constituencies are deprived and their geographic areas decay at an exponential rate. Is it a dream which says that the United States spends 700 million dollars a week destroying another nation while not finding ways to spend ten million dollars to clean up rats? The contradiction is too great and too obvious. It is one which a society will not be able to live with.

By the very nature of the situation with which we are presented it becomes necessary to face the ominous question of when the people may dissolve their government.

This is not a trivial matter, nor should one who raises it do so in arrogance or superiority. It can only be raised without being considered a pest when it is done from a sense of felt need and attention to the obvious. It is important in discussing this question to remember the basis of democratic action. As John Locke has said, there is a great difference between the dissolution of the society and the dissolution of the government. A society dissolves itself when it is conquered by a foreign invader. In that case, the individual has no choice according to Locke but to shift for himself. Governments, whether they are free or totalitarian, will invariably fall to the conqueror. Obviously, in our time a resistance would form itself. On the other hand, governments may and should be dissolved either when the single person or prince sets himself above the laws and authorizes what he wants, refuses to carry out the laws, or "when the legislative or the prince, either of them, act contrary to their trust."[16] The people always reserve themselves the right to act against a legislative which cause the people to be reduced to slavery. Where the annoyances are not petty but clear and major, the people who are willing to accept a great deal of mismanagement and even minor treachery will exchange murmur for mutiny. However, the people do not have to wait until a general castatrophe has occurred, for example, nuclear destruction, or a nuclear "accident" which destroys an American city, to act. Where the design is clear, according to Locke, the people should rouse themselves and "endeavor to put the rule into such hands which may secure to them the ends for which government was erected. . . ."[17] People are absolved from further obedience when governments are able to put themselves into a state of war with the people. They are "left to the common refuge which God hath provided for all men against force and violence." To the black man, his choices seem clear. Those of us characterized by the choices of people who undertook to build nuclear weapons in secret outside the permission of the people, and who finally built a military force which can destroy a whole civilization in a few hours while cities suffocate from pollution and inaction, are left to conclude that the American government finds itself in jeopardy because we are characterized as hostages.

Whensoever, therefore, the legislative shall transgress this fundamental rule [of not making its citizenry slaves to arbitrary power] of society, and either by ambition, fear, *folly* or corruption endeavor to grasp themselves, or put into the hands of any other, an absolute power over the lives, liberties and estates of the people, by this breach of trust they forfeit the power the people had put into their hands for contrary ends, and it devolves to the people, who have a right to resume their original liberty and by the establishment of a new legislative (such as they shall think fit), provide for their own safety and security, which is the end for which they are in society.[18]

3

The Plantation Colony

"If I knew that all I was going to do with my life was make 20,000 pounds of bubble gum, I think I'd call it quits right now."

—Factory worker applying for job as Washington policeman. *Washington Post,* March 15, 1970.

The economics of the West has traveled a long road since the time of Aristotle. To transform the United States from a mixed economic system of market and *diktat* to an economics of relatedness, it will be necessary to rescue some old Aristotelian principles that were misfiled. Aristotle points out that there are two sorts of wealth-getting. One is for use as part of household management, while the other is for retail trade—"the former necessary and honorable, while that which consists in exchange is justly censured; for it is unnatural, and a mode by which men gain one from another. The most hated sort, and with the greatest reason, is usury, which makes a gain out of money itself, and not from the natural object of it." Aristotle does not mean to censure the barter system per se, for example, as in the exchange of shoes for wine. Aristotle criticized the growth of that form of marketing and money power which distorted people into believing that "the whole idea of their lives is that they ought either to increase their money without limit, or at any rate not to lose it. The origin of this disposition in men is that they are intent upon living only, and not upon living well; and as their desires are unlimited, they also desire that the means of gratifying them should be without limit."[1]

Karl Marx in his work embellished on the distinction between the use value and the exchange value, siding with the Aristotelian view that there was greater meaning and authenticity for people in use rather than exchange value. The irony in practice of course is that the Plantation Colony in its market and regulated forms rhetorically favors the principle of use but follows the principle of exchange. The great insight of Veblen was that conspicuous consumption and, by extension, conspicuous waste and conspicuous obsolescence (a new model each year, whether weapons or cars) had given rise to the principle of disuse. The fact is that exchange values (the bread for the clothes) gave way to *gain* values which transformed the entrepreneurial instinct of man into an instrument for more things and more authority over others, so that particular men could do things while others remained as those who provided the labor for the few to do things.

By the eighteenth century, the principle of gain (in terms of power or wealth) silently eased the value of exchange and use to the side, when it came to be coupled with the Western technological revolution of the eighteenth century (and especially in the United States). Quantitative theories of economic growth in industrialized societies like the United States created a situation in which wants were created and needs went unmet. This system of political economy resulted in people *spending* their lives and making things that were neither useful nor necessary. The result of course was a human aliena-

tion from what was made, because what was made was
shameful or silly.

The Marxists were the first to remake the Aristotelian
point. The loss of control by the producer over what is
made results in a situation where that which he makes
but does not understand ends up exploiting him and the
user. In another sense, the aspiration to "become something," to become a thing, is the most literal result for
individuals in a market/feudal society. As Engels pointed
out in *The Origin of the Family, Private Property and
the State:*

> The rise of private property in herds and articles of
> luxury led to exchange between individuals, to the transfor-
> mation of products into commodities. And here lie the seeds
> of the whole subsequent upheaval. When the producers no
> longer directly consumed their product themselves, but let
> it pass out of their hands in the act of exchange, they lost
> control of it. They no longer knew what became of it; the
> possibility was that one day it would be used against the
> producer to exploit and oppress him. For this reason no
> society can permanently retain the mastery of its own pro-
> duction and the control over the social effects of its pro-
> cess of production unless it abolishes exchange between
> individuals.[2]

Yet technology seems to contradict the economics of the
market or the feudal economy, because the possibility is
clearly present to attain two ends: the liberation of people
to define their own tasks — self-controlled time, which in
modern history has been possible for only the few; and the
freeing of people to relate to people rather than to be
controlled by machines. This can happen if we transform
through the project the values of an economic system,
whether it is capitalist or socialist, which puts primary
emphasis on weapons, widgets and employment; that is,
doing the bidding of another. Very few people are

engaged in the making of food and fiber or related necessities as defined in classical Marxist terms.

Thus, making the staples of life is the task of the very
few. I should not be construed as meaning that there are
millions that are not working; that is, doing things they
don't want to do just to have money so that they can live
at a standard of life upon which the colonized society
subtly insists. However, it is interesting to look at the
question of how people actually "spend" their lives in
the United States, since that will give a clue to the argument that the "work" people actually do is either nothing,
or it is dysfunctional. Where people are actually "employed," we may find that the typical pyramidal situation is present. What is made or done is not as important
as the fealty and the psychological exploitation of having
one work for another. The worker becomes the commodity. This condition can be seen in bureaucracies in government and corporate enterprise, where busy-ness for its
own sake or for building authority over others is the goal.

In his classic essay "On Freedom," Bertrand Russell
points out how leisure could be distributed "justly without injury to civilization." He gives the reader an illustra-
tion which is less perverse than the American situation,
since in the American situation the potentiality for self-
controlled time on the part of workers is so much greater
than ever before, and the need for work in the sense that
many must labor for the few or for themselves to eat or
be clothed is now so clearly fatuous. But here is Russell's
example. "Suppose that at a given moment, a certain
number of people are engaged in the manufacture of pins.
They make as many pins as the world needs, working (say)
eight hours a day. Someone makes an invention by which
the same number of men can make twice as many pins
as before. But the world does not need twice as many
pins! Pins are already so cheap that hardly any more
will be bought at a lower price. In a sensible world, every-

body concerned in the manufacture of pins would take to working four hours instead of eight, and everything else would go on as before. But in the actual world, this would be demoralizing. The men still work eight hours, there are too many pins, some employers go bankrupt, and half the men previously concerned in making pins are thrown out of work. There is, in the end, just as much leisure as on the other plan, but half the men are totally idle while half are still overworked. In this way, it is insured that the unavoidable leisure shall cause misery all round instead of being a universal source of happiness. Can anything more insane be imagined?"[3]

The unfortunate answer is yes. In the leading pyramidal state the United States had millions work on necrophilia or activities that end up as necrophilic (for example, nuclear weapons, missiles, chemical weapons), through the corporate economic form. The authoritarian economic forms organize the profit system on needs which by their nature are pathogenic. Organizational forms, if they are to become something other than pathogenic, need to reflect changing human needs, desires and relationships. Obviously, the question which is always pertinent is "whose needs and desires?" We may assume here that we are talking about those needs, desires and relationships which reflect human feeling, not organizational function and class privilege which become encrusted in that part of the colonized reality concerned with economics. In America, such changes require the reconstitution of the economic corporation.

The economic corporation is central to American life. As Max Lerner has pointed out, the corporation is the way "by which Americans organize any project demanding group effort, impersonality, continuity beyond the individual life, and limited liability."[4] To deal with the Beast requires more than flaying it with a stick. Instead, the direction for an alternative structure needs to be

developed by which the present corporation can transform itself. Such a question directs one's attention further:
(a) What is the humane economic organization which produces man's needs?; (b) How should such an organization
be governed and controlled?; and (c) What are the standards which should govern the operation of such an
organization?

Since 1938, as a result of the New Deal, such questions
have been mediated through a complex system of business
guidelines and oligopoly, anti-trust protection laid out by
the federal government, trade associations, the labor
unions and leadership within the private corporate enterprise. However, the framework for the economy rests with
the planning boards and finance committees of the largest
corporate enterprises. They set the terms of what is to be
made, the quantity to be made and the profit margins
which they wish to obtain. Scholars such as A. A. Berle
have sat on such boards, titillated by the corporation and
its workings, building for it a corporate veil of respecta-
bility. While from time to time such corporations are made
up of scholars (note Kaysen at Polaroid), such committees
are peopled by owners of the corporations, their managers, and lawyers. The measuring stick which they
use to decide what is to be made relates primarily to profits, growth rates, long-term expansion and stability. For
our purposes the question of who makes policy in the
corporation, that is, whether it is the owner or the manager, is largely of academic interest since the standards
which each operates by and the methods they use to enforce those standards are essentially the same for both
groups. Their concern is instrumental in the narrow sense
of profits for stockholders and themselves. As Beardsley
Ruml has pointed out, "The search for profits is probably
the most important single motivating force in modern
business. Undoubtedly, many businessmen experience

other impulses in the daily affairs of their business than the sheer desire to make profit: the desire to retain an old and faithful employee whose usefulness is past; the desire to help customers who happen also to be friends by continuing their credit during depression; a genuine feeling of responsibility to serve the public. However, it is still probable that the most widely prevailing motive in modern business is the desire for profits."[5]

That emphasis in this economic system is on cost, price, obsolescence of the thing, and emphasis on "new models," there is no reason to deny. More important, the profit corporate structure does not make possible a means of judging value except in terms of price, nor does its mechanism help in determining the general environmental effect of what is made and the way people spend their lives. While there is a quiet rebellion among the college generation against the profit corporations, the vast number of people in this generation will continue to operate within the corporate structure or as servants to it. It is likely that they will bring their rebellion into the corporation. Such a rebellion will take the shape of new forms of community involvement and control over corporate life.*

---

* A social current which can affect the direction toward a profound transformation of the corporate system is one that is not usually considered important. The sons of the captains of finance and industry, if not the captains themselves, will yield control over significant parts of the economy because they cease to believe in the purposes of their class. In other words, the children of the rich and privileged see no reason to consume the goods that are being consumed, to spend money for accretion of military power (which leads to the building of potential rivals for control) and having power not directly related to forms of personal gratification. To put it another way, while the young may continue to favor the entrepreneurial model, such entrepreneurship of the young generation of the affluent appears to define good works outside of the economic profit model.

The importance of risk and purpose is not denied, but economic profit does not seem to be related to risk and purpose. Consequently, it is not a silly dream to think that those most likely to be attuned to the profit system's purposes will themselves force a withering away of the profit-making corporations. The young per-

As I have intimated, this extension is a necessity in corporate society if we intend to save ourselves from the devastating and inhuman results which our industrial system now is in the process of causing. While the democratization of the corporation might not, by itself, save the society from an inhuman result, certain consequences are more likely. There would be far less emphasis on honorific or humanly destructive activities and less error and more concern with the needs of people which are otherwise lost in the profit corporate system. Perhaps this view can be challenged. However, the burden of proof must rest with those who extol the present political economy. The figures which show what we spend our resources on reveal the difficulty of overcoming the indictment against the corporation.

There are ways to begin the peaceful democratization of authority structures such as corporations through the application of the Bill of Rights to the everyday activities of the corporation.

---

son whose class-consciousness is changed in school, through irritation and confrontation, will reject the purposes of the business corporation as foolish and the products which it makes as functionally unnecessary or indeed harmful.

Where the authority structure throughout the body politic comes under attack the assumptions of that authority structure in the economic sphere will also be changed to the point that the assumptions of the economic structure itself are reviewed by those most intimately involved in it. The long-term historic reasons for this reality can be noted in the effective division by stockholders, stock traders, managers and owners. While the distinctions between owners and managers as made by Berle and Means have little operational weight in the way corporations are run, one important fact should be noted. Interest by the stockholder is in profits either from selling the stock or from dividends. The average stockholder remains parasitical on the system and is a load to be carried by the corporate structure. This situation will cause tension within the capitalist structure as the stockholder is viewed as an appendage to the corporate economy.

But, while the young might abandon the corporate structure and seek nonprofit (but high earnings) activities and, as viewed by the corporate operator, might expel the stockholder from the capitalist scene, the power of the national and international corporation remains overwhelming.

Constitutionalizing the Corporation

In the United States, various attempts have been made by
scholars over the past several decades to offer plans for
the constitutionalization of the corporation within certain
prescribed limits. Unless specifically recommending na-
tionalization, as did certain socialist writers such as Lange,
or workers' control, as did John Dewey, the viewpoints
taken on this question centered around the ideas of con-
stitutionalizing or regulating the corporation within the
pyramidal context. In both cases, the purpose has been to
find ways for corporations to operate within the constraints of the national polity. While such positions assumed that the corporations should operate within the
polity, the purpose that the corporation was to serve
remained ambiguous. The reformist writers have taken
the position that the purpose of the corporation is to serve
the "public interest." Others take a view that the purpose
and motive of the corporation and business itself is profit
—the buying, selling and accumulation of wealth. Still
others have argued that the purpose of the corporation is
production of goods—either for or against the general
welfare. Whatever are the heavenly purposes or rationales
which the academics may find for the corporation in constitutional clothing, the owners and managers are clear on
its purpose as are the workers. The corporation is a profit-
making enterprise which sets its framework and the lives
of its participants for that purpose. The task of politics is
to promote profits for the corporation.

In his preface to the 1932 edition of *The Modern Corporation and Private Property* Berle states that the problem which he does not deal with is that of the relationship
of the corporation as an economic and political enterprise
to the State, " . . . whether it will dominate the state or
be regulated by the state or whether the two will coexist
with relatively little connection. In other words as be-

tween a political organization of society which will be the dominant form. This is a question which must remain unanswered for a long time to come."[6]

The present stituation in American political and economic life makes clear why this question must finally be resolved. Through the taxing structure the state bureaucracies have been spending tax funds which have benefited directly the largest corporate structures and the middle classes. On the other hand, while there has been a direct benefit to the corporate structure in such forms as defense contracts, highway development, education and manpower payments to train employees, neither the oligopolistic ones which sell predominantly to the public nor the national security corporations, which sell and manipulate the governmental bureaucracy and military, pay their fair share of tax revenue. Second, and more important, is that the formal political system of the United States (Congress, state legislatures, municipal governments, etc.) is unable to contain and balance the form of political power now exercised through unaccountable means by the corporate and banking sphere. That is to say, the corporate, banking and military forms of organization are no longer contained within constitutional and legal rules of the political system which make any socially ethical sense. The concentrations of these groupings, for example, is enormous.

As we come to analyze the corporation, we find that it is no news that the large corporations (say, the top 500) are the central staples in the life of the political economy of the society. The 500 largest industrial firms, according to Kottke and Reid, represent only one-fourth of one percent of all industrials while accounting for 60 percent of sales and 70 percent of profits.[7] These large industrial enterprises set the terms of life reference for the people who work within them. They produce the weapons for the national security state and the goods for the society. And by what is made, they set the contours of life for those not directly involved as workers or owners of the industrial enterprise. The extraordinary freedom which such private governments have so long as they operate within national security guidelines forces the issue of scrutiny and vast change.

Early in the history of the American law, through the *Dartmouth College Case* and *Terrett v. Taylor,* the Supreme Court made distinctions which, for most practical purposes, allowed profit-making corporations to be viewed as private bodies outside the scope of state interventions. This privilege and exemption assumed that profit-making enterprises were no different from non-profit-making enterprises, and consequently, could not be treated differently. (What is interesting is how close profit-making and non-profit-making enterprises have in fact become in their business activities, but that is another question.) "If, therefore, the foundation be private, though under the charter of the government, the corporation is private, however extensive the use may be to which it is devoted, either by the bounty of founder or the nature and objects of the institution."[8] No doubt the industrial development of the United States would have been considerably different had the courts held that there was control over profit-making ventures, rather than merely subsidies of them. The effect of the decisions of the courts in the nineteenth and twentieth centuries was to assert private government development in the industrial enterprise form at the expense of the body politic. Except through the market place, the people or their legislative bodies sacrificed the power to direct or focus the work and activities of the corporation. No doubt, an argument can be made that regulatory commissions belie this analysis. However, there is no question that the daily operations of regulatory commissions affirms corporate powers. Where it appears that the regulatory commission might challenge the "regulated" industry the regulators find that they are unable to obtain the funds necessary to do the studies from a Congress even aware of corporate power.

While the politics of both law and government has been to allow the extension of the meaning of private property to include huge American corporate enterprises which operate on a scale that three-fourths of the nation-states of the world cannot begin to operate on, it now appears clear that the nineteenth-century appeasement of the industrial enterprise has resulted in an almost impossible perversion of people's needs during the twentieth century. The reasons for this I have stated elsewhere. Suffice it here to say that the emphasis on the production of goods, the abuses of the environment, and the creation of situations which destroy the delicate relationship of man to nature and man to man, require alternative political structures that include control and democratization of the industrial enterprise.

There is a naive attempt to make the economic system "work" on the part of conservatives˙ who believe that competition will bring down prices and reduce political power of particular corporate managers and owners. Such attempts have not stopped the inexorable march toward pyramidalism, nor have they secured the rights of workers within the industrial enterprise. It is not likely that anti-trust laws or stringent forms of taxation will help citizens affected by the industrial enterprise live freely and in health.

Let us for the moment divide up the questions. The first question is worker control and participation within the industrial enterprise. No doubt, this issue may have been viewed as taboo in America although a growing number of firms use profit-sharing plans with workers leaving "management" decisions to "managers." However, most advanced industrial nations except the United

States have adopted some sort of plan which includes worker participation and control. Even the Bourbon, De Gaulle, understood the necessity of including workers in industrial enterprises who would share in the governing of the enterprise if for no other reason than the French government's need to keep labor peace. It is entirely possible that the American corporate system, which now prides itself on its multinational imperial character, will be forced to offer worker participation and local control in various democratic socialist countries where that objective is the local left trade union's price to the American corporation for allowing workers to be employed by the American-controlled corporation. The imperial and interwoven character of the American corporation abroad and domestically could mean that such a demand by non-American unions would stimulate the American worker to redefine the social contract within his place of work in the United States.

Even without such influences the crisis of work in the American corporation is so great as to cause a new generation to reject the goals of the corporation, its direction, the goods that are made and the quality of life that it creates. As I have suggested, the equilibrium of labor/corporate relations has just about ended as students and workers in universities who continue a left orientation seek to tame the economic beast through worker control, and as the corporation itself depends on rational relationships within its ranks beyond that of bureaucratic dictatorship.

In heavy industry, the average size of a plant within a large corporate industrial enterprise is approximately 1000 workers. Within that enterprise, the plant structure itself is decentralized. That is to say, while there may be some industries where the plants are located in one particular area, most enterprises now find it more useful to decentralize their operations in various parts of the country, for shipping and marketing reasons, more favorable worker conditions, etc. They operate on the basis of local control, with production goals set locally within general guidelines from the top. (I am not suggesting that this reasoning applies to mergers. Mergers continue to allow decentralized operations. Mergers are the creatures of modern management to increase managerial power.)

Recognizing that 1000 workers is the size of a particular plant, we may begin to see certain ways that the political and economic relationships can be reorganized within the corporate enterprise.

Justice Brandeis recognized the contradiction between the fact that the worker had a political vote but, when he went to work, he lived in a system of industrial absolutism. Professor Eells of Columbia has pointed out that the model that scholars have in mind when they talk about the constitutionalization of the corporation is to find ways of mirroring the political (voting) side of the American body politic for employees. The cry of American liberals in the first world war was that there was an "absurdity of conducting a war for political democracy which leaves industrial and economic autocracy practically untouched . . . . "[9] (Reading these words forces one to realize the regression in American political and social thought since World War I.) Under this theory, the corporation's charter could be changed by the states it was chartered or doing business in to reflect a new definition of constitutionalism. Such a mode of constitutionalism would now enable the development of a direct, but decentralized relationship between the political and economic side of the body politic in a legitimate public and participatory way. Surely no one would deny that such charters could be amended, revised or integrated along the lines put forward. Such ideas are still hidden. Perhaps, that is in part because of the labor movement which by the second world war saw its goal as *unionizing* (the closed shop), a dubious objective as compared to the idea of worker participation and control.

By the twentieth century Americans found themselves giving up on the idea of self-governing places of work which would have a direct effect on the political structure of American life. One should not forget that the ideas of worker management and worker control were practiced in the United States after the Civil War. The idea of cooperative undertakings, which were to be self-governing, floundered on the inability of such ventures to obtain capital and credit. And, in its initial stages worker control was not seen as a contradiction to the labor union movement. Indeed, William Sylvis, the head of the Iron Molders' National Union, saw that unionism was merely reformist and that the worker himself would have to control his work through cooperation with other workers.[10]

Yet, with the mass migrations after 1880, the idea of producer cooperation and worker control was viewed as a hindrance to the labor movement. It seemed that the values of producer cooperation specifically undercut the goals of the labor union which undertook to build class consciousness on the basis of confrontation with the capitalist, better working conditions and pay but consistent refusal to control any means of production. By the 1880's the idea of cooperative workshops had failed for lack of capital. Furthermore, the labor movement had now moved with the times as many immigrants brought from Europe the "new realism" which gave up on the idea of self-employment, self-controlled time and cooperative ventures in the area of work. In part, this situation was due to the incredible increase in corporate size by 1890, the growth of the city as a result of industry and immigration and the seemingly great power and difficulty of managing combines such as the size of Carnegie Steel or Standard Oil. It seemed enough just to get wages, and then as a dim goal organize the corporate structure away from capitalism. The method was to organize around the job and the job function. According to Perlman, "the class-conscious International of Marx was the cause of the least class-conscious labor movement in the world today."[11] The idea of the social contract in which the worker saw himself in control of his work and life was quietly laid to rest in favor of collective bargaining.

Since the "reforms" of 1916, and to some extent the patch job of the government during the depression of 1932, the American political parties have avoided the issue of the nature of the industrial system. The easy truce which existed between the political parties and the corporate system is ending. As a new class of people within the corporation question the goals of the corporation and the emptiness of their jobs, if they conclude that the most likely way of expressing their general dissatisfaction is through politics, the political parties themselves will radically change. The programs of political parties will come to include the internal workings of the corporation and its purposes as a way of integrating the economy into the polity. In a democratizing society, it is entirely likely that mammoth corporations themselves will become objects of new forms of governing and public election because of the profound effect that they have on the general body politic. This direction has been taken by John Lindsay, who urged stockholders to vote for public interest members to the Board of Directors of General Motors.

While the Lindsay and Nader impulse forces an opening of the corporation to public involvement and pressure it does not relate to the structure of work, what is made and the extension of the social contract to the person's place of work. But the fact that this definition of corporate responsibility does not start from the workers or the people within the corporation, or begin with an announced goal of worker community participation in the economic enterprise of the society does not mean the Nader approach is regressive. Rather it makes possible the laying out of another position within the frame of reference which assumes profound structural change in the corporate system.

The Failure of the Class Model

The roots of the labor movement in the United States were somewhat different than those one finds in Europe. In part the American labor unions have had to contend with the fact that there was an appearance of a non-class structure in the United States. That is to say, the ideology of opportunity meant that an individual could rise from his humble circumstances and become at least a member of the middle class or even possibly an owner. The appearance of a large middle class in the United States— shopkeepers, clerks, small businessmen—has always put limits on what union leaders thought they could accomplish. Men like Samuel Gompers, who read Marx to his fellow workers at the cigar-making shop, when he came to union power insisted on recognizing the limits that a trade union movement could accomplish. He did not believe there was a stable working class, that is, sons of workers who remained workers and lived in the same geographic area for their lifetime. He was firm in destroying any possibility for a political party which openly had a working-class base and indeed, he and the leadership of the AFL cut down the attempts of La Follette to stage a successful campaign for the Presidency in 1924. Some socialists believed that workers could balance the power of the capitalist through recognizing that the working class—as a class—was unstable. Worker strength would come through a trade union movement which could demand higher wages and material goods, generally accepted as "American goals."

It appeared to leaders of the trade union movement that it could not challenge the ideas of private property which supposedly were engrained in the American character. As I will suggest in Part Three, this view was a mistaken understanding of what was intrinsic to American civilization. Immigrants brought with them to the United States the straight Marxist class analysis and undertook to force that view onto radical reconstructive strains within the United States. They saw private property and the capitalist and believed that the issue was how to confront private property through welding a class consciousness. This they attempted to do around the issue of wages, hours and working conditions. They viewed as regressive cooperative movements which attempted to break up power and which attempted to develop the idea of self-governing workshops. Once having overthrown the idea of self-governing in the economic sphere the question remained as to how to organize against the capitalist.

The socialists assumed that in a capitalist corporate system there would be reluctance by the capitalist and the corporation managers to pay wages necessary to allow the working man a decent wage and a little bit extra. It was assumed that the inability or unwillingness by the capitalist to meet the demands of the worker would result in the radicalization of the worker who would see from his own condition how necessary it was to mold himself and his brethren into a politically conscious group beyond his own industry to force the end of capitalism. In this way, the individual worker would discover or recapture his humanity.

Contrary to this view, history followed a different course. American owners and their managers have been able to meet the demands of the workers without changing the profit system. They have been able to accomplish this end without giving up political power to workers and without reaching the general social question of who administers the state, and for what ends. They have been able to rationalize their power and control within the industrial enterprise. We may note as an example, Article IV, Section 1 of the collective bargaining agreement between the UAW and the Ford Motor Company, October 25, 1967:

> The Company retains the sole right to manage its business, including the rights to decide the number and location of plants, the machine and tool equipment, the products to be manufactured, the method of manufacturing, the schedules of production, the processes of manufacturing or assembling, together with all designing, engineering, and the control of raw materials, semi-manufactured and finished parts which may be incorporated into the products manufactured; to maintain order and efficiency in its plants and operations; to hire, lay off, assign, transfer and promote employees, and to determine the starting and quitting time and the number of hours to be worked; subject only to such regulations and restrictions governing the exercise of these rights as are expressly provided in this Agreement.

Alfred P. Sloan, the head of General Motors, in his autobiography noted how management was at first "unhappy" with unionism in its early days because unionism seemed to be challenging management prerogatives. The GM management soon learned that the tactics of the sitdown and challenging property "rights" of owners were merely tactics of the union to gain attention—if the union was recognized and wages and fringe benefits appeared adequate.

> What made the prospect seem especially grim in those early years was the persistent union attempt to invade basic management prerogatives. Our rights to determine produc-

tion schedules, to set work standards, and to discipline workers were all suddenly called into question. Add to this the recurrent tendency of the union to inject itself into pricing policy, and it is easy to understand why it seemed, to some corporate officials, as though the union might one day be virtually in control of our operations.

In the end, we were fairly successful in combating these invasions of management rights. There is no longer any real doubt that pricing is a management, not a union function. So far as our operations are concerned, we have moved to codify certain practices, to discuss workers' grievances with union representatives, and to submit for arbitration the few grievances that remain unsettled. But on the whole, we have retained all the basic powers to manage.[12]

An important reason for the failure of the Marxist prediction that capitalism would collapse (because it would not pay adequate wages) is that the market system (except in the case of technological innovation) has been transformed into an oligopolistically protected market where costs are passed on to the consumer and where the cost of a businessman entering into a particular industry which is basic to the operation of the economy of the society is virtually prohibitive (i.e., non-defense contracts). This positive situation for large corporate enterprises has meant that it could grant the economic demands of workers without fear of competition from other corporations. To guarantee itself against the working class, it was necessary for the corporation to pay high enough wages to ensure its own political and economic control within the plant. This was accomplished through a high profit system, oligopolistic markets and defense contracts from the State. Not only was it possible for owners and managers to maintain power within the corporation (the plant) but they believed it was possible to guarantee control over the state's direction. This conclusion on the part of corporate management was only partially correct. The corporate leadership now finds that power in the body politic is to be shared with the military and political elites. However, within the plant, the manager's power remains paramount. The corporations adjusted easily to the union leaders' conditions.

The ability of the corporation to adjust by offering indulgences in the form of wages and pensions* were objectives which union leadership sought. Such objectives caused workers to be involved in protecting gains that helped the worker see himself as part of the middle class. To protect them, labor leadership took seemingly liberal positions which ended as reactionary ones because labor ended up mimicking the authority structure of the corporation.

The industrial labor union leader protects the corporation in which his fellow unionists are employed by arguing that the corporation's success is the basis of material success for himself and his union. For example, workers believe that corporate profits dictate their economic well-being. Consequently, the labor leadership takes the stance of full employment for themselves and the industries in which they are employed. This stance is adopted notwithstanding the fact that workers may end up doing totally foolish things and producing destructive products. Where there are good contacts through the political parties with various legislators, union leadership finds itself used by the corporate management to obtain contracts from the government for the production of things which ideologically the labor leadership might have once rejected. Unions no longer talk about what work workers should do for the society and their leadership is caught in unmanageable contradictions (see pp. 93–94). For example, the UAW leadership organizes in aerospace

---

* Note the effect of pensions and how many people are tied to their jobs because of pensions. Pensions are of course an inherently conservatizing force among the middle and working class.

industries privately doubting the value, utility or validity of such work.

There are plaintive romantics who wonder about such questions as what happened to the moral force behind the idea of a labor union movement which would find meaning outside of the profit system but in a cooperative movement. Such direction has been lost sight of by a leadership which embraced the idea of job consciousness for decent pay as an end in itself without seeing what the job was, its purposes, and the function of such consciousness as a creation of the employer. The emergence of dissonance between human consciousness and job consciousness has caused a generational split within the labor movement between the men on the line, the leadership and the labor bureaucracy. Among some old-line union bureaucrats there is a powerful sentiment of contempt toward workers whom they refer to as "yahoos," a phrase used by a labor union leader describing the members of his union in a debate. While the status and privilege gap grows between the worker on the line and his national union leadership, there is little in the negotiations the unions carry on with the corporations which reflects the needs of the younger membership. There is nothing within the structure of the labor union which speaks either to the question of shoddy goods or to the social problems created by goods which are either useless or destructive. Some of the union rank and file see themselves as prisoners in an oligopolistic system which expects them to consume and buy on credit things which they question, or forces them deeper into a situation which is causing confusion and dissonance in their lives. The Dream Colony creates for them the image of material well-being through goods, yet they are aware of the slipshod quality of the goods they make, as well as the dysfunction and obsolescence built into the goods. The men and women know, through examination and use, the tawdry quality of the present consumer goods system. They are aware that the productive structure should be organized "to produce as much as possible, to last as long as possible, with the least amount of human effort."[13] Robert Theobald sees that both the labor union and the corporate system encourage none of these possibilities. In his working day, the rank-and-file union member is prevented from doing a humane, craftsmanlike job by the corporate and union structure within which he must carry on his work.

Except as he is provided with money, the worker's work may be meaningless. Is such a situation an indication of the worker's colonial status? Not in itself. However, there are other indications which make clear that the worker is colonized. He is employed by a corporation but protected through a collective bargaining procedure where if his voice is heard it is only through the voice of a bureaucratic union structure. The complaints he makes on the job must be made "through channels" on the basis of the collective bargaining agreement that his union bosses signed with management. Indeed, if the worker participates in a wildcat strike or a slowdown, he is generally not protected by the union. Again as an example, note the UAW contract with the Ford Motor Company. Section 3, Article V states that the union "will not cause or permit its members to cause, nor will any member of the Union take part in, any sitdown, stay-in, or slowdown in any plant of the Company or any curtailment of work or restriction of production or interference with the operations of the Company." Or under Section 4, Article V, "The Company shall have the right to discipline (including discharge) any employee who instigates, participates in, or gives leadership to an unauthorized strike in violation of this Agreement." Under this section, the umpire who interprets the contract has the right to review the reasonableness of the penalties. But the umpire services the contracts between the Union and the Company, *not* the workers vis-à-vis the company and the union. The wages the worker earns are spent by him in a market of things which prove to be socially dysfunctional, as in the case of new cars which clog the highways of cities. On the other hand, the services which he requires for himself and his family (health, education and housing) are very difficult to obtain as compared to socially dysfunctional things. His ability to control what is made by the corporation he works for is virtually nil. He has no voice in deciding what is to be made at his place of work nor does he have control over the amount that is made. He does have the power of sabotage which is continuously exercised by men on the assembly line. The thousands of defective cars made each year represent growing worker resentment.

Although advances made in the second world war indicate that the number of particular tasks performed by the factory worker has increased, making his life on the line somewhat more interesting, a fundamental fact remains. The worker is assigned a particular place on the line. He is organized in his work to the requirements of the machine and the profit system. The training he receives for his job is invariably oriented to a particular task which is limited and limiting, and is seen by those who hire him as a function of their purpose. The worker sees himself as functions to be performed. The union finds itself accepting this definition of its members since its own power grows out of that definition. The union finds itself functioning as the core disciplinary instrument for keeping workers in line. For example, one of the most progressive of unions, the United Automobile Workers Union, is central to the smooth operation of the automobile industry because it gives workers the basic job protections, without dignity or control over the life of the plant. (Of course, like any self-contained social system, each group is bound by the other and the acceptance of their respective roles.) No matter what the rhetoric suggests, the historic dominant power of capital/management to decide the organizational structure of plant life, what is to be produced, and what the profit margins are to be continues. The trade union leadership accepts this view.

There is a further irony. Because the present labor movement in the United States does not have any experience or perception of the management role outside of the profit structure, the probability is that the choices which would be made by the leaders of the labor movement, if they had the power to make management choices, would not be significantly different from those made by the managers of the corporation. Since there is little if any experience at worker decision-making and worker control, the trade unions would find themselves making judgments on exactly the same basis that management makes them. This conclusion derives from the fact that the labor movement has not developed its own political idea of what it wants outside of the reformist-opportunist success ideology of the managers and the society at large. By education and personal purpose, the older bureaucrats and leaders of labor are undistinguishable from corporate managers. Where the leadership of the labor movement has the power of investment, through pension funds, for example, their choices are as conservative (perhaps more so) as those made by the Chase Manhattan Bank.

In this situation, the worker now finds himself involved in a double alienation: at his place of work the union is the instrument which supposedly is his, although its purposes and ends are set by the corporation operating in such a manner as to make clear that the union's position in the plant is dictated by the corporate purpose. Labor leadership, on the other hand, merely improves its own stance without risk by blaming corporate powers and turning the frustration of the worker into a dinner-pail grievance. And second, the worker is told by the management that, as an employee of the corporation, he must operate and work on those functions and processes that are presented to him. Accept or get out. The technological base of the society has now sufficiently changed so that the usefulness of the union in this sense is now lost, and conversely the reliance which the union places on the corporation as an economic unit which needs the union is growing more dubious. The long-term interest of the corporation is identified, in the United States, with technology in the form of automation rather than mechanization in the form of human labor. This brutal fact changes the purpose of the union.

The technology system in the plant now seems to require two types of workers. One is an administrative worker who learns how to manipulate machines in the manner of a flight engineer on an airplane. This is the picture that those of us who grew up with the ideology of automation believe to be the present and future condition of factories. The second type of worker is one who is committed to operating along the lines set forward by the speed-up of the machine.

It is interesting to note that professional workers such as teachers also seem to see themselves in a profoundly immobilized and finally a reactionary position. In New York, for example, the teachers union has become regressive in purpose and outlook because it sees itself only as an embattled group that has to protect its rather tenuous position in the pyramidal structure. Teachers in the lower grades in schools probably have a view of themselves as not having any technical skills. Consequently, they may tend to respond less in terms of pride of craft (that is, their ability to educate and teach), but rather in terms of need to protect their class position. They do not see themselves as teachers of the community defining their work as teachers. They are paid to do work defined through pyramidal systems.

Transforming the Plantation Colony within the plant structure will occur when certain values merge into a serious political clash: a) when the corporate management continues to press for higher production records while cutting quality of goods and numbers of workers; b) when consumer boycotts are organized against shoddy goods; and c) when workers disclaim the utility of the goods made because they are patently unusable and the consumer credit advertising system falls out of phase with the shabby, obsolescent goods system; that is, when goods wear out too fast to explain away through advertising. (The worker addicted to consumerism buys more goods without having finished paying for the disposable goods which wore out. His consumer payments increase, while his human needs become greater. His needs go unfulfilled because he has "invested" in goods that wear out quickly.) A conflict will develop between the worker as one who is no longer necessary or who is worse off through automation because of time studies based on speed-ups to the machine, and the worker as consumer who is necessary to the successful and stable operation of the profit and social system.*

In this period, certain ideas will develop which will appear to go against the grain of American efficiency. For example, practice demands that groups of organizers develop ideas which include the establishment of independent worker-schools where workers would study questions dealing with the reorganization of the plant into a more modern technical system. They would have the opportunity of showing how factories could change so that

---

* Some have begun to note the contradiction between the two sides of the economy, the consumer system based on leisure and the production system based on speed-up. The contradiction has helped young people to reject both.

they were involved in choosing production schedules, the democratic organization of work in the factory, and the establishment of rules, duties and rights which workers decide upon in the plant. Since their work life is spent in the plant, they would be encouraged to organize workloads in ways which are happiest for them. Workers would be encouraged to band together with younger members of the union bureaucracy to set up schools which concern such questions, specifically the question of reconstructing the factory and work system to find meaning, feeling and control over the work process. Such activities will be stimulated through the worker community itself, the university and political action. Students in industrial relations departments, such as Cornell University or the University of Wisconsin, will probably organize among themselves to force changes in their school curricula which will reflect worker-community control methods of management rather than the corporate-labor mode of teaching and study presently fashionable in such schools.

In one sense, the unions have been extraordinarily successful following the path of Selig Perlman and Zwing who led the trade union theorists in arguing for an accommodationist position with corporate power and limiting demands to the economic contract of higher wages and job security. By following this course they have neglected the importance of the social contract and the need to establish its primacy in the industrial enterprise; that is, the participation in and control of the industrial enterprise. Where such social contracts are not achieved, the process of space and exodus would operate: the union would undertake to compete with the industrial enterprise itself, which did not draft a social contract.

The union finds that it undertakes three tasks while transforming its policing relationship in the plant.

One of its basic demands is that all workers who decide that they want to learn different jobs, the overall process of the plant, administrative skills and the general operations of the enterprise itself shall have that chance.

The second task which the union might undertake is that of stating that it believes that the workers should participate in deciding what should be made for the good of the society, how much should be made and whether what is made fulfills human needs. Obviously, in the present situation, unions cannot ask such questions for fear that the balance which they have worked out with corporations will be tipped, and the managers and owners of the enterprises will lock out the workers. However, if the nature of the technology is changing to the extent that we believe it is, then it is the case that the administrative and bureaucratic worker himself will undertake to ask such questions. It will then be incumbent upon the unions that such administrative workers protect the rights of workers on the line who are forced into speed-ups because of the machine. Beyond the technology itself, once a moral basis is rediscovered, a labor movement could begin to act in ways that now it cannot. It can begin to ask, for example, why the labor unions view themselves in exactly the same position vis-à-vis the Department of Defense, when it comes to contracts with the automobile industry, as does the management of General Motors. Can it not express alternative positions and strike for such positions?

The third task which needs to be performed is the development of skills, and the management of investment funds, so that the unions themselves can begin to operate their own plants under worker management. For this purpose it will be necessary to repeal those parts of labor legislation which now require that unions not operate businesses which are competitive to the corporation. The objective of the union's operating its own plant is to re-establish the nineteenth-century American idea of worker management and competition to the corporate organization. The modern corporation operates on marketing and profit principles which could now readily be challenged since there is a profound change in the technological requirements needed to initiate new production units. For example, a union which developed its own skills and retrained workers could produce for the public sector as against the private sector. It is within the scope of practice in the near future that the UAW (to continue with one union as an example) could challenge the Ford Motor Company to make public rather than private transportation and on its own initiative the UAW could set up its own economic production unit to manufacture public transportation.

As union members come to realize that there is a contradiction between the union as a human community and the union as a bureaucracy and the membership is prepared to undercut the authority of union leadership through wildcat strikes and reactionary political votes, the interests of union leadership will shift to concentrating on its role in the body politic. One way of changing the union's institutional role is for it to join with other groups in putting forward plans of reconstruction that its membership supports. Such plans might include the establishment of plants to fulfill the needs of the community. It would receive investment funds for this purpose from cities and other governmental units, counties, wards, districts to establish the plant. The union could offer to the city or other local authority the chance to become a legal part of the new industrial enterprise in exchange for additional funding made available through the taxing power. Members of the planning and governing group would be elected from the place where the product and funding emanated.

At this stage of development in the union movement, there are few leaders who are prepared to examine the root premises of the labor union which would result in such a reconstruction. But the dissonances are felt by the men on the line. Presently, there is nothing in the tactics or purpose of the labor movement to indicate that it is more than a corporate complement to the corporate structure. But conversely to the extent that the labor movement views itself as an institutional structure that is not tied to the oligopolistic system, it will begin to appeal to a class of people who see themselves as outside of the market system, because their interests and commitments, subjectively, are not for profit. Thus, professionals and craftsmen who now find themselves doing a shoddy job in the context of their work situation would join the labor movement in the preparation of those entrepreneurial activities which stem from the human purpose of use as against gain.

Unless the labor movement joins with the professional class in the context of a reconstructed political community there will be no way of controlling monopoly power which uses "free enterprise" as the shibboleth while it develops a form of regressive feudalism in which those who operate the corporation and bureaucracy attempt to dictate the form of economy, the program of an individual's life, and the political purpose of the organized society. There may be developing signs of such relationships. The New Party at the University of Maryland has encouraged worker student demands on campus. A new kind of union which is community-based could emerge.

It is possible, for example, that the organization of new unions in service industries and the breakdown of AFL-CIO with the alliance between the Teamsters and the UAW will result in an obvious and immediate reconstruction of the purposes of the labor movement. In such a case, the labor movement will see the importance of searching out humanistic values which go beyond dinner-pail considerations. It is likely that the relative ease with which things can be made and the obvious make-work tasks

which people perform in the bureaucracies will force
upon the labor movement and people generally involved
in the employment market to change their dinner-pail
concerns to the issue of self-controlled time. But such a
change would mean that the union movement needs to
re-investigate its root purposes. It would have to question
the twentieth-century direction of denying workers participation and control in favor of dinner-pail demands.
The idea of mirroring the class struggle of other countries
on the basis of people who profoundly believe in their
freedom or of becoming an instrument for corporate-
management power in the plant has been mistaken. Union
goals resulted in producing more of what is not needed
for the sake of employment, while specifically denying
productivity and creativity within work. Furthermore, it
has denied to workers the practice of workers' control and
a political citizenship within the work situation and in
the body politic itself. Through organizing at the work
place for worker/community discussions a new consciousness would be achieved which would both build the power
of the labor movement and simultaneously change the
consciousness of the workers. Another supplementary
plan would have similar effect. In a study at the Institute
for Policy Studies, a proposal was prepared which began
from the assumption that work as we know it now will
change and as a result it will be possible for people to have
more self-controlled time.* Once the idea of self-controlled time is recognized, it becomes possible to change
the economic system in striking and productive ways.
Suppose each worker had a sabbatical year every seven
years, similar to that which college professors and corporate management enjoy within the present economic

* The issue of the definition of work is not germane. It has generally been
viewed as a task required by others which I would rather not do if I had the
choice. It is clear that the structural differences between work and education
have broken down. That is one reason why I use the phrase "self-controlled time."

structure. If implemented on a massive scale, would a reconstruction result? In the study which we conducted, it was clear that the most difficult objective to accomplish was making people assume that a year out of the employment market should not have to relate to the notion of increase in economic productivity. Some government officials, for example, are willing to grant the utility of one year out of seven away from one's job if it is related to an increase in economic or social productivity. However, they neither believe in nor do they see supporting the idea of a sabbatical outside of the economist's conception of growth.

On the other hand, the idea itself, when it is implemented on a massive scale would lead to a radical shifting away from people willing to live in an hierarchic social structure, because they would finally comprehend the delicious freedom of self-controlled time. Self-controlled time could have the effect of stimulating dislocation in family and corporate life since it would enable the individual to judge the worth of how he lives his life, reconsider the social relations in which he is involved, and the social and economic structure to which he seems to be committed. The person is given the space to judge whether he is able to express himself in the economic, social and political ways he has built up through his job and through the social structure which evolves from his job and from his family situation.

Perhaps it is to assume too much, but it is possible that part of the effect of such a sabbatical program would be to cause people to work out human rather than functional relationships in their lives. This program I would view as a necessary next step in social security legislation. It allows people the chance of finding roots and security outside of the functioning demands made upon them by a colonized system.

It is obvious that demands such as sabbatical years cannot be made *in abstracto.* They are part of a program which calls for the changing of colonized life in America in all its aspects. Without changes in the other colonized structures, the sabbatical year as a new staple in the social security system would probably contribute to the all-encompassing Dream Colony, and the individual worker might feel himself thrown out of even that purpose and function which is provided by the Plantation Colony. Yet an individual given time to redefine and experiment with his life has the power to change whole social structures. He now has the chance to seek and find others in work relationships that he initiates. No doubt we will find many people unwilling to take such sabbaticals. In such cases, workers could negotiate for fewer hours of work each week.

The guaranteed annual income has received the support of a wide variety of groups. The idea, first proposed by Robert Theobald, is to feed and clothe people as well as give them dignity under the theory that the right of survival should not be dependent upon the mishaps or tricks of the market/corporate system. My fear is that in and of itself the guaranteeing of an annual income does not break the plantation colony, since it appears to leave the corporate/union form intact. Although the consumption level of the poor would increase, they would remain as the manipulated by an industrial system which remained a colony. In order to change the poor from mere consumers, who ultimately are exploited by the manipulations of the Dream Colony, there will have to be a total decolonization of the Plantation Colony.

4

*The
Channeling
Colony*

At any one time there are fifty-five million Americans in school, higher school, lower school, universities. What are they learning? Is it truth, beauty, scientific method to relate apparently unrelated phenomena, facts, wisdom and knowledge? Is it preparation for the next higher academic level? Or are these fifty-five million in the channeling process for more profound purposes which appear as the trivia of life, but which in effect structure the political, social and economic order? On all levels in the school, whether public or private, progressive or traditional, the young person is expected to learn the *basic* economic and political lessons which the modern nation-state teaches and requires so that it may remain authoritarian and pyramidal. The school thus serves as the training instrument for the state. The substance of what is learned—

Plato, zoology, *Silas Marner,* quadratics, woodwork and music appreciation — is less indelible in the young person's mind than other lessons which are taught and internalized. The student is taught and usually learns the importance of identification papers, records, tardy slips, no whispering to your neighbor, the acceptable dress, signatures, forms and tests. He comes to learn and respect the idea that in the colonized society authority dictates and individuals internalize the notion that papers are more important that the person himself. The physical and mental refugee of the twentieth century, whether he is trying to get out of a concentration camp, prison, hospital, school or corporation, knows that the papers about himself are the key to his being and to his escape. Papers are the means by which the modern state says that every individual's place in the world depends on the authorized organs of the state. There is a German phrase which makes clear the nature of this state authoritarianism on the individual: "Unless your life is certified with official stamp and seal, let me tell you, brother, it's a tough and dirty deal."[1]

Persons without citizenship papers do not exist, nor do people without passports. Stamps of approval are necessary from the colonizing agencies in the body politic for personal existence. Through keeping records and issuing papers, Authority legitimates *its* power. The individual is hounded by the relentless memory of the strokes which others have made of him for purposes of reinforcing colonized relationships. It is the task of the school to prepare and involve the student in such a relationship.

In school, students are readied for adult life through the synthetic process of tension with themselves about whom they are supposed to be in the pyramid. They are in dialectic with their records and profiles, which they come to believe are the definition of who they are. Since record-keeping and profiles do not describe the subjective feeling and potentiality of people, even if that is what such records say, and since the records and profile are to serve the needs of the authority system and describe where such an individual might fit (court fool, house radical, etc.), the young are taught bad faith. Students are urged to fulfill an achievement profile of themselves which is primarily derived from requirements and functions set by the colonizer's needs. Although the needs of the colonized system may be tempered by the interests and learning of the student, the standards applied to students which then become their profile are more accurately the reflexion and descriptive judgment of the needs or standards which the colonies require. But even knowing that the records and papers of a system tell us more about the system than the people who are stamped with them, the student seems unable to escape the image created for him—as him— through the hierarchic other.

The profile is the young's mocking shadow of the individual which pursues him and ultimately dictates his being. The student accepts the intrusion of "measurement" of his self made known to him by the colonizer. Schools continue this process by creating barriers to reinforce the "soundness" of the objective measure or profile that is created for the individual. (For example, the track system, "basic" subjects, etc. as a way of typing a young person for life.) Children in a colonized world find themselves on the bed of Procrustes through administrative determinations which are based on considerations they are not expected to know or to be cognizant of. They are expected to be tools of forces that they cannot see, understand or control. They are not supposed to know, for example, that poor textbooks in most schools are related to arrangements of convenience between book manufacturers and the bureaucracy of a school system. Or the issue of record-keeping of the child or student may be related to having bought a computer which is only economic if

it is operating continuously at some record-keeping task!
The last concern is the child.

Two forces pertain. The individual student is in school
for reasons not relevant to himself as a person, and he
generally learns things not relevant to him or to a subject
matter that one would want to know. And, he learns
that he is now secondary to the records and profiles about
himself. His personal insecurity is intensified because of
the dissonance he feels between what he believes himself
to be and wants, and what others want or expect of him
from pressures which they believe are on *them*. They are
slaves to the hierarchic other which becomes part of themselves.

Needless to say, such determination by the pyramidal
system is the individual's impediment to self-definition
and control of his future within the limits and boundaries
which he consciously and freely sets with others. Thus,
the school as a colonizing function is important for what
is *informally* learned. The student learns that others,
who have little interest in him and no lasting human relationship with him, set standards, rewards and payoffs for
him. As he gets older, personality and achievement tests
are taken with him as the object, which may decide his
job, whether he goes to the army, whether he qualifies for
places that then have their standards, qualifications and
records. Officials of the profile system readily admit the
meaningless or cynical nature of tests and records. It
is not unusual for the professor and the education administrator to say that grades don't matter while using
grades as their sole criterion for judging when they
are asked for recommendations. Of course, this situation
makes the student's position even more ambiguous and
intolerable.

Take a more profound and homologous case. Children
are taught and told by their parents and caretakers what

to do and what not to do in terms that are clearly for the good of the children. "Don't touch the hot stove, don't run in the street," etc. are the basis for acting forcefully with the child to limit the possibility of certain physical injury if the event occurs. This system of telling carries over into the general structure of how the child relates on all other matters which have to do with the interest of the authority or the colony. This process is seen in the classroom early in the grades.

Before he gets to school the child begins to find out about life by testing limits. (Note Chapter One, "The Psychology of the Pyramidal State.") The teacher and other school authorities become the arbiters and interpreters of these limits. They can give pleasure or pain, anxiety or approbation to the student. Thus, a very subtle game begins. The bright student and the dull student may find themselves dissembling or faking their understanding in return for approbation. (This system of relationships tends to bad faith—that is, the acceptance of role or function even though the person views that function as mad or meaningless.) Both of them may become expert at the system of mock understanding and knowing how to internalize dumbness so that they will more easily accept the hierarchic other and end up colonized.

John Holt, in his brilliant book *How Children Fail*, gives examples of the strategy of faking. The teacher asks a question. The child raises his hand when others do making believe that he knows the answer, hoping and betting on the laws of chance that he won't get called on. If someone else is called on he will have appeared to have known the answer in the mind of the teacher and his classmates. The child may become a body and lip reader, guessing what the teacher is answering in the question she or he is asking. The student watches the teacher's lips to see if she is giving the right answer.[2] (Of course the great teacher could teach probability theory and lip reading to his students from the strategy of teacher-student faking!) However, the unspoken interest of the channeling system is to get children to think defensively in terms of tests, right answers, or neatness per se. Other values such as creativity or analysis from student-formulated assumptions are eschewed because they cannot be easily contained in the pyramidal authority since the values and facts created from that social structure would come under scrutiny. Children learn and are taught an operational language or command and instruction, then in defense they attempt to create a private language for self and friend.

Once the student accepts the school treadmill, profilism,* and the informal lessons of the pyramidal structure,

---

* Since the society is enmeshed in the fact of investigator and investigated, one is no longer giving away his external self, but his very being, which comes to mean the external actions of the other to my colonized being. Since 1966, an important issue on records has occupied the attention of various members of Congress and the technocratic/bureaucratic part of the academic community. Carl Kaysen, the director of the Institute for Advanced Study, has argued for the importance of a centralized data-gathering center which in his mind would *not* include police dossiers, FBI reports and personal records. According to his Task Force Report, the "center would assemble in a single facility all large-scale systematic bodies of demographic, economic and social data generated by the present collection of administrative processes of the federal government — integrate the data to the maximum feasible extent, and in such a way as to preserve as much as possible of the original information content of the whole body of records, and provide ready access to the information, within the laws governing disclosure, to all users of the government, and where appropriate to qualified users outside the government on suitable compensatory terms."[3]

Kaysen's theory is that the present statistics do not help us make informed judgments about policy questions because they are spread about in dislocated and decentralized form. While he advocates greater centralization of data about people, he does not see the centralization of data as an extension of the principle of centralization of people. Unfortunately, the control mechanisms in a colonized society are related to welfare and education as well as the police. Invariably, all these functions are intertwined. Consequently, the assurances of the technocrat that he does not want to use the information for control purposes misses the point of what amounts to control in modern life. Furthermore, there is a certain amount

he usually finds that to survive he must become a master at the strategy of faking or totally internalize the channeling colony's view of where he will fit into the colonized reality. The price of the student internalizing the system's profile and expectation as mediated through the schools is very costly since the young person is in danger of giving up the choices and projects which he can potentially initiate through his own doing or in association with others. Under the theory of delayed payoff (study hard to get the good job or get to graduate school), the young person is mortgaging his future to activities of the pyramid from which he cannot easily extricate himself. The choices are not his but rather those structured for him.

There is a further irony in these matters. The student may fail at what the school wants him to be. Indeed, it may expel him even though he attempts to stifle his own sense of doing and intends to internalize the authority's purposes in himself to the extent that he is prepared to seek actively or imbibe supinely what the system wants and demands of him. For example, young people who are creative attempt to get Ph.D.'s. They swallow hard the arid academism of the classroom and find that they fail at turning themselves over to the colony either because the schools don't want them for economic reasons—too many Ph.D.'s—or the field of knowledge they have undertaken would be "poorly" served if the potential Ph.D. or high school diplomate graduated. The result is that the person,

---

of Pollyanna thinking which goes into an analysis that believes that data will protect along the lines one assumes in his proposal. An idea for change must be understood within a historical, political context. While efficiency of material-gathering may appear in and of itself to be good, and may help the technocrats in their rise to political power, the fact is that within the context of a pyramidal state where emphasis is on stability and control, mechanisms attending proposals such as Kaysen's add to the momentum of authoritarianism. In this sense, his idea fits as an attempt to rationalize the vertical structure.

on any level, may now accept the results of what is given
about him by others and is conditioned to attempt to meet
the "standards" which the channeling system requires of
him.

Until recently the phrases, "Is it going down on your
record?" or "Don't spoil your record" were enough to
strike horror in the hearts of the young. The schools,
corporations and the state needed the records to know
whom to reward and whom to punish. The young believed, and it was true in one framework, that they were
giving up their chance at success if they did not bend to
the will of the colonizing structure. Whole systems of
organization and knowledge were to be predicated on the
acceptance by the young of this pyramidal structure. The
young were to learn that by accepting this system they
would be giving away more than their external selves.

In first seeing the pervasiveness of channeling in Western industrialized society, I thought that this system
was the way in which the young were initiated to the se-
crets of the industrial culture. However, the industrial
system seems to be the exact opposite of ancient rites
of initiation. In the ancient rite the individual attained
the status of human being. There was a change in his
existential condition because the basis of his culture, its
guiding purposes and myths were revealed to him in a
profoundly religious and basic way. As a result of what
was revealed to him, the individual was able to locate his
place in the cosmos. He found himself to be rooted in that
cosmos. The person became another—a whole person.
The situation is profoundly different in an industrial
culture. Nothing is revealed to the individual and the
possibility of his wholeness is explicitly denied through
the Channeling Colony where the individual learns that
he is to see himself functionally in the performance of a
specialized series of tasks. Records, profiles, and identity

papers help the individual to make the adjustment to the anti-initiatory rite of seeing himself as less than a human being.

Even the Jews who have attempted to maintain some meaning in initiatory rites find that they are unable to withstand the pressures of profilism. There is a humorous story about a Jewish boy of thirteen at his Bar Mitzvah. Historically, the act of Bar Mitzvah signified the transformation of a boy into a man. His responsibilities and place among the Jews were revealed to him at that time. When this thirteen-year-old boy gives his Bar Mitzvah speech, he says—presumably because of all the gifts he has received—"Ladies and gentlemen, today I am a fountain pen." Taken literally, the boy is saying: today I have become a tool, an instrument in the hands of others. I have been characterized into something other than I am which I have no relationship to. (Obviously, there are psychosexual aspects to the story as well as that of the Jewish emphasis on learning as a trade, but they are secondary.) I have left my place as a human being to become a thing, the very reverse of ancient rites of initiation.

Politically, there are ways of changing profilism and of controverting the process whereby "selves" are reduced to "things." On the university level, which must now be viewed as a *body politic,* students would begin to organize against testing, grading and record keeping. In the Middle Ages the peasants demanded that records related to their serfdom and their reduction into property be burned. From such demands new movements emerged which gave rise to the roots of Anabaptist and Mennonite thought. They set the stage for the reassertion of individual meaning and conscience which unite the prophetic spirit with the social gospel.

In the Channeling Colony, students are essentially in the same position as the peasants of the Middle Ages.

While somewhat unbecoming, parents of middle-class children may find themselves demanding that records about their children be destroyed, since they are an impediment to the idea of teaching and the freedom of the child. Parents and children, as well as older students, will come to see that the power of the pyramidal structure is in the records kept by it, and in the controls which it exercises through the profiles it creates of others. Another's idea of the young person's being may be his occupation, but it dares not dictate the fate of the young person.

Is there a way to decolonize from the present structure of the school? Let us continue with the example of records and testing. When we analyze cheating* and cooperating, we find that it does not take a great leap in imagination to see that behaviorally such actions may be the same. The difference is the attitude brought to the relationship and the fact that the individual's motive is thought by him to be irrelevant. (This sense of irrelevance can only be changed through externally changing the person's sense of guilt, which the person feels because of his dissonance with an apparently "correct" external value.) Generally, students cheat because they have internalized the values of the hierarchic other. Thus, they use the system's methods of dealing with that failure. The individual senses the stupidity of what he is expected to know and then acts in bad faith by committing actions which reinforce the values of the system as they are. His guilt is most likely a political one. He accepted the colonizer's conception of himself as the student who is to be trained to be an opportunistic individual who cannot work with or borrow from another.

By professors, students and campus ministers arguing and engaging the school in a dialogue which makes clear that the university is not concerned with awarding

* Cheating is not faking.

place for the army or corporation—that is, the vertical structure—but is interested in knowledge and inquiry per se, they engage the vertical organization in the humane purpose of transforming itself into achieving community and cooperation in scholarship. Their political stand will change scholarship so that it fulfills the purpose of inquiry. If such a challenge is successful, the university will be impeded in its attempts to fulfill an external colonizing purpose which requires the awarding of status and place. An example of this limited success was the Columbia Student Movement, forcing that university to drop its plans for building a gym for itself at the living expense of the Harlem residents. Another was the MIT administration's suspending work on certain war research contracts.

If the schools did not grade and profilize youngsters for the corporation and the state, competitive relationships would give way to the practice of free inquiry in which students would borrow and learn from one another in groups, projects and experimentation. Consequently, they would be able to concentrate on the new practice of building community schools rather than acting as winnower and sifter of personnel for the corporate hierarchic machine or the state.

The Identity Beyond Profile

The young in the United States are less ready to internalize the values of colonization or the function and needs of the vertical structure as their own needs and purposes. This is paradoxical because, in terms of wealth and opportunity, the pyramidal system has never offered so much. This unfelt identity with the opportunities of the pyramid has meant that an unresolvable contradiction exists between the world view of the young and the actual operations of the vertical structure. The white middle class created by the organization and in part dependent on American imperial power, has produced "playful"* children who felt that they could rely on the democratic rhetoric of equality and less on the whip of economic necessity.

From the beginning of the twentieth century to the end of the Second World War, virtually everyone in the United States was caught in a fairly brutal economic struggle. One scurried to eat and learned skills which would make eating possible. The constant threat of economic failure which meant destruction of human ties, suicide and mental breakdown was present. By 1938–39, the United States still had not solved its unemployment problem. There were 18 percent unemployed and the ameliorating tactics of the New Deal, which swung between encouraging competition and monopoly, had failed. Historically, on the other hand, war has been an effective economic tool to restore prosperity to the United States. In this regard, the Second World War was a colossal success. Since 1945 the gross national product has increased by a factor of eight. By the nineteen-fifties place was easily attained for middle-class children if they stayed in line. Indeed, my generation became the generation of hipsters

---

* Young people have thought that they could be more "playful" without fear of losing their social status and place. Furthermore, they assumed that imperial power needed their brains and bodies in order to make the pyramid function. (There was a curious contradiction. Most of the young were too frightened of chance-taking. But others realized that the reformist colonizers liked people who did not totally internalize their values.) Those young people who learned the lesson of fake prodigality assumed that imperial power needed their brains and bodies to keep the authority system intact. The most clever realized that if they stayed within certain limits they would be able to return to the imperial bosom, the vertical organization, and at a higher salary for their prodigality. Indeed, after a certain stage is reached, it is even possible for the young to get jobs managing the young as instruments of the vertical structure. We see this phenomenon most clearly at the university, where a student leader of a particular political movement may in the course of time end up in the administration of the university as a manager and broker between the young and the vertical institution.

and psychological dropouts from the organization who disliked how we lived.

After 1960, the mood was lifted by those wonderful hucksters, the Kennedys. The silence of the fifties and the seeming "perfect fit" of that generation of young people caused apprehension among certain of the reformist elements in the country. Commencement speeches at universities were given which exhorted young people to take chances, have purpose and question their elders. All the rhetoric which the Dream Colony is so good at packaging was used by the mass magazines to find national purpose. President Eisenhower appointed a commission to search for national goals, its executive director being William Bundy, who was later to become the State Department's gauleiter of Vietnam. And, by 1960, Walt Rostow whispered in Jack Kennedy's ear, "We have to get the country moving again." The democratic rhetoric of the colonizers took hold. The young of the left and right believed that they could exercise personal and associative control (that is, control in agreement with others freely arrived at with their participation) and that there were political spaces outside of the vertical organizations in which to build their own institutions. The glossy rhetoric of another generation's leadership and teachers serves as the seed of contradiction to the young, who hear they are free but live colonized. Perception of the disparity between the rhetoric of the goals, ideals, and values of American society and their actual dynamic meant that a very particular legal and political veil was lifted (which shielded the social reality in which the American society protects organizational space while now finding itself limiting personal and associative space because people have forgotten how to "do" things, whether doing means fixing things or organizing with their neighbors). The young who have come upon this condition have become disenchanted and radicalized.

Those who find themselves to be in actual and immediate confrontation will bring about change in the particular colonial situations. We may include those who reflect the extreme situation in their own lives, or who through accident, study or contact, feel the need to change because there is no private accommodation which is available to them. It is like the middle-class ex-college student now living and working in the slums who had failed in his own colonized situation at the university, and his own family environs, and attempts to adopt and confront someone else's immediately felt situation. Once he decides that this is his situation, there is neither privacy nor adjustment; he accepts the stance of the wretched and dispossessed while undertaking to confront the might of that particular colony; in the beginning it is the powerless who must be changed first. For example, in civil rights, the struggle in the South at first was between those having only a surplus of power and affluence to guide them, and those at the bottom who were guided by their hunger, fright, and uneasiness. Neither group was bound by the rules the rest of the society accepted, although ultimately it is that group which sets the basic resolution of the confrontation when the society is still within the zone of stability. Ironically, those who "objectively" had power, in many cases thought that they had very little. But questions of power cannot be divorced from action and purpose. Power in any political situation is not an a priori matter. It can only be discovered in practice. Its shrewd exercise for moral ends depends on one's belief in formal liberties which are not found in a person's life in the world.

In 1964, at the University of California, the students rebelled against the administration in what was the beginning of a movement for profound political change at the universities. The Berkeley situation is a classic case of the historic series of struggles which will magnify within the

Channeling Colony at the university level until there is a change in the rights and obligations due the state and the economic corporation by the young. The struggle between students and junior faculty on the one hand, and the administration and the technological faculties on the other, concerned record-keeping, forms and administrative red tape, as well as an historically reasonable rule, which in practice turned out to be arbitrary and capricious. The regents of the University of California said that no political activity was to be allowed at Berkeley. But as a practical matter, how can politics be divorced from the university? A university is a place where politics is transmitted, analyzed and dissected. But for the warriors of the civil rights movement, "the university set about denying students access to those facilities and rights on campus which had made possible student involvement in the civil rights movement in the previous few years."[4] And it resulted, at last, in raising the question of what the university was.

It finally was raised to the level of consciousness in people's minds that defense laboratories, which were crucial in weapons design, were administered through the university for the purpose of rendering the United States top dog and imperial in the world. There no longer was a way to construe the American university as either neutral or non-political. The practice of such work being allowed and encouraged by the university for its reasons of profit and expansion meant that the university had become the fundamental shield and terrorizing instrument of the state. For this the state was prepared to pay handsomely to its servants. To left activist students such work was profoundly political, far beyond the issue of whether the students could distribute leaflets or set up political booths on campus. To them, the University of California had become a mask for the feudal society of top-down hierarchy where the interests of the AEC, the CIA, the

DOD, and the FBI joined hands with the local corporation. Within the university, senior professors and the
university administration had shamelessly exploited the
graduate or ex-graduate student to do the work of teaching and grading, and haunted and humiliated him for
living on the edges of the university once he could not be
exploited, or did not finish his Ph.D. which usually occurred because the Ph.D. system was run as a guild monopoly. The university seemed to have become a haven for
consultant-happy professors, protected by administrators
who consigned students to the lowest importance. This
was especially annoying since the economic power and
legitimacy (at least) of the state university rested upon
the teaching of students.

These students, some of whom had protested and gone
to jail for *others'* rights, seemed not to be afraid of the
consequences. Perhaps the fact that they were well-to-do
and assumed their own worth helped them now to tackle
their colonial status. They believed that the pyramidal
structure could be changed through direct action, either
by groups or the tenacious struggle of one person. There
is much political history which supported the beliefs of the
students. By undertaking a political risk which stems from
a shared pain, the possibilities of change (without pre-
judging the quality or kind) is very great. The condition
of shared pain is realized consciously by increasing numbers of students who have no vested interest in the present
vertical system since they see that their teachers and university presidents look to *them* for moral leadership, a
fact which is shocking. A vice-president of a Midwestern
university complained to me that he keeps asking the
students what they want, and he gets no answer. "They
are only against." But he does not stop to ask what he is
for. The old were once supposed to induct the young into
the civilization and show them the way. Now the old prat-
tle against the young: "You have no ideas." It is true that

students will have to be more explicit about their objectives—not so that they can be bargained out of them, but to be able to keep interest and commitment among themselves.

Students in the United States will find it necessary to go beyond mere revolt to work out their own projects and institutions. Their elders do not seem capable of guiding the direction of such a reconstruction. Furthermore, struggle or disorder as an end in itself only totalizes the power of the colonized structure. For example, at Berkeley, the university has attempted liberal mediation through better coordination of relationships of function (not of people) within the school. These changes, however, are merely mechanical, having as their objective a smoother running colony. Indeed, the final result of the series of events which grew out of the Berkeley revolt was the appointment of Charles Hitch as the president of the University of California.*

The present quality of educational leadership fulfills the disparaging comment of Veblen. In his book on higher education he referred to university presidents as captains of education; people who resembled the captains of industry in their style of thought and management methods. Presently, because of the great power of the state as manifested through the Violence Colony, the educational leadership has found itself integrating with the captains of violence. In some cases, the administrative and political leadership of the universities has fallen to men whose lives have been spent in a militarist direction,

* Hitch spent twenty-five years of his life in the theory and practice of the economics of defense before coming to the University of California. Before his appointment, he had served as the comptroller of the Department of Defense and was responsible for such important disastrous programs as attempting to bring counterforce into defense strategy, the TFX matter, an unlimited defense budget, and the capability and will to fight so-called limited wars. The university was now going to fend off the state with a civilianized warrior.

protecting and building the hierarchic structure, preparing for war and fighting it. This leadership has had a significant direction on the course of knowledge and its meaning. Those like Lewis Feuer who dwell on student violence would do well to review the relationships of universities as the fundamental purveyor of violent methods in its social science courses as they apply to manipulating the poor nations. It is not too much to ask that those involved in the natural sciences investigate the manner in which violent technologies are researched and buttressed by their discipline and university.

Knowledges for Channeling

Over the last thirty years the intellectual class has hidden from itself and others the relationship of the knowledges developed in the society to the groups being served by such knowledge. Such catch phrases as "value-free research," "objectivity," etc. helped in sanitizing institutional frameworks and grasping at miserable disembodied facts. This ideology of avoidance as to how certain knowledges come into being and who is served by the mode of analysis used, has not voided the stubborn fact that the knowledges produced in the knowledge industry as it has to do with the organization of the body politic, usually serve its ruling element. The knowledges developed attempt to justify and rationalize institutions and authority structures as they presently exist.

The case of Robert McNamara and the Department of Defense illustrates how calculations and objectivity are used as tools to hide political bargaining. He introduced into the Department of Defense a mode of rationality which made use of operations research, accounting technique and economics. With this method, one that had been used by General Motors since the late twenties and was used in the second world war to order priorities, he attempted to bring a new instrument into being which would give the appearance that defense decisions were arrived at in a reasonably scientific way. This method operated, of course, as rationalization and ornamentation. In 1961, McNamara brought to the White House numbers, formulae and charts showing why we needed 1200 Minute-Men missiles.* Antagonists on the White House staff showed that to do exactly what McNamara estimated it was only necessary to have 800 missiles. This was shown by using the same assumptions and numbers. McNamara responded, after being proved wrong, that he knew that the White House staff was correct. However, he could not go back to the Joint Chiefs of Staff after having cut them from 1600 missiles with the bargained position being "only" 800. Knowledge here served as pure ornamentation.

In both cases, we see a direct relationship between the type of knowledge developed and the power of certain groups in the society to have such knowledge developed. The "facts" and the institutions which produce them have a reciprocal and reinforcing effect, guaranteeing the continuity and enlargement of the institutions which need such "facts" as well as the support of educational institutions who produce and propagate them.

The facts developed by such institutions may be descriptions of realities created. That is, they are instrumental facts, those created by our own volitions as mediated through the demand of the vertical organization. Such facts and knowledge become instruments to shape power or justify it. Or, they may be used to ornament decisions arrived at by wholly different processes.

* It should be noted that by 1962 the civilians and military agreed to build and have in readiness 1800 missiles.

. . . large modern organizations are insatiable consumers
of scholarly knowledge, ideas, and theories. Any knowledge
that is remotely related to the activities of the organization
is fair game; it is an article of faith that in order that an organization will survive it must be at the "frontier" of knowledge.[5]

This form of knowledge does not help us get at the root
of what is going on, although it serves to strengthen the
particular organization which employs such knowledge.
Let us continue with the example of the Department of
Defense. Its brand of knowledge emphasizes management,
efficiency, facts and organization. Through Secretary
McNamara, the Department of Defense has become the
most powerful military war machine that ever existed in
history. However, if you view the Department of Defense,
the military, and the war system as problems to be solved,
not institutions to be preserved or enlarged, it would have
been necessary to develop a totally different sort of knowledge. Similarly, advertising firms use the latest polling
techniques and motivational research, viewing their
clients as institutions to be preserved. The consumer
becomes the object. This mode helps to enlarge the given
vertical structures by techniques of creating wants without fulfilling needs.

As many critics have pointed out, the university has
become a factory for suggestions of momentary and partial solutions which, upon analysis, end as mere irritants
and aggravators of the original problems. In the knowledge that they create and the people they train to solve
problems and to man organizations, the universities serve
particular purposes and classes (defined by a very particular point of view) which themselves *become* the problem. Momentary single purpose and expedient resolu-
tions are not tests of workability; for example, do we
really need bigger roads because we have bigger cars?

Many ideas which have been developed on public policy merely reflect such an expediential approach, and for awhile we were not conscious enough to understand how foolish were the arguments which were reflected in the expediential approach.

In the 1950's the nuclear strategists and various scientists, for example Kahn and Teller, were fond of pointing out that many more people were killed on the highway than would be affected by fallout from atomic testing. The values of the hierarchic other had so been internalized into us that no one stopped to question why so many had to be killed on the highways, whether there were mechanical reasons stemming from defective cars which the society blindly accepted, or correlatively, whether the reasons for committing suicide on the highway were socially or mechanically caused.* Once we accept internalization or are defined by the systems so that we dance without knowing either the tune or why we are dancing, we ratify the vertical organization which forces its colonized to think of responsibility only as it is defined by bureaucratic situation or function. "I am only doing my job" is the statement of the defense secretary, the motor company president, the hangman, the prosecutor, and the social

---

* Even as decent a man as John Kenneth Galbraith cannot think about how to humanize corporate power and has concluded that we must accept it and live with it. Instead of facing the basic problem, he concludes that the vertical structure in terms of the economic and social organization cannot be tampered with. People, he suggests, must find their freedom in aesthetics. We must, he says, stipulate the importance of aesthetics and art to the survival of people; indeed, they make their art from their own suffering, joy and striving. But it should be obvious that the way art and aesthetics are used by a self-conscious elite in the context of vertical structure is not totally irrelevant to the work which the artist may find himself doing. For the artist and aesthetician it should be obvious that art and aesthetics, when viewed as ornaments and soporifics, will have lost the battle for art as a humanizing activity. Is General Motors to set up an arts division to subsidize artists and use their works? Or, is the cause of art served when a foundation buys paintings to be used in the American ambassador's home in the country to which he is accredited? (Robert Komer, who was an ambassador to Vietnam, ordered forty of these paintings for his home in Saigon.)

worker who spies on the poor. They see themselves only as their job, which in turn is defined through the pyramid.

What, then, did the growing class of the educated find itself committed to and what did it think education was? Since the second world war, the educated class established itself as a prime supporter of the New American Feudalism—the feudalism of *national security* with its emphasis on structural stability, growth and more of everything within the framework of the corporate organization. The university acted as the servant and mediator for the colonizers. American society, based on consensus of those at the tops of the different pyramids, created the knowledge to serve more of what is—more military technology, larger national security institutions, greater control through television, more mass-produced goods, more poor education and more consumer credit.

Politically, the effectively operating vertical organization was to identify the ruling elite of the organization with the members of the organization and then the organization's identity of interest with the rest of society. The heads of the organization were then delegated to trade and broker with other like-minded leaders whose organizations were also built on the assumption that more is better than less, whose organizational corners are centered on process rather than purpose. Held together by command, economic need and threat, the mailed fist, class laws, and authority symbols, vertical organization internalizes its values and legitimacy onto individuals whom it characterizes. This has had disastrous consequences. It encouraged us to accept our situation as victims of nuclear disaster as if it were a natural phenomenon caused by natural forces or God.

The problem of the vertical organization and its relationship to knowledge as its instrument and justifier is exhibited by those whom society recognizes as the most enlightened and clever people. Indeed, they were thought within the elite groups to be enlightened mediators who stopped the Neanderthal.*

Consider this: McGeorge Bundy, former Dean of Harvard, and President Kennedy's advisor on national security matters, bragged at Yale University in an important speech about having nuclear weapons in "all shapes and sizes." A former President of Harvard, James B. Conant, said that we must develop a warmaking capability in which "surviving a thermonuclear barrage, we would be able to deliver thermonuclear weapons to such an extent and in such a way that at least three-fourths of the industrial complexes of the Soviet Union would be utterly destroyed."[6]

The reconstruction of democracy based on associations of equals is not the operational purpose or goal of the American educated class, which is dependent on instrumental social knowledge needed for manipulation. The status and sense of privilege of its members staples to the society that type of individualism and opportunity which assumes open doors (in which the keys are held by the professional classes which develop standards and operate as a monopoly), ladders (over which they control the rungs), and structures organized on the basis of merit, style, language use and the threat of exclusion which can be used as the power to punish the doubters. The present Mandarin group of the educated class assumes special "responsibilities" (another word for power) for the system because of its facility in rationalization, reflecting a knowledge which is rooted in "objectivity." (Rationalization is used in the sense of arranging into an order which best fits into the going social organization.) Whether these mandarins are in Washington, Cambridge, or Detroit, whether their organization is the university, the

* The "bomb them back to the Stone Age" theory of Curtis LeMay would be mediated by a civilian intellectual like McNamara to bomb "them" to the Neolithic Age.

government or the corporation, their actions are governed by the same operative principles. Emphasis is placed on execution without concern for purpose. Interest in purpose is feigned through rhetorical statement and rationalized through public relations. Whether the issue is nuclear weapons, cars, missiles, or body counts, the habit of mind is the same. It is quantitative and abstract.

Knowledge of things and knowledge of living beings are merged into one method of understanding by the mandarin elite which uses measurement and calculation as the primary tool for manipulative purposes. This "object" knowledge in practice is aimed at ascertaining the behavior of people, and then manipulating them to behave according to the norms set through the vertical organization of the society. In this context, such knowledge becomes handmaiden to the production of disastrous moral and political consequences. Such "knowledge" in sociology and psychology becomes part of the "helping" professions which, without reconstructive intent, act as a control mechanism that causes political immobilism and reform without change.

In operations research, a field of social science developed in World War II, the activity of political manipulation of one person over another appears as a form of objectivity because it uses that form of quantification which easily transforms subjects into objects. This is not a new problem in the social sciences. Now, however, we can discern the pernicious effects of "objectivity" when university-trained bureaucrats and professors take problems and transform them into abstractions.

Through abstraction and "objectivity" we find that the mandarin group has developed a ritualistic language whose social consequence is the exclusion, exploitation and manipulation of other people. It is directly antithetical to the idea of participation and democracy.

The twin problem of abstract, non-referential language

and of knowledge which has lost meaning and generally adds to our colonized situation, is part of a spiral of intellectual, political and economic forces that began with the industrial revolution.

> The materialistic or positivistic trend prevailed throughout the country in the nineteenth century. It imbued the sciences with factual reality, and we owe it much knowledge. On the other hand, its rejection of any spiritually-selective principle, its levelling and disintegrating activity, brought about an immense overcrowding of the disciplines with unorganized material, so that in the intellectual field, just as in the practical field, the material, the instrumental world of research, overpowered reason, and man, and became his master. Today, even the specialist can scarcely master his field; he is rather mastered by it. It is his field that dictates collective questions, and a collective method of working. As a result of overcrowding, there is continuous specialization to narrower fields that can no longer completely deal with the unorganized mass of human knowledge. Scholars and scientists of every subdivision have evolved a special terminology of their own that nobody else understands. Modern learning has become a Tower of Babel. [7]

As Karl Mannheim has pointed out, no knowledge exists *in abstracto.* No knowledge (specialized or otherwise) is by itself even though it may be presented in that way. Knowledge exists within a time period. It also exists within an institutional structure which has certain primary and secondary values which are passed on from one generation to another. The knowledge itself comes to reflect institutional structure which reflects the will or the interest of particular groups. Obviously all knowledges are open to this analysis. That is to say, whether the knowledge is colonized or reconstructive knowledge, the sociology of knowledge analysis still applies. But the purposes served and the assumptions taken by those who buttress colonized knowledge as against those who attempt to build a reconstructive knowledge is quite different.

Colonized knowledge walks on two legs. The person must learn the trivia of the classroom (note p. 112) so that the individual is characterized into a function, using his creativity for that function. And he must learn specialized subject matter. In this way the individual learns his place and his particular opportunity in the pyramid. The basic ingredients of a channeled education for an individual are familiarity with a particular area of specialization and learning to come on time to a particular place so that a diploma can be awarded. In this sense, the Channeling Colony operates to insure that the individual accepts the social and epistemological framework of reference as it is given. If he were innovative the individual would be urged to develop his creativity through improving the assumptions of the organization. Organization, whether it is of knowledge or of a social organization itself, is to be viewed as set. It is obvious that to some extent this will always be true; that is to say, conventions of thought are necessary and continue to be so. Yet even conventions of language which have shaped social reality are now under question. We may note the new typography of the free presses. But other examples quickly come to mind which force such a change.

Wolfgang Köhler points out that he was forty years old before he asked, "Why is it that we go in order A, B, C, D, E, F, G, etc.?"[8] What is the fact of teaching ourselves to see the alphabet that way? What does seeing the alphabet in that way teach us about the structure of the society? Now, at one time of course where letters in an alphabet grew out of religious and moral tradition those reasons could be found, but those traditions have long since been forgotten and we begin to see in my view that the structure of the society will probably dictate the new way of learning the alphabet. It may be in terms of the typewriter—Q, W, E, R, T, Y, U, etc.—or in terms of those letters we use most of all coming at the beginning of the alphabet. In this way, it would be clear that our society was totally different and tied to a technological and functional basis of operating.

But take a case dealing with knowledge and language that attempts to define communication outside of the usual frameworks: Suppose I describe a particular situation to you on the written page. I am usually forced to use language which masks the situation's real meaning in terms of its emotive content. Suppose I say, "In Hiroshima the United States dropped an atomic bomb which equaled twenty tons of dynamite. Today we have nuclear weapons which are each fifty megatons and the United States drops three megatons of bombs a year on Vietnam. Furthermore, with the methods we have we are able to destroy the world many times over." After stating this point I might go on to the next sentence about a related matter. By the structure of that sentence I have undercut the emotive and warning meaning which I am attempting to communicate to the reader. But suppose I leave six blank pages except for the word "reflect" at the top of the first blank page. It is conceivable that the reader would see my meaning more clearly. In this way communication outside of spoken or written language becomes the instrument of changing political responses. Existentially, such a mode of communication becomes the way to reflect the motive content of self as subject to another as subject.

In dealing with specialization which has given so much impetus to objective knowledge, we are always left with a partial or incomplete picture of what it is that we want to know. This is, of course, the direction knowledge has taken over the last several hundred years. The wags say that we come to know more and more about less and less until we finally know everything about nothing. Yet the truth is that the knowledge which is learned is basically that of staying within one's particular niche or framework. It means that the assumptions of the larger frame of reference or the problem of the larger organization itself is not open to question. The disastrous consequences of this are seen when we examine the Department of Defense, which until recently was viewed by very few as a problem to study with the view of performing radical surgery and not as an organization to assist. The specialized knowledges that the Defense Department developed fitted into the framework of the Violence Colony, thereby amassing a whole storehouse of facts and values that now come to be seen as problems.

Suppose I am a physicist at Harvard, MIT, or Chicago. During the cold war period I am put the question, "How do you stop an ICBM?" I ask the question, "What is the formula and the method that would have to be invented?" and then I ask, "What is the technology that is needed?" In this process I set down and begin to work through a whole series of ideas which are supposedly facts or factors, and I develop a theory and technology to answer the problem put to me. By undertaking that mode of analysis and creating a technology I have worked out a knowledge which creates the problem.

Put it another way. I have an ICBM system. You have an ICBM system. I am told to answer your ICBM system with an ABM system. The result is that I attempt to relate those two systems together and I work through a whole system of knowledge that gets us absolutely no closer to the solution of the basic problem than I was before I began working through the most elegant techniques of science and technology. The result is that we pile layer upon layer of silly, incomplete objective knowledge to support the most soggy social frameworks and frames of reference.

For example, someone questions, "How do we destroy the world?" In a government agency or a university that may become the problem that an individual puts to himself. Now obviously I am setting this problem in a value-loaded way. But take another way of putting it. Suppose I say, "How do we take out all the cities in China and the Soviet Union?" It is obvious that a whole system of values is built into this way of looking at international relations or relations among people. One which I will explain shortly is the whole issue of objective knowledge and false consciousness wherein people and things become interchangeable. But for the moment we may view the question of destroying China and the Soviet Union as a problem within an organization of epistemology. It is a problem of efficiency, of developing certain sorts of analyses, of seeing things getting to other places at a particular time. Very specialized sorts of knowledge develop as a result. The result of course is that each piece of knowledge developed becomes related to making the organization larger and more efficient.

Quantitative knowledge and objectivity turn out to be related. When I use the word "objectivity" I don't mean seeing things as they are, but rather I'm describing a relationship to subject matter in which you are "cool" about it and make the judgment of that which is going on as quite separate from who it is that you are. The individual maintains distance. In one sense, of course, this is good. Yet this definition of objectivity may also give rise to the idea of false consciousness. In one's own thought he begins to invent a language and a way of acting which says that the people of a particular city become a thing—an entity that others are able to play with—at first in one's head and finally in practice.

Thinking about other people's problems at a time when

the technology to affect other people and the power to do so rests in the hands of very few is, of course, a colonizing activity. One of the problems of objective knowledge is that it easily can be used by those with power and an understanding of technique to further the ends of their own colonizing power.

The philosopher and the minister are not without responsibilities and potentialities in this area. The task that they must undertake for clarification is to familiarize themselves with subject matter which passes as knowledge in the sciences, social sciences and humanities so that within the university and the society they are able to stand up and say, "Hey—why are you asking that sort of question, doing that sort of research? Why are you not taking up this sort of question? Why do you not research areas which will have the following likely consequence?"

Finding ourselves in the world we become aware that our problems rarely divide according to the disciplines which have been developed; nor does the knowledge which has been developed help in the resolution of the social or political problems which may be in store. More likely, the reverse is true. The knowledge which has been developed is man's problem, in part because the knowledge serves as a screen against seeing himself as he is—a part of the whole socio-political dilemma. In this context, knowledge can be understood only as an object of study for those interested in seeing a complete and intersected picture of knowledge as rationalizer and rhetorical tool of the system in power.

Let us continue with the example of "defense knowledge." (The reason I feel justified in using examples from national security is because most of this generation's collective material and intellectual wealth has been spent in defense. Its influence has been enormous.)

In recent years, as a result of work done at the RAND Corporation by Hitch, Enthoven, Rowen and others, there was developed a whole system of cost effectiveness by which to judge the validity of one weapons system as against another. This strategic systems theory was supposedly superior to the less pretentious one put forward by the Eisenhower-Wilson administration which was charmingly known in its day as "more bang for the buck." The RAND view, plus the ideology of using nuclear weapons for diplomatic bargaining purposes and of building an imperial armed force ready to strike when it suited the fancy of the national security leadership, resulted in a vastly enlarged defense establishment. The methods of accounting and cost effectiveness which were brought into the Defense Department have now permeated the entire federal bureaucracy. Indeed, government policy planners are now sent to be trained in the vagaries of this pseudo-science in order to apply "The Method" to education, urban problems and transportation problems. RAND men and RAND mentality are found throughout the federal bureaucracy. Those who adopt this method end up not asking fundamental questions about the purpose of their activity or the purpose and effect of their programs. Hence, if the order is given to destroy the world, the question for those experts is how—for example, between competing programs put forward—to do it most cheaply. Or, if the RAND man concludes that the poor are going to the city, the government should encourage their irrationality by allowing subsistence conditions on the farms to remain. The methods of the "think-tanks" reflect social techniques based upon computers and all other forms of paraphernalia used in the defense of foolishness or just plain madness. The basic question of value is never asked either by the planner in the employment of his social techniques or in the body politic itself. It is always the assumed or given. Technique brings its own values which themselves are regenerated in more technique.

Abstracted technique is not the same as practice. The methods which are developed in complex hierarchic organizations do not relate to participation and practice for people except as they are instruments in the fulfillment of the mission. The mission—that is, the purpose— of the institutions remains intact while the activities of the individuals are judged according to the criteria laid down for the unexamined mission. Consequently, the split remains between the judgments men make in their roles as experts for the mission or the organization and those that they make in terms of themselves as selves relating to other selves. Objectivity in this context takes on one-dimensional characteristics.

What the corporate or government bureaucrat thinks about, "objectivity" as an object, lifeless, detached, is not a part of his living biography. It is not his life in the sense that the laws which the scientist discovers in nature are laws within which he must live. Obviously, in the best of all possible worlds one cannot identify totally with another to comprehend existentially his situation. Just because that is the case, the types of knowledge which are developed are so important. They operate where they are instrumental to serve as that ingredient which makes up for the fact that one cannot identify with another.*

---

* In bureaucracy the issue of objectivity is central. Let's take a look specifically at the case of how objectivity works in a bureaucrat's life. The scholar or the bureaucrat thinks about and works on those sorts of questions that are not his in a personal or biographical sense, whether past or future. They are really not part of his life. For example, the bureaucrat sees as his problems whether he gets home early or late, whether he gets tied up in traffic, whether he is invited to a particular meeting, not what the substance of the meeting is or the position he takes except as effects his possible attendance at the next meeting, whether he gets promoted, whether he has a good sex life, whether he gets sick, slighted, or frustrated. This is his subjective reality. But that is very different from the objective reality which he thinks he deals with.

Now, what is the objective reality? It may depend, obviously, on what his job is; it may be whether the Vietnamese get napalm today, whether the cities will be strangled in polluted air, whether or not we build more nuclear weapons, and so

In the area of social knowledge the attitude which dominated among scholars and practitioners is that the problems with which they deal are other people's problems. They hardly intersect with the other people. The result is that their knowledge is cold and manipulative. When they do intersect they no longer see problems but rather people who are "transformed" because they learn that the people have their own ideas and consciousness. When this happens the "problem" then threatens the power or sanctity of the practitioner or scholar because they are forced to interact rather than act upon inanimate things. The problem "bites" back.

---

forth and so on. Those are the problems which he comes to think of as abstract and objective questions, when, indeed, they are highly subjective questions which define and affect his existence as well as ours. The very important task of education in all of this and the historically important task of education is how do you get people to comprehend that which is indirect so that they feel those indirect things existentially. That really is what the basis of education and what the basis of knowledge should be. Now, part of this is seen in statecraft in the following ways. We know that we can't do everything ourselves and that indeed what we have to do is trust an indirect structure. Now you see this in a number of ways. We trust the pilot when we get on an airplane. We also know that he lives with the same sort of strictures that we do. He will crash with us if a mistake is made. But, the point is that what we have to begin to do is to take a look at how we make indirect things direct and, in the political area, how we begin to redistribute what is indirect to what it is that is direct, so that we can begin to have the responsibility of our lives which we have turned over to other people or the colonies. As I have suggested elsewhere, the basis for this exists in the dissonant— in the personal dissonance and in a descriptive prescriptive method.

5

The
Dream
Colony

"It's just like in the movies."
Collective American anonymous,
in describing the reality of
life situations.
"All the American people want is a little sunshine
up the asshole."
Former network television
executive.

According to a report of a congressional committee, "Television viewing alone occupies nearly one-fourth of the waking hours of the average American."[1] The people of the United States spend approximately 1.5 billion hours a week listening to the radio and watching television. As a base of comparison, the aggregate work week in America is 2.8 billion hours. The process of television and radio media involvement is roughly half as important as the nature of work in this society and far less varied in its substance.

Communications as a thing in itself turns out to be more important than what is communicated. There are certain objective power relations which support this view. Historically, in the television and radio industry in the United States, the goods advertised have been more important than the media themselves. In the early stages of the radio industry, stations were started by stores that wanted to sell their goods or by universities that cared to experiment. While radio stations separated themselves (literally) as independent business entities from the showrooms of automobile dealers early in the history of commercial radio, advertisers were able to dictate the content of programs shown on TV as late as 1963. As the television and radio networks increased their power politically and economically, communications became the goods to be sold in themselves. Corporations that make cosmetics, soap, cigarettes, and beer, were less important economically and politically than the carriers of national communications, while communications as a product—that is, the sale of air time and telephone time— became more important politically than those particular corporations that produced material goods. This reflects a basic and historic shift in the society. As products communications and information have become more important than goods themselves. Indeed, whole studies are given over to the organization of information and communications in which the argument is made that such "knowledge" is the new technology.

The transformation of communications into a consumer product has had profound effects on the body politic. While people might once have petitioned the government for action, they now attempt to get action—as Kenneth Cox and Nicholas Johnson have pointed out—through petitioning the media. "Those who have proposals for action must reach the media before they reach the people or the government. They need the media to put their needs in the forefront of the community's consciousness."[2] The shift of power to the communicator, AT&T, RCA, NBC, etc. and the organizer of the bank of communications, IBM, etc., has *not* changed the fundamental colonized relationship of the mass audience to those who

control the medium of communications.* The change
merely means that the economic and power relationships
between the program-maker, the sponsor and the television network has changed so that the "communicating"
owner and those who operate in colonizing roles in the
broadcast pyramid have increased their economic and
political power as against the corporate consumer maker.
This change is indicative of the importance of information over things as an example of power transference to
those groups in American society which control and
disseminate information. In the United States, where the
economic system is based on the negative productive
growth, that is, obsolescence, waste, needless change in
models and styles of goods, the important business reality
is the *relationship* of buyer to seller and the shared mind-
set which is developed for the buyer and colonized seller.
One way of putting this point is the mind-set, the dreams
and illusions (besides profit!) which will get an auto

---

* Yet, through the use of opinion research modes and techniques which give
the colonizer "objective" correlation with the profit motive and the hierarchic
structure of both his industry and the industry's view of the public, the colonizer
can also be terrorized. He may be reinforced or terrorized by the incantation of
numbers, ratings and polls supplied by the social scientist, who becomes the high
priest to determine what is on the minds of what they suppose is an inert, acted-
upon mass audience. The priest must be listened to since he now has the task of
interpretation for the colonizer. The priest and his expertise become the interpreter of the "popular will." The people think that the way they are described,
and their will (tastes), as interpreted, is really who they are. The colonizer also
then believes in the priest's power.

Once a relationship is secured between the "scientist" and the colonizer, the
colonizer is able to accomplish two ends. He is reinforced in his view of what the
audience wants and he is able to characterize the audience along the lines which
he decides upon and which the audience itself may come to accept as who it is.
The fact that the audience is "influential" in showing its support or disgust at
particular programs which are not in form different from each other has no meaning except to the individual producers and performers who have put forward a
program they want to keep on the air. The fundamental power relationships
between colonizer and colonized remain the same. What tunes and pictures the
colonizer uses to strengthen inertness is secondary to the fact of the power relationship.

salesman to sell a Mustang and a buyer to buy the product. In this sense, the goods that are sold are incidental to the communications relationship which is engendered through the media. The communications and relationship process reflects the struggle between the goods-oriented society as against the newly evolving communications-oriented society in advanced industrial nations.

It is important to note that communications is not communication or relatedness. Communications is the means by which one person relates to another through technological or fabricated devices. It is not a system of actions which, by its inherent structure, builds or "produces" a community or common humanity. Yet communications could begin to have such a task and lead in that direction.

Who Needs Goods?

The telephone and airplane have destroyed the geographic boundaries of distance and extended people toward each other through technological means. Movies and television have removed boundaries (for the time being) between what is real and what is make-believe. The transistor radio has connected people, almost like robots, one to another, as either friend or controller. The phonograph has allowed music to become a constant in our lives. All of them stimulate dreams and potentiality. But it is the television medium which has been especially successful in fusing dream and reality.

In and of themselves, these are delightful and creative developments, since from our personal dreams comes the possibility of union with humanity. My dreams relate me to a common humanity and consciousness. But what happens, for example, if the dreams of corporate gain and continued violence are the over-arching reality with which I am presented through television. What happens when the hierarchic structure *dreams for you* and its dreams are only those of a corporate Moosbrugger? My own actions, or the biographic past I created for myself — that is, my events — are secondary to the sensations I receive through the canned experiences that bombard me through the communications media. I am inundated with immediate and minimum-reduced experience of the described other through the hierarchic other.

Viewers respond to and live in that which is presented before them. They accept the pyramidal structure as the god which operates to decide what they should be presented with. The television presentations are determined according to economic requirements of the media, leaving viewers as non-participants in deciding what reality they wish to participate in. Viewers are presented with a way of looking and responding which is modish. People subjectively look and respond to that which fills their senses and helps them to continue to look and respond and accept other realities which then become a part of who they are. As usual, such realities are kaleidoscopic, unrelated, and free-floating. Technology is used as the vehicle for the free-floating dream which swoops them up into a whirling buggy ride. Yet that dream is felt individually. I am exhorted to accept the immediacy of what I am presented with as important. I accept it because the networks possess the technical equipment to decide whether or not my television set will show anything at all. This power enshrines as paramount the substance of what they present, a substance that is continuous and which runs together. In this way, it is usually incorrect to view TV programs as separate from each other. Instead, they are thought of by the networks as forms which are expected to run together in people's minds. Thus, the television industry treats individual programs as part of a general program theory of what they want people to watch. Each program is functionally related to another.

There is an irony to all of this. The Communications Act created a scheme of locally-based radio stations so that each of the stations would be attentive to the needs and interests of the local communities served. A very different situation has emerged with the growth of the networks. Empirical studies since 1962 show that the network system virtually blocks out any creative programming on the local level. Monitoring of television in Chicago, Omaha and Oklahoma has shown that there is relatively little programming on the local level. The networks have created the colonizing idea that there is a common culture in America which is mediated through advertising, fashion and little morality plays. This ersatz culture has taken the place of the rich culture that does exist in America and which is not totally dominated by the fake and inauthentic. Where they can, the networks work in setting the terms of the fake and inauthentic by coopting ideas from such cultures. Their scheme of what I watch, plus their controls over the technical equipment force me to pay—and pay attention. It may happen that I will be exhorted to respond in dialogue, but not yet.*

The vertical organizational structure of the media, television and radio networks, which now own publishing companies (originally for their profit value and ultimately for their value in centrally controlling the experimental life of the viewer who is reduced to a consumer or "student"),† sets the terms and the content of the individual

---

*Clearly the content of the program and a more and more sophisticated technology finally forces a change in my relationship to technical equipment and the human other. Such equipment either becomes the mode to destroy the other of the vertical organization or the other of our common humanity.

†Herbert Schiller has detailed this merging activity in *Progressive* magazine, May, 1969:

Radio Corporation of America (RCA) acquired Random House. Interviewer's fantasy and experience.* Operationally, whether what I see is high or low culture, the media control is predicated on my participation and acceptance of an assigned role as a listening, seeing man who is expected to be passive except in the case of his relationship to advertisements. When the issue is buying and consuming, the sponsors and advertisers undertake to employ those strategies which will change us from passive viewers to active consumers. The advertisers open to any possibility of active consciousness, in any part of the American society, attempt to package back that sense of active consciousness for their product.

Take the case of the new politics. For the networks and advertisers it became an instrument for selling products. Note, for example, "pucker power" and "cold power"

---

national Telephone and Telegraph bought out Howard W. Sams & Company, a textbook and technical book publisher. The Columbia Broadcasting System took over Holt, Rinehart & Winston, a trade and textbook publisher, for which it paid $280 million, the highest price ever offered for a publishing company. International Business Machines merged with Science Research Associates, which in turn bought out Howard Chandler Company, college text publisher in San Francisco.

The list goes on and on, Litton Industries, the industrial conglomerate, absorbed the American Book Company. Raytheon Company, in electronics, acquired D. C. Heath, the textbook firm. Xerox bought University Microfilm, American Educational Publications *(My Weekly Reader),* Learning Materials, Inc., and R. R. Bowker, the publisher of the leading trade magazines, *Publishers' Weekly* and *Library Journal.* Ginn, one of the two largest elementary school textbook companies, has also been taken over by Xerox. Time, Inc., together with General Electric Company, created the General Learning Corporation, and along the way, Time, Inc. acquired Little, Brown & Company, the venerable Boston book publisher. Sylvania Electric Products, a subsidiary of the General Telephone and Electronics Corporation, has formed a joint group with *Reader's Digest* to investigate the potential of electronic systems in education. Harcourt, Brace & World, a major book publisher, has joined with RCA to explore the learning process. The list of such acquisitions, consolidations, and mergers grows more massive month by month.

---

* It is not far-fetched to envisage an individual as an NBC/Random House man as against a CBS/Holt-Rinehart man.

slogans, and picketing for products as an instrument to sell the "goods." Obviously, the idea of the advertiser was to channel any active impulse in a passive public which might have political manifestations back into consuming. "Join the Dodge Rebellion" is another example of taking political impulses toward activism and cooling them through active consumption.

Most canned programs expect and encourage the viewer to be an active buyer and a passive acceptor of the authority structures. Except where the paradoxes and contradictions of the authority relationship are too great, the colonizer/colonized relationship is presented in a positive way, using any new fashion trends or authentic cultural changes, after proper sanitation and cooptation. These programs become the new myths of the colonized relationship of the society. The TV medium is an example of how isolated and separated from one another people are. At any one moment millions may be listening to a specific program, but reinforced by the nature of television itself no one would think that there is any control he could exercise with others on the media itself, or that he had a *right* to use the media, because the media was publicly owned. TV becomes the pyramidal instrument to give the appearance of understanding participation and sensual participation, so that the dissonance of one's life, which could be activated through personal recognition of one's feelings and related to the dissonance which other people feel as people, is destroyed.

In the fall of 1966, the Marine Corps undertook "to bring the boys a little closer to home" by starting a television network in Vietnam which would pipe such programs of individual heroism as *Twelve O'Clock High* and *Gunsmoke* into the front lines. The presentation of the dream reality was offered to counter personal loneliness, group discussion about the meaning of the war in which they were involved, their situation and what they as feeling men were doing and having done to them. The Marine Corps High Command's purpose was to replace the authentic—what people feel and do on the front lines in a war—with the fraudulent and authoritarian—what the pyramidal structure wants them to feel and do. (Of course, this method is also meant to counter any similar propaganda by which the enemy attempts to instill doubt in the opponent's fighting men.) The purpose of the pyramidal structure is to break the relationship of a group (and their lives now depend on the quality of relatedness which emerges) which forms out of human need back into a non-group structure where people become a series of isolates whose concerns are with ersatz realities and fantasy dreams of personal heroism beamed through television.

Outside of the armed services, the task of the Dream Colony is to package modishness and the cosmetics of rebellion (thereby making a profit from it) while ensuring that the structure of the Authoritarian relationship remains. In 1968, a television program called *The Mod Squad* made its appearance. The three major characters of the program are a beautiful blonde girl, who is the hippie possibility, a young black man from the streets, and an upper-middle-class rebel. They represent the beautiful, young, alienated, poor and black people. In the background is a stern man of technique and principle who is trying to relate to the young generation. The three people have been rebels, living on the other side of the law, smoking pot, perhaps even a *ménage à trois,* but having as one of them says, "a little bit of soul." They adopt the language of the next generation. Of course, the extraordinary thing about these four people is that they are policemen; the older man is their captain and the three younger people work for the captain as a special police team. The message of this program is that the new, brooding, law-and-order authoritarian relationships can easily encompass hippie language and style. The "enemy" in this drama is the square, middle-class man. He is usually portrayed as someone who does not know how to relate to the young. He appears in the film as the confused, older generation that has fuzzy attitudes toward authoritarian values, who is alienated from the language and style of the young people and from the authority role of the police.

It is not surprising that television, in its more avant-garde programs should mirror the strongest clearly emergent elements in the society and show how the authority structures are able to finally have one of those elements work for the perpetuation of settled authority relationships. Networks not only seek this role of "preservation" with their little morality playlets, they also attempt to perform the same role of authority preservation in their political reporting. Thus, in its own way, the Army-McCarthy hearings taught the same lesson as *The Mod Squad.*

In the case of the McCarthy caper, people watched with fascination as the demagogue attempted to destroy the basic authoritarian institution of American life, the armed forces. The citizenry was not going to have any of that once they saw the uncouth (by any advertising standards) Joe McCarthy. Television helped to save the authoritarian structures of the Department of Defense by showing Authority in its best light (Welch, General Zwicker, etc.). Once McCarthy stopped serving Authority and started attacking it—for whatever reason—he was able to reassert himself only as a dissociated thug. He was bound to lose support of (the Greek chorus) people who feared the loss of their mobility and authority more than any ornamental threat such as communism.

In politics, television's effect is to stimulate the cosmetic as more important than the substantive positions taken by candidates. (It is not accidental that President Nixon favored advertising and public relations executives for his White House staff.) Under the guise of presenting everything in a continuous stream, the viewer is inundated with the individual as a character without dimension, except as defined or mediated through the colonized system. He is neither human being nor thinking being. He is a role who plays out a particular plot. One candidate for the Senate told me that he is stopped on the street and congratulated for being on television. "What did I say?" he would ask. "I don't know, but you looked good." In other words, the actions of the individual while on television, without reference to what he says, become more important than his rhetoric. He appears as an authority who is there — but who has no meaning or content.

The system of ersatz Authority was presented in the quiz shows of the late 1950's. For example, *The $64,000 Question* attempted to show how discrete pieces of knowledge and information were the way to success. It encompassed the traditional emphasis in America upon winning, losing, hierarchy and mobility. These programs attempted to show the audience that winners and the authentically knowledgeable were rewarded in America. Knowing scraps of information defined one's place on the ladder of rewards. To the public, the quiz programs were an extension of the American dream; luck, self-education and working hard were the elixirs. Thus the viewer thought that if one contestant knew the answer and the other did not, the one who knew the answer won. However, the mechanics of putting the program on television showed that the ideology of winning is a less chancey affair. Predictably, sponsors dictated which contestants would remain on the program on the basis of what the sponsors thought was·best for the sale of their product. While the general public may have believed it honestly rewarding that those who know absurd bits of information win money, status, or goods is the personification of the American dream, those who were brought into the sponsor-programmer relationship learned, and then taught, otherwise.

Since the information and knowledge that individuals have are disembodied scraps that have no inherent value, it is no wonder that, in the colonized reality, the sponsors dictated and insisted on their own interests according to more traditionally understood principles of power, control and profit. Those principles are accepted and extrinsic for all to see, understand and admire.

In 1959, a subcommittee of the Interstate and Foreign Commerce Committee of Congress uncovered an interesting memo between the sponsor-producer and advertising agency of a quiz show. In a meeting between three representatives of these groups, it was decided that there was "a definite need for more losers." This was explained to the committee as meaning "that there were too many winners." The sponsors felt that the emotional electricity was going out of a contest if people got on and won consistently; it didn't have enough meaning. They wanted more people to lose to "highlight the winning."*

It is a mistake to assume that the colonizer is not trapped by his own functional and role behaviors. He accepts them and acts on and believes that which is described for him through a media system which he creates. Certain examples of this dynamic reinforce the dissociative aspects of American life. As we shall see, there is a contradiction in the frame presented by television which may be more powerful than the dissociative effects: television points out contradiction.

The news at 6:30 PM is by now a hallowed institution. Events which are reported seem to change, but not the

---

* Through the media, the colonized reality is concerned with appearances— how to look good, how to win, and how to guarantee losers.

meaning of the advertisements and the structure of
presentation. They continue to be concerned with violence, with sexuality as a tool for selling something else
or with goods as a tool for climbing the hierarchy. During
the American war in Vietnam, there has been an especially
debilitating quality which positioned the viewer as part
of a rectangle of unreality. I sit down to eat my dinner and
watch the latest napalming in Vietnam, knowing that this
is "Marlboro Country" where men ride alone and tall in
the saddle, dependent only on *their* cowboy, the ciga-
ette. I am objectified through the Dream Colony in which
communications present me with the violence colonizers
who napalm for me, the advertiser who brings me the
napalming in exchange for seeing myself dependent upon
his product to survive, while encouraging me to identify
with the sheriff in *High Noon*. It is a busy minute between
the roast beef, the screech of the jet bomber over the
Vietnamese villages that drop 2.5 million tons of bombs,
and the whinny of the symphony orchestra playing the
Marlboro song. The media become the instruments to
help me become these actions and presentations. Or to put
the point another way, the television industry objectifies
the rectangle and collapses the lines of the rectangle into
a single line continuum which connects me as a trapped
puppet through technology's extension with other, like
puppets. We are a single line with no beginning, separation or end. The elements of that line are the cigarettes,
Vietnam, the television industry and my canned fantasy.
The colonizer is attempting to achieve the kind of satisfaction for me which assures my passive state or my sense
of dissociation. This sense of dissociation is added to by
the manner in which the news of reality is presented to
me. (In the schools, reality is presented as a series of discrete events and harsh specialized courses which are not
even pasted together through a system of mock relationships. Likewise, in the media one is presented with the

"news" of the indices of reality in discrete unrelated ways, thereby stimulating the individual's sense of free floatingness.)

Take as an example news broadcasts "heard every hour on the hour." Within the space of five minutes, fifteen subjects may be touched upon and run together with one minute out of the five used for advertising. The dissociative ways that "news" is presented to people through the media appear to have psychotic aspects. Certainly, we would have serious doubts about an individual's mental stability if someone spoke to us about various matters face-to-face in the way we are talked to through radio and television on five-minute newscasts. Here is a sample of a five-minute newscast over a radio station from a major network, these words and impressions perhaps having reached twenty million people:

NBC, Station WRC, December 18, 1967, 3:00 PM Washington, D.C.

NBC Radio, News on the Hour, brought to you by Bayer Aspirin. Bayer is pure aspirin, not just part aspirin. Bayer works wonders. Now here is Virgil Dominic. . . .

Doctors are keeping close watch over heart transplant patient, Louis Washansky, who is reported to have grown weaker from lung complications, apparently brought on by the body's attempt to reject the fifty-three-year-old patient's new heart. A report from Sidney Lazard, NBC News, Capetown, South Africa.

Washansky's doctors believe that he may now be rejecting the heart transplant and . . . next twenty-four hours will be crucial ones.

This is the first serious trouble for Washansky, who underwent the history-making heart transplant fifteen days ago. More news after this for Bayer aspirin.

When you or someone in your family catches cold or the

flu and brings on a fever, fever that saps your strength and wilts your spirits, that's when Bayer works wonders, Bayer Aspirin. It's truly wonderful how two Bayer tablets actually reduce fever, help bring temperature down to normal, so you feel better fast. So, when a cold or flu strikes, remember all three steps doctors recommend: Rest in bed, drink plenty of liquids, and take aspirin to reduce fever and relieve pain. Yes, aspirin is what doctors recommend and Bayer is pure aspirin, not just part aspirin. Ask your pharmacist, mothers, when your youngsters catch cold or the flu; be sure to get orange-flavored Bayer Aspirin for children in a special pediatric dosage. Aspirin relieves pain and fever the way doctors recommend. Just as Bayer makes the best adult aspirin, Bayer makes the best children's aspirin you can give. So, you and your child will both feel better fast. For adults and children, Bayer works wonders. Here, again is Virgil Dominic. . . .

There is speculation that President Johnson may fly to Australia Friday to participate in memorial services for Prime Minister Harold Holt, who disappeared while swimming near his home. The government has given up hope that he will be found alive. Deputy Prime Minister John McEwen today was named to succeed Holt until the ruling Liberal Party elects a new leader.

The US Command in Saigon announced today that American planes bombed the bridges, missile sites and rail facilities in the Hanoi-Haiphong areas of North Vietnam today. The announcement made no mention of the enemy claim that eight aircraft have been shot down, but did confirm the loss of three planes yesterday.

Michigan Governor George Romney, who is a declared candidate for the Republican presidential nomination, said he heard some new ideas on Vietnam today in a meeting with fifty Soviet leaders in Moscow. He declined to give details.

The Chairman of the Joint Chiefs of Staff made a strong attack on anti-Vietnam war demonstrators today. General

Earl Wheeler called acts of dissension the single most important factor in prolonging the war. The General claimed Hanoi leaders sincerely believe that such demonstrations will force a change in US policy in Vietnam and refuse to negotiate for that reason. Wheeler's statement came even as 2,500 protestors staged a new demonstration outside of the Army induction center in Oakland, California today. They held flowers in their hands and chanted "peace on earth". At least 140 were arrested.

Air Force helicopter pilots are braving heavy snowfall today trying to find Indians who may be marooned in up to six feet of snow on the Navajo Reservation in Arizona. At least two bodies have been found, including a two-year-old boy who froze to death.

A massive clean-up is under way in the area of Huntsville, Alabama, which was raked by two tornadoes this morning. Two persons were killed and thirty injured. Property damage in Huntsville was about one million dollars.

A sharp earthquake jolted the San Francisco area of California today. The second of two quakes caused a thirty-story building to sway but there have been no reports of injuries or damage.

Divers continued their search of the Ohio River today for more victims of Friday's bridge collapse near White Pleasant, West Virginia. Another body was found this afternoon raising the known death toll to 17. Forty-one persons are still missing and feared dead.

The US Supreme Court today banned government eavesdropping on private telephone conversations, calling it a violation of the constitutional guarantees against unreasonable search and seizure. The court made an exception, however, when the security of the nation is involved.

A former aid to New York City Mayor John Lindsay was indicted by a Federal grand jury today. James Marcus was accused of participating in a Cosa Nostra plot involving an $8,000 kick-back on a city contract.

Again, this hour's top story. Heart transplant patient, Louis Washansky has taken a turn for the worse. Doctors say next twenty-four hours will be critical. Virgil Dominic, NBC News, Cleveland. . . .

Listen again on the hour for NBC Radio News.*

Such information is internalized in us. The events go unexplained without a history and without an analysis. The world appears as discrete events and behaviors that are related through the presentation. But I become this unconnected puzzle piece. I understand things in undigested form without context. My public voyage is on a sea of unrelated behavior which screams at me to say that society and its method of communication are dissociative. Yet, the communications media are now central. I am their object and link. Now I find that I am engaged in a public subjective stream of consciousness. Radio and TV present their world to me as a stream into my consciousness, without beginning, middle or end—in which events run into each other, one to another, each as important as the other. The world becomes a perverted form of *Finnegan's Wake,* where each word is different and every message is the same. The shock of television and advertising is their symbiotic success in using the public. Both forms turn out to be well-matched instruments in making, and then fulfilling, mass society.

Until the present, perhaps reflecting the dream response to television, there have been no groups, except the most *ad hoc* and ineffective, which have attempted either to boycott television programming or control the structure of national television. The attempt to "uplift" people through alternative programming does not change

---

* It would not have mattered had an audience seen a televised account of these words. Television news coverage is very sparing indeed in its moving picture shots, although each of these programs is so constructed as to create the illusion that there is a formidable amount of "on the spot" picture coverage.

the basic colonized relationships between those who are telling and those who are told.*

It becomes impossible to see a pattern of political and economic relationships unless we participate in the control of such instruments which "manufacture" and send messages through the media. That is, while the events of the world may be presented by colonizers to an inert mass, as if each event is as important as the other to each and every viewer, there is no possibility of making sense out of the meaning of events unless there is participation which would help in defining the roots of participation and relatedness through the media. The interesting and ironic contradiction is that the media itself may force the transformation of the authority structure.

Elsewhere, I have mentioned the tragic fact that changes in technology have not successfully transformed the pyramidal relationships of industrial and post-industrial society. There may be some proof of the contrary view as it is demonstrated by television. Because of its "you are there" nature, TV seems to help in doubting official statements of other pyramidal structures. Thus, the ability to believe what governments say, or to take them seriously as having specialized knowledge of an event is considerably lessened by the immediacy of television. The opera-

---

* I do not want to be understood as saying that goods seen through television do not have dislocating and perhaps revolutionary consequences — although I suspect they have anti-revolutionary consequences with the appearance of change — but, in fact, the reality of giving greater power to those who attempt through their own methods to build a new middle class in poor countries which is the stable "responsible" element according to modern American social scientists.

As Sukarno said, "The motion picture industry has provided a window on the world, and the colonized nations have looked through that window and have seen the things of which they have been deprived." It is perhaps not generally realized that a refrigerator can be a revolutionary symbol to a people who have no refrigerators. A motor car owned by a worker in one country can be a symbol of revolt to a people deprived of even the necessities of life . . . [Hollywood] helped to build up the sense of deprivation of man's birthright, and that sense of deprivation has played a large part in the national revolutions of postwar Asia.[3]

tion of propagandists of other pyramids as a mediating function to "explain" to us what's happening becomes almost laughable.

It is possible that each advance in the media of communication gnaws away at the authoritarian pyramidal structure. The length of time that such a gnawing process takes is dependent upon the spread of transmittal to the number of recipients who are either in the process of decolonizing or who have already decolonized. In such a situation they are reinforced and the process of decolonizing moves faster. Although it may still remain as an instrument to promote passivity, what comes out of media has the potential of contradicting the pyramidal structure for those who watch it. Take the case of the Vietnam war: the immediacy of presentation to the different publics that watch television strengthened the opposition to the war. This quality of immediacy struck down the idea of specialized information about the war. Official American propaganda was constantly undercut when it took the usual government line of how well, technically, the United States was doing and how moral was the enterprise.

Abstractions such as morality and justice, as they are handed out by governments, are under serious attack because of the immediacy of television, which contradicts the mediating or explaining function of governments. TV shows the means used to obtain justice—"napalming villages," "killing women and children," "destroying crops." These "means," when shown on television, in one's own kitchen, living room, or bedroom, turn out for the viewer and the person harmed to be the ends themselves. Since television, when it is presenting an event while it is happening, deals only with the *now,* it can define justice and morality only in the *now.* Consequently, the idea of deferred payoffs, which is what warring governments view as justice and morality, is undercut by the immediacy of TV's presentation of felt realities against the government's abstractions.

The contradiction between presenting the simultaneous event of the *now* against the abstracted view of the potentiality of the deferred payoff, through present suffering by whole nations and classes, is not likely to be bridged. Young people in the warring nations will experience the contradiction in the immediate just because TV does give the individual a sense of simultaneity with the event rather than cause-effect of the event. In the case of simultaneity, he knows only the now and does not believe in the means, except as the ends are immediately projected by what he sees and is surrounded by.

In the instance of the media (whether TV, radio or printed matter), so long as the instruments of control are held in the same pyramidal authority structures, it may remain only a potentiality that TV can build continuous new relationships between people in an associative, democratic way. Presently, it can only be seen as a political control mechanism of the society which is colonized by the few who themselves are trapped and ultimately colonized. In their more conscious moments, the warriors of the Violence Colony will use TV as an important instrument in stopping personal communication. They will use it to undercut community or the formation of the group. Through television, vertical control is perpetuated. The radio transistor has this extraordinary aspect in which the individual is successfully cut-off from his own thoughts and is totally externalized by being tuned-in with the now through the radio transistor which he finds that he cannot be without. He is plugged-in to a one-way relationship. Yet, even in this case, there is a contradiction. Call-in programs in which individuals express their opinions and speak with announcers or other people, are the beginning way of engulfing the structure of the pyramid, which assumes that relationships can only be top-down.

They are the beginnings of continuous communication and, consequently, continuous creativity and dialogue. Such programs could begin to relate to town meetings where people are joined together in different places for discussion rather than the more alienating "sounding-off" process. However, note what the basis of the relationship is when the purpose of the user is for control.

We may accept the optimistic view that the wonderful new reality which is presented to us through the media extends our being into relating in the now to others, destroying the walls that exist between people. Yet the Procrustean bed of pyramidal, non-democratic control that TV must sleep within, means that the viewer at present is little more than the extension of his dream colonizers. He has little chance of controlling or cross-communicating through the media. He is the string of the economic and political arrangements which bind the television systems to the major networks, and then to AT&T.

PART TWO

CATEGORIES OF COLONIZATION AND THE RESPONSE TO THEM

6

Immobilism

In this chapter I am attempting to provide a basis for reactions to the pyramidal structure in modern post-industrial life. I have not adopted a class analysis of the United States, not because classes do not exist in this country, but because American society is imbued with a series of values which cut across all classes. The rich are not different, to reverse Fitzgerald's assertion, because they are members of a particular class, but because the role that they assume stimulates the will to either domination or submission. On the other hand, the concept of colonizer and colonized asserts that the lives of individuals, while they may appear distinct because of money or status are inevitably the same as they relate to the fundamental aspects of control over life (schools, violence, media and economics). In this sense the lives of Americans who are active members of the colonized system are tinged with a classless base. There exists a collaborationist mentality among the people from different economic classes partly because of the appearance of quick social mobility and partly because of the understanding on the part of people within the middle and upper classes that the economic reality in their lives reveals them to be as starved as the poorest beggar in the Bowery or the most exploited worker in the Appalachians. The syndical fascist system which is generally spoken of in the United States as a series of partnerships between business, labor, the university, the military, is of course an attempt to replace the social contract in terms of a corporative system of agreements between leaderships. The result is that power and agreement attach to role in the pyramid—not to human agreement. The colonizer and the colonized are all of us simultaneously in the pyramid. As I have suggested elsewhere, this analysis is the reverse of that put forward by Luther where *because* we are inwardly free we need not concern ourselves with the pyramidal roles assigned to us in life except to be obedient within our station. The possibility of approaching inner freedom emerges when we become aware of the colonizing role we are assigned or seek. Thus the value transformations in America which are going on cannot be viewed as limited to one economic or social class. They cut across all classes of society. The result is that in each major institution and economic class there will be insurgents and splits along lines that cannot easily be seen with classic Marxist analysis.

Habit and Immobilism

By nature people are creatures of habit. And habit, by its nature is conservative. We may say that habit is the glue

necessary of a body politic to develop the social character of the beside himself. In *The Public and Its Problems,* Dewey cites William James approvingly for having discovered the social fact of habit. James tells how people stay tilling the soil, working the mines, fishing, and so forth; they do so out of habit. Thus the rich are kept rich and unintimidated, and the poor allow the rich man's son to remain rich. In just this way David Hume believed that government did not rest on consent through the social contract, but rather on habit. But the present American appearance is radically different. Young people feel freer to define their own situations in which their responsibilities can be self-imposed. Thus, because the habitual is no longer a fundamental characteristic of American society, there is little chance for large groups of people to remain politically immobile, since the basis of their being in the world is now changing. Consequently, they will undertake to protect what they have through a reactionary political intervention, or they will find projects which break the bounds of colonized relationships. Once the basis of man's moorings, habit or rootedness, is destroyed, political immobilism as his social condition is no longer secure. To take a case in point, technology continues to offer those who occupy colonizing roles new and more profitable ways to organize the technology, while the colonized find that they cannot live within the changing and arbitrary rules of the colonizer. The market system is replaced by a new feudal system in which technology changes the life style of colonizer and colonized alike. For example, *all* classes become users of birth control pills and inner-space pills. While technology adopts rote procedures so that those working with machines don't understand their purposes or innards, technology *as a force* negates the habitual, by emphasizing the new, the now and the non-habitual.

Political Immobility

Besides crumbling social roles, people confront a powerful contradiction to their pitiful wish to accept their lot. Technological forces in American society do not allow habit to dominate one's life. They force change of social character and life style. Yet even though people's lives can no longer stand on the shaky foundation of habit we would be mistaken if we assumed that people are any the less politically immobile. Such immobilism in America is related to fear that the relative consumer affluence which the individual may have achieved could be taken away or lost if the individual were anything *but* politically immobile. The converse, however, should be taken into account. When inaction appears to be a key to losing one's possessions, man's engagement to doing becomes strong. Doing, for particular purposes, becomes the instrument to conserving or retaining the position of social status or position no matter how tenuous or meaningless that status might be. Conservative support among the home and mortgage holding lower middle class seems to be directly related to their fear of losing possessions for which they worked hard and which they now believe define who they are. Such possessions are assigned positive value to them by the colonized system and they internalize that series of values. Their lives were used up for those goods and fear of losing them becomes equal to losing their lives. The *beside-himself* demands acting "responsibly," immobile, because of real commitments to others, a nuclear family, friends, who are caught in the web of their own social character which is equally ersatz.

Suppose I am a worker whose weekly take-home pay is the national average—seventy-eight dollars. Obviously, I will be very careful in risking anything that I have, for fear that I will lose even more. If I were able to express dissatisfaction in a relatively risk-free way, my reluctance might change, through the vote for example. I might become politically more active if my mortgage payments were high, my take-home pay small, my house deteriorating, my family in danger of physical attack from the poor, my food contaminated, and I appeared to be invisible to the leadership of the state whose values I had so internalized that the leadership thought I had accepted my lot without another thought. In this case, I would indeed find myself in a situation similar to people like Vincent Imperiale in Newark who sees that small property-holding power is heavily taxed while the "liberal" institutions such as the churches and the universities are excluded from taxation. Furthermore, in their rhetoric their leaders seem to side with the poor against the small property holder and working-class man. In such a situation, political immobilism changes into finding leadership among those individuals and groups who had internalized the values of opportunity and God-fearing America to lead them against the vast pyramidal institutions which they see as favoring the poor over themselves. This grouping is now beginning to discover that their energies and funds are used for the national security state, empire and military force. Once this discovery is internalized into a political framework with the fact that their food and consumer goods are rotting, the lower-middle-class anger against the young and the poor could be mollified.

In the middle class the problem of political immobilism is directly related to social immobility. *Political immobilism is the inevitable result of social mobility and characterization.* The politics which the individual comes to develop is the politics of climbing the pyramid. Some would calculate in the following manner: "Supposing I tell off the boss, or supposing I undertake the project which I really want to do. I might lose a promotion, or that raise in pay. Indeed, I could be fired, and then I would not be able to pay for the mortgage or the refrigerator or car. My pension rights would lapse. What I had better do is keep out of trouble, accepting the personal unhappiness I feel in the rat race. In any event, if I keep rising, then I will be able to make the break. I might still be in the system; yet, I'll be outside of it." This person's life is virtually one of slave to the future, as it is defined through the hierarchic other. He learned his lesson well in the channeling colony. He hopes that he will be mobile enough to shake his personal political immobilism about his life. For the interim, the fear of losing place appears total because he cannot conceive of himself in a political situation outside of colonized relationships. Consequently, he has to rely on mythical characters for satisfaction. They may appear as people who have escaped the colonized reality and have done so through playing the colonized game. The Horatio Alger myth is a case in point. In 1968, the presidential candidates of the three major parties trumpeted Alger's theme. The middle class finds heroes whose mobility through and beyond the colony becomes the rationalizing force for remaining in colonized relationships. It is the theme of making it.

The power of deferred payoffs is an important element in holding the entire lower and middle class in the schools, factories, offices and media. Suffer now for nirvana later. The reward system, with its method of conferring privilege and potentiality establishes the colonizer's control over the future of the colonized. Mobility or the potentiality of mobility, is accompanied in American life by technology as the apparent guarantor of political immobility because of the need which technologists and the elites claim exists for expertise in machines. The complexity of technology seems to require experts who are the only ones to comprehend difficult matters. This class then takes over any political role that might exist. This question is viewed by some philosophers as beyond politics. "In all areas of his existence, man will be encircled ever more tightly by the forces of technology. These forces, which everywhere and every minute claim, enchain, drag along, press and impose upon man under the form of technical continuance or other—these forces, since man has not made them, long since have moved beyond his will and have outgrown his capability for decision."[1] Heidegger's view of despair may be correct. But its despairing quality allows the technologists the task of being our pall bearers and choice-makers.

There is a more serious aspect to the question of immobilism as it relates to the orgy of technological revolution. If technology determines our freedom, how can we freely choose a project which stands outside of a colonized relationship. Obviously, if we are choked by our technological freedom, we gasp for our own breaths and fear to risk or give as beings to other beings. What we undertake to do is protect ourselves individually, which means that our doings and our actions fail at relatedness. One's actions may be a personal tour de force, but they do not escape the colonized relationship.

False identities in which the colonized see that the rhetorical panacea which is created by the colonizer to reflect identity of interest contradicts the experience of the colonized—the contradiction between the colonized description of what people are supposed to feel according to the colonized relationship but cannot perceive in *their situation,* or in the one which they consciously seek—means that the conditions for the self-defined project emerge in each man's life. Not only is the project a condition of man; it is a social necessity. He sees no other choice if he remains in the world. He cannot fit into the mold of the hierarchic other. Where mediations are used by the colonizer to buy time, and where expectations are raised in which consciousness occurs without changing self with other, many people will withdraw into psychosis. They cannot find a way to pro-ject a different reality. They are not free to pro-ject because their colonization has been total.

For others, the contradictions and pain will show them that there is no choice but to pro-ject because there is no present place or space outside of beginning an alternative. They feel that their simple instrumental needs are not met. In this sense, the problem of colonization is beyond economic class, although in capitalist societies it may appear to manifest itself in economic terms. For example, the southern Mississippi tenant farmer who would like to have fifty cents a day to pay for public welfare food is not politically and psychologically that different from the middle-class person who does not understand why he is not happy after doing everything his teachers, the commercials and the corporation to which he is indentured set for him to do.* Nor are they different from the man who builds his civil defense shelter but, by so doing, reaps the unhappiness of knowing that he justifies nuclear war and the leader's right to use nuclear weapons. The fact which all share is that they are all objects, who have lost the will to ob-ject. It should be noted that while the pyramidal state puts more and more people into a custodial relationship (note figures of schools, military, those institutionalized for other reasons, indentured relationships), the power of dissonance within the society is extensive. Free enterprisers (for whom supposedly capitalism exists) feel castrated because personal economic risk in the capitalist system was the way to show one's existence as a man. In the pyramidal structure of society, this feeling is denied to him. (The entrepreneur was like the mountain climber or the warrior who courts extreme situations of risk.)

---

* It is an extraordinary event of modern corporate life to see how the junior executive and his family must move every year or two at the command of the corporate lords.

He does not see a place for his commitment that stemmed from a sanctional need to risk, pro-ject and define his place. Consider the dissonance which the engineer feels who does an uncraftsmanlike job in the name of profit, which translates into more goods that entrap him, such as a second car, or a color television set that may cause cancer. Such people are powerless and colonized. The dissonance involves the marginal worker who sees wealth around him and who is expected to steal from his boss in a way to make up for low earnings.

A question might remain why, in the long run, the immobile person who is afraid to lose anything will risk emergence on the side of reconstructive or revolutionary change. Perhaps the answer can be found in the social change of the values of property. What was once held dear cannot be held as such in a system where property is related to consumption and obsolescence as against utility and longevity. Consequently, by the nature of the change in the worth of goods in the society, the values of what is important will change even among those groups who seem most tied to the consumption society. Attempting to protect what they have, their intervention into the political battle will be reactionary. But as that fails, they will attempt to find a different rationalization to their human situation.

The material and technological conditions for radical change are present among those who would not ordinarily be thought of as the dispossessed or wretched because they are not allowed to settle in as slaves.

The burden of the existential argument in the society that is changing its definition of property is that class position fails to define personal happiness or unhappiness.

7

Reform

There is a momentous sameness to the history of reform in the United States. Perhaps it stems from the literal meaning of the word "reform," which has been defined in some dictionaries as the improvement or amendment of what is wrong, corrupt, etc. It has a piecemeal and judgmental sense to it which accepts the frame of reference of what is wrong or corrupt. Its method is piecemeal and *ad hoc.* The intent of the reformist is not to see relationships outside of the partial or the momentary. Obviously, in discussing the nature of political reform, it is hard to separate out its meaning from the reformer himself. The reformer's attitudes are reflected in the work which he undertakes to do and the limits which he proceeds to set on his purpose. He pretends that his position is supremely objective, well-motivated, and outside of class interest. He is the correcter and the amender, usually for others. He is disinterested.

In politics, of course, there are various men who adopt the rhetoric of reform, see its validity as a tool to achieve or maintain power, but whose commitment to even piecemeal reform is slight. Because the critique of the reformer is not basic, or he is prepared to accept the *ad hoc* and expediential, he is ready to see power-seekers or reactionaries as reformers or instruments for his reform, thinking that he can trick them.* The result is that the reformer ends up serving such political men whose interest is power. Men like Herbert Croly, who began the *New Republic,* saw themselves as rationalizers and "consciences" of the powerful men like Teddy Roosevelt.

In public life, Theodore Roosevelt was known as a radical reformer. His rhetoric was punctuated with the sort of fervor that one usually finds among the anti-wrongdoers. Yet, while he saw the rhetorical importance of the reformer's critique of American society, his own activities as President were conservative, as he was invariably finding ways to serve as the broker for the rich and powerful. From his point of view, his task was to save the capitalist from the excesses of the capitalist system. This was a rea-

---

* Even William Jennings Bryan could not resist being used in this way. After the war against Spain, a treaty of peace which included provisions to annex the Philippines, was placed before the Senate. Because of their forthright stand in the spring of 1898, it appeared that the anti-imperialists would have enough votes to defeat the McKinley Administration's peace treaty. The anti-imperialists feared that the ceding of Puerto Rico to the United States and the acceptance of protectorate status over the Philippines would thrust the United States into the quest for world empire.

The imperialists needed a helper, and the reformer William Jennings Bryan came forward. He undertook to lobby the populists to support the Roosevelt-McKinley position in the name of national honor. Through his efforts, the U.S. entered the world arena with a bang. The treaty was ratified with an exceptions clause for the Philippines that was wiped out in 1899 by events.

sonable position to liberals at the turn of the century who saw efficiency, growth and destiny as served by the capitalist.

While the Rough Rider's ears seemed to be tuned to the poor, his inner ear connected up easily with representatives of the houses of Morgan and Rockefeller. For Roosevelt, when George Perkins, Nelson Aldrich or Mark Hanna spoke, it was as if their voices ranked with the objective truth of the medical scientist whose conclusions were drawn from seeing a dangerous tumor spreading. What was the dangerous tumor?

At the turn of the century, radical reconstruction seemed to have been on the minds of many people in America. Socialist literature was widely read and it was having practical effect. The Socialist Party, as James Weinstein has shown, attracted immigrants and poor Americans to its banner. At the beginning of the twentieth century the Socialist Party could claim over 1200 officeholders in municipalities and legislatures. The labor and anarchist movements were making systemic critiques of the society and they had an active political audience to whom they spoke. Professors, such as Richard Ely, were pointing out that the only interest of the wealthy was the accumulation of more wealth. His kind of analysis made it necessary for the rich to find a way, through government, to give the appearance of amelioration while continuing to accumulate. During the Roosevelt reform period, specific piecemeal suggestions such as the right of labor to organize and strike, regulation of factories for safety and health, public education, and equal suffrage for men and sometimes women, were not viewed as sufficient by the dissenters. They were making a systematic critique of the capitalist structure. But Roosevelt was not the dissenters' champion. Nevertheless, he found support for his views among the reformers of the period. Roosevelt was not interested in muckraking, analyzing or systemic changes. He was interested in keeping the game of imperialist expansion within rules that the biggest players formulated, understood and accepted. That the nature of the game itself might have been crooked was hardly his concern.

In his own way, Theodore Roosevelt performed for America what Count von Bismarck had performed for Germany. In Germany, socialism was taken over in its rhetoric and in a perverted way by the Count, because he had failed in his attempt to outlaw the Socialist Party and trade unions. However, Bismarckian socialism performed the task of rationalizing Germany in such a way as to build the bureaucratic and military idea of the total state. In America reforms in rhetoric and cooptation spurred the game of expansion. While Bismarck was claiming that Germany was arbiter for Europe, Roosevelt was reiterating this position for the United States, at least as it related to Latin America and parts of Asia.

The great-power theory of imperialism as developed in the Roosevelt era was continued through President Wilson, who also viewed himself as and was thought to be—both in his foreign and domestic policies—a middle-of-the-road reformer. Economic reforms such as the passage of the Federal Banking System were examples of Wilson's attempt to insert governmental regulation into a chaotic monetary system. Attempts were also made, through the passage of legislation establishing the Federal Trade Commission, to straighten out competitive relationships. The problem, of course, was that the limitation of competition meant the strengthening of oligopoly. The reformist worked for changes which assumed the basic soundness of the economic and social structure with its attendant principles. Wilson's domestic reforms strengthened the New Faith with its twin pillars. The "system" is basically sound. However, from time to time it requires the intervention of government in keeping business enterprises honest. But no more. Its purpose was to protect the hustler, the get-up-and-go fellow, busy-ness. As Wilson said in *The New Freedom:*

> What this country needs above everything else is a body of law which will look after the men who are on the make rather than the men who are already made. . . . The man who is on the make is the judge of what is happening in America, not the man who has made good . . . that is the man by whose judgment I, for one, wish to be guided.[1]

Here was the contradiction liberal reform could solve. While the individual was to be on the make, his political views were to be immobile, stemming from the habitual nature of man. Reform was necessary to update one's traditions and habits. Such reform was not meant as a challenge to the habits of greed, competition and avarice, which supposedly defined human nature. Reform could be brought through a national government powerful enough to deal with at least some of the big players in the competitive game. The reformers might be from new strata of American life. These new strata were indeed men on the make:

> . . . trained up in the pragmatic dispensation, immensely ready for the *executive ordering* of events, pitifully unprepared for the intellectual interpretation or the idealistic focussing of ends.[2]

These men, as Randolph Bourne pointed out, were a wholly new force in America. Their technical aptitude was great, but it could be in the service of any purpose. They learned the lesson of instrumentalism with a vengeance. They could adapt their instruments (knowledge) and their beings in the service of the state. During Wilson's time it meant in the service of war, and in the first-stage process of rationalizing bigness in the United States *through* the government's power and through the idea of a new group that knew about technique as scientific method and ordering who could work with and mediate the old Robber Barons.

The building of the new national government also had another important role to play. As a result of the war, Wilson put over the idea of the sanctity of the state. It had lofty unquestioned purposes that were translated into such ideas as "world responsibility," patriotism, and obedience to those who held the state's reins of power. America emerged as a new international power, quite willing to fight war as a means of keeping the state healthy. Internally, in Wilson's administration, it was clear that regulation meant rationalization of relationships among the largest corporations and government. It was necessary for foreign policies to reflect this new form of stabilization. The people who ran the reforms internally and the policies externally, were essentially the interest groups that were able to co-opt reform and use it for securing the faulty assumptions of corporate organization and corporate power.

The impending first world war was supported by the reformist intellectuals and part of the Socialist Party. The *New Republic* in 1917 showed how the Wilsonian policy toward war followed its own editorial line. The war itself brought reformers into the government as the "President's investigators," advisors, conciliators and arbitrators in industry and on boards which would serve the war effort. Yet something was missing in all of this. The American system was not being changed. It was just growing larger. Wilson the southerner hardened the lines of segregation and discrimination against black people. Under his direction the federal government became committed in its internal regulations and folkways to discrimination and not so genteel racism. And on the issues of social reconstruction the reformers under Wilson had given up.

The New Freedom Presbyter was not speaking to the issues John Dewey had talked about prior to and during the war. (John Dewey mistakenly believed that if the war could not be prevented, its purposes could be made humane and idealistic.) Unfortunately, the issues that Dewey raised fifty years ago remain the basis of the American agenda for social reconstruction:

> . . . a right which is enforceable so that the individual will always have the opportunity to engage in some form of useful activity . . . insurance against accident, insurance against illness, insurance against the contingencies of old age, and . . . greater ability on the part of the workers in any particular trade or occupation to *control* that industry, instead of working under these conditions of external control where they have no interest, no insight into what they are doing, and no social outlook upon the consequences and meaning of what they're doing.[3]

The next time the reformers had their chance at reform was fifteen years later, during the New Deal. Reformist intervention by Franklin Roosevelt was an attempt to press for those reforms which would shore up a collapsing economic and social structure. As William A. Williams has pointed out, Roosevelt continued the program of rationalizing the corporate systems. The extraordinary part of the Roosevelt Era was how easily people were ready to accept social tinkering in welfare at the cost of participation and control from below. Such new banking, labor laws or agriculture laws that were passed ended up providing a measure of regulation and protection of the kind which guaranteed political immobilism in the people. Organized groups, whether bankers, unions, or farmers, were protected through reactionary means; that is, by creating artificial demands on markets. Yet, the economy continued to fail. The problem of men out of work, empty factories and meaningless jobs could not be resolved until it transformed itself into the second world war. Problems which mainly fixed themselves in the cracks of the major economic and social institutions were hidden behind the stroboscopic war ideology—flickering, demanding and all-encompassing. The war ideology transformed itself into a cold-war ideology, which continued between 8 and 11 percent of the economy on a war/cold-war footing. The feisty haberdasher, Harry Truman, went on organizing the national government by using the threat of communism as the great fear. His programs assumed a permanent war mentality, invariably being explained to the country in paranoid security terms. He was pressed from the left liberals to build a social welfare system which was to be managed in military socialist fashion—top down. Somehow, through booms, busts and wars, America could not find creative and meaningful work for its people. In the place of such work, workers were kept *busy* making the instruments of war and imperialism, surrounded by propaganda and a style of consumption which risked their sanity. The reformers emerged from the second world war believing that the major issues in American life had been resolved. A theory of American exceptionalism was developed that asserted that the problems that had engulfed the nation during the Depression had disappeared in the maze of legislation guaranteeing some measure of full employment and social security. According to this view, American problems merely required the adjustment of interests among competing groups that somehow were equal in their morality, purpose, and need. Liberal reformers and technocratic intellectuals were to be the gods and goddesses holding the balancing scales in their heads and in their calculating machines.

Through this period, liberal reformers who occupied the White House concerned themselves far more with foreign policy. Indeed, foreign policy and its co-habitant, national security policy, turned out to be more to the liking of the manipulations of groups of people such as reformers and businessmen who saw the world as something to make over and believed that they had the power, the will and the right to do so. On the international security side was the grand design of the white nations joined together in a new "holy alliance" against communism and the third world. There was "nation building"; that is, the rending of other people's societies and cultures to match the thoughts of America's bureaucracies, corporations and internationally oriented volunteer organizations. Vietnam, Laos, Latin America—all were the playground for the American middle-class war and peace planner. And for spice was the nuclear arms race—a new dimension in brinkmanship.

On the domestic side, Kennedy brought forward various reformers who saw their purpose as that of narrowing the differences among the huge feudal units of American society. One of the favorite words during this period, was that "partnerships" should exist between government and business, government and labor, government and education. Such partnerships were similar in their mode to a system of agreements which emerged in the twentieth century in other authoritarian states. While such was the grand plan, concentration of energies of the bureaucracy was on keeping the arms race going, controlling it, and finding ways of using such power in imperialist wars. Problems of conflict were to be avoided through economic growth, new frontiers (space), and the sportive instinct which would put emphasis on being first in all things— largest growth rates, highest turnover, biggest tonnage, fastest crossing, greatest altitude, etc. Style was to be the measure of man's understanding in statecraft. Technique was to be supplied by the intellectual managers.

During the Johnson administration, new attempts were made to address social problems. The anti-poverty program, which apparently was meant to help the poor, merely ended up building a new bureaucracy. The civil rights laws, over a hundred years late, attempted to integrate into the society a new middle class of black people who would be "prepared" by education and style to be ready for the exigencies and ecstasies of middle-class living. Social legislation (maximum feasible participation) in its first stages appeared to have as its purpose aiding blacks in ghettos and in tenant farms to generate their own politics and demands. However, the institutions that were challenged quickly feared the results. Old social welfare wine in old bottles was the result. But now it was accompanied by a national policing system which was rooted in the assumption of the importance of strong national government with regulative authority.

Since the New Deal, the emergence of the centrist ideologists such as Hartz and Schlesinger and right-wing social-democratic political groups such as the ADA at the time of omnipotent military power of the United States resulted in an extraordinary channeling of ideas and events. People saw things and events as they were characterized into seeing them by the colonizing structure of the society. The world was seen by the young of the middle class through the eyes of what the colonizer saw. I remember how foolish Marxist propaganda seemed to me in the middle nineteen-fifties when the Soviets and their propagandists would say that there was a ruling class in America and the Rockefellers had something to do with the foreign, domestic and national security policy of the United States beyond that of pulling a lever at election time. This view was invariably pooh-poohed by centrist ideologists who claimed that such ideas were either simplistic or lies. That certain groups, families or classes had power which made them the problem because they insisted on continuing the pyramidal structure as it was, was an unthinkable notion as it applied to understanding America.

In terms of practice such rhetoric and ideology meant that people in their political lives operated as colonized people. They saw things as they were not and could not be. The words and phrases as used in the media and in the schools gave people a view of reality which ensured that people operated in a characterized condition. However, events and time have the habit of shocking people out of a dream state. The Vietnam war, of course, had such an effect as did the civil rights movement. Young people were shocked out of such roles as the colonizing structure dictated for them. In this sense history plays a cruel joke on parents. The very fear of the older generation, which played out its views of reality through the pyramidal structure, found that its greatest fear—that the young would somehow buy Marxist-Leninist thought—now finds the campuses full of such talk. In reaction to the liberal rhetoric which no longer could take the place of what people saw and felt, some young people have begun to hug the clichés of the Marxist leaders such as Stalin, Lenin, Mao and Giap. Having been denied access to such thought for twenty years in a manner where it could have been understood, and challenged, for the purpose of changing the society, many of the young left leap to this thought as their establishment ideology. Such is the effect of repression. It creates its own contradiction, but without a synthesis.

What, then, can we learn from all of this in terms of the nature of reform? The liberal reformer in the United States assumes that the basic hierarchic structure of the society is correct. America is viewed as a pyramid in which people should become unequal when they are given an equal chance. The task of government is to give the individual more "skills" and "opportunities" to climb the ladder of success.

As Elinor Graham pointed out, the American ideology is to evoke "an image of a goddess of peace and plenty rather than lanky Uncle Sam [with] Johnson [declaring] that both at home and abroad, 'We will extend the helping hand of a just nation to the poor and helpless and the oppressed.' In the American reality, however, 'we' take care to see that the 'helping hand' doesn't contain money or tangible goods—just opportunities to earn a better way of life and opportunities *to learn* [emphasis Graham's] to 'want to earn in the American way.'"[4]

Thus, the reformist comes to believe that no fundamental changes are necessary, that adjustments are necessary by the colonized if they are given the option to change the clothes of their colonization. Such adjustments are introduced to him on the basis of "objective" need put forward by the mandarin class of experts, who are turned out by universities to fill the exploitative roles of ordering others. Reform is then separate from any popular base except as the people can be manipulated and "educated." For example, the reformist might work out a program of manpower re-training so that the individual can keep up with the changes in the economic structure or the technological base, that are made by the colonizer. He attempts to find ways of controlling wars so that they don't get out of hand once they begin.

But such activities merely serve the colonizing institution. (The limited warrior of the cold war thought of himself as an objective liberal like Kaysen, Hitch, Kahn, Rostow and Kennedy.) The reformist addresses himself to formal requirements such as the right to vote when the question is whether voting takes away power from people, since it gives the appearance of participation, but in fact reinforces the principle of plebiscite. As the society reaches for a tighter pyramidal control while the people attempt to escape from their place in the tomb of the pyramid, the reformist will help to devise and implement—

through education as the tool—various forms of political repression such as buying off gang leaders and bringing them into the feudal system of organized political power, in effect turning over the cities to the gangs to keep order for the smooth operation of the corporate system. It means rationalizing monopoly control. (Reactionaries will not allow this reform to take place.)

Liberal Corporatism and Its Relation to Reaction

The reformist considers the corporate system with awe and views it as the basis of American power. His conception of growth is materialism in the sense of more goods, or just plain *more*. It is the way to keep things going. The assumption is that, through a powerful material base, quality can be achieved.*

As a result of liberal reformism in the economic area, a sad situation has developed in the United States. We are enveloped by crackpot Keynesianism, which assumes that a dollar spent on anything is equal to a dollar spent on something which has human value. To the reformist technocrat this formula means that the political economy could be as successful if money were spent on atomic bombs as it would be if it were spent on community schools. Such reasoning never questions the idea that spending builds certain classes at the expense of power in others. The result of this misguided ideology has meant the building of a military-industrial class in the United States similar in scope to the kind described by Neumann

* This method of governing is dependent on two qualities: charismatic leadership which uses rhetoric in such a way as to hide the basic deals and power relationships it protects; and expertise (super-juggling) in matters such as control of the economy. I doubt if there is any liberal expert so clever as to make reformism successful in the last quarter of the twentieth century. (No doubt there will always be demagogues who will attempt mass manipulation. They will be found in all political directions.)

in *Behemoth.* Although there is some competition among its various elements (Navy *vs.* Air Force, aerospace *vs.* the auto industry, etc.) in politics it merges with the conservative-reactionary Southern and small-town business coalition in the Congress. Geographically, the ideology of growth plus the cold war aided the economic development of the South through space and defense contracts to large corporations built by federal subsidy.

There is a more traditional reason for this coalition. Besides economic benefits which come to his area, the congressional conservative views the military as a necessary stabilizing force in the body politic. As a result of the civil rights struggle, he sees that the churches are not monolithic. In fact, churches are destabilizing. Consequently, the conservative depends more and more on the police and the military as the church withdraws support from the state in the spirit of ecumenicism and confrontation. The family and the church, two traditional authoritarian forms, are so changed in their own internal structure—that is, reaching toward equality—as to cause conservatives and reformists to depend finally on armed force as the basis of their protection and the inevitable and dependable arm of the state. The reformist can only get aid for his plans from the conservative if he is prepared to accept order as the purpose of the State. This is the lesson of the reformer in government who now knows that his plans for the American slums are social control mechanisms similar to those used by the United States in Vietnam. Either to implement his schemes, or for the illusion of power in the pyramid, the reformist may be prepared to pay that price.

There are two questions to consider. The first is that the liberal reformist begins his analyses and suggestions for change from the motive of good will. For example, he sees problems which need solution and then he undertakes to find a way which will bring together contradictory groups to iron out their differences. As I have suggested elsewhere, he serves as the mediator between colonizer and colonized, attempting to find a happy road which both may travel on. The reason for this approach is that either he does not want to confront the basic power realities of the society or he does not believe that the colonized themselves are able to mobilize enough power against the colonizer to bring about change. His insider role is necessary to help the colonized.

The reformer knows that he must accept the pyramidal structure of society and the existence of the colonizer. He finds that his place is dependent on the authority structure of the pyramid. His suggestions have to fit within that authority structure if they are to be adopted. He cannot put forward ideas which are antithetical to the pyramidal structure. But the result is that the reform itself is antithetical to the reconstructive project which stems from a system of relationships and ideas that by its nature must confront the pyramidal structure. For example, the suggestions of the Urban Coalition, in which corporations are put to work by liberal reformers to help in the slums, turn out in practice to mean nothing more than a new market for the corporations, with very little change manifesting itself for the poor. A few jobs here or there, a training program and the sense of movement among the middle and upper classes are the result of such programs. There is no attempt to redistribute power or rights in the society.

The second motivation that may be attributed to the reformer is that, because he views his work as other peoples' problems, by necessity he identifies his personal interest with the authority structure as it is. His only task is to find a way wherein individuals are able to accept the opportunities of finding their niche in the authority structure. If he is a reformer of good will, he would add, "just like we have." But no matter what the motivation is, the fact remains that reform itself is a necessary instrument of colonization because it is the one specific method which updates the colonized structure through presenting new modes of entry into the hierarchy and through presenting methods of adjustment.

Elsewhere I have referred to the Tufts University example. In this context, it is useful again to see that example. A university decides to put a health center in a black town in the South. That town cannot support a health center of the size and scope which the university wants to put in that town. It is necessary for Tufts University to bring in doctors and other specialists, since the standard of medicine is the standard of specialization that most of the society now accepts. The doctors brought in don't live in the town. They are usually white. The result is that the town now ends up serving the hospital structure with blacks continuing to serve as maids, janitors, etc. in a traditional colonial relationship. This remains the paradigm case of the reforming method which merely updates the relationships of colonization.

8

Revolution

There are two stubborn facts about the twentieth century. One is that in the people's quest for new roots of authority in themselves, they have instead invested authority, and indeed their total being, in pyramidal states. The social experiments in the major industrial and popular nations of the West and East, with their revolutions, counter-revolutions and technological modernization buttress this deplorable fact. Such situations as occurred in Germany, Russia, France, Japan, the United States, China, Africa and Latin America justify the premise that twentieth-century politics is the history of authoritarianism and totalitarianism. The second notion is that the means by which people collectively attempted to achieve new roots of authority in themselves—new roots of freedom—

was through war and revolution. Perhaps such methods dictated the failure of the objectives of freedom.

In their own way, war and revolution may be intellectually distinguishable. However, the reality is that one merges into the other. War usually is thought to be between two different groups of people who have defined that they live under different political organizations— one rule as against another. On the other hand, revolution is fought among those who live under one rule, over who will rule and govern and what the shape of the political system will be in the particular place that both groups of contestants recognize as being the nation or political entity. The revolutionary's theories of society may be universal, but his actual political purposes are limited.

The leading scholar on the nature of war does not see great differences between war and revolution except operationally.

> Revolutions are concentrated manifestations of the conditions of opinion underlying all social violence, whether denominated rebellion, insurrection, or war. Starting as new symbols in local areas, revolutions spread ideas of violence by contagion and opposition. All revolution starts in principle as world-revolution. Their symbols and principles must, in the opinion of their initiators, become universal or nothing. While the sobering experience of local success usually tends toward geographic limitation, before such limits have been established, friends and foes of the new symbol will have come into conflict and will have heightened tension levels in remote areas.[1]

But more important than the idea of whether or not in the twentieth century ruling groups accept distinctions between war and revolution is their intertwined result. Wars incline countries toward their own internal group or class revolution. The Russian ruling class, for example, by forcing Russia into the first world war, defined the misery, anxiety and class conflict which stimulated a revolutionary zeal within Russia that would insure the success of the revolution. The 1904–1905 wars by Russia also defined the character and possibility of revolution in that country. Wars have a brutal habit of showing contradictions in a political system and widening the fissures in societies where there are deep and consciously felt class conflicts. The Russo-Japanese War showed the weakness of the overblown military, the bureaucratic state and the Tsar's court lackeys. These groups became more dependent on the workers and bourgeois as the Tsar needed revenue, bodies, and machines to fight his battles. They lost sight of their own interests, ideology and sense of legitimacy in their crude attempts to hold onto their palaces, seats, jewels, and horses. The groups which insist on prosecuting such wars while depending on other classes for fighting such wars give rise to an internal revolutionary situation in the imperial power.

Depressed, alienated groups and classes in the imperial nation begin to see their struggle as parallel to those whom the powerful in the imperial nation define as the enemy abroad. In modern times, individuals who see themselves as individually against the government find that there are other individuals who hold the same view in their country. They build a group and then they find "soul brothers" among the "enemies" of the state they live in. Black people, students and new left professors in the United States see their own situations as similar, in part pointed out to them by experiencing the American war in Vietnam as an imperial war. The misery and chaos, the sense of loss of understanding over what has gone on — as in pre-revolutionary Russia—teaches that the effect of failing in war, once it is undertaken, causes powerful dislocations which can lead to revolution. Where such a result occurs, we may assume that there is an irreconcilable split between various groups on the nature and purpose of the war or imperial undertaking. Ruling elements attempt to get disparate groups to accept the ideology of unity as central, in order to cover a failure in war. Where the war is an ambiguous affair—which modern imperialist wars by their nature must be—it is virtually impossible to break anti-war groups if the war continues. The more the war continues, the more likely it is that those groups opposing the war will seek revolution or reconstruction.*

I have attempted to describe here a phenomenon which occurs almost without variance in the history of imperial nation-states. If a state makes war and its leadership is

* To discuss the means of the revolution, that is, whether violence is used, might at one time have appeared to have been an unnecessary question. Violence was the purifier and violence remains the chosen instrument of the struggle in the revolution. Once war is used by the State as its means of enforcing its will elsewhere, who but a Pollyanna would think that violence is not the method to be used at home to stop those who used the violence power of the State to deprive others or enforce their will.

Yet today there is a new reluctance about the use of violent methods. In part, this reluctance is related to a new consciousness about the nature of revolution itself. The revolutionary means, if successful, become the revolutionary ends. To put it another way, the day-to-day activities of attaining power become the life style of maintaining it. Furthermore, there is a new, powerful ideology of non-violence which appears to give the colonized a weapon that can channel revolutionary zeal into processes that are more humane.

The reasons are tactical as well as moral. Unless they are military palace coups, revolutions usually result in civil wars. A civil war, as for example in the Russian case, was fought to destroy or protect the revolution for four years. Imagine what a civil war would be like in the United States given its present lead of military technology. Simone Weil has taught us that "The man of the right forgets that no political regime, of whatever kind, involves disorders remotely comparable to those of civil war, with its deliberate destruction, its non-stop massacre in the firing line, its slowing down of production, and the hundreds of crimes it permits every day, on both sides, by the fact that any hooligan can get hold of a gun. The man of the left, for his part, forgets that even on his own side liberty is suppressed far more drastically by the necessities of civil war than it would be by the coming to power of a party of the extreme right; in other words he forgets that there is a state of siege, that militarization is in force both at the front and behind it, that there is a police terror and that the individual has no security and no protection against arbitrary injustice . . . And both of them forget that during the long months of civil war an almost identical regime has grown up on both sides."[2]

unsuccessful, a fundamental violent wrenching of the political system is never far behind. If a series of small wars are fought in the name of imperialism, which by their nature are "losers," is there a likelihood of revolution? Perhaps there is an "iron law" of nations. Where countries are imperialist and where there is an emphasis on the product, presented through communications, violent dreams and myths, either mass or personal, the likelihood is that in its internal confrontations the imperial nation will be wrenched by mass violence. A content analysis of American movies and television yields such a conclusion. Furthermore, where there is a patent dissipation of resources and a virtually total misallocation of priorities so that resources are used for paranoid purposes rather than for day-to-day human needs, there is a likelihood that the conditions are present for violent change. Here is an example of what I mean: If I have one hundred dollars a year to spend and know that my family needs medical care, but I fear a robbery and spend eighty-five dollars to protect myself from robbery and don't give medical care to my family, I have made an irrational choice and have dissipated my available resources. This weakens the basis of relationships among the members of the family and indeed endangers the lives of members of that family.

In an imperialist country, the order of priorities and dissipation of resources is also turned around. From that situation, the authority structure itself is called into question by various groups because of the foolish choices and judgments that the authority structures have made. War, which various groups among the violence colonizers might have believed is the way to keep the imperial state healthy, in fact turns out to be the way to destroy the basis of the authority of that leadership. Support from society at large is shaken because those holding power refuse to make choices that would fulfill needs which would keep people contented and immobile.

While media establishments may want to flatter young people by saying that those who wave the flag of revolution are making it (except as they may be the beneficiaries of the moment because they have thought of taking advantage of the moment earlier than others), the real revolutionary is the Establishment itself, or the ruler or the ruling class which undertakes—out of passion or stupidity or economic need—activities of war that cannot be concluded. In America, the theory of exceptionalism has allowed people to believe that America could fight small wars without danger to the pyramidal structure of America and to those who believed in their pyramidal roles. Americans could have guns and butter, and indeed some would say that for the American economy as a whole it was necessary to have both.

Eliot Janeway has argued that the Vietnam war was the first war in American history which did not materially benefit the society as a whole. However, costs of defending empires are far more expensive than the cost of obtaining them. It was relatively easy for the United States to make commitments to forty-five nations through pacts, treaty obligations and military assistance. It is quite another matter to be able to fight wars as a continuous way of life without changing the power balance at the heart of the American Empire—within the United States. The first problem is that there are organizational relationships which are developed abroad in maintaining empire that are followed in continental United States in order to maintain power. The bureaucratic organization of that power in terms of military and police relations usually results historically in threats to one's own citizenry. In response, citizens themselves begin to act in their own defense. What begins as defense may end up as revolutionary challenge as the spaces for individuals and groups "dry up" and such groups are forced to see themselves the way the rulers see them: as criminals, even though existentially the colonized do not feel criminal and attach that concept to the rulers of the society once they have found their consciousness. Both groups address themselves to the person as role.

While it is true that revolutions in the short term are judged harshly in history because of the number of people killed and dispossessed, and in the long term are judged more positively because of the new social systems brought into the world that serve Progress, the potentiality of nuclear weapons being used in the short term to protect power, changes the possibility of anyone's being able to make a positive judgment favoring revolution. Yet, the contradiction remains. Suppose the colonizers use nuclear weapons to protect their power, either in Southeast Asia or the United States. Then?

In the United States in the latter part of the twentieth century, the war in Vietnam has taught Americans in an existential way the relationship between war and revolution. If such wars continue in other places in the world, and the United States initiates or commits itself to them, then it will be virtually impossible to transform the society by reconstructive means, because of the symbiotic relationship that seems to dictate that revolution follow war. I do not mean to suggest that this is an iron law of history. It is enough of one, however, to give pause. The task, therefore, is to persuade political forces in a coalition to bring about a situation wherein the national security state is *dismantled* before it undertakes a series of wars that will cause revolutionary coups from the right, which will then cause a full-scale fascist repression and other glories that twentieth-century man has invented. This task is incredibly difficult because of the nature of American military engagement all over the world. The national security state is an engaged nation and not an interventionary one. It has already intervened and is engaged militarily in nations. During the process of dismantling, it is obvious that repression itself against political dissidents will continue and grow in America as that struggle is internationalized. The question is whether the size of that repression can be kept at a level which is low enough so that relatively peaceful reconstruction can go forward. That question requires a further analysis into certain tactical considerations such as the emergence of a new political party. But I am getting ahead of the foreshadowing events of revolution.

Scenes of Revolution

It is useful to examine the way revolution-repression may emerge from the present American situation if no reconstructive action succeeds or is undertaken. The situation is assumed to include a national security state that is unable to supply guns and butter because those parts of the business classes not primarily in defense contracts refuse to pay for both, while the military classes continue to support the American national security state and its indulgences in different parts of the world. A split develops among the military and business groups with an attendant split in the labor movement. The problems of the urban areas appear insoluble since no reforms work. The political system itself is at a standstill because there are no ideas, and the reformers are drummed out of executive position. They are replaced with a law and order mentality of immobilists who view Mayor Daley as their idol. Ironically, at one stage the law and order grouping of the lower middle class disdains colonial wars although its commitment to property forces it to call on the military for protection in its own cities, thus causing it to be beholden.

On the assumption and felt reality that the piecemeal efforts of people do not bring about either obvious or lasting change which *matters,* that is, which has substance, the brightest of the young people now turn their thoughts to revolution. Instabilities caused by the need for higher profits, an inflationary spiral caused by banks charging usurer rates while the percentage of consumer goods sold falls, or the constant sting of the whip of necessity among the poor, or the casual introduction of technological innovation which has far-reaching consequences, or continuing undefined wars which have no accepted ideological purpose—all of these invariably result in widespread social disruptions that elicit violent response from the colonizer and the colonized. Groups organize themselves for protection and the possibility of preemptive violence. For example, in Mississippi, the tenant farmer realizing that voting means nothing without economic power, proceeds to burn the crops of the plantation owner who had previously beaten or kept him at subsistence wages.* After this confrontation, the plantation owner calls in the violence power of the state against the person of the tenant farmer. The local state and the plantation owner join to kill the tenant farmer. Revenge is sworn on the plantation owners and a group is formed which no longer listens to the advice of the young organizer who is now suspect because he eschews violence. This group now attempts to destroy the plantation, the plantation owner and the state machinery which he controls. The police, vigilantes, and the national guard are called in to "restore order."

---

* Fannie Lou Hamer told me about voting day in one county in Mississippi. The plantation owners pay double the usual rate for cotton picking on voting day. Since few black tenant farmers are working and the condition of the tenant farmers is very depressed, they pass up the "opportunity" to vote in favor of cotton-picking wages.

More tenant farmers are killed. The tenant farmers run away to the big cities. Some of them are more militant than ever although most become frightened and lose their militancy to the deadly status of the welfare client. The state remains intact with greater alliance and cooperation among the military, the police and the plantation owner. The corporations sell war technology and hawk war products such as gas grenades and Thompson tanks, etc. as necessary complements to keep the peace at home and on the farm.

In the cities gangs organize for the purpose of providing institutional supports and barriers against the threatening outside world. They organize to get money either from the city or the rackets, and they occupy turf. In other cases where political contact develops, some of the young organize to burn city hall and the slums. Those groups that can be bought by the city police or federal government are used by the city to spy on the revolutionary groups. (The police and undercover agents do not destroy these groups because their power depends on the apparent existence of revolutionary groups. Indeed, the police work hard to *build* the revolutionary spirit.) When the riots come, political gangs which do not stay bought, burn property. In response, the police and their gangs, as well as the military, now turn their violence against the people. The police and the military attempt to coordinate their activities nationally and then unify them through communication and technology. The mayors lose control over the police. The police end up being absorbed in a national system whose directions are given, through the guidance and active involvement of the military, OEO, FBI, CIA and other intelligence and social control agencies, which now discover analogies and parallels between the wars against insurgents and revolutionaries which are fought in Asia or Africa, Latin America or Canada, and the ones which are fought locally in the cities.

The cities become armed camps as the Violence Commission predicts. The middle class attempts to find ways of protecting itself while surrounding the cities which are inhabited by the poor, deracinate and the very rich with friendly police and armed forces. The cities are looked upon as the enemies of the young whites who attempt to find places to escape to. And the small town and rural proletariat have a vision of the city not unlike that of Mao Tse-tung. Yet there is no peasant population to support an army of guerrillas.

In the armed forces black soldiers who fight in such wars as Vietnam wonder why they are fighting for America. Indeed, they begin to see themselves as colonial troops similar in role to the Algerians who fought for the French against Vietnamese in Indochina. The blacks return home, having mastered the arts of war, with no reason to see why they should not be practiced at home. The military leaders are asked—for planning purposes—to show how they would solve security problems in the cities. Their methods are at first rejected by civilian bureaucrats, but they are finally tried in the American city, as the crime rate appears to increase and social experiments end which were the bureaucratic answer to aiding the cities. The same personnel who work in counter-insurgency abroad and then domestically are put in charge of the domestic "war on crime." The will of the "order makers" is worked through the Federal Bureaucracy which becomes the work of the national security apparatus. Detention camps are readied in makeshift fashion from existing army camps. First they are thought of as summer recreation camps "for the underprivileged." Then they become camps with rules and orders to hold the black young during the summer. They are "captured" through dreams of basketball and swimming. Here they will learn to become either policemen or prisoners. Middle-class college students organize against the armed

services, refusing to go into the armed forces. They
occupy draft boards, set up their own, or begin holding
elections for them. They occupy buildings or universities,
attempting either to get power or confront the militarization of the university. The police and the military respond
against the students with gas and clubs. The students
respond by taking their personal anguish and turning it
into a continuing commitment for change. Many talk
about revolution without knowing its meaning. They
hope for personal liberation or identity or human solidarity. Some of them now see violence as the only way
to bring pressure on the society. They undertake to organize a national movement, not eschewing violence but
seeing it as the only way to bring down the American
empire. Then rhetoric follows class struggle language.
Some organize military cadres committed to blowing up
buildings. Others "drop out" by building their own pro-
tective associations and cooperative communities. Their
organization and fear of the blacks now give rise to
authoritarian right-wing organizations which are already
armed. Such organizations stop fighting the reformists
and see their legitimating role by serving as the vanguard
of the police. They are pressed into more extreme acts.
Some have served from time to time as paid assassins of
national security agencies. Leaders who are non-revolu-
tionary but militant, or who want to bring changes in the
governing structure, find their lives in peril. As the
society becomes more dislocated, the rhetorical emphasis
and public expenditure are on the obligations of order.
The political cases are brought almost wholly against the
left.* The right authoritarians who act are at best ad-
monished.

The liberals who run the universities exclude and

---

* In this sense the pattern is similar to the Weimar Republic where the left
incurred punishment while the authoritarian and totalitarian forces of the society
escaped punishment and indeed became the Law.

punish students severely on the grounds that they must protect the university. The students and the people in the slums call for revolution, but they don't know what will happen, nor do they care about programs to be implemented after the revolution succeeds. They say, like Lenin, that the struggle defines the program. The military, now fighting on two fronts, at home and abroad, occupies various American cities under martial law. They fear their own power, but intend to use military means to protect that power—and the state. Some of the more militant in the military call for the use of powerful weapons on the cities. The technological revolution now gives the military the most exquisite weaponry which is used continuously on blacks, students, and finally on workers. The geographical areas of their use are delineated, of course, to teach lessons and to respond to a system of selective terror which is initiated by street gangs. Mini civil wars occur which give vent to and test the violence inherent in the economic and technological system. But nothing good results. Instead we are treated to murder, repression and unexamined totalism. In the back of people's minds are the nuclear weapons first to be used for defense against others, now used as a threat to the cities. In a revolution/civil war situation in the United States those in a resistance are forced to reckon with a military class that literally has the keys to tens of thousands of nuclear weapons. It is not possible to dismiss with casualness the idea that the colonizer in defense of his prerogatives would use nuclear weapons in the United States.

And what if, by some "miracle," a revolution were achieved? The probability is that the pyramidal state would remain attractive to the revolutionaries as a thing to run and control. As a movement for the new, revolution and revolutionary fervor calls forth those critical and

creative impulses that create consciousness and potentiality among those who want to hear. But revolution
in power is false because it usually does not prepare the
way for wholly different social structures that are humane.
Because it is unprepared, the revolutionaries catapult
themselves into power through the means of the old
regime and then must use such means to protect themselves.

In Orwell's *Animal Farm,* there is a description of the
animals after a successful revolution against their owners.
The animals end up acting exactly as their owners acted.
They now sleep on the beds in the big house. They now
talk la-de-da talk. They now make the same rules which
their former owners made. De Tocqueville showed how
even after the French Revolution the governance of the
society stayed the same. There was no difference in the
administrative structure and methods prior to and after
the revolution. Revolution is like the face of the clock
in which the hands of a clock start at the bottom and move
to the top. Perhaps as the Bible says, the last shall be first,
but as it is looked at by the outsider, the dynamics of the
dialectical flip which occurs merely causes a new class
to come forward which uses the same tactics and strate-
gems to stay on top as the ones who were replaced through
force. As Berdyaev has pointed out:

> No revolutions ever have loved freedom; the mission of
> revolution is something different from that. In revolutions,
> new social strata are thrown up to the surface, strata which
> had not before been permitted activity and which had
> been oppressed, and in the fight for their new position in
> society, they cannot display a love of freedom: they cannot
> be overcareful in their attitude to spiritual values.[3]

(I am reminded of Lenin, who could not bear to hear
Beethoven's "Appassionata Sonata" because it took his

mind off the need for revolution.) The hierarchic structure remains.

Even those who put forward socialism as the goal of
revolution have only the poor examples of state socialism
to show. In state socialism, of course, as Lenin has pointed
out, the authority of the state grows stronger, the planning
which goes on is from the top, with little emphasis on the
"-ing" and great emphasis on the "plan." Thus, state
socialism itself merely turns out to be the bringing forward of a new class of people committed to hierarchic
authority. The difference is that it is now their authority.
It is an authority which invariably stems not from either
the excellence of their work or the sense of creative relationships which they themselves then build. It is rather
again from the authority of power and the assumption
that, because one is at the top, his rules and views are
correct. The history of the Russian Revolution is the
taking over of the Russian bureaucracy, the strengthening
of the Secret Police, etc. The state socialism which occurred merely turns out to be the mirror of corporate
socialism in the West. *Thus, revolution in its present
form will mean little more than the natural progression of
immobilism and reform.* The difference is that revolution and its aftermath will be accompanied with a greater
amount of violence than we would ordinarily find in a
society which becomes, through natural progression,
more authoritarian. It is necessary, therefore, to break
this dynamic vise in which man is caught. While the
appearance may be that revolution itself is a total rending
of the system into its opposite, its opposite turns out to
be the same.

A question may be asked, and rightfully so, about
whether the American Revolution itself meant the repeat
of what existed prior to the revolution. Here, my argument is, of course, that there was no real revolution in
America. Instead, there was a decolonization from En-

gland. After the colonization occurred, a group of states, attempting to solve their own problems built—through a series of compacts—the sorts of relationships they believed should exist. In France and Russia, the new social contracts were built on authoritarian state structures already in existence; in America, there were no such structures. Spaces existed—and were postulated—of a political and geographic nature which attempted to limit the nature of hierarchy. The spaces that now exist for reconstruction are political and psychological. But the protection and extension of those spaces demands an approach to politics and knowledge which at times will require the kinds of sacrifice that may cause both the colonized and the liberated to wonder why *they* should bother.

9

Elements of Reconstruction: The Project and Social Invention

"Do these men who make pronouncements
realize the implications of what they are saying?
Are they thinkers? They claim to be intellectuals.
I submit to you you'd be warranted in finding they
don't think. They feel."*

Two methods of social participation are available as instruments of groups and individuals to bring about decolonization and reconstruction. One is the project; the second is the social invention. I use the concept of project differently than the reader might find in existential literature. In such literature the project refers to any action taken by someone. I have narrowed this meaning because under its usual definition it becomes difficult to differentiate purposive from non-purposive behavior. The meaning of project which I suggest is that the action taken is purposive behavior which matters to the individual and the group, but it is not so fixed and purposeful that it is

* Prosecutor John Wall in his summation to the jury in the case of US *v.* Coffin, Ferber, Goodman, Raskin and Spock, for conspiracy to counsel, aid, abet and hinder the operations of the draft. Criminal case # 1-68-F.

mechanical and not the individual's own action. In its dynamics the project takes us from a pyramidal structure to a series of horizontal, interdependent relationships. The project attempts to transcend the usual political relationship which operates around a father or authoritarian figure, replacing it with an egalitarian and associative relationship. In this sense, the project is related to the idea of the social contract which tries to break the authoritarian political relationship.

The project is man's way of feeling and acting as being to being which asserts that he is not thrown into the world or programmed through a series of steps which define the being of some in the world at the expense of others. And there is a pragmatist context to the project. It starts from the injective sense of an individual or group acting in ways which it defines. It endeavors to extend the initial creative or injective impulse into a continuous systematized situation of liberty. Hence, in its first stage the project begins as an act of potential freedom; it is sustained by a series of doings that are based on intentionality (purpose) and reasoning feeling. The individual attempts to share his actions with others and others with himself. In its initial stage the project is an expression of man's aliveness since he is acting in freedom with his feelings and senses for himself and with others. Through the project he attempts to express the formerly dormant, now alive, lust for freedom that is aborted by a colonized system which is only prepared to give the colonized person his freedom to lust. (In authoritarian and totalitarian societies, the characterization of individuals includes freedom to lust—note the Dream Colony—but the people are carefully stripped of the lust for freedom which would force new boundaries and new relationships between individuals and groups.)

The project is more than an abstract concept to describe actions. It is prescriptive in that it is a method of action which defines how we act and how we describe and judge our actions. Projects may begin in the space developed through decolonization, although once under way the people in the project may end up repeating the habits of mind and the ways of acting and relating which the colonized structure follows. The people fall back into their pyramidal social character which they are unable to shed through the action of their project. Another problem is that ideas which appear as projects may in practice end up as fool's gold. Such projects are like broken lances against the shield of impenetrable authoritarian relationships, merely repeating the colonizer-colonized roles.

In one sense the communists first mediated the Marxist ideal through the concepts of Power and Authority. They failed in their projects because they built into the habit of mind the same colonial attitude, when faced with the problems which derive from wanting to keep order and power. The project which may begin as the transformation of human relationships may end in the old ways. That is to say, those in the project become panicky since they find themselves beset with problems which occur when the values of the group have changed. People find they are unable to build beyond the immediate. Order and discipline, the old values, are then called upon because they give people security. Trivial matters of administration are used as the basis to shape the formal and continuous relationships of people to each other within the project. As Djilas, that wise and arrogant man, said:

> All the demons that Communism believed it had banished from the forthcoming as well as the real world have crept into the soul of Communism and become part of its being. Communism, once a popular movement that in the name of science inspired the toiling and oppressed people of the world with the hope of creating the Kingdom of Heaven

on earth, that launched, and continues to launch, millions
to their deaths in pursuit of this unextinguishable primeval
dream, has become transformed into national political
bureaucracies and states squabbling among themselves for
prestige and influence, for the sources of wealth and for
markets—for all those things which politicians and governments have always quarreled and always will.[1]

As I think about this book, *The Unperfect Society,*
and Djilas, I am forced to wonder whether revolutionary
projects necessarily borrow and use the methods of
the colonizer to survive. Now this fact will always be true
but the question is to what extent. For example, if we
want to start a school, it has to be done with the currency
of the realm. We either have to get the money from rich
people, rob for it, work for it, beg for it or entertain a
public subscription. In each case the appeals will be
different. Yet the nature of appealing to those not part
of the project for basic help shapes its direction. The
chances are that the project will be first defined in terms
which reflect the needs of the pyramidal structure.
Another problem is that we may build too quickly. What
was a project becomes a movement before we know
whether the first notions of the project had any merit
beyond the immediate few involved. Once people feel
disparity and dissonance in their lives (and they have
decided to act outside of characterized roles), they are
anxious to find their potentiality and any ideas they
can use for this purpose, it would seem, are fine. Well-
meaning people will try any experiment because the
opposite admits continuity and victory for the colonized
structure.

It is also obvious that necessity (the state coming down
on you) dictates the limits of the possible success of the
project. Suppose you are characterized by the state as a
conspirator with people you don't know. Your time,

energy and being are now taken up with the matter of attempting to find out whether you are or are not a conspirator. You are defined by others into the make-believe world of courts, lawyers, legal fees, contradictory advice, and the strong sense that what is going on is unrelated to you or your tasks. Yet the realities are defined for you, and the project in the context of repression may appear as a luxury, a never was for the space in the public realm which does not exist or can be wiped out by the pyramid. But this is a tactical question. It is the meaning of getting a beachhead, one's foot in the door; or if he is a camel, his nose under the tent. The project is built whether or not the space exists, and so can the social invention be built. Even easier.

Reaching for another is the basis for the project but it is not enough. To change relationships and things as they appear or as they are in the way we use them, we are required to develop a method of knowledge-action which is instrumental in seeing things in new ways and in acting on them in those ways. In this sense we are required to develop a theory of action which helps us understand what we want to become in the world, what we can bring into it and what others, by what they are or have been, bring into the world. Is man a clean slate, without limits and always free, having meaning and giving meaning to choices? This is an old debate among the existentialists. It would be well to review a part of it for a moment.

Jean-Paul Sartre, the non-believer in God, argues for the recovery of one's freedom. Give up on God-talk and face up to your choices. "Life has no meaning a priori . . . it is up to you to give it a meaning, and value is nothing else than this meaning you choose." Martin Buber sees this as demagogic. To Buber we are under penalty to use our freedom properly. "He who sets in the place (of freedom given to us) the postulate of the

'recovery of freedom' turns aside from true human existence, which means being sent and being commissioned."
Buber cannot abide the idea that God is dead, because
then all is permitted. In this way he appreciates Heidegger (but not totally because of Heidegger's insisting
that current history does not stand under divine judgment, and for this philosopher Hitler brought the "new").
For Heidegger, being is bound to "and attains its illumination through the destiny and history of man, without
its becoming a function of human subjectivity." God
rises from history and the dead in this formulation. For
Buber, God is. (It is not as if Sartre threw over God. By
1952, its form seemed to take that of the Communist Party.
He believed that the workers could express their true
being, their freedom through the will of the Party. The
Party becomes the means to introduce the working class
into history. Thus is man's fate unfolded.)[2]

Buber's idea of the established is in the relation of self
to God. I would accept this view as given. But accepting
this view forces us to doubt even more the pyramidally-
established which has nothing to do with God or Being
unless we are impertinent enough to believe that God
our Father (the idea that man must create authority figures who happen to be rulers and who might call themselves God's representatives) is what God is. God is at
the top of the pyramid. Surely that is merely the verbalism
of the monks and clerks trying to please those at the tops
of the pyramids. What we can only begin to understand
is that building from the subjective ("I feel, therefore
I exist"), that is, recovering the subjective which then
opens the individual to the potentiality of freedom, is
the only way we can begin to expect and define the un-
anticipated and work with it. This notion becomes the
basis to build a framework which attempts to pro-ject
another future from one which is likely if we mistake
the established for the Established, the Being of God

for the being (the coming to himself) for man. Each to his (His) place.

The being of man in a future is his attempt to pro-ject the systematized and continuous framework or situation of freedom: the absence of *external* or externally caused constraint. If in one project the individuals are able to succeed at bringing about a systematized situation in freedom and personal liberty which sets off other such projects that relate to each other in purpose and view-point, the beginnings of reconstruction are under way. The project in this context has particular values and purposes which are to be replicated and added to through each projection of another group that shares the injec-tive impulse and the need to structure its own impulse into a basis of continuous existence. The project is a continuous process between internal and external rela-tionships of those who live the project, those who start similar projects and those who are unmoved or outside of the project. The internal purpose of those living the project is that of sharing and building, over a period of time, spaces which define freedom and its new bound-aries. The internal political purpose of spreading the project to others with similar concerns will strengthen one's own project and then make the project in its values, not necessarily its particular activities, the basis of a movement.

The outside purpose of the original project and others that may grow from it is to change and confront the colo-nized reality. The likelihood is that the project will be forced to such a confrontation because of the challenges it offers and its non-cooptable nature as it grows or is replicated on the basis of values that clearly conflict with those of the colonized reality. The project itself may be eminently practical. For example, it might grow out of the need for a school which is different from those pro-vided in the Channeling Colony. The result is that parents

and children take their individual objections and dis-
agreements as the basis to build a school. Or a group of
young people who drop out of school and leave their
parents attempt to build a new community outside of the
structure of the plantation and violence colony. Or a
group of workers begins reordering the relationships
within the structure of their industry and in their work
(e.g., worker councils of reconstruction). By their nature
such activities, if they are maintained and spread, become
the basis to confront the pyramidal structure. The solidarity which builds outwards from human association
rather than mere adversity is the basis for long-term
confrontation and change.

As I suggest in Chapter 12 the method of protecting
and building on such projects demands political activity which means the formation of a political party.
So long as the American nation-state remains liberal
authoritarian rather than totalitarian, the political party
(if it is racially integrated) becomes important as a method
of protecting and extending the movement. It undertakes
to mobilize political support and legitimize political
space in the protection of the new project, the school,
the intentional community, the shared vision of dismantling the national security state, because it speaks to an
objective need and the humane interests of groups which
serve as the ground for the project and the political party.

While such actions confront the pyramidal structure,
it does not mean that the cooperative basis of relationships within the project is lost. Individuals undertake
to comprehend the desires of the other and to share his
pain, to a degree which does not contradict one's personal
coming to oneself. Instead, the emergence of self through
relating to another is strengthened just because the projects are based on the rigors of empathy and the magic of
induction. Take the meaning of empathy: it is being with
another. In political terms it translates itself into meaning

standing with another after seeing him, that is, after feeling with his condition. However, empathy is not the idea of losing one's self by so identifying with another that the individual becomes another. If this should happen the basic meaning of empathy is lost. As Heidegger has pointed out, such a situation denies the uniqueness of self and other and assumes that each is the mirror of the other. Politically where such uniqueness is denied, the self easily becomes the tool of the other and we return to the colonized reality. Arthur Waskow has pointed out in re-applying the teachings of Rabbi Hillel, the existential pragmatist position can be found in the Talmud. The Talmud has said, "If I do not stand for myself, who will stand for me? If I do not stand for others, what and who am I?"

When I speak of the inductive method as having magical qualities, I mean that it is virtually impossible to justify induction logically. As Bertrand Russell pointed out, "To justify induction as such is impossible, since it can be shown to lead quite as often to falsehood as to truth." Russell points out that in the first instance we must rely on "feeling" which rules out fallacious inductions. The inductive method becomes the way of mediating this feeling through something which is "more explicit and reliable."[3] This feeling includes the personal qualities of the situations we are in. The project and social knowledge can only be accomplished through the development of an experimental and inductive method which does not deify standing off from the data and so-called objective observation. The project does not let this occur since it is the complex of experimental operations which change formerly existing conditions so that a new insight may be obtained which will indicate and test proposed methods of solution. Thus, the mode of solution is formulated, as Dewey points out, as a hypothesis to be tested existentially. The project method is a way to develop knowledges and structures whose values will allow further liberation of thought and energy. In turn, the values developed through the practice of the project could give impetus to other actions that begin to define for us what the practice of freedom might be. In this sense the project energizes a society to struggle with a new system of freedom in the present which then reaches out for others in a political movement.

Quick change in a society results from technological innovation and the social invention. The social invention is a method of thought-in-action which uses the spaces in the colonized structure and which starts from the idea that thought and action are objective and impersonal. This method also depends on practice, but the programs presented are for others to live within. Once ideas are put forward for others to live within, we are on a slippery course. The social invention alone is endowed with the quality of the I-It relationship at its best. It only knows and appreciates people in their aspects. As Buber says, it is a different I which exists in the I-Thou than in the I-It. In the I-It we may know and appreciate another, giving him help, finding ways of observing, reflecting or being solicitous to him. It is not the same as I-Thou where one stands with the whole of one's being "and steps into an essential relation with him."[4] When we put the I-It relationship into the political context, it becomes the primary reformist and revolutionary ideology for massive confrontation and change. Its programmatic tool, the social invention, is intimately connected with the amassing of power for either profound change or merely the updating of the political authority relationships to the technological level of the society. In reconstruction it is the secondary method for massive transformational change. The project method holds as primary the idea of terminating colonized relationships upon which the state operates but asserts the day-to-day goal of I-Thou as the

objective of reconstructive society. Obviously, this goal
is virtually unreachable. But it is necessary as the framework for social action.

> Both build up together human existence; it is only a ques-
> tion of which of the two is at any particular time the architect
> and which is his assistant. Rather, it is a question of whether
> the I-Thou relation remains the architect, for it is self-evi-
> dent that it cannot be employed as assistant. If it does not
> command, then it is already disappearing.[5]

Otherwise, the changes which occur become mechanical
and functional. The project protects the potentiality of the
I-Thou and creates an I-in-We relationship. That is, a
joining together in essential aspects of doing and standing
with another without the totalization of one over another.
In modern time the I-It relationship has emerged un-
contested and dictates a mock form of totalist I-in-We that
destroys the essentiality of one to others and gives back
the pyramid over one. Our difficulty is that the knowledge
of I-Thou and I-It are intertwined. Knowledge becomes
the knowledge of manipulation as well as the knowledge
for knowledge as being and understanding. The project
in the knowledges which it attempts to develop includes
the separation of these seemingly inseparable practical
results of knowledge and value. If we are able to separate
out the knowledge of understanding from the knowledge
of manipulation, that is to say, eschewing the knowledge
of manipulation which is laid bare in Machiavelli as the
way men operate, then we will have begun to work out
the basis of insisting on the priorities of knowledge, what
is taught and what is learned, as favoring the knowledge
of I-Thou rather than I-It. But this is a hard objective.
The question of knowledge and value is determined and
studied in practice and it is always easier to manipulate
than relate, using that technique and then passing it on to
others.

The knowledges to be learned through the project and the means-ends process emerging from the project for reconstructive change, begins with the framework of the I-Thou and I-in-We. It uses I-It knowledges as helpers which are seemingly objective and impersonal but within the I-in-We framework. (I say seemingly because they may have a profoundly humane basis to them upon examination. Where they do not, one could then argue that epistemologically and ethically the discipline has gone awry.) The projects which develop in this way are part of our uncharacterized consciousness which therefore begins by rejecting the characterized personal situation and the colonized situation of the society. Projects are required to meet two tests: One is that of personal relatedness to form an "island of reconstruction," but with plenty of bridges to others. The second is that of advancing the decolonization of the society.

The I-Thou framework for the project becomes its basis for operating as a reconstructive activity because it is the only way that an individual or group can reach out in a human way, respecting the humanness of those who occupy the colonizing role in the pyramid. They are seen as human beings who are in one aspect enemies, not as enemies who in one aspect are human beings. The chosen project, while it may be personally satisfying, must in its social nature transcend us as individuals because its success depends on committing and involving others while we become reflections for each other in cooperative activity. In this sense of cooperation we are to enter the project with openness, naïveté, and self-examination. In effect each must be willing to be changed himself, coming out of the experience with perceptions and actions which are based on the framework of the I-Thou and I-in-We relationship. Each gives part of self to make the project part of self and finding part of self in the projection of the project.

One should not be fooled into thinking that, by giving part of himself into an activity, he is building a project or escaping the colonizing structure. Most activities are pseudo projects because, in the structure of the action and relationships of them, the individual reinforces colonized functions. Suppose I distribute food to the poor at Thanksgiving time. In itself this is not a bad act—but only I feel good in the process. I am looked at as being good because I have fulfilled a role of being good. But the facts are otherwise. There is no sense of equality or association between me and the one who gets the food, the object of my affection or need. There is also a perverse reinforcement of scarcity and my role as giver in that act. I help the taker reinforce the colonized reality. I am the representative of the hierarchic other now reaffirming the object state of the taker-beneficiary.

Suppose I put forward an idea for a project to a group of economically poor which I will live within. I say (and do), "Let's organize a food cooperative in which we buy food cheaply or grow our own and we share the distribution and agricultural aspects." I have begun to participate with others as an equal. Suppose I say, "I will join with you in striking against the gougers and their principals so that an alternative system can be established." Through my personal actions and with others, I make clear that it is an alternative to welfare and high prices or the A & P food chains; I have begun a project which meets the prerequisites for fundamental reconstructive change. The group has now formed and is living an alternative to the colonized structure. Those who are rich, bright, industrious or lazy are prepared to share their individual quality and themselves, taking from the group other qualities for themselves. Each offers himself up for change, first in a common purpose and then in a way of being. The group as a group is to determine with itself its purposes and directions. In bringing such a project into being I am myself changed. I am more than the giver and the other is more than the taker. I have left my role as giver. The dynamic of the political invention or project which involves others will have to fit the needs of others who have joined with me as equals and comrades. Together we define our personal limits in practice and break down old categories, transforming what were the givens in the political and social landscape. We learn experientially what Buber has taught. "He who takes his stand in relation shares a reality, that is, in a being that neither belongs to him nor merely lies outside of him."[6]

While we may successfully define our limits within the group it can occur that what we attempt as a project may internally meet the requirements of personal relatedness, but it may also operate as an instrument for colonizing other groups. Suppose a group of students decides not to live in the dormitories because they are similar in their day-to-day operation to reformatories. They leave the dorm to set up a housing cooperative near the university. The relationships within the cooperative are based on sharing a certain amount of privacy and intercommunication, clustered sex, and the sense of solidarity which develops among those who share a system of values which they live with but do not have to fight for. The university administration may be very pleased with this development, especially if the university is in a black community. As a practical matter, most university administrations are frightened of the blacks in the city. They hope to find ways of building a Maginot line around the university against the intrusion of the blacks. Whatever their attitudes toward sex and drugs the university official would rather have cooperatives around the campus than the black poor. The cooperative students find themselves faced with the problem of building an internal island with purpose and intentionality, while being used as the instruments against other parts of the society and other projects which it should attempt to reach towards. Thus, the project is to be concerned with the continuous relationship between people in the project who live it and the external needs of participation with some groups and confrontation with others. The project of cooperative living cannot be separated from how it relates to the university and the blacks. If the cooperative makes a common cause with the blacks on terms which they fashion and accept, the project has initiated decolonizing action which attempts to show how to live nonexploitatively with those who might otherwise see the project as another intrusion or burden on their day-to-day being. To succeed, the project has to find an I-in-We larger than the project itself. It accomplishes this purpose by not shirking the political need to confront the colonizers. The colonizers are confronted in the context of a human relationship which accepts that humanness as beyond the issue of confrontation.

The Project in the Spaces of Pyramidal Politics

On the one hand, we participate with others in actions which may or may not have a common end. We discover each other as being to being in a common experience through our roles that may even be self-generated. Yet, when a project which we ourselves initiate takes on a shape which was not intended and is different from our purpose, we are thrown into personal dismay; then we want to terminate the project if it does not follow our original vision.

Take a project of a congressman and his assistant as another case where functional and role failure related to the failure of going beyond the initial-step question. In 1959, Congressman Kastenmeier and I organized a group of congressmen and scholars into a group called the Liberal Project. The efficient condition for this possibility was the election of a strong group of young Democratic congressmen who, by the standards of the fifties, were willing to examine American society critically and offer a different direction to the way the United States was going. It was a time when ideas as rhetoric would become important in the attempt of the Democrats to recapture national power.

Congressmen without seniority (almost anyone but committee chairmen) are like small-town businessmen. They are entrepreneurs who watch a political market, who believe and internalize the idea that they can affect very little except that of remaining in office. On the other hand, in 1959 we believed that since politics was entrepreneurial, there was space for a group to move. Their action was limited only by fears which I thought were illusory. I had high hopes—a new platform for the Democratic Party, indeed a very different Democratic Party which was not tied to the national security system. Although I did not realize it until some time later, it is now clear that national security was the backbone of liberal-corporate power. That is to say, the new industries which emerged after the second world war owed their status to the Democratic Party. I found that the spaces which I thought existed for the American entrepreneurial politician did not in fact exist. His legitimacy was defined by the colonial system. Consequently, the project itself was doomed to failure. The only positive result was a book, *The Liberal Papers,* edited by James Roosevelt, a sensible group of essays which were hooted on the right and which frightened the liberals (one congressman who participated in some of the discussions, when asked by the press if he had ever heard of *The Liberal Papers* said, "No, a thousand times, no"). The thrust of the book would have meant ending the cold war and hence those institutions which in fact were predicated on or used liberal talent. (President Kennedy, while I was on the White House staff, sent a letter to Congressman Roosevelt telling him that he could not accept the views of the book although he once held them. The historian in residence at the White House proceeded to draft letters to Republican congressmen telling them how foolish the book's views were.)

If the project is directly dependent on a part of the colonial structure for its success, and particularly if its purpose is to develop new values and alternative associational structures, the project is bound to fail. Thus, for example, a group of Quakers thought they would be successful in changing the values of the organizers of violence in the Department of Defense if they could convince that department to start its own program of non-violence. This did not make for a change in the Department of Defense as the violence colonizer. The Department of Defense merely added the program to its kit of violence.

In the case of the Liberal Project, there was no other reference point but the entrepreneurial and colonial relationship which gave each of the congressmen (and their assistants!) legitimacy. If one does not believe that his project is legitimate, and must find the objective correlative for it in the colonial structure, he is lost. The act of withholding or awarding legitimacy is the colonizer's method of supplanting authenticity of any project. For the average congressman, security is more important than authenticity.*

---

* Examples, unfortunately, of this point abound in work that we have undertaken. Obviously, an analysis of the project requires also an analysis of where funding is received. One of the most important aspects, therefore, is to analyze carefully the effect that the type of funding which is found has on the character or quality of the project. For example, will the funding dictate the character of the project? Once a question is resolved satisfactorily, other questions remain.

Several years ago, Leonard Rodberg, a Fellow at the Institute and professor of physics, and I began a Neighborhood Science Center. The basic idea was, in its initial stages, to assume that science could be integrated into people's lives, at least to the extent that public libraries had served that purpose. People would be

There were two other failures of great importance attached to the political/intellectual Liberal Project, which we should come back to. One of the failures, according to Waskow, was not relating its work to the people in the various congressional districts. Without such a base, there was no easy communication between what the scholars and congressmen were doing and groups which would have helped the congressman in his district. Without such help, the congressman in some cases was an easy target for criticism and attack. He was unable to find help within his own district, since no groups knew what the project was. Nationally, no help was possible, because the project itself was too much related to manipulation and keeping people apart rather than helping to build an associational relationship. This error was mine. I thought that the only way to continue the project was to keep people in the project away from each other, since if they talked with each other, it would lose its "radical" character, whereas if they did not talk to one another, the character remained

---

invited to undertake experiments with help from "librarian-teachers." The idea changed so that it became the establishment of a neighborhood science center for children in an integrated, poor neighborhood. In this framework, the idea worked. There was much individual attention given to young people between the ages of six and thirteen. There was control and participation of older people as well. It operated as a summer activity out of a basement store.

The following year, the project was tried again, this time without the actual participation of the initiators. Instead, we pursued the idea of the spin-off. That is, it was turned over to the local community. The local community itself, not having enough money to fund the project, received aid from the City Recreation Department. That department then staffed it. It did so in an area where there were few children, and where the basic notion was transformed from that of individual attention and actual involvement of young people in scientific experiments to one in which black children were brought into the makeshift laboratory thirty at a time to stand around for an hour or two. In this context, the project turned out to be a disaster. Simultaneously, however, the neighborhood science center was tried in a poor neighborhood adjacent to the University of Maryland, staffed with graduate students who worked day and night with young people from the poor neighborhood on a continuous basis. That project turned out to be successful. The funds in this case came from the graduate students themselves.

defined by actions a few of us might want to take. How to relate to another in consequential activity too often falters on one's own wish to be Authority. In all of us there is the residual feeling of Ayn Rand's architect hero.

Yet, as the character of the nation changed and the congressmen themselves became more secure in themselves and operated together as a group without feeling the need for an internal broker or a commander, the project began to succeed. Through the sixties, as a liberal and radical movement began to be built in the United States, the congressional group found that it was not isolated from the country if it intended to act. There was support for its activities. This group developed its own methods of relationships and rituals which were based on their independence against others and the sense that they sought and achieved a position of dignity in their combined actions. By 1969, they had begun to carry the rhetorical and the economic battle against the military and industrial complex to the people and the Congress in an effective way which for a period of time seemed to promise the rescue of liberalism from its fate as veil for the corporate and military thug.

This group is now referred to as the "Sisyphus Society" in Congress. They now operate as a group to bring together the toughest issues, raise questions and take stands which open spaces for others in the society to undertake their projects. From their role they have, in a unique way, built a solidarity of human relationship. As is usually the case where the human relationship remains and the authority to act is present, the commitment necessarily flows to continue the action. Where the authority to act does not flow from their role, people find their commitment and solidarity from the pain of where one is in the role to the potentiality of what can be developed humanly. Rosa Parks and Eldridge Cleaver are people who as colonized saw their respective roles as unbearably painful and acted from that pain to a different human potentiality. Most of us find that our situation of powerlessness forces us to act away from our function and role, since authority to act in human freedom is not defined in the role and function, but as a negation (and hence, potentiality!) to it.

The Social Invention and the Project

What is the relationship between social invention and the project? Both may have separate roots but overlapping branches. While the social invention assumes the intellectual nonparticipatory method for others to live within, and the project assumes that the inventor will live within the idea, both accept certain assumptions which border on social myths. One is that a change in the world can be made and can make a difference. And second, that the change which we devise and the myth which we employ to implement the scheme is the vehicle and the social structure to which we want reality to conform. Because our ideas outstrip how we live, we usually propose realities which others are urged to live in, but which the social inventor is privileged merely to write about.

One might almost think of the social invention as play. There are similarities. Huizinga has said that play is an activity which operates within certain limits of space, time and meaning, according to fixed rules.[7] Much of science can be included as a play activity. In the Introduction I asked why science fitted right into the hierarchic mold. Scientists, as Kuhn has pointed out, start with a puzzle or game attitude. They accept certain rules as given. Besides accepting certain rules as given and certain paradigmatic rules to prove, they also accept as given the social structure which will either help them or allow them to solve the puzzle or play the game. The scientist will tinker with a particular puzzle or game until he realizes that the rules he is using to solve the puzzle are no longer applicable. He concludes either from intuition or analysis—is there a difference?—that a major change in method and assumption is necessary to comprehend his *problem;* that which his puzzle is part of. It is at such a point that the liberal attitude of tinkering within a given framework gives way to a revolutionary one. Yet if one's attitude remains with a revolutionary stance, the rules which will be invented will be for a new game or puzzle. The perpetuation of the game method contradicts a reconstructive view which rejects the game/puzzle mentality, especially as it is translated into political practice.

Social inventions are not play activity. They are not defined too rigorously as in the case of a game with set and rigorously defined rules. Instead, the rules are open to constant modification. Yet, paradoxically, they are the ultimate game since it is not necessary to live *within* them by those who put the invention forward. Historically this was an important aspect of the meaning of game. In the pyramidal state games are played for the amusement of others. Consequently, they are played with great seriousness by the players who in a commercial and human sense find that they are on trial. As the entrepreneur pointed out in the movie *They Shoot Horses, Don't They?,* the audience does not care who wins or loses, that is the concern of the contestants. The audience is interested in the show.

But the question of the game is a digression. Imagine that the social invention was put forward with rigorous rules which governed the logic of action and doing, and with an understanding of the liberating emotions of the people involved if the invention were enacted. It is clear that the method of the social invention would not be able to guide action with the existential precision derived from the project. Nor would it have the same meaning to those who initiated the invention. The latter point is unnecessary to over-analyze. What starts as one person's invention becomes another person's project. Thus, in both cases we attempt to discover, through the means, purposes and events which the invention passes through, the definition of what the structure is and the final outcome of what the invention will be.

In this sense the social invention and project are to be analyzed in terms of their political and ethical purpose, their utility, their means and consequences and their reflection of the democratic principle of participation. I do not invent that for which I am not prepared to suffer the consequences. I am able to understand the question of project only in terms of subjective commitment to live with that which I create and to be its object. This becomes a standard of acting in the context of governing where one has received authority or shared authority wherein he is responsible for another. Would I like nuclear weapons dropped on me? Would I encourage pacification for me? Am I prepared to share this question with the objects of my action and then share the consequences?

I live by the subjective corollary to the Kantian imperative. Or, as children say, how would you like it if I did that to you? This question is one which cannot be answered by the reformer except in an abstract colonizing way. Take the case of Jeremy Bentham, the father of modern reform. His notions of the project are the paradigm of activities that justify the colonized relationship and accept the assumption of master and servant.

Jeremy Bentham's formulations of social inventions and social projects are the exact contradiction to the reconstructive, decolonizing idea of the project. Bentham attempted to channel one's energy to two directions which he did not view as being in conflict—the will for personal monetary profit, and the personal need to rationalize such profit as serving the public weal. The British Utilitarians in their work attempted to integrate the two goals, which were of course the nature of enlightened reform capitalism. Personal profit and public service, however, are not the basis of the new definition of either project or social invention. Just for that reason, the idea of profit and service to others does not signify a modern project which can be termed morally successful.

During one part of his life, Bentham designed a pentoptigon, which was a new kind of prison. His prison made it possible for the guards to see the inmates in the jail at all times. They were always to be watched, at every moment, and his building plans attempted to totalize the life of the prisoner so that there was no personal being for the prisoner outside of the guard's command. Bentham sponsored legislation which attempted to get the British government to set up such a prison and to pay him handsomely for the idea of the pentoptigon. He failed in getting the British Parliament to accept the idea. However, Bentham's method of action is critical. Was Bentham prepared to live as a prisoner in his pentoptigon design, or did he see himself only as a guard/reformer? Was he prepared to be the object of the criminal law, the project, and the social invention that he had created? If not, his suggestion is both irrelevant and dangerous. (We accept the doctor's nostrums because he is expert and because it is assumed that he would accept the same medicine if he were in a like human situation.) But this test is a minimum one. Because one is prepared to live as an object of his own project, we cannot a fortiori conclude that the project has worth for others. It is only the negative that is shown. If I am not prepared to live within the idea I put forth as a way of life, the likelihood that there is a basic failing as it relates to human feelings is great.*

---

*Over the last several years at the Institute for Policy Studies a project was developed by Kotler for inmates of San Quentin, which attempted to turn San Quentin into a four-year liberal arts college with the same quasi-freedoms and problems which a college has. While it may have been the case that those who de-

Or I may be repeating aspects of the old authoritarian mode. This we may refer to as the fountainhead complex.

Subjectivity and Social Knowledge

We all are aware of the complexity of human motivation, although this does not mean that there is a complexity to immediate feelings in a situation. Sartre's analysis of motivation and feelings as being sado-masochistic is open to profound question so long as it does not comprehend the pyramidal structure of authority as causing the basis of sado-masochistic behavior. Hence, that aspect of existential psychology which sees the world of human action and relationships as only within the framework of sado-masochistic behavior can only be accepted if what is being described is man in his colonized role within the pyramidal structure. Such a psychology does not describe relationships outside of roles and functions, or roles and functions which are derived through shared authority relationships. The purpose of the project and the reconstructive social invention is to *escape* the sado-masochistic structure of the colonized reality.

In the colonized society, my energies are utilized, as I have said, on what is expected of me. I am the slave to the other. As a colonized man, my needs are judged wrong and I come to believe in the judgment that they are wrong. I can only understand the hierarchic other, not the other being as coming to being. But once, through whatever means I am given or that I wrest time to daydream or do something beyond what is expected of me, I can begin to

---

signed this project were prepared to live as objects of it, the basic question was whether the redesign of the prison into a college would result in a reconstruction which changed human relationships from that of authority and force to one of persuasion and empathy. What is clear is that it was a social invention which could not make the situation worse for the inmates.

ascertain what it is I want. I can begin to distinguish and judge. I can now set limits and boundaries in concert with others. In this search, old truths are rediscovered, namely, that such ways of life as finding of personal space are best achieved in horizontal rather than vertical relationships. In democratic theory, society was to be held together on the basis of equality of membership and participation. One freely chose membership. Through such associations the qualities of empathy and dignity are developed, it was thought, which would help the people in a society accomplish two objectives: self-judgment through personal re-shaping, and the re-shaping of the image which others have of him. That is, of course, the central virtue of democracy. The democratic society was open to change, experimentation and discovery by individuals and groups. Authority was doubted and operational legitimacy passed from group to group. Its method reflected the style derived from science and technology which appeared to be contradictory to hierarchy, status, privilege and structures that represented feudal organization of society.

The task of social knowledge is to incorporate subjectivity into itself. Historically education has attempted to find ways of incorporating what was indirect and outside of an individual's experience so that he might understand and feel matters indirect to himself existentially. Subjective knowledge stems directly from the dissonance of the sense of pain in the situation—that is to say, from the Jeffersonian sense of "I feel, therefore I exist." The analysis, then, goes something like this. I feel. I am within a situation. I cannot really divide up what the situation looks like. I must be aware of every part of it. The sorts of knowledges which I require to understand what's going on are the sorts of knowledge which are not specialized. The sorts of things which I have to know to understand that situation have to emerge from a descriptive/prescriptive method.

Subjective knowledge leads to participation and, therefore, its own definition of freedom that is *not* predictable. This is the irony. We attempt to develop a total method of knowing which when applied yields freedom and, therefore, unpredictable results. Consequently, the purpose of the method is not to yield total knowledge for control, but subjective knowledge for freedom which is comprehended in practice.

If I am a scientist in a laboratory, the only way that I can really understand what is going on is through self-participating in experiment—self-performing an experiment on an object which I am aware of as interacting with me. It may be a natural phenomenon in the sense of rat or a monkey, or, indeed, it may be an atom. Whatever the case is, the I and it make up part of a totality. I am self-participating with the phenomenon and I am controlling the various parts of it. In the colonizing social sciences, the sorts of knowledges that we develop which should be participatory end up being exploitative. The problem of social knowledge in action is how to participate with others to bring a project into existence on the basis of a mode of action which includes self as subject. This can only be achieved through the project in which participation, empathy and experimentation are the primary aspects of acting. The individual comes to understand himself, not as somebody separate from the problem itself, disinterested or objective, but as part of the problem that he is attempting to resolve and part of the project that he is attempting to bring into reality. This mode of doing contemplates a religious basis of self and world knowledge which changes the person.

The work-study program of colleges such as Antioch, the building of intentional communities, and middle-class idealists living with the poor as organizers, are attempts by the young to change their consciousness in practice. Yet changes of life style or mere participation in an event are not sufficient unless the felt consequences to others, in the immediate, are comprehended. Where we have already given over ourselves as the colonized, our sense impression is deadened and our participation in the situation will merely yield a quality of meaninglessness and unreality to ourselves and to our fellow participants. Students who "tour" the poor without understanding their problem situation and who are reluctant to work on projects which they should be prepared to live within, merely reinforce abstract empiricism which has no referentiality to reconstructive change.

Participation in an action does not make for understanding of consequences, nor does it make for decolonization, unless there is pain or openness and willingness to free oneself of those colonized relationships which obscure the meaning of the experience and the event. Where events are screened through abstraction so that the meaning of the sense impression, and hence the experience, is confused, an existential knowledge—that is, one which changes the self and the problem—will fail. (What would it have meant had the pilot of the *Enola Gay* made a choice and decided with his crew that they wouldn't drop the atomic bomb?)

A project which attempts to go beyond colonization and which attempts to bring out reconstruction must be predicated on naivete, an attempt to see ourselves only as a part of what we create. A person comes to know himself by the chance to create himself, yet we must still prepare to see, to participate and to do naïvely and undogmatically; otherwise, our senses and actions will not escape the pre-existing authoritarian forms. Whatever doubts we may have about the method of sense impression and the project, it remains the fundamental way to break through the wall of abstraction and mediation in knowledge, and the hierarchic organization of society. Such a method is not without its risk, since education in this framework considers technique as secondary to empathy. Feeling precedes technique. The danger is that people may come to believe, as some already do, that good *feelings,* humanness, make technique unnecessary. The crucial action is to bring technique into feeling. How?

The fact that it is impossible to devise systems and experiments in which all apparent options are tried and carefully studied need not retard the acquisition of reconstructive social knowledge, because the method contemplates and starts with the clarity that the problems which one studies, whether or not he wants to think so, are his problems, that he is in them, they are part of his life situation, and that he is the object of its solution. This may be one way of controlling foolish knowledge, and at the same time of teaching us how class position impinges on the direction research and action takes. In its best sense, if the existential mode is adopted, the students and educators will begin to comprehend that certain knowledges are not worth knowing or pursuing because the consequences *in practice* are disastrous.

The development of a method for social knowledge will help in seeing the relationships and the common solutions to the questions which are at the heart of the colonized structures. It will help in the development of a method which will show that each of the systems of colonization are fundamentally the same and that the types of studies which are developed will point to common solutions for decolonizations. Although reconstruction is to have a rational base built from specific situations, the result which may emerge does not necessarily restrict the method to the particular area or social problem to be resolved. The specific result may vary but the method or critique will invariably stay the same. The requirement is that we show the relation of knowledge to the problem in the situation and then to the good which people obtain in the particular case. We are then able to judge the system and institution to see how it hurts, manipulates or destroys individual freedom, and encourages destructive group choices.

The analyst himself is to be governed by the fact of his being part of the problem under analysis. As Dewey has suggested, we can undertake criticism of "beliefs, institutions, customs, policies with respect to their bearing upon *the* good."[8] No doubt it is difficult to know a good or a good purpose, and it is especially difficult when we realize that man's situation leads to circumscribed situations by the choices which not only are made for him but by the choices he himself makes that set a pattern—a reality which he draws for himself. Even in freedom this will not change. But to know that is only to know that we must begin again to understand the concrete, the sense perception and basic feelings. When we begin from this base point we know what is not wanted. It is the way we begin to know what we do want.

As I have suggested, the method of the project is an inductive one. Its values are heuristic. Its requirement is the continuous analysis and reconstruction of one's own relation to his work and to the body politic. No method for social change or inquiry is *outside* of roots in the moment, and this method is no exception. The project method seeks its intellectual and political roots in risk-taking and the populist formulation of the student and protest movement. It views numerical calculation and quantification as a deceptive mode of analysis because it assumes a static description/prescription of human relationships. It deals with *becoming* rather than *being*. It doubts highly analytical techniques in which the frame of reference is wrong, or the assumptions are foolish. Consequently, it seeks intellectual action and rapport with those who act against the passive violence of a society which denies participation or well-being to people. It does not accept the principle of elitism on central matters. While there is an undeniable need for certain forms of calculation and statistics, this method doubts that the form of subject-into-object objectivity are aids in inventing new social structures. The reason is that the purpose of such structures is the opening of personal-relational space and anti-colonial relationships. If such relationships can be created, the openness necessary for meditation and self-controlled action results. But meditation is subjective. It is where I can learn *who* and *what* is the *other* who is like me, that is, outside of role and function. It is how I can see through the hierarchic other to reach the others. It is how I can learn what I feel. A praxis predicated on withdrawal helps me to know my need. When I am active in the world as one who is still colonized, I cannot begin to know, except through immediate pain, what I cannot abide.

In one sense the project is an attempt to recapture the original spirit of science and democracy which hoped to define authority as not based on blind acceptance and obedience. In another sense it may be related to wholly different modes of thought that are usually viewed as unfashionable. Within the history of thought there are ideas and subject matters and traditions which have much to teach us and relate. The existential pragmatist tradition may not be so far from some elements of gnosticism. The gnostic felt alien in the world that he was in. He was encompassed on all sides by limitations placed on him from time, body and matter and of the even tighter structures of temptation. His situation, according to the gnostic Valentinian Theodotus and his modern day interpreter Henri-Charles Puech, is unacceptable: "Who are we? What has become of us? Where are we? Whither have we been cast down? Whither are we going? What is our birth? What is our rebirth?"[9]

Such questions are constantly asked and have been used in the political sphere to avoid the situation which is created for man through the authority structures which appear and are accepted. Where man has a future he asks those questions as if they have no political meaning. Where there is doubt as to whether he has a future, such questions become immediate and practical in the interlocking realm of religion, politics and epistemology. They are religious because they deal with man as the terrorized self unto death and toward Being. They are political because they teach us what structures of our existence need changing to make man able to stop and question what he has done as a result of his acceptance of a situation in which the divine spark is smothered or "allowed" to lie dormant within himself. The gnostics understood the importance of awakening that spark which is allowed to sleep. The questions are epistemological because they deal with attempting to develop a method of self knowledge, conscience and science as the primary method of knowledge and of things to be known.

Thus, the projects and social inventions will be concerned with fundamental questions, although the actions undertaken in practice will appear simple and naive. They will question the bases of the colonized society, the emergence of ideas in practice which allow no escape for the individual, or the colonizing assumption that suffering is undertaken in the name of a higher goal. In practice, this will mean asking why and how politically one gets to offer up another's life. In its most gross terms, it may ask by what magic and authority does a general offer up his soldiers to the slaughter. It may mean what hubris was there in Abraham to think that he could offer up another in sacrifice to God? By comprehending how the chooser obliterates the political and life-space of the one for whom he chooses, we will develop a wholly different set of facts, knowledges and actions than we would otherwise expect when we approach the question of a new politics and social science.

If we begin with the operative principle of humanizing (subjectivizing) knowledge, we will find that certain judgments of an *obvious* nature can be made. As Wolfgang Köhler has said, if obvious judgments are denied, man is lost.[10] We begin to see the creation of a series of facts and values which were mistaken because they objectified people. For example, in our best universities and institutes the nuclear and non-nuclear war system was rationalized and justified as a tool of American imperialism so that the type of facts and factors developed made the problems of life greater, rather than more soluble. Institutional structures are then strengthened and predicated on the "facts" and needs of such an interchange. What is eliminated in this search for facts and factors as a rationalizing tool for the violence colony is the central human issue: man's destruction. Although some scientists might think otherwise, such a destruction is more than the rearrangement of matter in new ways.

Knowledge for the Project and Social Invention

The project and social invention as social knowledge are the important *sine qua non* for creating a reconstructed knowledge, and hence a reconstructed society. The approach for such a method asserts the gestalt for man in his situation which can only be described by a knowledge which itself is gestalt in approach. It does not accept, a priori, disciplines, subspecialties or specializations except as objects of study, since such disciplines in their original motive and continuous operation are experienced as and reflect administrative and political convenience among competing groups within a university and corporate structure. Contrary to some aspects of natural science, when we analyze a social situation by dividing it into constituent parts (making related parts unrelated by our method), we lose the meaning of the person or the situation under analysis. We do not understand man separate from his situation or knowledge when it is divided among specialized lines.

In the United States, we are hard put to recognize the continuous wholeness of either knowledge or man. In the university, specialization seems to have triumphed over general education. As a social fact, general education is taught in such a way as to prove its lack of seriousness and thus to enforce the seriousness of specialization. Marxist thought, which attempted to develop understanding of the problems of society and man outside of non-specialized lines, has not succeeded in achieving that end. The Marxist failure in this regard does not mean that a descriptive/prescriptive method of thought and action is unnecessary. If a critical and creative method is not developed, we are left with the psychological and political quest for it in a colonized society. Such a need is spuriously fulfilled by the mandarins who invent a rhetoric and a method which gives the appearance of relatedness. The new epistemology of the vertical structure (some forms of systems analysis and quantification) is predicated on thinking of people in terms of function within the hierarchic social organization, while simultaneously it will create an unexamined political rhetoric of stereotype such as we use when we think of the Vietcong, Nazism, Capitalism, or Communism. To overcome the problem of abstracted and functional knowledge—"knowledge" which is the linguistic and psychological manner of hiding our colonized relationships—we need to create a social knowledge of action which begins from a far different point. We will find that social knowledge which is predicated on behavior patterns that are manipulated by the colonizer, is antithetical to the meaning of a public philosophy predicated on freedom.

The ally of the colonizer is the rhetoric of objectivity

which steers us away from trusting the subjective. That is, this rhetoric attempts to deny our immediate feelings, sense impressions and concrete experiences which present to us our situation as *a* totality, even though it may not be *the* totality of the situation. The historical roots for a descriptive-prescriptive method are present. It builds on the development of our senses to comprehend a totality, to add to our understanding of the totality, and to show that our actions in the form of projects lead us to a situation of social reconstruction.

The experimental method within moral boundaries is the most fruitful way in our century of finding out what the choices of social and political organization are that we want to live within. During the seventeenth century, man looked for the answer to political organization by following the method of Galileo which eschewed sense impressions and appearances in favor of the underpinning of natural phenomena found in the triangles and rectangles of geometry and mathematics. But this method assumed that man is further along in his political development than he really is. Before we can be deductive, we are bound to be inductive, especially as the events which come through the colonized reality toss and impinge upon us. The development of a set of projects and new facts which we care to live within will show us how we can understand and control ourselves. Such projecting of the future into the present may set the limits of what cannot be permitted so that the inquiry may be continued.[11] The development of such projects and facts, *which take root in ourselves,* will necessitate the conscious surrendering of power beyond limits which, if attained, would end human freedom.

In our schools and other institutions that would educate, young people would learn technology and non-literary activities for the purpose of judging their worth and seeing their interacting effect between themselves (people) and other institutions and other extensions of man's being. For example, high school students might undertake the following curricular study: airplanes, telephones, movies, missiles, television, radio, phonographs and cars. They would be expected to learn how these things are built, show their interacting effect on people, the types of social institutions which are built from them and the kind that might emerge in a non-hierarchic, associative community. They would also be expected to judge the meaning and effect of the interaction of these various "extensions" of man's being to see how many people really participated in them and how in the end many only suffered from their existence. By this sort of preparation, we might begin to sift out and transform those extensions which are destroying the basis of human relationships and social groups. Or we may find ways of setting the terms of integrating them more successfully in our lives.

As I have suggested, in the hierarchic other there is loss of self as *self* as a result of man's extensions and inventions. In the pursuit of knowledge in a decolonized system, we can begin to retrace the extensions of people and decide which contradict his very being and potentiality with other people. In other words, insight and experiment will have to go on about the obvious and the technologically accepted.

If a method is developed which helps us to limit ourselves, we can avoid a situation in which we are mired in romanticism and action qua action leading to exoticism. Invariably, such action resolves itself into a new form of totalitarianism and hero worship. Sartre's formulation that a man's action changes the world is a truism, but the paramount question—in what way and for how long—remains unanswered where the action is merely action, without purpose.*

---

*The fact of the failure of education and the success of canned dreams and violence is found in our young. There is an underside to the present revolt of the

Until new patterns are developed through other sorts of experience than we presently have, we are unable to know with very much precision how to prescribe or predict. We can only experiment with new patterns. But experimentation has very specific meanings. It means that the projects undertaken do not buttress what is obviously foolish. Methods and projects come from practice and an image of the situation which a person finds himself engaged in. It is not an elite activity but a popular activity. It is not a liberal mediation or reformist trick both of which now reinforce the objectifying method. Where the intention is to decolonize and to contradict the fundamentals of the particular colony, we can even afford the trial and error of practice. If, as Dewey has pointed out, nation-states ended the war system, they could then experiment with a variety of legal and social inventions for the solution of problems. Where they continue to operate in the wrong frame of reference, there is little room for intelligence, flexibility and experimentation. In the right frame of reference, the perception of an individual or group may be wrong, and what they do may be wrong. Yet, one transforming change has occurred. They become aware of what they are doing.

This consciousness becomes a primary mode of handling problems according to the basic experience which the group feels. A new measure of authenticity is felt. Such authenticity is found in the scientific method and in subjectivity. Barrett has pointed out that we can begin to reject ideas on the basis of understanding of the obvious and the necessary.[12] Thus, when we construct a method

young. They are taken over by drugs, hippiness, and cosmetic forms of revolt which the colonized society then packages back to the young at a profit. Exoticism is then seen in the Nazi decorations, black leather sado-masochistic thrust of literature that surrounds such groups. Whether the question is theological or political, it must be practical; how can action be made integral to the good consequence? It is unfortunate that very little knowledge developed at the universities now helps in that direction.

for social knowledge, it is hard to avoid looking to the natural sciences as a way of bringing about change to resolve problems. John Dewey said that "policies and proposals for social action are to be treated as working hypotheses, not as a program to be rigidly adhered to and executed. They will be experimental in the sense that they will be entertained, subject to constant and well-equipped observation of the consequences they entail when acted upon and subject to ready and flexible revision in the light of observable consequences."[13] Even if we accept the truth of that statement, we are still left questioning how this can be accomplished so that the experimenter or innovator is not the new exploiter in his projects and inventions.

One way is that the experimenter embraces democratic roots. The educated class again needs to realize that "the man who wears the shoe knows best that it pinches," even if the expert shoemaker is the best judge of how the trouble is to be remedied. Dewey's idea is to be broadened to include the fact that some people don't want to wear shoes nor should they have to if they don't want to. Thus, we are bound to accept the idea that "the world has suffered more from leaders and authorities than from the masses."[14] This question can now only be answered by attempting to support and fashion projects and structures which emerge from four themes: (a) that the political judgment of the wretched about their condition is better either than an elite which decides or causes the condition of the wretched; (b) that the educated class, to comprehend its own position, must understand how and when it stands as colonized and colonizer; (c) that the method for decolonization is understood as involving elements of confrontation and reconstruction which will be undertaken in all classes and institutions of the society; and (d) that by the nature of the colonizer-colonized relationship and the authority principle, there are parallels in all vertical institutions in whatever their apparent functions, be they school, army, factory or institutional dream manipulation, which will yield to confrontation-reconstruction and rational-reconstruction, the processes of the project.

Confrontation-reconstruction and rational-reconstruction lead to new facts and result in the development of a new fact-value social system. Consequently, these actions will lead to new knowledges that will help create new forms. Just as the development of a massive civil defense system would result in a whole new knowledge of social control over people, of changes in the ecological environment as a result of nuclear attack, of new industries and skills involved in burrowing underground, so it is the case that decolonization in the attempt to build a non-hierarchic horizontal structure of society will result in a new series of facts and values.

10

*The Cooperative
Other and
Reconstructing*

If an individual breaks out of the hierarchic other and does not fall into the trap of self-serving egoism, the fountainhead complex, he is likely to begin seeing self and other outside of hierarchy and in associative relation to each other. At this point he attempts two activities that are political and immediate. He may undertake to destroy the idea of characterization of others, and he may attempt to free others by allowing them to choose authentically for themselves outside of the system of characterization which they accepted and followed in their relationships with other people. George Herbert Mead believed that such relationships occurred naturally and, of course, he saw this need and relationship as creating an interdependency between self and other. However, he did not take into account the pyramidal structure of society, thus continuing the myth of equals as the way the self's character was formed from others. Mead refers to the interdependence of self and other as the generalized other.[1]

Mead argues that if the human individual is to feel whole, he must undertake to adopt the various aspects or phases of the common social activity and internalize them. He believed in the "internal" voice of socially limited attitudes, language and logic that one could not escape. The broad activities of any given social whole must therefore be experienced within the life of an individual. We may stipulate that Mead's notion is correct. Yet the question remains, "How are those activities internalized? Are they presented as a given to the individual?" Mead avoided this question. If the individual is not presented with a situation and hence, his personality, the beside himself, what are alternatives to the hierarchic other and how do they form?

For the moment I would ask the reader to waive my rejection of the game mentality, because of its pernicious aspects, in order to consider an example. This example would reflect the *best* sense of the operation of the generalized other. Yet it has little relevance once we attempt to translate this example beyond the confines of the playing court. It is then that the individual may begin to feel the fullest development of self. Suppose I am a member of a basketball team. The team organizes the experience of each of its members. How other teams played the game in the past affects the team I am on and the way I play the game. A series of accepted rules exist that I play within. In effect, there are traditions and ways of acting which I accept when I play ball. I accept my fellow players as having had a valid set of experiences, which I accept from their performance and their being on the team. When I join the group, I help to organize that experience cooperatively for myself and others. I have space to run, I throw at the basket, and I score points. I can be infinitely creative and fulfilling. In this context leadership has a very special meaning. In 1969, the most valuable basketball award was given to a player who, as one of his teammates said, gave the "kind of leadership that allowed each of the players the possibility of doing our own thing."

> . . . only insofar as he takes the attitudes of the organized social group to which he belongs toward the organized, cooperative social activity, or set of activities in which that group as such is engaged, does he develop a complete self or possess the sort of complete self he has developed.[2]

Mead sees two general stages in the full development of the self. On the one side is the individual's development on the basis of particular attitudes of other individuals toward himself and toward one another in those actions in which he participates with others. In the second stage, which he refers to as full development, the self is constituted not only by organizing particular individual attitudes, but also "by an organization of the social attitude of the generalized other or the social group as a whole to which he belongs. These social or groups attitudes are brought within the individual's field of direct experience and are included as elements in the structure or constitution of his self in the same way that the attitudes of particular other individuals are; and the individual arrives at them or succeeds in taking them, by means of further organizing and then generalizing the attitudes of particular other individuals in terms of their organized social bearings and implications."[3] The self, therefore, reaches its stage of maturity when it organizes its individual attitudes with others into a social or group attitude which is solid enough to act from and provisional enough to change from. There is a cooperative dialectic between the individual and the social group (as he organizes the attitudes of the group and as he, in his own thinking and actions comes to reflect the attitudes of the group). What is important to Mead's view is that an individual does not precede the social group—he is a part of it from the moment of birth.

Furthermore, it is assumed that his attitudes build on what has existed and that the individual comes to add to the attitudes that do exist. Mead's society builds from the assumption of cooperation and equality. The problem with Mead's view is that it *assumed* an egalitarian or democratic society which did not exist except as ideology. Mead did not seem to see the society as organized in a pyramidal structure in which the attitudes that are held mirror elite groups which use others to enhance their own ability to act freely. And finally, not even the minor elite groups would see themselves as becoming roles without human attributes.

As Anatol Rapoport has said despairingly, "The United States is ruled not by human beings but by a vast program of decision rules built into the nervous system of a super-organism that I have called the war-waging state. To be sure, the cells of this organism are human beings; but in their roles as the cells of the super-organism they do not behave as normal human beings are expected to behave in normal human contexts. In those roles they are insulated (often physically) from normal human contacts. Messages about human needs, human aspirations, human suffering, human despair, addressed to the cells of the war-waging state cannot change its behavior because they cannot change its decision rules."[4]

The generalized other of Mead becomes a program of abstracted and then internalized messages of the kind which one receives from his radio and television transmitter. One's task, what he is commanded to do, is little different from what he is told about the world through the media. But what then is the means by which there is a way of finding the cooperating or cooperative other which stems from feelings and experiences which are immediate, sensate and such as to allow the return to humanness? The cooperative other is developed through challenging and changing existing authority relationships and developing new ones through the project. If such challenges do not occur, the psychology developed in the body politic remains pyramidal and role dominating, since individuals learn who they are and what they are through the dynamic operation of the hierarchic other.

Thus, while the cooperative other assumes the internalization of society's values and the socialization of the individual to those values through dialectical and cooperative relationships, the hierarchic other does *not* assume socialization. It rather assumes the characterization of individuals who may or may not accept the attitudes of the society but who, *as a group,* are manipulated through the hierarchic other. They are characterized into situations created through anti-human systems.

Space and the Choices in Action

In a rhetorically democratic, or in fact democratic society, the individual breathes in the possibility of space—the sense of movement by self through his own actions. Even beyond the democratic society giving sustenance to this sense of space, the individual *needs* space as a life function. This need is the individual psychological contradiction to the hierarchic other (and is the reason why the generalized other has a chance of coming into being). In highly socially mobile societies, becoming the colonizer is the way that individual needs for space are satisfied. (But they fail because being a colonizer is no fun either—as Camus pointed out in Caligula and Fitzgerald showed in Gatsby.) The beside himself is the body politic's receptacle for channeling the internal subjective need for space into the pyramidal forms. Yet, the self's need for space is the contradiction to the hierarchic other, and the hope for the cooperative other as the basic psychological characteristic of this society. Space is not external to the person nor is it a void. The need for and the image of space is carried by a person through situations which, by plan or accident, he may create or which he would wish to define differently than they are within his physical and biological limits. In its political and social meaning, space is derived from this idea of sense perception and participation. In politics, however, such consciousness is achieved only through participation either in a project which one has helped choose or in a situation of confrontation. In those cases, the fact of psychological space (the spatial organization of thought and memory as well as desires and needs) and the space at hand, outside of man himself but within his physical reach, is brought together through the project, which must include the subjective sense of the individual's view of himself.

Some argue that no matter how many projects are undertaken, how many confrontations a man participates in, there is no way to escape the mythical or collective past, and so there is no physical space outside of self which is not determined or self-defeating, and no project which liberates from the hierarchic other. There is merely the immobilism of man's limitation through this innate weakness, vulnerability, and fear of risking what he has or might have. This view assumes that freedom can be achieved only within man's mind, since that is where freedom is defined. (Man can think what he likes. Activity imprisons. There is infinite time and space in man's mind.) But this is a metaphysical and essential view which allows what is externally, to be. It assumes that there is no *beside himself* which is the crucial psychological vessel for the operation of colonization. It is the objective view of the world in a hierarchic structure. When I see myself as part of the world, I see myself as objective and external. My actions and existence are characterized by others. I am assigned place or path. Thus, I am easily seduced into acting or feeling differently from the image which I have of myself. The external characterization of myself is that I have neither being nor space in the world except through the pyramidal structure. When it applies to the present, objectivity becomes a statement of another's view which denies me the right to act outside of characterization by others, or the hierarchic other. The profile and record of me are the objectification of me. It is the hierarchic other's way of controlling my actions.

In the mind, the existence of space to wander is infinite, playful and purposive, but potentially captured by those who understand that the mind's space for abstraction and purposiveness can be controlled by the hierarchic other. Where there is personal realization (by whatever means) that such space can be related to practice, social inventions and projects result. External space is then filled with political action which can lead to confrontation and community—assuming that the action begins from the impulse of self with other—otherwise, traditional colonized actions result.

In this regard, we may note three modes of action which define a person's place and association with a political stance: standing off, standing on, and standing with. More precisely stated, these modes define what a person's subjective and objective position is in relation to the colonizer and colonized once he is able to make choices—a condition which is made possible through economic well-being if he is a member of the middle class. One of these modes redefines the authority principle away from pyramidalism.

Imagine a lecture hall. A professor stands on the stage and talks about ethics and stands off from others as a result of the physical nature of the room and the expectation of being separated from others. Someone yells, "Get off the stage and come *down* with us." A colonizing role has ended and his humanness has been reached. The students are attempting to develop a cooperating other outside of role. When a group of students at Howard University jumps on stage during a Founder's Day ceremony in which honorary doctorates are given and the students make demands for changing the university while some pour water from the President's pitcher into his glass *for themselves,* "standing off" as a viable authority principle has ended. Such actions speak to virtually everyone's colonized condition, in which the students are seeking political space which will re-organize their experience and therefore themselves.

Take the meaning of "standing off"—to "stand off" from others occurs because of fear of involvement or of the personal penalty which may result from involving oneself with others. It also is the natural outgrowth of a petty bourgeois competitive view in which standing off protects one from contamination from another. An arbitrary set of standards are put into motion. For example, a country club or a private school is built with standards which have the purpose of keeping others out. Its requirements, which protect one individual from another and one group from another, invariably declare our distance from our fellows and reinforce the mode used for divisions based on class, race, education or income. "Standing off" is primarily the way which assures privatism at the expense of community. Immobilism is its political counterpart.

"Standing on" may be viewed as behavior in a competitive society in which an individual or group ends up using and manipulating another. Imagine the case of the missionary whose power in the church is built on the souls he has saved and the crosses he has given out among the natives in religious social centers. Or imagine the liberal reformist mediation in which economic aid is given to another. In exchange, that aid builds the power of the giver and the beneficiary can only deal or trade with the giver.

The usual economic relationships between the classes can of course be described in exploitative terms. In a society transforming itself from one of scarcity to one of affluence, the political, economic and social power of whole groups within the middle classes emerge from the accepted perception that there are groups of people who may be viewed objectively as problems. While the standing off relationships apply here—that is to say, psychiatrists do not socialize with mental patients (unless economically they are members of the upper classes)—the standing on relationship is more relevant. The existence, for example, of the social work profession is predicated upon the poor as our problem. Their income and status specifically depend on "helping the problem" or giving the appearance of so doing. We may structurally translate this phenomenon by saying that standing on is the case of personal and class imperialism in which a group begins by doing for another but in fact remains on top of the other. Reformism and revolution are the political playing out of the standing on relationship.

"Standing with" starts from the assumption of self in relation to. We may assume that a person who stands with another begins by knowing who he is and being prepared to open himself enough to relate to the humanity of another. He is prepared to take the chance of being penalized for standing with another. It does not necessarily mean that this person is a martyr who stands in for another. That is to say, he does not efface another by standing in for him. Instead, he is prepared to accept the penalties of asserting that he is part of the "problem." For example, if an individual is exempted from danger of the draft because he is over-aged, but that individual identifies with the young people who are part of the nation's "draft problem," he has chosen clearly a value system that asserts standing with. He does not assert by his action either a mediation between groups, a separating himself from other groups or a standing on top of them for personal advantage. Standing with, which may be the political prerequisite for me in relating to the project of another, means that I have undertaken to accept the other's humanity and the need for me to join with him in recognizing that humanity. In this way, the possibility of the psychology of a cooperative other in sharing and association is formed and reconstructions can then begin.

11

Confronting
and Persuading
for Reconstruction

The reasonable people's failure is obvious. With
the best intentions and a naive lack of realism,
they think that with a little reason they can bend
back into position the framework that has got out
of joint. In their lack of vision they want to do justice to all sides, and so the conflicting forces wear
them down with nothing achieved. Disappointed
by the world's unreasonableness, they step aside
in resignation or collapse before the stronger
party.

—Dietrich Bonhoeffer[1]

Confrontation-Reconstruction

As I have suggested, the methods of thought and practice
which create new fact and value situations are confrontation-reconstruction and rational reconstruction. Each
method attempts to pose in a stark way the values and
directions which one group in the society wants the body
politic to take. Both are active methods and attempt phe-
nomenologically to clarify the differences in practice so
that even the colonizer will renounce his role because of
the starkness in which the values are presented to him.
Both methods are based on reaching that aspect of the
individual which is not hidden by the *beside himself.*

In the spring of 1969 an example of confrontation-reconstruction occurred in California. I refer to the People's

Park incident, where the University of California razed an uninspired student cooperative and allowed it to become a swampy parking lot for the breeding of mosquitos. The university's long-term plans for the area were not palatable either. It intended to put up new dormitories which the students viewed as unwanted prisons. The students and street people applied—without knowing it—common and American Indian law principles: land was not to be destroyed or despoiled. It is for the care, use and benefit of people and nature itself. Land is not to be used in such a way as to become a public nuisance.

The people, according to Art Goldberg, undertook to change the swamp. They "laid sod, planted trees and flowers, built a sandbox and swings." This was viewed by the university as an attack on *its* property. It did not matter to the state or the university to what use the land was being put since the university had purchased the park site for 1.3 million dollars. It could not allow "unauthorized" persons to use the land. Out of embarrassment and as a tactic to stop the young people from planting flowers, dancing, digging and having open sex relations in the park, Chancellor Heyns said that he intended forthwith to turn the park into a soccer field. He defended his decision with National Guard troops and local and state police. Army helicopters were used, 2000 National Guard troops held sway at the University of California through the urging and acquiescence of Ronald Reagan and Charles Hitch, who had done similar planning for riot control and brushfire warfare for the Department of Defense.

The result, horrendous and painful in the process, was that the police fired on demonstrators and several young unarmed people, who were either seriously hurt or killed. Tear gas flowed from guns and helicopters played the historic role in Berkeley which they played in Vietnam. What is so shocking about the event is that there was not enough life in the University to allow for reconstruction: that the knowledge which is developed at the university did not give vent to humanistic values which would have allowed for a peaceful reconstruction. It was not knowledge which would have led the Oxonian Hitch, to see the university as the instrument of *humanistic* values. But two important long-term effects emerged.

First, it became clear that people could work together whose life styles were quite different because they understood the obvious: that a swamp or a soccer field or a dormitory is not equal to a park which gives space to people and nature. Students, hippies, ex-students, the upper-middle and working-class people in the area came together to defend a life activity against a situation in which a mammoth institution was using the lot for cars and mosquito-breeding swamps. Secondly, the bravery of these seemingly disparate groups who embraced their humanity had the political effect of withdrawing legitimacy from the colonizing apparatus, the State and the University which depend on the support and acquiescence of people because they maintain some sort of moral and legal cloak.

Each situation such as People's Park delegitimatizes the established structure when it refuses to accede to the obvious and the necessary. And just as important in such situations the people who build and challenge by what they build are practicing the kind of liberation which should be allowed, in real places, in real time, with friends and associates.

There is a further effect that such events as People's Park have on administrators. Those who occupy the colonizing role become shaky in their own identity because of what they are aked to carry out. A dissonance operates between their colonizing role and what they think of themselves as human beings. Over the last several years various college presidents and university deans have left their positions of power. The usual explanations which are given relate to being caught in the cross-fire between students, faculty and trustees. The other explanations usually revolve around the power of the SDS. One wonders. Those who have left see that the university has failed and that their role as colonizer is wrong and *humanly* impossible for them to fulfill. The statements of Buell Gallagher of the City University of New York and James Perkins of Cornell suggest that they saw themselves as men who were better than the situation which their role created for them.

Confrontation-reconstruction can lead to forms of violence. During the People's Park struggle the violence was in the form of the use of sanctioned power by the state which saw its various forms of authority attacked by "unauthorized persons." Rock-throwing did occur after the National Guard and police moved in against the "unauthorized people." But it was as nothing compared to the activities of the authorized and officialized who saw themselves defending the entire colonial structure of American life. The state forms of violence are totally delegitimized by the State itself in such situations because that which is defended cannot be believed by its agents, whether police or presidents. The State legitimacy is lost. Yet the fact that legitimacy is lost by the State does not change its violence power unless those doing its bidding no longer see *themselves* as legitimate. By what it is they are required to do they come to see themselves as outlaws. Those who confront them, by the way they confront, light the spark which destroys the oppressors' colonized being.

In the Mississippi Delta there is a place called Tribbitt where the cotton grows. As a result of a cotton subsidy, a program in which the federal government now pays the white plantation owners not to grow cotton, the black farmers who originally came to the Delta because it was "an opportunity," or remained because their grandparents were slaves in the Delta, find themselves kicked off the land and with no jobs. What are they to do? What do they do? At first, of course, they do nothing. They seem to have as their choice the right to wander. They can travel up and down the Delta as they did in the past, "adjusting to economic realities and to automation." They can continue isolated, abused, nomadic and suffering. But even this course is open to them only if it appears that the situation in which they exist can continue; that is, where they believe that there is a possibility of plantation work. It is the tenant farmer who is expected to adjust if the plantation owner determines that he can make more money by changing the tools of production or what is produced. If there is a national reformist mood, the tenant farmer may be confronted with a social mediation that is advanced by a liberal bureaucracy within the government, church, foundation or partnership of these groupings. In fact, mediation may be nothing more than a modernized version of the plantation system. Yet the rhetoric which describes and announces the mediation, plus the activity of these groups, which appears to be created to solve "the problem" assuages those elements of the middle class who feel guilty about their economic well-being and the wretched condition of others. The middle class is satisfied if a government program is advanced for a "disadvantaged" group which will help that group prepare itself for adjustment to changing conditions.* There may be a manpower

---

* The ideas advanced by the liberals invariably fail in their own terms. The monies available for such mediations are enough only to irritate, not to help people to adjust. For example, turning on the fire hydrants in the summer and making available more summer jobs which disappear on Labor Day when the school colony takes over at the end of the summer vacation. Or undertaking a national air conditioning program which will keep poor people off the street during the summer when riots (presumably because of poor housing and heat) occur; but then starting only a model program or paying only for the unit and not the cost of operation.

retraining program to train people for jobs that will disappear in a few years because of the pressure of technology and profit on the local plantation owner. This program was tried in the Delta where tractor drivers were trained several years ago, although now none are needed or wanted. As in the summer programs set up to keep young slum children busy and off the streets, the primary purpose of manpower training is to keep people occupied. If the manpower training program is staged carefully, the tenant farmer will accept himself as "manpower" to be treated objectively — as an object. The manpower training program is quickly accepted by the tenant farmer, since he is confronted by the whip of necessity. What should be noted of course is that the manpower training programs have been failures even in reformist terms. In ten years, only 904,800 have been trained.* The information-minded middle classes are content because something is being done and their conscience is assuaged. Yet, why does the tenant farmer so quickly accept this largesse?

It is understandable. The tenant farmer is at the butt end of society. Any show of interest in him by the government will be enough to seduce him. It is not difficult to achieve this end by a clever administrator, who utilizes the American genius of packaging marginality. The ingenuity of American staging, packaging or mediation through the Dream, Channeling and Plantation Colonies results in the acceptance and internalization of someone else's interests, or of some other class's or group's interests as his, or their own. Such internalization of the others' interest and values is a fundament of our society — from the hat-check girl who lies and says that the money dropped into her cup is hers rather than, as is generally the case, the owner's, to the car engineer who destroys his

*This figure is from the Office of Manpower Management Data System, Washington, D.C., and represents completions in the Manpower Development and Training Act through March, 1970.

sense of craftsmanship by saying the cars he designs are safe when he knows they are not.

Whatever the initial intent of such programs, the reformist hopes that his ideas will serve as the synthetic mediation between conflicting groups. In this case, the mediation is between the plantation owner class and the tenant farmer class. But there can be no mediation between a system which assumes inequality-in and inequality-toward and another which assumes equality-in and equality-toward. Synthetic mediation as a political and philosophical method is relevant only where there is an acceptance on both sides of a new value structure predicated on the colonizer's giving up power and living in the system of equality-in and toward, and the colonized giving up his sense of powerlessness and profile of self as colonized. If such changes do not occur through the method of synthetic mediation, the liberal reformists end up doing the bidding of the plantation class, since the ability to make deals remains with those who have real economic power. Too often, men of good will, unaware of their own habits of mind and action, introduce compromise as a solution where its only result is that of consigning the claimant to his former position or to a new one which the status quo system, now updated, *chooses* for him. The costume changes but nothing else. The liberal reformists accept the plantation class's assumption of manipulation and "responsibility" for the tenant class. Such a conception is an easy compatibility with the liberal ideology. Hence, as one observes the dynamics of the relationship between the plantation colonizer and liberal reformist, we find that both are agreed in their habit of mind. The tenant farmers are manpower who are objects of the goals of another class. They are neither men nor citizens. The liberal reformists assume and create in reality the fact of inequality for a new generation.

When it is finally articulated, the disagreement between the plantation owner and the liberal reformist is in the question of who gets to run the colony. Even if the liberal mediators are able to try their compromise of mediation and characterization, they are bound to repeat the previous hierarchic structure because no new political structures come into being except administrative ones which begin from the assumption of treating the colonized as objects. The tragedy of present-day liberalism is that it does not know how to apply the concept of freedom and self-responsibility to those who have been colonized. It has nothing to say on this question except to expand administrative structures and create more meaningless jobs. Ironically, revolutionaries invariably find themselves in the position of the reformers, since they also build pyramidal social structures to bring about massive change or use the very structures built by those whom they replace.

In the Delta, once the land is played out and the web of national and local law makes it impossible to adjust because the older class of plantation owners does not see the liberal mediationists as doing their bidding but replacing them on top of the pyramid, the tenant farmer is forced and disciplined by the whip of necessity. For him there is no program of mediation. Open to him is one of three courses: He can die. I mean that in the most literal and physical sense. Secondly, he is "free" to leave the Delta and go on the welfare rolls of the great Northern cities where he becomes the object of the liberal industrial welfare system. In this case, if the tenant farmer accepts this course he becomes part of a spiritual and psychological death. Third, he can force a full-scale personal onslaught and reconstruction of the system which colonizes him.

Once he places himself against the plantation system

where he is born, and says "There are other ways and other values," his very existence now depends on successful opposition. He has created through his opposition a political and geographic space for himself. In the initial stages, he can maintain his space only through continued opposition. His new being is not dependent on the plantation owner, nor is he the owner's creature. He is no longer characterized by the plantation owner. The tenant farmer comes to the idea of an onslaught against the plantation owner through the emergence of a group of leaders from his midst. More likely, in the present generation it seems to occur because the young—those who do not or cannot exist in other parts of the colonized society—undertake to initiate the old and the isolated into a different mode. These are the new teachers. The catalytic effect of the young, plus the solidarity of the group, or the commitment even of only one man, is dependent on the task of confrontation. For as I have suggested, the meaning of decolonization and reconstruction is achieved through the assertion of the will to act in ways that are not set by others. Revolution may have that appearance, but its method in practice totalizes the relationship between the plantation owner and farmer. The tenant farmer acts in revolt against the owner. But such revolt may end only in vengeance. The tenant farmer may shoot the plantation owner, but he will be shot as well.

Reconstruction starts from the assumption that democratic hopes and aspirations are not theoretical expressions of liberty and equality. In political reconstruction, as Dewey has pointed out, "every existence deserving the name of existence has something irreplaceable about it," in which "what is specific and unique can be exhibited and become forceful or actual only in relationship with other like beings."[2] For such sentiments—Jeffersonian, communal and individualistic—to have practical effect, certain actions are necessary. Let us assume that the tenant farmers know that the ghettos of the great cities are industrial and social plantation colonies. He learns this from his relatives who have gone to the great cities. Consequently, he decides to stay in Mississippi. But as a free man. He must convince his brethren that they be prepared to wrest power or he must find those who are prepared to give power in the form of money, land, and skill to them — to organize themselves as citizens in Mississippi.

Analytically, the distinction between revolution and reconstruction is very great. However, one should not expect the wretched and dispossessed to carry those distinctions on their back even though, extraordinarily enough, the movements of Elijah Muhammad, Malcolm X, Panthers and SNCC, spoke to the urban dispossessed and rural wretched, start from the assumption of self-reconstruction and finding one's own consciousness.

The tenant farmer's analysis has several immediate consequences for those who have political and economic power and who are prepared to help. The churches and universities become important sources for the redistribution of land, industry and knowledge. To begin the decolonization of the Plantation Colony and the first tentative steps to the reconstruction of the political economy, the churches, universities and the insurgent groups within them are now charged with the responsibility of forcing these institutions *as* institutions to train people and to give their own resources to set up schools, community colleges, and farms and industries which will be transferred to and controlled by those who were the objects of the Plantation Colony. For example, Harvard University, which has over one billion dollars in endowment, should now divest itself of part of its holdings to neighboring Roxbury where many of the people are no better off than the tenant farmers. Students and faculty in such an institution should change the policies and nature of *its* body politic, the university, so that Roxbury can have its rights.*

The struggle in the churches by the young ministers can revolve around similar issues. The church's theological necessity of building community could take the political form of voluntarily removing their exemption tax status by taxing themselves. For example, the amount of tax that a church would pay on its property should be paid by setting up non-sectarian non-profit communities to be owned in part individually by the inhabitants, and cooperatively either in the form of a local community corporation, a kibbutz, or a neighborhood government. Such programs should be organized in seminaries by students and faculty.

In the university and the church, students and faculty, ministers, rabbis and laity would organize groups which would deed and transfer substantial proportions of their property to local communities of poor people. Whether this method can bring about wide-scale political and economic change in which the poor control their own destinies, is dependent on those people in the churches and universities who see themselves as responsive rather than reactive.

The partial embodiment of the reactive class today is of course found in the university. While it cannot stop radical social action or technology, the university can make change bloody and repressive on everyone, including itself. To no little extent it becomes the choice of the educated class to decide whether future confrontations will be reconstructive, repressive or revolutionary. It

---

* Indications of this growing consciousness at Columbia University where many students felt two things: that they were in a colonized situation at the university which for them was painful and similar to those in the neighboring ghettos and the immensity which they were a part of exploited the ghettos.

decides this question by its methods, the type of knowl-edge it views as important and the actions that it under-takes in the world—in short, where it stands. If that class becomes part of the repressive machinery of the state, one can be sure that the inhabitants of the Plantation Colony will not believe that it can attain any objective except through continuous violence. It will not be inter-ested in reconstruction.*

If the educated reactive class cannot distinguish exis-tentially, and feel the difference between the repression of the police in Watts and the passive violence of a system in which a high percentage more blacks die each year as a result of malnutrition, poor housing and mercenary ser-vice which gets expressed in the black uprisings in the cities, then reconstruction cannot result, and the univer-sity will become the velvet glove and rationalizing voice for the brutes who manage the repression. It will send into the ghettos social workers, professors and crime special-ists who will write reports and study the poor as objects.†
After all, the university is proficient in such a role. The military defense establishment has spent 8–11 billion dollars on the educated class in and out of the university

---

* An interesting argument can be made which would lead one to conclude that the plantation mentality necessarily emerges from the competitive ideology of buy cheap and sell dear. The mentality of price is built into a system of thought so that even the most well intended in the educated reactive class end up paying maids who are usually black a low wage, because low wages are the going rate for maids. Perhaps, as the basic economic structure is transformed, value as deter-mined by price shifts to other ways of determining worth.

†The National Crime Commission study which brought together honorable sociologists and law professors by the group resulted in an excuse by the Congress to pass an extraordinarily repressive piece of legislation which strengthens the police and transforms them into a class instrument. In Sartre's visit to the United States in 1945, one happy comment he made was that it appeared that the police were not a class instrument. Now it is the case that the police will specifically serve as a class instrument as more and more of the crimes in the society take on a political character.

to rationalize nuclear war and to make that class the fulcrum of military power.*

As I have suggested, while ostensibly taking sides with the economically colonized, the educated can become the exploiters through the path of liberal reformism. The most difficult thing for an emerging group to comprehend is that while their intentions are noble, their knowledge translates itself socially into a powerful exploitative instrument for their own purposes. The government bureaucrats have invented something called a demonstration project. Its purpose is to get a program started in a particular area at a level approximately one-hundredth the level at which they believe the program should be funded, although they do not know how to get budgetary support for it through the conservative-military alliance which dominates Congress. In many cases the money is obtained by a university or anti-poverty agency, which then hires people to do research or help in setting up the program. Once the demonstration money is used up or the program fails, the university employees now undertake to secure a new opportunity elsewhere. Nothing is left behind. There is no project left. While the government might have been successful in giving the illusion of doing something, very little is accomplished for the recipients. The program ends up as little more than an opportunity for faculty members and other college-trained persons, who were employed at a rewarding and affluent level.

Take, for example, another situation where there was a real commitment. The Tufts Medical School, located in Boston, is setting up a health center in an all-black town in Mississippi. The town's total budget is $200,000 a year. The health clinic is a two million dollar project.

* Note the speech of Rowland Gaither, Chairman of the Board of Trustees, RAND Corporation, on its tenth anniversary. "Decision Making for Defense," p. 4.

The white doctors don't want to live, understandably, like the local black men, so new houses and new facilities have to be built. The poor can now serve the whites as maids and janitors. The health center is too important and sophisticated to be left to the locals, so whites have to be brought in. Thus, the colonial system continues in a new costume through the work and good intention of liberal mediation. Robert Kennedy and his Senate staff attempted to help the Bedford-Stuyvesant neighborhood, a Brooklyn area of over 400,000 people. They brought industrialists and finance bankers in to set up "industries" in this area. Cheap labor is one attraction, it is said. While performing a public service, these industries will be guaranteed a high profit margin. Since this is an area of small buildings and face-to-face politics, the Senator and advisors planned to build a big state office building for a bureaucracy that will live elsewhere and commute. The residents of Bedford-Stuyvesant were restricted from working on the construction projects because of labor unions, although they would have been able to get jobs in the building as janitors. The structure itself becomes a pyramid, and the habit of mind is pharaohistic for the memorialization of the architect and the political patron. The plans for such programs are drafted by the technocrats in our best universities.

Perhaps such situations could be corrected through the development of a new social knowledge and ethic. If social science and theology is concerned with knowledge beyond rationalization for an affluent class, its primary task is to show how that class can stand with the urban and rural poor without exploiting them. How can you or I stand with the Mississippi tenant farmer in useful and non-exploitative ways? To accomplish that end, the educated and the rich will have to realize their own situation and stand with the tenant farmer who says, "This is where I stand and you must take cognizance of me as a man and as an equal." "Standing with" is not the same as "standing off" or "standing on." (Note Chapter 10.)

When a tenant farmer or the urban welfare client says, "This is where I stand and I am a man," he is attempting to recapture a sense of space and equality not that different from Francis Bacon, who attempted to change the basis of knowledge so that it would end the tyrannization of the feudal world of man. Through the tenant farmer's confrontation, he established his own existence, and he projects a future in which new social organizational forms can come into being. When the Mississippi tenant farmer pitches a tent in front of the White House to confront all of us with his situation, he is also showing us how we reinforce that situation. By his act of confrontation he begins to define for himself and us a new definition of freedom. When he says, "We squat for land and money to build our houses and towns in Mississippi," he breaks out of the Plantation Colony and *hopes* that he no longer relies on welfare rolls and liberal mediation. By ending this nomadic part, he has begun the process of self-definition. That action begins to create an inductive value system which gives rise to new avenues of social knowledge predicated on equality toward, standing with and non-exploitation.

In the university, for the aware professor and student in the social sciences, this becomes the basis for reconstructing curricula around the question of how to build communities which are not colonized. The plight of the Mississippi tenant farmer was joined by two former SNCC workers, Frank and Jean Smith. Frank Smith was a student at the Institute for Policy Studies and now a Fellow of the Institute. He worked with Milton Kotler on a series of ideas of the body politic which were developed at the Institute with broad implications for the Mississippi tenant farmer. The ideas evolved from the democratic anti-technocratic assumption that the poor are not unintelligent, that if they saw themselves outside of the context of being serfs, they would be able to manage their affairs very well. Smith also assumed, perhaps because of the tenant farmers' sense of rootedness, that they would be better able than those who had lived in a transient urban neighborhood to build a community which could serve as a model in the rest of the rural society. In this theoretical model, advice to the poor was to be viewed as the kind which the prosperous might receive from a specialist such as an accountant, doctor, psychiatrist, or lawyer. Armed with this theory, Smith intended to help the people confront the Plantation Colony in ways which did not require them either to die or to migrate to the cities where they would very likely die spiritual deaths as welfare clients. He hoped for them, and they wanted for themselves, a self-sustaining economy in Mississippi which would be organized, controlled, and owned by the black poor. The purpose of the project for the organizer was to build a political and economic system which would fulfill the democratic ideal and human fact that the black man is a citizen who is a subject, rather than a powerless object to be used, manipulated, and tossed about by the colonizer.

The tenant farmer, who now pitted himself against the Mississippi plantation system and who had been expelled by the plantation owner, wanted to build houses and a community, to learn skills other than cotton picking, and to initiate economic ventures which would be integrated into the political life and control of the community. But risk capital is not readily available for poor people, black or white. As a general rule, the great foundations, religious organizations and universities which hold large appreciating capital funds support only the middle class or the extension of their own institutional power. Although the gifts of such eleemosynary institutions are beginning to trickle further down the economic mountain, the investments of such institutions remain in the safest and often the most reactionary enterprises.* Their clients are not the poor, although the poor may be the political opportunity of the non-profit institutions to obtain funds from the city, or federal government.

So where do people who live in tents and shacks turn? Although a few "patrons" helped this Mississippi group with funds to build a handful of houses, such aid did not change the fundamental reality of dependence and thrownness which the people felt. They had spent the winter living in tents when they had been thrown out of their plantation shacks by The Man. They decided to confront the federal government, namely the White House. In the spring of 1966, they came to Washington to set up their tents directly across the street from the White House in a city park.† They hoped that this dramatic act, in which the poor slept in tents across from the President's palace, would result in a willingness on the part of the federal government to recognize the crisis of their economic desperation and to fund the poor directly through a self-organized structure which would not make them dependent either on the plantation system of the South or the welfare-plantation system of the North for their survival. Some of the people had hoped that they could live outside the competitive market system as well.

The Mississippi people who camped outside of the White House were stood off by officials of the federal anti-poverty program who said that the Office of Economic Opportunity had no authority to fund the building of houses. This was a bureaucratic truth. That is, it conformed to one reality of truth as is known by people who

---

*Note the study at the Institute for Policy Studies by Barnet and Lockwood. and attempts to change the direction of investment of eleemosynary institutions.

†One of the results of the sleeping in the park decision by the poor was the decision of the liberal Secretary of the Interior to disallow sleeping in the park in the future by either the rich or the poor.

live and work inside the bureaucratic net. Under the Office of Economic Opportunity Act, Section 203, authority existed to build houses. However, in the Washington political swamp a gentlemen's agreement had been previously negotiated between the Director of the Office of Economic Opportunity, Sargent Shriver, the heads of certain of the federal housing agencies and Senator Stennis* of Mississippi, relinquishing the authority granted under the act to the OEO to help the poor to build houses. That particular section of the law was a direct threat to the housing industry and to the public housing bureaucracies. In one case, the free enterprise of the builder and mortgage market would be challenged. In the other case, the political and administrative authority of the bureaucracy would be challenged. So the special interests effectively destroyed the rights of the poor under the law.

No help came from the government in this project. Instead, it was demonstrated again that a far more massive effort must be mounted in order to get help from the government to build a community. In Mississippi, the federal government owns 5 percent of the land,† another 1½ percent is part of the soil bank program (which in effect means that the federal government is paying farmers, many of them plantation owners, substantial sums of money not to grow food nor to develop the land).‡ Although we can readily admit that some of the same elements are present which were controlling after the

---

* A word should be said about the white Mississippi legislator. Mississippi is a poor state with a fascist-racist base. It sends to the government set in Washington representatives who live with the double image of being legislatively powerful and racist. On the other hand, they view themselves—as do most white southerners—as the conquered who cannot reconcile themselves to the national system, which they believe conquered and emasculated the white people of the South. The white southern politician sees himself as both the conquered and the conqueror.

† Source is Table 7, Public Land Statistics, Bureau of Land Management, GPO, 1969.

‡ Source is ASCS, US Department of Agriculture, GPO, 1969 and 1970.

American Civil War, there is a major difference which could cause a reconstruction where one hundred years ago the result was repression. After the Civil War, Negroes were not in command of their own revolution but were used by whites who had their own purposes and motivations.[3] Now the blacks have developed their own leadership and have the power and will to make the sort of demands which will cause large-scale reconstruction in the South and in the cities. While the white-dominated governments may attempt to destroy militant groups to protect order, that is, the status quo, the fact is that more and more self-conscious leadership groups are appearing within the black movement.

Another extraordinary change has occurred. Reconciliation and reconstruction after the Civil War seemed to be opposite political principles. Today they are the same. Reconciliation of people with one another is predicated on a radical change of the hierarchic social structure forced upon everyone by technology.

In the case of Tribbitt, the federal government failed the people. Anti-poverty remained a struggle between the plantation-owner class and the liberal reformer. Funds and programs neither related to nor trickled down to the poor. Smith continued to work with the project through an entity called Neighborhood Developers which built houses for the people. Those who built them were the tenant farmers who then ended up owning them. The new citizens of this town have worked out a democratic political structure as well as a rudimentary economic system which is not controlled through the Plantation Colony although it is dependent on the existence of the market economy. The people own a business which sells to the Tufts Hospital Center. Their houses and land are held cooperatively and individually, similar to the way the cooperative system operates in Israel on the moshav.

In the Mississippi project we attempted to develop a

non-exploitative knowledge which said that the poor could decide for themselves what they needed most, and thus we could relate to them without having to manipulate them. In this we acknowledged and reinforced their right of confrontation and exposed the social knowledge of the federal anti-poverty program as primarily class-biased against the poor.

That we have attempted this project and have had limited success means only that the process must go on with others starting similar projects. In some cases it may require more emphasis on confrontation, which results in what Arthur Waskow calls "creative disorder"[4] so that attention will be paid and so that those who have become objects of other people's history will themselves be the historians and judges of what they are and need. One aspect of the history of the twentieth century concerns the changed definition of what and who is history. The objects of history are now the subjects. This situation obtains in the United States where people think of themselves as subjects, but in fact are objects. They hold a colonized status (thinking of themselves as "free") without realizing that they may be something other than the way they have been characterized. The most stark case is the plantation colony of the city where the real poor, not those organized into unions who have already accepted their stake in the colonization, are totally characterized by the system, but because they have not been included in receiving largesse from it, remain without loyalty to it.

Rational-Reconstruction

By 1963 the rhetoric within radical and liberal thought revolved around attempts to recapture the local partici-patory control arguments of Jefferson and G. H. Cole. Milton Kotler, Ivanhoe Donaldson and Christopher

Jencks attempted to formulate the theory of parallel institutions in which the poor and the dispossessed, where they cannot be integrated into the society as equals, take advantage of social space and start their own political governing units within the city, to give them greater political power in the society at large. Donaldson, Kotler and Pastor Leopold Bernhard, in a project in Columbus, Ohio, called ECCO, got the Lutheran Church to transfer "the government of an existing church settlement house agency . . . to the people of the neighborhood it serves."[5] Although the church transferred political power to the poor, in that the poor now can change the types of social services they want and have the power to decide whom they want to hire, as well as the responsibility for getting funds from various sources, the church did not deed over the property to the poor.* On the other hand, it is an extraordinarily uncommon situation in the history of social welfare in the United States that the poor themselves vote on what they want and need, as well as who their officers should be. It is very seldom that an educated class from which social welfare agencies draw their staffs and boards is prepared to be responsible to the poor.

In ECCO, the people have chosen the services they want — pre-kindergarten nurseries, day-care centers, credit unions, legal and job placement services. In the ECCO model, the corporation is governed by a Neighborhood Assembly "conducted in the manner of a town meeting" which meets several times a year. The members of ECCO, defined geographically, elect an Executive Council and a full-time staff. Kotler's notions stem from the idea of the Jeffersonian ward republic and the East European *shtetl,* in which people developed community bonds from face-to-face relationships, from family ties,

---

* The deeding by an Episcopal church, St. Stephen's, to a local community occurred in Washington in 1970.

and from *continuous* participation in the transaction and formulation of their rights and obligations in and to the community. The question is whether a society in which communities are breaking up and re-forming themselves can accept traditional notions of place.

Kotler's thesis with regard to the question of place and citizenship follows the importance which thinkers such as Ardrey have placed on territoriality. Citizenship in this framework then stems from the place one finds himself, that is, from the land one occupies. But the problem with this view is that in the United States and in the West generally, place is not something which binds someone to an area. People move around. The question is whether citizenship can follow the individual without doing hardship and destruction to the inhabitants who already live in a particular place. The Roman and American notion of incorporation and federation clearly leads to imperial design and finally ownership over others. In the United States as one travels to the southwest he is struck with the fact that Mexicans are now citizens of the United States but that does not mean the land has not been taken from them. Nor does the fact that the United States offered citizenship to the losers of the war mean that they are any better integrated into the American state except as objects.

The New Left and the right agree on the importance of localism and place. There is a sense of the need to recapture the roots and the belonging which evolve from a situation in which a person is able to "reach out" and have effect and authority, while he has affect, feeling with.

Building on Kotler's work and the traditional conception of geographic place, Gar Alperovitz has added the idea of neighborhood groups organized together as units for economic power. We may accept the Kotler-Alperovitz model for the establishment of a small community of voluntary home rule within the city. This political-economic model has aspects of the small towns of eighteenth-century America. In the cities, such neighborhoods could deal with public and private financing authorities, and they could become a new level of governing in the American system. As Glick has pointed out in speaking on Kotler's model of self-government, "Neighborhood residents could be delegated authority, within their territory, over aspects of such important municipal functions as elementary education and land planning and development. The new units would be part of a federal system in which national, state, metropolitan, and municipal government would perform most functions, prescribe minimum standards and general plans, collect and redistribute revenue, and provide central purchasing, audit research and other services. These higher levels of government would neither organize nor administer the neighborhood governments, but would aid residents of urban neighborhoods who so choose to form self-governing politics and control certain delegable functions."[6] Such activities could be carried on within the structure of civil rights and constitutional law without damage to the rights of any minorities, but rather with recognition of their self-governing rights. The economic part of the model which becomes an important, indeed an integral part of the community is the establishment of income-producing businesses which are controlled democratically by the community. In turn, the community decides through its town meeting process what social and welfare services it wants from the "profits" derived from the community-owned business enterprise. We may view this method as the new theory of basic economic development. Under this model a group of social development banks would be established in all regions of the country with funds from the federal government, foundations, universities and churches. Such banks would loan money to non-profit businesses and enterprises that operated under community control. In turn, non-profit enterprises would invest in the local community from profits (surplus) and savings. There are partial examples of this method in various nations. In Canada, Rochdale College has received government loans for the purpose of setting up housing cooperatives which are operated to obtain comfort and community. This project seems to be profitable as well. And the profits from the cooperatives are then invested in service functions such as health and schools.

We find these ideas in Borsodi, G. H. Cole, Jefferson and Paul Goodman, but the most significant practical economic model can be found in the New Deal. Since 1933, under the Farm Credit Act, thirteen banks were established by the federal government to provide capital to farm cooperatives. These banks were viewed as a source of aid beyond mere loan services. The bankers apparently spent a considerable amount of time in the field, similar to the activities of the farm extension agents. (The federal government, for all practical purposes, has withdrawn from loaning government money. At present, the banks receive their loanable funds through debenture sales from commercial money markets.) In my view, such banks are now absolutely necessary for urban reconstruction. We may designate them as social development banks which would operate as cooperative banks for non-profit ventures and neighborhood communities which borrowed money from them.

The national bank would operate outside of the appropriations process of Congress with a substantial capital fund, twenty-five billion dollars, and with additional authority to borrow from the commercial market for non-profit ventures which would be guaranteed through a federal insurance program. The governors of the decentralized banks would be democratically elected by the borrowers so that the policies of the banks would be set by neighborhood communities and community controlled boards. Besides being borrowers, communities would also become shareholders in the bank, with surpluses also being reinvested into the cities for social services. It is obvious that such community models for democratic economic development will cause tension with the mammoth corporate plantation structure that may view the poor communities as their next market opportunity and the cities as a profit-producing institution for the corporation. Indeed, some have argued, including Alperovitz, that the corporation's expertise can be utilized without surrendering more of the public weal to corporate power by contract. My disagreement rests in the likelihood that national economic power is predicated politically on the great corporations.

There is no countervailing political power which poor groups are able to exercise in the cities to withstand advantage-taking corporations which would undertake programs for the poor. The only possibility open to confront the corporation and the police is massive violence, which would have the effect of discouraging corporate intervention in Black neighborhoods. On the other hand, it would also have the effect of destroying for the time being any possibility of economic development. One problem with corporations that work in the cities which might want to provide services is that their past performance is inefficient. Aero-space industry, for example—an industry that would like to enter into the "poor market"—is a state-subsidized enterprise that operates totally by negotiating its losses with the government. While there may be plans on the part of Xerox or education groups to sell schools as one would buy consumer goods, with appropriate warrantees to parents that the children will learn a prescribed curriculum, the likelihood is that such methods could better be applied by people who were hired directly by the poor or new neighborhood government units without corporate intervention.

12

The Political Party and Movement of Radical Reconstruction

There is an argument which borders on the persuasive that rejects the idea of political space in American life. This view holds that the state is protected by a shield of laws, penalties, police actions and investigating harassments, which are meant to render discussions and actions of individuals and groups relatively meaningless and controllable. This shield is turned into a sword against the citizenry through charges of conspiracy, sedition, and drug abuse, against those who test the limits of the state or merely attempt to live in a liberated way, which in itself tests the state's limits. There is much empirical and painful evidence which suggests that the forces of the State and political parties which represent the large parts of the colonizing structure will not tolerate any citizen or human activity that shifts political and economic power relationships and controlling values in the society. The fate of the Black Panthers, various leaders in civil rights and peace movement activities and workers in these movements, as well as those who dare to create a situation different from the dominant culture, may suggest the limitation of the idea of political space.

In his book, *The Roots of American Foreign Policy,* the brilliant historian Gabriel Kolko has made this point:

> If the history of left politics in the United States is cooption for some, it is also repression for many others: grandfather clauses, poll taxes, and other means for applying the stick when the carrot was insufficient or deemed inappropriate. Authority and power exist quite beyond general social sanctions and rest on specific interests and ability to impose restraints, and the ruling class has never permitted decision makers in the governmental apparatus who do not advance and conform to the interests of the State.[1]

Yet, this analysis is not objective enough. That is to say, it does not take account of either the subjective or the dynamic. By not allowing for subjectivity, this analysis loses the place of accident and the survivability of the human spirit. As I have suggested, political and social spaces are subjective psychological needs and facts which, when they are acted upon, can become the basis for the creation of objective frameworks. Such needs interact with the frameworks of social existence outside of one's mind and heart. That interaction can cause profound change. In *War and Peace,* Tolstoy tells us about the French soldier who, for whatever reason or sense, begins to retreat from battle. It is then that Napoleon finds that he has lost. No doubt this poetic view can be accompanied by a more material analysis of what is happening in American society.

The acceptance of the theory of political space means operating in the context of a politics which both rejects and accepts old forms. While there is political space, the present electoral system in the United States leaves precious little room for either a fundamental reordering of priorities of the society, or reallocation of political power to groups other than those already represented. Even if it were possible to jump beyond the base which the Democratic and Republican Parties represented to other constituencies and other interests,* the mechanics of voting, getting on the ballot, and the intent of voting (which is to give away control to administration) deny the kind of continuous involvement with power to make decisions which would change the meaning of voting and the process of governing. The purpose and setup of the two major parties are antithetical to direct democracy. Day-to-day active participation in decision-making in the major economic and political institutions of the society as citizens is not contemplated by the two major parties.

Elections of the two major parties' candidates engage people in the plebiscite system.

The voting process encourages people to vote a yes or no without any further involvement in the decision process. The established groups within the pyramids of the society are reluctant to encourage or allow an active electorate, since such a result would mean that a reshuffling of power with presently-unrepresented groups might occur.

---

*The Democratic Convention of 1968 in Chicago was a visual proof of the groups that were not and could not be represented in the Democratic Party. Here I mean the radical, the Black militant, the hippie, the poor, and the soulful, even though some of these categories were "honorable" sons and daughters of the middle class. The problem was even more acute in Miami Beach. Whereas these groups showed up at the Democratic Party Convention to mill about in the hotels and be beaten on the streets, they didn't even show up at the hotels of Miami Beach. Hosea Williams and Ralph Abernathy's S.C.L.C. appeared in the Fontainebleau. Their appearance was not a challenge but viewed as a freaky accident. At the same time, those excluded from both parties—the Blacks in the ghetto of Miami—were being shot and maimed by the police of Florida with a ferocity that wasn't matched in Chicago a few weeks later.

This reshuffling would be accompanied with an analysis which showed that particular groups were benefitting financially or politically from the presence of problems which they caused. A reconstructive voting system would also mean that areas of public life hitherto closed to public analysis and scrutiny (media, military institutions, hospitals, penal institutions, schools) would become open to such scrutiny.[2]

The development of a consciousness among certain groupings within the poor and middle classes has meant a direct conflict among the closed nature of the two-party system, the electoral process which it reflects, and this new-found consciousness. For example, the active, educated middle class which earns its livelihood from involvement, information and scrutiny, does not fit with the plebiscite method of decision transfer which is reflected in the American voting system and the two parties.

The conflict of new consciousness against the pyramidal structure is of course an ominous situation. As such groupings gain strength, those who manipulate and operate the pyramid feel themselves threatened to the point where political space seems to have to be filled either by the pyramidalists or insurgent and dropout groups. The irony is that so long as those who operate the pyramidal structure remain authoritarian rather than totalitarian, the new groups challenging their own new-found consciousness will mature and grow in power as well as anger, if changes do not occur quickly. Authoritarian structures do not deny the existence of political space.

Once the managers of the pyramidal structure are unable to use law and order as an instrument to protect and buy off the middle class, and they can no longer co-opt people into the corporate structure because of their own conservative views, the managers may be forced to respond only as repressors and intimidators. In such a situation, members of the middle class will be warned to mind "no one's business" except their own, as isolates from each other or as ciphers of the colonizing institution.* There will be a strong attempt to reinforce colonizing knowledge and reduce the critical faculties of individuals and groups within the universities in an attempt to internalize into individuals the signs that appeared a few years ago in the RAND Corporation: "Compute, Don't Think." In other words, general attempts to enforce the clerking status of this new educated grouping will be made through the professional associations, universities and corporate structure. This repressive direction is of course a dangerous one to pursue for those who hold elective office.

Former Secretary of Health, Education and Welfare Finch, who deals with the new class and the poor, understands this situation, whereas President Nixon and Attorney General Mitchell do not. Since politicians must still deal with the magical value of voting which grips the middle class, it is possible that by accident or organization, intimidation of active groups could result in the repressers being kicked out of political office. This is not to say that the continuing repressive situation would cease. It is to say, however, that managing repression is indeed a complex activity when it is aimed at an active middle class.

Besides the older, active middle class, the young between the ages of fifteen and thirty-five have invented their own life styles which attempt to avoid the weight of the pyramid. In this way, they have invented their own decision-making process which may be viewed as a new social contract between individuals and small groups. The most profound sense of this group of people, hippies,

---

* This warning was made manifest by Vice-President Agnew in his attack on news reporting. The purpose of his criticism was to warn the owners to keep their employed in line.

commune lovers, is that they reflect traditional American values, emulating in some cases Indian dress, wearing frontier costumes, and favoring individual anarchism. But such groups do not believe in the United States as a nation or political entity. Instead, America is looked upon merely as land where different groups want to live in new ways and then sign their own social contract to establish a body politic. Such groups view themselves as the new pilgrims. They do not see themselves living in utopias as the people in the Brook Farm or Oneida Communities saw themselves. Instead, they see themselves as a *class,* which by its nature, life style and sheer numbers, challenge the present structure.

In both cases—that of the older middle class with a professional, expert or "modern" mentality, and the younger people who are attempting to break radically with the pyramid and with work as it has been defined over several hundred years—allegiance to the pyramid has ended. The authority of the job and of the state no longer provides the thrill of collective acceptance and identity it once did. This new phenomenon can be understood by the changing nature of work. Self-controlled time and self-definition of work can no longer encompass the narrow industrial clerking or selling task which historically has been the content of the social character which individuals acquired to exist in their colonized role.* Thus, the social aspects for challenging the colonizing structure by the different elements of the middle class are present in the new culture of free personal expression through drugs, sex and sense relationship, and a new definition of expertness that does not follow the traditional lines as laid out in pyramidal authority.

---

*Where automation has been practiced, the lives of most workers have been made more miserable, since their personal movements on the line are geared to the machine. This situation in the factory is one reason for the great increases in wildcat strikes.

The success of this challenge and the possibility of for-
mulating a new definition of political participation is dependent on three assumptions: (a) acceptance by people
who live vastly different life styles of the need to join
together in resistance and reconstruction; (b) the practical
determination of whether spaces exist within the authoritarian structure to build alternatives to authoritarianism
and to replace the pyramids while their legal structure
continues to appear to function; (c) the need to bring about
profound change without relying on a political party
which holds to the revolutionary dogma of internal discipline and blueprints for change and control.

It was on this series of questions that I believed a new,
anti-authoritarian political party could be brought into
practice. This party would serve as an instrument in decolonization of American life. Such a party would protect
the young and the changing roles and lives that both
young and old are now experiencing.

The early summer of 1968 seemed to me to be a propi-
tious time for the formation of a new political party. A
confluence of forces and events occurred which could no
longer be contained by the media as entertainment. The
resistance campaign against the war in Vietnam, the cultural rebellion in America, the McCarthy presidential
campaign activating the rentier and professional class,
and the flagging civil rights minority power struggle* led
to powerful political impulses that were not going to be
internalized through the two-party system. I hoped that
such a party would accomplish several objectives. First,
it would split discerning liberals and conservatives who
are non-authoritarian from the established forces of society and it would cause them to begin looking at the

---

* This series of events was symbolized in the death of King and Kennedy, who
had been accepted as the symbols of American potentiality. It was thought that
these men knew how to control violence in America and relate the white working
class to the black poor.

roots of the institutions which they built or accepted over the last several generations. Second, I believed that the candidacies of Nixon and Humphrey would be seen, upon examination, as reflecting different modes of the same set of crises in American life. Given the mini-civil wars in the cities (and the crime rates have to be seen as part of the economic and political crises), the continuation of the Vietnam war, an inflation which threatened the worker and pensioned classes of the society, each candidate, in order to govern, would be forced to appeal to the most reactionary elements in American life. Third, because such a direction was likely, there was a chance to bring together liberal, radical and anti-authoritarian groupings around candidates and ideas which reflected far different publics—specifically, those who felt themselves disfranchised, passed over, and yet the "next wave." I had hoped that the political consciousness of people was far enough along and that their personal financial commitments, causing political immobilism, were not so great that they would be able to see the two-party governing frame of reference as merely an instrument for the cooptation of people and ideas in changing them into the status quo.

The issues which presented themselves for debate and confrontation, while monumental in one sense, were merely the top of the iceberg of unhappiness in American life. Everyone running for public office seemed to acknowledge that the fundamental question was that of powerlessness and impotence as human beings and as citizens. (Even Sisyphus would get the rock to the top of the mountain before it rolled down.) Whether rich or poor, mean or saintly, quick or slow, the spaces for people to do anything were swallowed by roles and functions which meant that people lived out their lives being mediated through the corporate enterprise. This newly conscious sense of shared misery, or shared non-being meant that the usual ways of describing class structure did not fit into the advanced

industrial system because misery and unhappiness caused
by the structure was no longer a mere province of the poor
but in fact reflected everyone who found himself part of
the corporate collective enterprise. The basis of the enterprise had broken down and manifested itself in wars, in-
flations, riots and spaced-out behavior.

After the Democratic Party Convention in 1968, I com-
mented in the following way on this question:

> Where the policies which result from the political parties
> and the bureaucracies cause basic structural and institu-
> tional deficiencies, and the policies cannot be changed
> through the party structure because the parties created the
> institutions and the deficiencies, then a new party must
> emerge to make a structural analysis which shows the new
> politics and policies that are necessary and the structural
> changes that are required. Unless such a new political party
> comes into being the revolutionary repressive situation will
> grow. . . .[3]

This mood had already emerged on the left, although it
had not manifested itself in electoral politics of the new
politics variety until the Peace and Freedom Party gained
attention in California. Its efforts had spread to other
states, finding its strength in various socialist, Trotskyite
and New Left groupings. My view was that the Peace and
Freedom Party's base was not broad enough to appeal to
the middle class. It had already embroiled itself in a
number of factional disputes. Members felt hopeless.
They had cut themselves off by a form of consciousness elitism. In this view, I thought that the issue of
style and substance had become mixed. Dress, long hair
and eccentric appearance were scaring middle- and working-class people away who would otherwise be prepared
to listen to the positions taken by the "dissidents." At
the convention of the Peace and Freedom Party in the
summer of 1968, I pretentiously suggested to members

of that party that the requirements of American politics were such that they should be radical in thought and action but conservative in manner and style. As Thomas Mann pointed out, the fact that one dresses in a particular way is not necessarily a clue to either his politics or his inner life. Style and cosmetics in a consumer society, I believe, are easily co-opted. My own view about this matter has changed somewhat. If the style is integrated into one's life and reflects a new direction for that person, the first requirement of a new politics is that people be taken on their own terms and style. Once that occurs, a shared style—and existence—can begin to develop.

Since the 1968 elections a liberal grouping within the Democratic Party has developed who believe that they are able to get power over public affairs through their party. They have formed themselves into a New Democratic Coalition (NDC). One of its proponents, Arnold Kaufman, argues its radical purposes and aims although its views in various places in the country are more traditional. It is much more in tune with what might objectively be regarded as a reformed ADA. But self-characterization is important. Some of the NDC sees itself as the "democratic or radical" wing of the Democratic Party, appealing to some students and professors and "pragmatic" political types who have a yearning for old-style power, legitimacy and public office. The NDC is a distinct minority in the Democratic Party. In most geographical areas which the Democratic Party counts on for its votes it is dominated by those with a right-wing authoritarian direction—those whose class interests at this moment appear to demand a law-and-order mentality. The result is that those people who continue to cling to the symbols of the Democratic Party, such as the New Democratic Coalition group, may find themselves going in one of two directions: Some will be co-opted to accept the new authoritarian basis of Democratic leadership. Others may find themselves forced to embrace a new political party, especially if this group attempts to be even a fraction as militant as they now claim. Activities such as Vietnam Moratorium confrontations border on political strikes. The result is that the roles of the colonizing structure will come under severe attack. Where political consciousness is high, actions such as political strikes relate issues such as war, racism, inflation and empty social roles.

There is a basic political interest question which those who continue to participate in the Democratic Party must concern themselves with. It is the illusion that people with quite unequal roles and places in the pyramidal structure stand equally in their demands, interests and power. The idea that each is equal in the Democratic Party means that each person's role as it is perceived and played out in the pyramid is essentially a correct one. David Friedman has formulated this point in the following way:

> No mass movement would allow the heads of GM or Columbia to become spokesmen and to formulate its demands . . . yet all these things which no other ruling class institutions could do are accomplished by the Democratic party, relying on the fact that people feel impotent to act in their own name or to put forward their own political leaders. This party legitimizes class rule in America by pretending to represent the interests of the "little guy."[4]

When I argue that it is possible for the new party to operate across class lines and roles, it is because people who would join it recognize either the bankruptcy or the need for the transformation of their roles. They are prepared to admit to the existence of class exploitation through the pyramid either by them or to them. This *raison d'être* cannot be the *basis of the Democratic Party where the idea is held that the class structure and the roles fulfilled in them are inherently and operationally sound.* As I have suggested elsewhere, the Democratic Party, with the exception of particular individuals in that party, is unable to go beyond its most important clients, the pegs of the national security state which it built and was responsible for since the 1930's. It is conceivable that within a party, even those whose motives are directed toward obtaining office would now undertake to dismantle those institutions which are either their primary constituencies or which in fact reflect their getting power. While from time to time in history we may see the atrophy of certain positions like sheriff or coroner, there are few who at this stage in the Democratic Party would see the necessity for the abolition or dismantling of the entire intelligence or spying apparatus. The reasons for this, of course, are not because such apparatus gives "intelligence" about the "enemy" but because fantastic power is achieved by individuals through those roles. Would the politicians in the Democratic Party be prepared to dismantle the FBI or CIA?

Besides the need to protect personal power, there is an equally difficult problem which those in the Democratic Party face: that of undercutting one's own constituency. The ABM debate of 1969 was one in which the Democratic Senate opponents to the administration yearned for a victory against the Department of Defense, and the President, *and* a curtailment of the arms race. Yet as one examined what liberals would have called a victory, he is immediately struck by that victory's pyrrhic character. The majority of the Democratic Senators rallied around an amendment which would have meant an increase in the research and development of the ABM system while delaying the emplacement of anti-ballistic missiles. One interpretation of this position was that it would slow down the arms race. However, a more substantial analysis is that the position taken by the Democratic Party was that of

straight military Keynesianism. In effect, they were voting
to keep state-subsidized corporations operating, including
their unions, as well as the upper technical elite employed. The liberals closed their eyes to the nature of the
employment and to the final structural effect that such
employment would have on the arms race and on the nature of the society. In effect they were voting for continuation of the arms race and the pyramidal structure. The
irony, of course, is that even that victory was denied
to them. The delay they sought was not achieved and
yet there is long-term technological unemployment.

The question remains as to what the character of the
new party will be and where its support will come from.
It is obvious that in politics movements work out their
character in practice. We may note that there are break-
away groups from the Democratic Party and non-authoritarian conservatives who see that the issue at this stage
in American history and indeed in the development of
industrial societies is the confrontation between authoritarian and non-authoritarian structures. It is not to say
that such groups themselves can form an identity of interest, although they may be able to work together for the
purpose of coalition of interest around the issue of participation, political space, and non-authoritarian relationships. In this sense, anti-authoritarian and non-authoritarian groups might be able to build from the practice of
the activities which are necessary to undertake as citizens.
For example, libertarian rightists might join with the new
left in a tax resistance project or in some school building project, reaching out for those groups that now find
themselves disdained by the political parties. Where
individuals find that they are in a custodial or nonparticipatory relationship to the life situation in the
organization that they are lived, political organizing for
decolonization can readily occur.

Organizing activites of the new party should emphasize

the relationships of people within apparently different groups to the sameness of their desperate condition in the light of modern technological and political structures. When people are colonized they are in the same condition and robbed of the potentiality to relate to each other in a human way. The new party must assume the tasks of:

(1) The establishment and creation of projects, social inventions and reconstructive confrontations.

(2) The delegitimizing of institutions which have outlived their usefulness or in their nature have become positively detrimental to society. . . . (To that part of the delegitimized institution which performs a useful function, the new party would put forward alternatives to it which would then become wholly legitimated. Examples of this abound in schools, health centers and certain forms of economic activity. The political party would include the establishment of councils of reconstruction and the organizing of shadow cabinets nationally and locally for the operations of governmental tasks.)

(3) The participation where possible in established elections. That is to say, the new party would embrace electoral politics with the understanding that such politics represents only one part of participation and involvement in the body politic. It would be understood that all electoral politics needs to be accompanied with councils of reconstruction from people in so-called non-electoral institutions.

Projects, Social Inventions and Confrontations

I have suggested various forms of such actions elsewhere. Their political content would depend on what the people who performed them intended as their purpose. Organizers of new party activity would initiate those activities chosen by the people and would move on once the activity could be sustained without their aid. The organizer's task would be that of attempting to sustain projects so that they became reconstructive institutions, which, by their nature, challenged other institutions and within themselves had continuous reconstructive activity. Thus, a school by its nature challenges, performs its own task, allows for its own redefinition, and teaches others to do the same. As I have suggested, confrontations per se are not reconstructive activities.

In recent years, confrontations have become a popular means wherein protesters show to themselves and to others that the state wears bare knuckles all the time. This becomes a fruitless exercise in political sado-masochism. Those who needed to know it for themselves should have by this time found out the grim truth. It is not to say that confrontation is forbidden or should not be held—indeed, it will. The question is different: What is the character of such confrontations and over what issues should they occur?

Some people favor confrontations of personal *machismo* which attempt to help individuals prove that they are alive. The more exemplary form of confrontation follows that of projects and social inventions which by the nature of their structure confront existing institutions. Such projects then become the basis of people defending them and confronting others. The confrontation becomes a continuous life function rather than merely televised street brawls which may be heady to watch or participate in but do not help in the creation and sustaining of a new society. In this sense, the establishment of coffeehouses near Army bases has resulted in changing the outlook of members of the upper middle class who set up such coffeehouses and bringing soldiers into a situation where they could begin seeing their own colonized role.

In such projects as coffeehouses we begin to see the establishment of a continuous life function for those involved. It attempts to take advantage of a new culture of the young which cannot fit into the colonizing activities of the state or economic system. The culture which exists within such a place as a coffeehouse on the first level may appear to be innocent in its intent. However, if the colonizing system attempts to demand allegiance from the new culture by jailing or intimidating its new members, the likelihood is that any political allegiance which may have existed to the colonizer would cease to exist. The function of the new party in this context is to find ways of organizing and protecting social inventions, projects and alternative life styles, such as hippie communities or other new forms of social relations which by their nature have the seed of the future in them and confront the present, hierarchic, pyramidal structure.

Delegitimizing Institutions or Roles Within Institutions

In the delegitimation of institutions, we are required to analyze what the purposes of a particular institution are, how it is organized, whether such institutions have a humane mission and, if so, in what form. Once such questions are answered, institutions can then be reorganized and reconstructed through establishing alternate forms of governing or through those activities which cause the particular institutions themselves to wilt. The new party could engage in a series of activities on a state and local level to determine how public institutions and institutions which operated publicly could be formed (as the new party has done in Washington state). One might form a series of investigating committees which would look at the asylums, schools, etc. Such investigating committees would hold public hearings and meetings and organize in such a way as to show how those institutions could operate differently and how they could be democratically controlled. This activity could extend to the corporate structure itself wherein groups within the institutions would join in their reconstruction. In such cases, councils of reconstruction would be set up once it was clear that community support within and outside of the institutions perceived the legitimacy of such an activity.

The new party's task, then, is the limited one of initiating a council of reconstruction. The council would lay out the rules of operation. In some cases, once the council of reconstruction begins to operate within the institution, it becomes plausible to work with the established structure. A group which starts with a clear view of what it is, can serve as a magnet. In this sense the coopting process will flow from the council rather than the institution.

In the history of resistance and in the attempts to redefine the social contract, certain forms of political activity continue to emerge. One of those is the idea of the shadow government. The shadow government of course is a part of the established European and British style of governing. In the United States, however, this form has not been used, supposedly because of the looseness of the political party's structure. In recent years the idea of shadow governments has emerged among Black groups and even among various people in the Democratic Party. Part of the purpose of this activity is to legitimate those who find themselves members of shadow governments prior to the time that they have legal power.

The view of Jaurès was that it would be possible to substitute such new officials either through election or otherwise because the legal state and those who operated it could no longer rule. The constituted authorities were feeble and flabby. Jaurès argues the point of continued de-legitimation and legitimizing new groups that have their basis with the people.[5] To extend this notion in the United States would mean the holding of elections within the new party which would be public. In other words, those who put themselves forward would say, "The new party stands for the following actions. You have a right to vote in the election and I'm running for the following office." It would be understood that a shadow government which came to light from such elections would always be as responsive and not as important as councils of reconstruction.*

By asserting and acting in such a way that councils of reconstruction as they formed were the paramount governing activity, charges which are rightly leveled against socialist, national security state, and communist parties as elitist and bureaucratic would not be applicable. (Note: see Part Three.) Coincident to such awareness and consciousness are the attempts to organize needed services which are now denied through the pyramidal system. For example, such services as garbage removal, health care, preventive legal service and education could be organized in new ways, in practice by new party organizers.

Participation in the Present Electoral Process

There is technical and legal activity which is necessary to undertake in the name of a new political party, viz. fulfilling those requirements to get on the ballot in all the fifty states. This action should be seen as allowing for the

---

* It should be noted that the arguments of "A Call to Resist Illegitimate Authority" were essentially the ones raised by Jaurès in attempting to understand the French Revolution. He argued that the rebels were in the Tuileries and the people were the law.

potentiality of running a presidential candidate in 1972. There are those who believe that little could be done by a President at this point even if one were fortunate enough to elect one. But that view misses the point.

Participating in certain (not all!) elections is a tactical question and not one of principle. By participating in certain elections it is possible to stimulate the transformation of the body politic without winning. This is not a paradox. Winning or losing in any particular case, whether for President or County Supervisor may be important but not controlling. The purpose of political activity is to make clear that there is an organized, active community which can simultaneously challenge colonizing groups and define its own position through dialogue with those people who are viewed by the colonizers as immobile and quiescent. Challenge and the potentiality of it helps to ensure political space. But in the immediate a party of radical reconstruction should generate councils of reconstruction in work institutions of the society. Simultaneously new party organizers need to find ways of relating to and protecting new modes of life through such councils.

The reconstructions which I have outlined in the remaining chapters of this book reflect both goals and process which in one measure could be tested through a political party and groupings which find identification with each other once they begin to challenge and transform the colonies.

PART THREE

RECONSTRUCTIONS

13

The
New Social
Contract

From the position here taken, reconstruction can
be nothing less than the work of developing, of
forming, of producing (in the literal sense of that
word) the intellectual instrumentalities which will
progressively direct inquiry into the deeply and
inclusively human,—that is to say moral—facts of
the present scene and situation.

—John Dewey[1]

The attempt to reconstruct the social contract will occur
throughout this next generation. The contradictions between what is necessary and what the few demand for
their power will continue to grow even more obvious and
more dangerous to each person. The purpose of people
in politics will be to define through their projects ways
in which they can reassert and redefine control which is
theirs and which rests with others. The question remains
as to how such political structures will emerge, what form
they will take, and which models will be replicated by the
people.

The new social contract undertakes four objectives:
First, is direct participation of citizens with each other
such that there is shared responsibility; and governing is
done in a shared way. Second, the group itself defines its

character in terms of self-fulfilling and self-denying ordinances. For example, a self-fulfilling one may be a series
of social and community services. A self-denying one may
be the specific limitation on armaments, both among its
citizens and its police. Third, attempts are made to find
ways of representation that limit the possibility of tyranny
of the chosen governor over the governed. Besides the
method of election, there is a question of finding denying
ordinances, that is, limitations of power upon the government. Fourth, the social contract is defined in terms of
economic and other institutional activities such as education, media, or health because each person lives within
them, without choice, We may see certain methods for
achieving this end.

The urban church and the university have found themselves in the situation of encouraging and being part of
new communities. As a result of the insurgent renaissance
in the churches and the ideological belief in education,
the probability will be that the power of the church and
the university as against the state will increase. In the
case where the churches view themselves as either exempt
from or challenging of the state, they will begin to operate
as a secular authority whose task will be the spinning off
of new political communities. Churches could fund such
communities and give allegiance to them. At present of
course, churches are exempt from taxation. By surrendering this privilege it does not necessarily mean that they
have surrendered the right of choosing the secular authority that they intend to pay taxes to. For example, in a city
it may well be that the church would pay its share of taxes
to the neighborhood, or to an intentional community
which it started or was involved in. These communities
would be authorized and run by people who would feel
their allegiance growing from a new humanist or religious

definition of community. They would be prepared through the way they lived on a day-to-day basis to accept the challenge which the state would thrust upon them. Church lands, church properties, funds and impetus will become another crucible in the task of challenging political authority.

The university faculty's educational duty will be experimenting in and showing ways of shaping new communities. The universities themselves become the prime units attempting associated communities since their political and economic structure could easily be integrated. Because of the student and younger faculty influence at a university the ideas of Kropotkin can be tried without embarrassment and with the possibility of their practical success. Kropotkin's view of mutual association and cooperation as the actual precondition of man's being (the reason he seeks society), will be the basis of a decolonized project.[2] In this case, the project is the new community. The idea of cooperation and mutual aid becomes natural to man. We are able to see this where the project which I begin is one in which you join. And where you are equal to me in the maturation of project into structure, we have correlated in our actions the meaning of cooperation and mutual aid. Once we have the beginnings of such structures which organize freely, we are able to confront the question of a new national and transnational compact. What are the relationships in peace which New York could have with Berlin, Hanoi and Moscow? Should there be transnational mayoral assemblies? But first we are to recognize our roots.

As Erich Kahler has said, "The United States was built step by step, by covenants, compacts, declarations of rights and liberties between free individuals, among whom every one had the same right and the same opportunity."[3] Clinton Rossiter has pointed out that America's debt to the social contract is so great as to defy measurement.

The importance of this conception remains as we attempt to define the basis of legitimacy to citizenship. The idea of the compact and declaration of rights is not the same as the emergence of memoranda of agreement between various elements of a police system, such as between the FBI and the CIA, to lay out the territory of what each can exploit. It is not the same as the collective bargaining agreement between a corporation and a union which in fact is a memorandum of understanding of the acceptance of a particular feudal and pyramidal role. Neither the agreements between the leaderships at the tops of the pyramids or the agreements between various leaderships within the national security state define the basic notion of citizenship and relationship for an individual in a group which he feels himself a part of and to which he knows he contributes. We may speak of different meanings to the social contract in the models of reconstruction.

Coleridge spoke of an ever-originating contract. By that he meant that relationships among people reflected an act of continued creation. As a result, the social contract "was a means of simplifying to our apprehension the ever-continuing causes of social union." Coleridge appeared to have accepted Paine's and Jefferson's view of the social contract.

Bringing into being such new compacts requires the reconstitution of the body politic outside of the private government enterprise and national security state model. As we have noted, it is impossible to reorganize the body politic without reorganizing the economic base of society as a cooperative one. The plantation corporate economy will be changed in the rewriting of the compacts and covenants so that it is transformed into a horizontal participatory rather than authoritarian structure. This reorganization requires a new social contract and qualitative cost analysis as well as a new political interpretation of the corporation in the democratic society. (Note pp. 303–04.) It also requires the importance of ending the contradiction which asserts that political freedom exists for the individual with an attendant bill of rights in the social contract, but that the same rights do not exist for workers and employe in the economic sphere.

Within the context of resistance and reconstruction there will be experimentation with the kinds of compacts that would serve as the building blocks for new laws and values. They may come as a result of a violent or non-violent confrontation with colonizers. Such energy will cause people to turn their attention to compact writing and drafting of constitutions as the society gears itself for a confrontation with a public and private government that controls by folly and indirection a person's life in the world. Indeed, we shall see a new Constitution, and the right wing will ensure that this event happens. By 1969, the thirty-four states called for a constitutional convention. Yet this will only have meaning in the context of resolving the purposes of governing, and the rights of the other upon me.

Making one's weight felt, mattering, is accomplished through the political vote and through the economic vote. The political election on the national level is no longer effective because the national security bureaucracy and the military do not respond to elections. The options which the present party structure offer the voter are in the wrong frame of reference so that choices which are given him in terms of ideology and personality are virtually meaningless and almost invariably disastrous. Finally, the political vote has marginal effect on the course of the nation because the institutional and bureaucratic structure (vertical organization) dictates the function of the elected officer so that even if he wants to change the course, it is virtually impossible. Even if the elected officer acts for us successfully, he is merely representing us. We neither participate nor have power in the changes that occur.

The electoral process becomes trivialized as people do not participate in decisions of a day-to-day nature, thus achieving deliberative power, or finding representatives who can effect the deliberative bureaucratic system on basic issues. The political vote, as it relates to the continuous direction of the body politic on basic issues, is dead. The political vote as it is now defined buttresses the national security state authority. Accordingly, what are ways which resurrect public discussion, public participation, public limits on representation, and public limiting of authoritarian controls of bureaucracy?

In the Declaration of the Rights of Man and Citizen, the French attempted, at the height of their revolution, to work out the basis of a representative and a participatory democracy. Georges Lefebvre points out that "All citizens," according to Article VI, "have the right to take part, in person or by their representatives," to vote taxes. While the Assembly did not act on this notion, reserving itself full power, Lefebvre believed this language authorized the direct democracy system which was "attempted by the electoral districts of Paris."[4] Whatever its meaning the need for democracy will not be denied in the drawing of new compacts in America. The political vote might matter in the following way: We may begin to see the emergence of new constitutional forms from two directions. The first is that which builds on the post-industrial civilization. Here I mean young people who don't "work," start new communities, experiment with new forms of governing and then reach out to other groups similar to their own. In the reaching out, they form a new national assembly that stems from the councils and assemblies which emerge from such new communities. These people will view their participation, their obligations and duties, in such groupings as more important than their nominal position as members or citizens of the body politic. They undertake to choose their citizenship in groups which they want to join. They do so without the panoply of privilege, hierarchy, police, armies and bureaucracies. Touching examples of this direction are now in evidence.

At a meeting between various students and professors with an assistant deputy attorney general, which included the turning in of draft cards and the challenging of the legitimacy of the war, one of the young people, Dickie Harris, got up from the conference table. He said to the government official: "Man, for me, you and your government no longer exist. In Berkeley I live in a cooperative community where we protect each other and where I owe my allegiance." He then left. This example will multiply as young people experiment with new living arrangements, as the nuclear family breaks down and as the national body politic becomes more dependent on police structures to survive.

T!.e second direction which will increase in importance is the continued and growing attempt of people to participate in the governing of those institutions which directly affect them. Thus, as change occurs, it is likely that councils and assemblies will be initiated by people in industrial enterprises, the school, neighborhoods, hospitals, social and leisure groups, armed forces and bureaucracies. If the past is any clue, it is likely that such assemblies in each of these institutions will not necessarily follow class or role lines. The political and administrative functions will be mixed together and the people who are on the "top" and the "bottom" of the enterprise will begin to participate as equals-in or equals-toward each other in such councils. These two directions are the basis for profound constitutional change, and constitute the seeds of a new national governing mechanism.

Hannah Arendt speaks of the French, Russian and

Hungarian revolutions and the attempts of the people to develop councils which would fulfill the ideas of egalitarianism. She points out that such efforts were hardly recognized and, when they were, they appeared as a threat to the party and the bureaucracy and were snuffed out.[5] One may speculate that the demise of these councils stemmed from the seeds of their flowering, revolution, which by its nature gives the appearance to the participants of chaos, and the need for authority, in which the participants and onlookers are forced to act quietly and ruthlessly.

In the Hungarian revolution, the UN reported that the councils which did form attempted to link up with other councils that had formed. If such link-ups had occurred, over a longer period of time, outside of the revolutionary moment, and where there was a history and ideology of participation, as in the United States, the answer might have been quite different. Perhaps political reconstruction could be successful in the United States just because of the ideology of participation.

A longer time span of intense confrontation and change, for example, a generation, may be the way of bringing new forms of egalitarian governing without risking the danger of totalitarian or authoritarian ruthlessness from a party or bureaucracy which destroys the original purposes of profound change. In this sense, political reconstruction is the attempt to find legitimate authority and sanction in the activities which are undertaken by those communities and places with which the individuals identify. It can best be achieved where the work to be done is carried out by everyone through an entire generation.

But is there in fact an economic vote?* We may assume

---

*One notable figure has suggested that "flexible tax rates are now simply indispensable to the effective management of economic policy—and so to strong and stable economic growth." McGeorge Bundy suggests that the power of changing tax rates perhaps "up to 20% in either direction" should be given to the Presi-

two models. One (Case A) assumes the viability of the nation-state as an instrument of a national community. The other (Case B) assumes that the national community grows out of new local compacts.

Case A — Suppose the following: The federal government and the Congress set the scale in which each citizen would be paid through the tax dollar. The individual citizen, however, then has the right to allocate proportionate sums of his tax dollar to specific cabinet departments, agencies of the federal government or required services which are based on estimates of his needs and whether a particular department is doing a useful or needful job for the country. Assume that my tax bill each year is one hundred dollars to the federal government. The obligation to pay remains. However, I have the choice of allocating forty dollars of the one hundred dollars to Health, Education and Welfare and media; ten dollars to the Department of Defense; ten dollars to Housing and Urban Development; thirty dollars to foreign aid; and ten dollars to Commerce. It would of course be necessary to put a ceiling on how much each citizen could give to a particular agency. Thus, a man who paid a million dollars in taxes would not be able to choose his agency beyond, say, a limit of 100,000 dollars. Beyond that

dent — that is to say, his staff of advisors. The Bundy argument in this particular frame is consonant with his general theory that the executive and the mandarin class should be given authority to undertake all aspects of domestic and foreign policy. He relies heavily on the omniscience of bureaucratic or mandarin intellectual power, whether the issue is tax rates or getting involved, or making limited wars. The idea of changing tax policy is a reasonable one, although I would argue that it should not go the direction that Mr. Bundy has suggested. At present, of course, the National Security Establishment dictates the general contours of what tax policy is to be. The real question is whether there are ways that taxes, that is, voting with one's money, can be effectuated. Thus, the issue is not one of placing more power with any single individual and his mandarin staff. The issue is how to undertake taxing in such a way as to measure the will of the people and to engage their participation in governing. Maintaining the present direction or adopting a solution which assumes greater authority in the President and his staff for tax policy, merely builds toward an inevitable authoritarianism.

amount he would be bound by the choice of the majority of the society.

What I would expect is that the Cabinet officers would compete for funds either through the President or individually to the people in order to get a share of my money. This would have the effect of making government a continuous dialogue and continuous experiment between the people and its government. My conjecture is that it would also have the effect of decolonizing ourselves from a national security state which spends 80 percent of the federal budget on war-making and its preparation.* Some would agree that such a scheme would have one of three results: that people would vote 100 percent for defense, that orderly processes would be destroyed, and that governments are predicated on expertise and people would not understand at all what they are voting for.

Through the next decade we are obligated to find the correct procedural formulation which would assert the way the people's will would be made manifest. In the suggestion of voting taxes up to certain limits the agents of the people would know more clearly what the citizenry wants, and that they are the active judges. It would allow the people to act as the judges of whether their agents were acting in trust, and where they were not, the people can act for themselves.

Case B — There is an alternative which I think will come to be the more realistic and favored political direction. The citizen begins to pay his taxes to new political units on the local level which give services that he understands and to which he can relate. What we now require are new political structures in which authority and legitimacy no longer follow the pyramidal structure.

---

*It should be noted that this figure has stayed constant since the origins of the federal appropriations. What has changed is *actual* amounts without serving a twentieth/twenty-first century definition of the common defense.

Mumford points out the democratic method in practice was related to neighborly intimacy and customary usage. The surplus, that is, the affluence in American society suggests that we may now afford a system of relationships not organized along the industrial and military model. The citizen now has no choice but to experiment with the question of where authority is and where his allegiance lies. It is a project which cannot be denied. The kibbutz and the new neighborhood corporation which show the direction of where personal allegiance should lie are such experiments. It is not in the violence colony or in the pharaohist enterprise.

The search for the practical redefinition of authority in the building of free communities, small communities or cities is found now among the young and those who have turned away from power as the primary way of deciding fundamental questions of one's being.* The notion of

---

* No doubt one may find a trend which will relate other cluster cities in the rest of the world to the cluster cities of the United States. In one way, the reasons for this are obvious. The problems of the American urban dweller will be more similar to the problems of urban dwellers of other advanced industrialized societies than they are to the problems that the American citizen in the same nation may have. The difference between living in a small town as against a megalopolis will be exacerbated as the advanced industrial countries find that their industrial and political structures are similar in scope and type.

The fact of the emergence of the large urban region does not mean that the present population exodus to the cities is going to alleviate the problems of the city. They will have the reverse effect. No doubt it is a fool's paradise to attempt to find the maximum or efficient size that a city should be or that a group should become. Yet, the negative can be stated with some sense of certitude. Clustering around specific areas only and emptying out the countryside will not improve the sense of participation that individuals want to have in their political and social life. The question is whether or not options should be provided for people who want to build new communities. The serious consideration of such an option would require the building of new towns on public land and the reconstruction of old towns. In the history of American development, approximately 1.1 billion acres of a total of 1.8 billion acres has been transferred by the federal government

shared and fractionated sovereignty which operated on the principle of dialectical persuasion and scientific method is only operative within the small community where the rules are set and reset by those who participate in the operation of the community. When the young, who have been taught that they are free and sovereign, find out that they are neither free nor sovereign, they will develop alternative models for living. By their presence and nature, those models will challenge the authority structure of the Violence Colony. It is the work of reconstructive philosophers to comprehend the new knowledge and wisdom which will serve as the basis for such models: the horizontal, associative community. It is their task to see how the colonized structure can be challenged to decolonize. When such models are developed either through accident, experience, necessity or plan, the individual will begin to see himself as part of a horizontal association which he helps to develop. The development of his per-

---

to individual citizens, businesses, and non-federal government organizations. For example, 229 million acres were granted to states to help support public schools, develop transportation systems and aid economic development. Presently, the federal government administers about 765 million acres of land in the United States. While the legal authority for such land resides in the federal government, it is administered by different agencies such as the Department of the Interior, Department of Agriculture and urbanizing development.

We may imagine an urban development department which would have the coordinating power and technological skill necessary to build new towns. Revenues for such a department would come directly from taxes paid out of earmarked funds chosen by the taxpayer. One of its tasks would be to charter new towns on federal land and encourage non-profit, tax-exempt institutions such as universities to work with groups of people who would now care to leave the city and build new towns. One can conceive of the New Nomads, groups of 10,000 or more citizens, organizing themselves as new town groups or through labor unions, churches, universities, who would seek federal land and economic subsidization from the government for a certain period of time to start new towns. Advisors and technicians would help such groups begin towns and would develop systems of communication through the establishment of universities and international television systems that would enable people in such small towns to have both a sense of rootedness and a sense of world participation. Another method also becomes attractive for this purpose.

sonal subjective space with the action which he undertakes outside of himself with others spells the demise of the State structure in its present form. In that frame of reference, taxes and conscription, political authority's basic staples will cease to be readily available for the state's purposes. Obviously, the accomplishment of this end is no easy matter. Human freedom, the injective sense, however, has its practical moments which not only illumine but incite fundamental change. As Riesman and Maccoby pointed out, they would never have believed that the Southern Negro college with its white bourgeois emulation and frightened demeanor would give rise to the civil rights movement, a movement anything but timid. And so there may come a politician who, when he is mayor of a great city, announces that he will pay that amount of taxes which he ordinarily would pay to the federal government for war, to his city, and he would ask his fellow citizens to join in that effort. According to Arendt, the greatest failing of the Constitution may well have been an unwillingness to relate the governing processes as described in the Constitution to face-to-face groups such as wards, towns and cities. As Jefferson said, "As Cato concluded every speech with the words, *'Carthago delenda est,'* so do I every opinion, with the injunction 'divide the counties into wards!'"[6] The social contract relationships which develop in practice in such communities and neighborhoods could become the basis of what a new constitutional relationship should be.*

Basic political choices made by dissatisfied groups within the society, such as the young refusing to serve in the armed forces or the middle class's refusing to pay taxes for war, may become the primary political and moral instruments to bring about a restoration of constitutional

---

* But that is not enough. As I suggest on p. 306, there is no other way to obtain stable participatory democracy except to include the economic enterprise as open to the reason and voice of the workers in the enterprise.

form of government. As Rexford Tugwell has pointed out, the President's power grew out of the rule of necessity in which the President proceeded to act according to his view of what was important. However, the rule of necessity only operates as a non-authoritarian tool in the democratic society in the instance where the President has the support of the people and is not guilty of manufacturing such support.

For example, at present, the forces of restoration are helped by the New Left when it says that allegiances should be found in local communities rather than in the national state. The result of such "militant" demands may make it possible for Congress, which is more directly responsive to local concerns, to attempt to restore to itself the war-making power. In this next generation the issue then will be attempting to find new authority in the local community while forcing conservatives in the society to find ways of making the constitutional form of government work. This can only be accomplished through a continuous series of confrontations by the Congress which insists that the executive has no power to make war on its own or commit troops to fight in brush-fire wars or to put down insurgencies in other countries. Such confrontations between the executive and the legislative may appear to be bourgeois, unromantic and dated. However, the fact is that in the attempt to obtain a return to divided authority between the executive and the legislative we will find numbers of politically active people becoming radicalized because of the difficulty in bringing about a change in the present political structure to meet the constitutional objective of divided authority. Beyond the dynamic of personal radicalization which will occur to those who assert constitutional arguments, demands themselves are inherently important ones to make. The pretension of being big brother to the rest of the world, dictating what its ideology and goals should be, is an impossible way to be *in* the world.

Conservative ideas, for example, such as the traditional-ist argument that the President cannot act militarily without the Congress and that the United States acts in foreign affairs within the context of decisions made by a universalized United Nations General Assembly and United Nations Security Council, attract those who are not militant revolutionaries, anti-imperialists or isola-tionists but whose concern is that of proper procedural form. The constitutional or procedural mode of confron-tation between the constituted authorities will proceed while the more direct method of confrontation for indi-viduals and groups with the state will continue with draft resistance and non-payment of taxes so long as the policy of intervention, misallocation of resources and the hostage form of authority persists. While the confrontation con-tinues, such groups will attempt to find their own roots of authority outside of the present structure of the nation-state. Their activities will force the constitutionalists who follow the procedural mode of confrontation to take more militant stances. When the attempts of the constitutional-ists fail at the restoration of the balance between the exec-utive and the Congress in the control of executive power (that is, the national security structure), in part because of the mandarin class of educated who see their power related to executive authority, rather than constitutional forms, the constitutionalists could be forced to merge with a younger generation which attempts to find new alle-giance and authority outside of the nation-state structure and in new constitutional forms.*

* There is a question of political education which should be noted, since cer-tain models of political education toward reconstruction beyond revolution and compact writing are useful to follow. A new political education will include the way television and continuous communication might ensue between the citizen

It is well to close with a note on the nature of active violence as it relates to reconstruction. Over the last several years, because of assassinations, groups within the elite public have been concerned with individual terrorist violence. The general attitude which has been expressed by the press, government officials and most social scien-

---

and the body politic. It is not difficult to imagine a technology in which the people would be able to participate and discuss choices and alternatives through the media of telephone and television while remaining in their homes. Cities are usually divided into wards, districts or parishes. Each of these units could continuously communicate with one another and *in* one another about ways to handle problems which happen within a rather specific territorial area. With the method of continuous communication, we will see the emergence of a new group of people who themselves would be new teachers, on the level of the organization of the body politic.

Such social inventions have usually been accepted by the conservative because he sees them as a way to ensure hierarchy and authority. The question now is whether there can be an intellectual extension agent who would help interpret what is going on, call things by their right names, and dare to suggest alternatives which require drastic changes, the working out of a new social contract in practice and the development of de-colonized knowledge. The energies of the young are sapped by attempts like the Peace Corps which end up buttressing authority. The young do not have to be fooled or trifled with. Perhaps the intellectual extension agent could be organized through the campus ministries and the universities which would bring together old skills of persuasion for opening up vastly different questions for analysis and discussion in neighborhoods. In part, some of the methods of the intellectual extension agent have been tried in recent years. In 1964, elements of this method were present in the voter registration drive in Mississippi. It would be the task of the intellectual extension agent to learn, teach and confront. At one time, and well into the twentieth century in many nations, there was a person who was a village reader and writer; communities again need such a person who will help them see for themselves what it is they do and do not want. He must stand outside the system of colonized power. He cannot be a social worker for the state, or a social psychiatrist for the country. Nor can he view himself as organizing people into an authoritarian union which itself will confront the colonization in such a way that nothing will change except the formation of a so-called countervailing balance in which the new leaders or the organizers turn out to be interchangeable with the original colonizer. Indeed, the leaders of the emerging or rebel group come to share the attitude the interests of the colonizer. Where the emerging or rebel group share the colonizer's attitudes, the reconstruction will have failed and a new colonization will have manifested itself. Such a result need not be inevitable when we shape the new social contract.

tists is that either violence is part of the American landscape and very much with us or is based on the madness
of the expansive American spirit.

I had occasion to testify in court in my defense on the
question of violence. I pointed out the obvious: The state
is the spearhead of violence in the society since it is the
chief organizer of the individual's experience. People,
whether left, right or center, take their cue from the state
as to how to resolve disputes. In its international relations,
that is, in the state's relations with other states or other
people, the reason of the state reduces itself to the manner
in which it employs violence. In turn, its attempted monopoly on violence is its reason for being. In America, violence itself can become translated into the worst kind of
war-making power against others by the few, and ultimately against the people of the state itself. It is true, of
course, that it is not only the state which has the violence-
making power; in a technologically rich or class-stratified
society it also includes those who own property and who
have easy access to the military or police power of the
state.

Marxists point out that the rich "control" the military
and the police structure of the state. They write the laws
of the state. They manage the institutions of the society—
institutions which, themselves, operate as social controls.
Those who decry the use of violence are of course ready to
use violence at any moment when they believe that their
personal or class situation is threatened. That is the general meaning of order. They are anxious to keep order
when it appears that what they have is threatened by
others, and they are prepared to resort to violence in
order to protect what it is that they have. As John Dewey
has said, "They do not need to advocate the use of force;
their only need is to employ it."[7] The very nature of the
social dialectic in this system is predicated on the survival

of the fittest. Where the system is competitively organized or is organized in an authoritarian structure, it is a mistake to believe that coercion is not the basis of both the competitive and authoritarian system. Thus, this coercion which is mediated through the social control mechanism, merely protects from our eyes the mailed fist, and from our ears the clanking of the jail doors. But the fist and the jails are invariably present. It is not mysterious that those who either control or use the military or who have great economic power and use the police to protect their personal situation, talk about the need for law and order, when that law itself is predicated upon a violence function which protects their real or apparent role as colonizer.

On the other hand, those who argue for a revolutionary view, again saying that violence is the only way to break either the passive violence of the state or the active violence of the state, are telling us that man is an unchangeable animal, that his human nature cannot in any way learn a new series of methods and new way of life which would make it possible to bring about a profound change outside the frame of reference of violence. Those who are indeed revolutionaries and who argue the case of violence, reject the obvious connection between means and ends, where the means used are the ends achieved. There is nothing outside of the day-to-day meaning of the day-to-day acts which individual and groups of people perform. Consequently, the revolutionary is in danger of repeating the authority structure of those whom he replaces whether or not very great bloodshed results, so long as his persuasion stems from this use of violence. The series of mediations which are created after the revolution turn out to be merely a new variation of the ancient theme of the pyramidal structure. In this regard, historical evidence is merely a series of constant changes which tell us in detail and in broad stroke the general possibilities which man can become. Where non-violent methods are used to bring about profound change, man himself becomes changed and the human nature which he projects into a future becomes his human nature and, in so doing, the structure which he brings into being does not necessarily have to be the former structure which violence dictated, that is, the old authority structure itself.

14

From Plantation Colony
to a Social Contract
of the Political Economy

**Assembly and Free Speech
in the Democratic Economy**

The political, economic and social questions which need
to be discussed by workers and managers within the
corporate or bureaucratic structure—whether in the
assembly plant or the office—will necessitate profound
changes in attitudes toward free speech and assembly
within such institutions. The idea of industrial and managerial absolutism which pervades the American economy
is protected in law as a result of the unwillingness of the
courts to apply the Bill of Rights to an individual's place
of work within the plant, bureaucracy or industrial enterprise. Private property as it is defined in terms of place,

land, machines and things where held by the few is viewed in our folklore as more important than the rights of people within the industrial or bureaucratic enterprise. Order, stability and production within the corporation are held to be more important than constitutional rights. Of course there is another meaning to property. Without re-asking the question of whether property should be collectively held, there is an alternative view within the context of private property which rejects the idea of external things as being of prime importance. Instead, the alternative view would hold that property includes the uniqueness of self which is inviolate even in situations which are not of one's own making. This view would hold by extension that one's speech and ideas serve both his uniqueness *and* his relationships to other people. Such uniqueness and relationships take precedence over that view of property which in operational aspects reflects accumulation, material constipation and control by others.

In America 91 percent of the working force population lives within the context of being employed, serving another within the corporate form. At work they are limited in expressing their views about what they do, who controls, what should be changed, etc. Obviously, it is fatuous to continue the fiction that the denial of free speech as it relates to the place of the individual's work does not cut down his political rights as well as reinforce the political economy's authoritarian aspects. Some would argue that since the corporation is "private" its authoritarian nature is hardly a political concern. But that view cannot be right. The largest corporations in America are in fact private governments. Perhaps at one time the economists and rationalizers of capitalism could have maintained the fiction that the corporation was separate from political power and authority in the state. One need only study the state's subsidy to corporate enterprise or look at the people who make up the top echelons of government, the large corporations and the banks, to see the extent of interlocking relationships between business, finance and government. Institutional economists who sang the praises of corporations (Galbraith) recognized the power of the corporation as a private public government which sets the basic framework for the national body politic and now plays an important role in international politics. But this is an aside.

In the work situation, free speech and the right of assembly aimed at discussing problems of a political nature are not allowed except in a highly restrained and formal way. When it is allowed, the worker and the union accept the notion that the worker does not have free speech and assembly as a right.

As an example, one might note the 1967 UAW-General Motors agreement which is as advanced an agreement accepting and favoring labor as one can have within the present corporate structure. The agreement states that the bulletin board is restricted to notices of meetings and union elections. It excludes notices that are "political" or "controversial in nature." Article 92 says that: "The Union will promptly remove from such Union bulletin boards, upon written request of management, any material which is . . . detrimental to the labor management relationship." Article 94 states that: "There shall be no other general distribution, or posting by employees, of pamphlets, advertising or political matter notices, or any kind of literature upon corporation property other than as herein provided."

Historically, in constitutional law, free speech and free assembly stopped at the door of the plant gate or office building. The serious business of work excluded the possibility of free speech and assembly in the context of work. The assumption is, of course, that an enterprise such as General Motors somehow is private and it would be an infringement on free enterprise if the Bill of Rights extended to individuals working for such free enterprise. Once we accept the idea that a social contract not only includes participation in the political life of the society but also in the economic and work life of the society, then it is obvious that protections and rights extend within the economic sphere of the society. There is some evidence to suggest that even now, where the corporation is effectively the political unit of the area, there is a right of free speech and assembly for people who work for the corporation even though the corporation argues that no such discussion can go on in the "territory" that it owns. Thus, Justice Black has said in *Marsh v. Alabama*[1] that corporations cannot restrict political liberties in company towns. Indeed, at universities professors (are they employees or entrepreneurs?) reserve free speech and assembly to themselves *in the context* of their work situation. This right has now been extended to school children in the *Tinker v. Des Moines School District*[2] case, where free speech cannot be denied to children.

Once one establishes the fact of the rights of speech and assembly on enterprises where people spend or rent most of their lives, then it is important to find a way for the free speech and assembly "open door" to be applied, because without the rights of free men—participation, power and deliberation—workers remain slaves. It is an important right which would allow students, organizers, the consumer to come forth to discuss problems of the corporation within such a closed unit as an industrial or bureaucratic enterprise, so that they could help to organize the basis of a different corporate life. Opening such corporations during the day at appointed hours to discussions from "outside" about what is made in the factories, how work is organized, etc., can become the basis of profound change in the economic, corporate and bureaucratic life.

The question of the "open door" in which other people besides workers may come forward to talk and explain their views within the industrial enterprise is not totally foreign to American life. For example, it is assumed that the economic corporation is able to recruit on a university campus for its purposes. It is only in the last several years, as a result of the Vietnam war, that the profit-making corporation has been politically challenged within the university corporation by students. While corporations may recruit within the university, students are unable to reciprocate by recruiting on the grounds of the corporation or within the corporation's offices and plant. In the spring of 1968, a group of Columbia University students undertook to organize Dow Chemical employees, trying to convince them that they should stop working on napalm and that they should resist the war in Vietnam. This group attempted to present their questions on company time and in company quarters. The students and faculty members who participated were arrested for trespassing.

Because the work force will be represented by people whose skill is in forms of communication rather than mechanical manipulation, such people will see free speech and assembly as a natural extension of who they are and what they believe their work to be. The industrial absolutism of the plant and the bureaucracy can be confronted through demands made in the unions and by white-collar workers.

Lawsuits assaulting the primacy of the narrow definition of property which excludes gigantic corporations from the constitutional requirement of the Bill of Rights should now be brought by workers against their unions and against the industrial enterprises. Demands within the union and among the bureaucracy of the industrial enterprise could be raised once the right of outsiders to involve themselves in the industrial enterprise is won.

Once outsiders gained access to such enterprises in order to discuss relationships between the corporate enterprise and what is happening in the society itself, new groupings and relationships would develop in the offices and factories which would work to transform the tasks and jobs of workers. Such ideas should now be developed and presented in the context of free speech and assembly — that is, as a positive right to guarantee that the social contract is not a hobbled notion made applicable in instances which are not part of the individual's life. It should be noted that the right of assembly and speech in the industrial enterprise is merely a procedural suggestion. It does not tell us what people will say, or what the substance of the transformation which would take place in the enterprise. Such judgments are for the people in the industrial enterprise to make. But there are certain clues which can be found in socialist and non-socialist literature on the question of what might happen to the industrial enterprise.

Economist Peter Drucker, not known for his radical views, sees the necessity of developing a third kind of law called organizational law which would apply to organizations in two ways. It would "make organizations perform" and "safeguard the individual's freedom."[3] Obviously this definition of the law can only be worked through in a democratic way if there is a redrawing of the social contract to give citizenship rights to individuals who are now considered employees within the economic organization. This view is based on the idea of changing the nature of employment to one of citizenship within the organizational unit. Such changes are not administrative but emerge politically through new forms of organizing within the corporate unit in relation to groups outside of the particular corporate unit that have legitimate and continued interest in the activities of the particular corporate unit as part of a larger community.

To begin the process of democratization of the factory in which workers control their life on the assembly line, and in order to allow workers the right to comprehend the effect of the goods which they make—as well as decide questions about hours, wages, and administrative conditions of the factory and investment questions in social services from profits—workers would elect representatives among their number who would serve in the local worker-community assembly. Within the plant itself workers would choose their own foremen and supervisory officers. Representation by workers in the local assembly would be complemented with representatives elected by people in the local community where one of the plants in the industrial enterprise was based. Citizens in the locale of the factory as well as workers within that factory would choose representatives who would comprise the non-worker group to the local worker/community assembly. The local assembly would concern itself with problems of the plant, what is made, its relationships to the city, its effect on environment, and its investment policies in social welfare projects. Representatives of the local worker/community assemblies would then elect representatives to an executive parliament of the national corporation. The executive parliament would be made up of workers and administrative personnel, citizens elected from the different local communities, and appointees of a proposed environmental and ecological agency. Agency representatives would also serve in an advisory capacity to local assemblies. While the executive parliament would be chosen and politicized through local elections, the President of the corporation would be chosen by his political party to run nationally as president of the corporation. For example, the president of General Motors would stand for that office every four years. He would have the power to bring with him a group of advisors. He and his advisors would operate the corporation within the limits of the proposed new federal environmental and ecological agency, along the lines established by the executive parliament and within the investment for social services context set out in the local worker/community assemblies. Under this view the enterprise would undertake the support of local, state, national and international agencies. Besides regular taxes to the first three units, the amounts reinvested in the enterprise would be fixed through the worker/community assembly, the executive parliament and the president of the industrial enterprise. Beyond taxes and reinvestment, the surplus would be invested by the parliament in projects' of rebuilding, health, sabbatical, education, social-entrepreneurial and artist activities.

One question of profound importance remains. Suppose workers would say that they wanted, with a community, a controlling voice in the operation of a plant. What would be the response of the middle class which appears to be conservative? There are several answers to be given. The new middle class comprising young, educated people will view such participation by themselves and workers as a matter of course because of the profound changes which are taking place in the Channeling Colony, where participation is demanded and received. But more important is the fact that the middle class still believes in a form of producer cooperatives. America is also a nation of small businesses. The purpose of that form in the United States is that the men or people who join together in such an enterprise attempt to achieve self-governing in the economic sphere. Is the primary issue for the middle class and the lower middle class one of profit or self-governing? If it is the latter, then the middle class will not support the owners of the great corporations or the police. If the issue is one of profit and fear that its economic situation will be challenged, the middle class will support the corporate owners.

A favorable answer to this question cannot be given until the issue of workers' control and participation is raised by the middle class where it is *not* self-governed.

Certain questions immediately emerge. What are the relations of various of the assemblies to each other? We may presume that a level of cooperation will exist which is no less efficient than the relations between General Motors and those from which it may purchase steel. No doubt a healthy meaning to planning would emerge. It would be a process that emphasized the on-going, the "ing" side of planning. It would be predicated on a judgment of people's wants and needs except as stipulated through the proposed environmental and ecological agency.

The second question to take up is what contours should the parliament of the corporate enterprise and the elected president of the corporate enterprise operate within. This question should not be answered within the classic socialist context of the "big plan" with control from the top. Instead, the answer to this question is found within a more classical idea of citizenship. It is that the public has a right to control industrial enterprise so that the environment and ecology of the society are not destroyed.

The nineteenth- and twentieth-century argument for bureaucratic socialism was its efficiency in building a floor of services such as health, education and social security from which people could not fall. Of course, the utopian kind was always present as the spur to practice and the mask of bureaucracy. This more adventuresome socialism included the belief in changing the nature of man by ending economic exploitation. The maxim was that once exploitation ended, then the problems of economic necessity could be solved. And if necessity were no more, the practice of freedom could begin. The free market capitalist argued that exploitation stemmed from human nature and once the state attempted to interrupt enterprise because it appeared as an exploitation of others, freedom would be lost forever. Bureaucracies would begin to operate in the name of an authoritarian welfarism (supposedly a necessary concomitant to socialism), and the individual would have lost custody over himself. While such arguments are interesting theoretically, we now see that in form and substance there is a considerable togetherness of method in the practice of capitalist and advanced socialist systems. The United States and the Soviet Union, as Fromm has suggested and as Galbraith believes, have become mirror images of each other. Both are attempting to relate the demand of the consumer and the technical demands of the tasks which are performed by workers within the a priori purposes laid out by the bureaucracy of the polity and the industrial enterprise.

Since the problems of distribution and exploitation remain the same in the third world as they once did in the West, the socialist analysis which calls for a central plan has powerful force and relevance to third-world nations. However, there is less relevance to the idea of accepting socialism in the Western world because the models of socialism and capitalism are bureaucratic, controlled through hierarchic institutions without roots or accountability outside of the bureaucratic structure. In the two great powers both socialism and capitalism are hooked on defense and consumerism. The people living in both pyramids until recently appeared to be content with the system of denying oneself now for consumer goods later or alternatively, using consumer goods now and denying oneself of them later if necessary. However, such a statement of either socialism or capitalism does not tell us about certain fundamental problems caused by the twentieth-century way that state socialism and state capitalism in advanced industrial countries use people and materials. These problems have less to do with price and distribution and more to do with ecology and environment. The argument which *I have assumed* is that rational production is based on either cost factors or rational behavior in the economics of the advanced industrial society which is totally different than the kind of judgments made in a scarcity society *if we* have the good of the society as the economic purpose.

The redrafting of the social contract to include responsibility, participation and some measure of control on matters that are real will cause citizens to concern themselves with conservation, ecology, and the environment. It is possible to argue that such matters could be dealt with even in the pyramidal society and through the various colonizing agencies of the society. (For example, the TV exposing the soap manufacturers for killing fish in streams.) But at best reformist intentions in the context of rhetorical hopes are presented. On the day the United States began intensively bombing North Vietnam the President sent a message to Congress imploring it to save Nature and the countryside and streams because of man's spirit (February 8, 1965). The contradictions are too great. Without redrawing the social contract and grabbing hold of an economy of death, does anyone really think it possible to stop the number of cars (good or bad) produced by the automobile corporations? And if not, then what? It is not enough to see socialism as the answer to this question.

The socialist method of setting limits, for reasons of distribution and price, is essentially a method to deal with scarcity problems in industrializing society. And the methods which they use to set price and distribution are merely the next stage in the rationalization of the economy as found in a corporate capitalist system where the managers of the great corporate units act from their preference to control the economy's direction. It is obvious that issues such as scarcity still maintain their importance and meaning, especially in the poor nations. However, in a nation such as the United States, the issues once presented through the socialist scheme for political control and the setting of limits of what is to be made have been transformed into far more meaningful ones. We now find that what we spend, and the way we spend it is causing a negative result on the ecology and environment of the society. Even in socialist nations, attention may have to be switched to the environmental and ecological health of the society.

Much of what we import for a high-level technological economy has a debilitating effect in the United States while simultaneously robbing the third-world countries of resources which it needs. In an authoritative book put out by the British Political and Economic Planning organization, entitled *World Population and Resources,* the statement is made:

> As, in 1950, the United States was using about half the world's supply (of minerals) and was increasing its demand at about 3% a year . . .[4]

During that period, the United States consumed, according to the Paley Report, more than half of the 1950 supply of such fundamental materials as petroleum, rubber, iron ore, manganese and zinc. In that report there is a listing of the demands for minerals made by the United States which have proven quite prescient. For example, our metals, fuels and non-metallic needs have almost doubled since 1952; the demand for timber has risen substantially, etc. As the PEP report showed:

> . . . the U.S. consumes about half the world consumption of leading materials and the remaining countries of the West consume another 45%. This means that the consumption of the underdeveloped countries—nearly 3/4 of the population of the world—is only 5% of the world consumption.[5]

That is to say, as the PEP people have noted, the mineral and resource consumption of the underdeveloped countries is relatively insignificant. In other words, the third-world anti-imperialist argument against the West has its basis in fact. The United States has done nothing to change this remarkable imbalance. In its UN votes it has consistently voted either against the entire membership or against third-world nations on trade/aid matters. The problem of this form of imperialism will intensify as Americans need more to live because of technology. It should be noted that over the next few generations the United States will become more and more dependent on materials and resources from underdeveloped countries. Technology is voracious in its appetite and dependence on particular items such as nickel, cobalt and chromium. The standard of living in the West—especially in the United States—reflects this appetite.

In America, we moan about the fact that we are poisoning ourselves with our products, our ugly cities, our pollutants and our inability to study the interplay of component actions that we undertake politically and technologically. We have not found a way to manage natural resources or relate knowledge to human beings so as to be able to understand the interplay between the various forces operating in the modern world. It is obvious that the questions which get studied in the society do not reflect the challenge to those institutions that, in their course of doing business, add to the problems of man. Thus, it becomes paramount that we see the scientific bases for setting limits to what the face of the society should look like which will stem from humanistic purposes. This will be translated into a politics which sets limits for those forces and institutions of the society that can destroy man himself. There are certain practical proposals which one may consider. First, perhaps, is the establishment of university programs in environmental and ecological study and health. Another is the establishment of a national institute of environmental and ecological health which would undertake to do the basic research necessary to comprehend the effects of pollutants on people and all those various questions which related to the scientific and political degradation of man as caused by the interactions and interplays of people, by what they make and what they do. Thus, seemingly unrelated matters must now come to be related together. For example, such questions as the building of a 2000 mph airplane and its effect on the psychological well-being of people within the air route of such a plane; or the effect that such a plane has on the rebuilding of highways and therefore on the cities and tax bases of those cities. Or another example: the poisoning or changing of the atmosphere as a result of the kinds of jet gases which are emitted from such a plane.

What we require is nothing less than the studied control over technology, the dismantling of that system of economics and politics which presses man forward in a technology that spells his own doom.

While one may propose, as I would, the establishment of a national and international environmental and ecological agency which undertakes to set limits on the political or industrial enterprise, there remains the first step to take. It is the development of those ideas which deal with the interrelationship and interplay of natural forces and man-made institutions which now escape our study. As René Dubos has said:

> The more life becomes dependent on technology, the more it will be vulnerable to the slightest miscarriage or unforeseen consequence of innovations; hence the need for studies of interrelationships within complex systems. Science will remain an effective method for acquiring knowledge meaningful to man only if its orthodox techniques can be supplemented by others which come closer to the

human experience of reality. To serve human welfare, action must be guided by a better knowledge of fundamental human needs. A truly human concept of technology might well constitute the force that will make science once more part of the universal human discourse, because technology at its highest level should integrate the external world and man's nature.[6]

We are left with wondering how the operations of such an agency can be democratically controlled. Some would argue that the replacement of managers with the environmentalists as the authority which calls the tune for the rest of society may end up no more helpful or democratic than the system of controls that presently operates. No doubt, it would be argued, it is better to breathe clean air, but it is not possible to argue that the system is more democratic. An operational answer to this argument is required, since we have begun to see that scientists in politics act out of personal interest in ways similar to any newly emerging class that grasps power and money in any way that it can get them.

Over the last several years, a conception of advocate-planning has attempted to play some part in determining the shape of the cities. For example, some planners undertake to serve poor communities as advocates to prepare alternative plans which would protect the poor community against the incursion of a highway system. We may extend this form by suggesting that not only would there be official agencies that would operate with worker-community assemblies and the national government, but there would be advocate planners whose tasks would be the analyses and independent evaluation and monitoring of what the environmental agencies undertook to advise.

In the *Report of the Environmental Pollution Panel* of the President's Science Advisory Committee there is a detailed discussion of the "unfavorable alteration of our surroundings, wholly or largely as a by-product of man's actions . . ."[7] The discussion suggests how and to what probable degree we are poisoning the atmosphere and the land, the cities and people through the things we make and the systemic relations which occur between things and men once they come into contact. Let us follow this point through in terms of the effect the automobile has had on American life. The motto of the largest auto company was best expressed by its president, John Gordon, and its new emphasis on diversity: "Our objective is not only a car for every purse and purpose, but you might say, a car for purse, purpose, and person."[8] Once the automobile had the effect of freeing people to go places outside of their place to seek nature, friends, to escape parents or to find and go to work. Now we begin to see a different ecological, environmental and social result of the witless direction of cars for every person, purse and purpose. The number of cars which we have and continue to produce each year (8.4 million) has caused us to adopt a particular kind of roadway system which has the effect of killing small towns. By the highway system which we have adopted, the cities in the United States are divided by class, and race, with a constantly shrinking urban tax base. The cars and buses themselves pollute soil along major routes of travel through lead poisoning. "Studies have shown that the lead content of soils and plants along roadways varies directly with traffic volume and decreases exponentially with distance from the highway."[9] Gasoline consumption in the United States rose from forty billion gallons per year in 1950 to about seventy billion in 1964. "By 1980, the use of gasoloine in the Los Angeles area will have increased by a factor of four since smog was first noticed around 1945."[10] The result of such increases on life expectancy and illness is very great. There are "striking increases in illness and death . . . [where] acute air pollution incidence" occurs above a certain level. Besides this marked increase where there are acute air pollution problems, there is a continuous problem at lower levels of exposure to eyes, nose and throat as well as damage to vegetation.[11] This condition is partly caused by incomplete combustion in the automobile engine and losses caused by venting of noxious gases into the air.

The life expectancy of an automobile is little more than five years. Each year approximately five million tons of cars are turned into scrap which is then loaded onto valuable land now used as dump sites. What then is the result of an endless orgy of cars on the road? (a) Increased highways which kill small towns and divide up cities to the point that they are merely festering adjuncts to highways; (b) increased incidence of death, irritation and disease in America as a result of noxious fumes emanating from the transportation; (c) use of raw materials from poor countries for purposes which are harmful to us and useless to them; (d) defacement and devaluation of the land as a result of obsolescent cars which wear out and are quickly replaced; and (e) an irrational pattern of production which focuses on profit and growth rather than the total effect such production has on the society.

We may begin to make an environmental analysis in many arenas of American life. A first step in such an analysis is to trade off the social benefit, the personal benefit and the long-term effect of using up materials for things in the way we now use them. The unfortunate fact is that there is no planning unit attached to political or economic publics which either compares such relationships or suggests ways, either by law or reason, that would cause industrial and other economic enterprises to choose a different purpose than the present one, viz., deciding on the basis of high, stable profits and more power for the managers who press mergers on their corporate enterprises to increase their personal authority.

To control the junk of the economic system now encouraged under the guise of economic growth,* the worker-community parliaments would operate with a federal agency which would work out a national plan that operated solely from principles having to do with the ecological and environmental effects of goods made. Their task would not be to dictate price or distribution except as consideration of such questions was necessary to save the countryside, the city and people from harm and extinction. Their recommendations would be open to cross-examination by other scientists.

This program would operate in various industries after a sufficient number of public studies were conducted that concluded the industry in question was clearly affecting in a significant way the body politic. Three tests might be considered to determine the public character of industries: (a) that the industries are using public businesses and operating them as private institutions; (b) that by their size they are so great as to dictate the character and contours of American society; and (c) that by the way they are operated they can cause sufficient public damage to the health and welfare of the society that in their present conditions they are hazardous. In the first class of cases we might begin by studying the electronic communications and radio media. In class two, we might think of the weapons industries, airlines, telephone and automobile industries, insurance companies and banks of a certain size and magnitude. In the third class of cases, we might think of the drug industries. Consequently, democratization and worker-community assemblies would start in-

---

* The standard of economic growth is so imprecise as an analytic tool that negative and positive activities are both counted as adding to economic growth. For example, carcinogens packaged as cigarettes are counted as part of economic growth, while anti-carcinogenic lobbies and activities are not counted as part of economic growth.

itially in those industries which in fact were private governments. They would now be governed by democratic principles of participation.

During a transitional stage private stockholders of the corporations effected with the public interest would be protected to the extent that they continued to hold the stock. They would be paid on the basis of a fair return. If the stockholders cared to sell the stocks, they would be required to sell them back to the industrial enterprise. Such enterprises would be mandated under law to sell or redistribute stock ownership to public bodies such as cities, neighborhood corporations, public investment funds or eleemosynary institutions that were democratically controlled.*

The environmental and ecological agency would operate to set limits for the corporations which could adversely affect the health and welfare of the society. It would, therefore, include various of the democratically voted-upon corporations while excluding others. On the other hand, it would also set standards and limits for other corporations which by their size did not, a fortiori, adversely

---

* A word is in order about the function of the stock market. For the most part, hundreds of billions of dollars of paper money in the form of stocks changes hands on a yearly basis. An infinitesimal amount of such funds find their way into productive capital use. Productive industry and enterprise no longer depend on the stock market to obtain capital. "The purchaser of stock does not contribute savings to an enterprise, thus enabling it to increase its plants or operations. He does not take the 'risk' of a new or increased economic operation; he merely estimates the chance of his corporation's share increasing in value. The contribution his purchase makes to anyone other than himself is the maintenance of liquidity for other shareholders who may wish to convert their holding into cash. Clearly he cannot and does not intend to contribute managerial or entrepreneurial effort or service."[12] And, as Berle concludes, why have stockholders? Stockholders neither work nor earn their rewards by giving their capital. They are, as W. H. Ferry has pointed out, bettors very little different than those who put money down at the gaming tables of Las Vegas. But for the fact the players are attempting to maintain a rentier position without concern for the productive utility of the goods of the corporation, we would see this entire class of players as parlor pícaros.

affect the environment and ecology of the society. It followed. Thus, for example, the city of New York might would be understood that each industry would hire ecologists and environmentalists who would help in the operation of the plans laid out by the new agency. Such an agency would operate locally and regionally with the corporations and the cities to ensure that the limitations were now feel free to ban cars from Manhattan and a politician in New York could demand such an action without feeling that he was undercutting General Motors or his own political life. Instead, it would become his obligation to work as part of a political party which attempted to bring forward such a program and to bring into line the politics of the society with its needs.*

---

* Obviously, numerous studies should be undertaken to ascertain how such a plan might operate and in what ways. No doubt there will be arguments of style and method. For example, should a local plant have local representation on its board? Should national corporations operate abroad under the Webb-Pomerene Act; should there be competition between the corporations; should the United States give and lend money to other nations in order to buy American corporations abroad so that they may be owned by nationals of other countries? In other words, should the United States encourage expropriation of American corporations abroad in order to protect itself against the facts and charges of imperialism? The seeming retrenchment of American economic influence outside the United States may be the only way to survive in the world.

15

From Channeling Colony to Educating Society

When we begin to think about the purpose and utility of the modern school, whether it is elementary, high school, or college, we must be aware of the functions it serves which are not immediately apparent. Besides acting as a control mechanism, compulsory attendance "frees" a parent from worry about the child during a six- or seven-hour period. In that period, the parents may work or engage in other activities. This is not a bad thing. It is only to say that there are many motivations for school. As Philippe Aries has pointed out, the historical justification for the school in Catholic countries was to teach morals to the young who were influenced by their parents in the ways of the profane. The children were taken out of the home to learn the ABC's of morality.[1]

The moral criterion is no longer applicable since the

definitions of who or what is moral seem to be under scrutiny by the children rather than the adults or the schools. Schools and adults have lost their authority to set out the basis of moral definitions and limits; that is, they are no longer believed just because authority says so. Once the mock definitions of morality were broken because of this onslaught on authority (knowing your opportunity, and minding your p's and q's in the way the Channeling Colony laid out the framework of the p's and q's) we are left with other justifications for the school that are real but not as "high-minded." An economic justification remains.

It is the accepted dictum that the more children there are in school, the smaller will be the burden on the economic system for jobs which it might be unable to provide or give training for. The hope is that the longer people remain in school the likelihood is that they will someday be able to get jobs because of their education. There may now be evidence to suggest that this view is merely myth, for while it may be correct in the particular, it no longer seems to hold true as a general practice because of the profound shifts in requirements of the society. So long as there is stability in the society, what is needed seems set in concrete. Where the goals are no longer determined and the structures themselves are under attack, the jobs that one plans for appear foolish. Thus, the screening and channeling which the school may do for the corporate system is no longer a viable function in its own terms as the economic basis of the society comes under scrutiny and profound change.

Once the Channeling Colony begins to deteriorate as a well-oiled machine because there might be too many children in school, or the authority systems in the school are under challenge because the knowledges taught seem empty as compared to what can be learned informally and by personal experience, the brightest children reject the school and the sorts of education which would lead them to the Plantation Colony. They begin to use the society as a place to study and change, rejecting the more contented idea of their parents and the authorities that the school and learning in it are for the purpose of mediating oneself into a priori notions of what "reality" demands. Children and their teachers begin to act on the basis of what they see, the contradiction between the schools (higher and lower) as a place to learn and what goes on becomes virtually impossible to contain in the old structures. Perhaps because of the great social movements of the nineteen-sixties, the civil rights movement, the attempt on the part of some educators to recapture the idea of spontaneity in education, certain truths were rediscovered by children, students, and teachers. These truths when acted upon, subvert the framework of the Channeling Colony with its extrinsic rewards and delayed payoff assumptions. It is no longer possible to deny the obvious.

A child or person who wants to learn and think does so either in isolation or in discourse and play with friends and adults whom he respects. Persons use private moments in the bathtub or on the toilet to explore questions that are important to subjective understanding. It is in such situations that a person turns questions over in his mind and considers avenues of investigation and thought. For a child the experience of learning is in the context of play and playfulness. The child learns physical and mental activities, language and walking, in an atmosphere of love and self-testing and personal experimentation. He tests his being in the world. He finds what is useful to him, to his parents and peers by this system of testing. In his play where rules emerge between himself and others they are of the kind that he accepts because he enjoys the activity that the rules make possible, as in checkers or marbles.

In games such as tag football he believes that the actions are negotiable. Consequently, he undertakes to negotiate the actions on the field against the rules. Before his beside himself is developed the child learns and attempts to find his being in the world through love and rule making which flows from the activity he undertakes. Such activities can have useful content. Where children and young people are organized in terms of tasks which they learn about and work at in the community, the malaise of not having "something to do" or feeling useful could become unknown. Real work and learning—not mock disciplined work as in many Montessori schools—becomes an attainable and immediate activity where results are felt in children's time.

Given this measure as the standard of how to learn, it is no surprise to note that the schools are utterly incapable of providing this framework. In the last decade the breakdown of the schools (except in terms of offering anything but the sort of "excellence" which was required to beat the Russians to the moon) generated considerable discussion of innovation. They included massive doses of federal legislation and monies which were to shore up the Channeling Colony. The practical result of this interest was an increase in jobs for those with guidance and other social control training. It also meant the extension of the economic corporation into the field of "education." Such firms as Xerox and Time-Life undertook to get a piece of the education market with government funds. In this process they undertook to challenge the school bureaucracies and administrators who saw a challenge to their power from teachers who know equipment, and from equipment that might need different (or no) teachers. But little changed for the students except that they became pawns in the struggle between the old administrators, the new learning technique people and the young Peace Corps-type idealist. The fundamental institutional result of those efforts has been to build the importance of the school within the community as a central place for the teaching of hierarchy, competition and submissiveness to the young while serving as an employment and opportunity market for adults not otherwise gainfully employed.* These opportunities are not very meaningful to the young. The schools still remain the encapsulating instrument against them—especially in the cities.

There are ways of turning schools around. We might begin by changing the "have to" quality of them by repealing the compulsory attendance laws. These laws operate to keep the children in line, off the streets and out of the factories and teach them how to be punctual and deny to their parents the right of educating their young in the way they choose. That is to say, the compulsory laws are an instrument to rationalize pyramidal discipline in the body politic.

There is no need for compulsory attendance of children when parents and children (as they get older) agree upon what a child is supposed to know after a certain length of time. Parents and those nominated as "teachers of the community" would work through a program for children which the parents could join as aides and resources. Parents and teachers would prepare materials and places where the child could learn what was mutually agreed upon for and with the child. In this situation, the school would merely be an occasional meeting place but not the place where a child is expected to learn. The teachers of

---

*During this period I served as a member of the Panel on Educational Research and Development. I first suggested that the universities should take over the schools in the cities on a contract basis from the local boards of education. They would be responsible to local boards of parents. Thus the schools of New York City (Manhattan) or other cities where there were great universities would operate the schools, setting up curriculum with the parents who would be on school boards—one or two schools to a board. I had hoped that this would have the effect of bringing back the whites into the public school system while at the same time offering an exciting radical educational experience for children. I had hoped that education by such a system would not necessarily mean merely educating for the next rung in the ladder, although this was a naive view on my part. On the other hand, the idea itself very quickly came to be changed until it was unrecognizable in practice.

the community would be paid by the community either to organize much smaller new schools, start neighborhood science library centers where small groups of children could attach themselves, and prepare teaching plans and materials to show how quickly and thoroughly areas of knowledge can be taught to children. The teachers of the community would work out of a school or television station, a cooperative house of young people who gave up on family life, a university, art gallery, and would serve to organize learning and action experiences to show children how to bring about change in the society while comprehending and appreciating nature. Their classroom would be the institutions of the society and the natural phenomena of life.

Over the last several years I have been working at the task of setting up such a school. Following the idea of the mini-school but rejecting Paul Goodman's notion that the curriculum must be open and unstructured, we are beginning two such schools in Washington with rather clear purposes. Each school will have thirty children. Reflecting the neighborhood, one school will most likely have an all-black population and the other will be integrated. Each school would be divided into two groups so that greater individual attention can be given to the children. The members of the school will be between the ages of nine and twelve. I have chosen these ages for two reasons: One is that by nine, children are usually at the point of giving up on formal knowledge and learning except that of learning the trivia of staying in line and faking. Second, it is a time when they have achieved internal discipline without having lost curiosity, creativity and risk-taking forever.

Each school will have two teachers. The two schools together will have a coordinator whose task will be to make arrangements for activities which I describe herein. Over the years I would view this task as a rotating one between the teachers. In advance of the schools' beginning a group of representative participants from the various institutions met on a regular basis to plan a curriculum and thrash out their own biases.* Children between the ages of nine and twelve met in seminar discussion to plan the nature of the school. We found that the children wanted to analyze institutions simultaneous to creating new ones. Thus, in the process of creating something new they wanted and needed to know how it was done by others. The institutions of the city were the classroom and it is intended that about twenty half-day sessions would be spent in each institution. The rest of the day was to be given over to the child's own projects which related to analysis and reconstruction of institutions. In planning the school I started with seven purposes: 1) To encourage children to analyze institutions and what they do with clear eyes; 2) To encourage children to use their creativity and imagination cooperatively in ways which will get them to know how functions now performed by institutions either should not be performed, or could be performed in different and more democratic ways; 3) To give children the strength to be misfits in a colonized world by igniting their own creative and active political impulses through their ideas and practice; 4) To get beyond the confines of the classroom and involve in teaching people who work in the world and who have things to say and offer children; 5) To open institutions for scrutiny and discussion by children and people within those institutions who have responsibility for their operation; 6) To train teachers in seeing institutions function, to learn administrative skills in setting up schools and to develop new curriculum; 7) To study ways through a mini-school task force in which ideas and suggestions developed in the

---

* Funding for the first year was private. It ran first as an after-school activity. The school was operated by Phil Brenner and Ken Fox. Strong support for the school came from members of the District of Columbia Board of Education.

mini-school project can be made relevant to larger numbers of school-age population.

The following questions are taken up in curriculum materials by the representatives of the institutions in dialectic with the children and their teachers of the community, who go with the children to the institutions:

Scientific Method: The development of a program operated at an in-town science laboratory, such as the National Science Foundation or National Institute of Health. The scientists explain why they work on certain questions, why they follow certain procedures. They also undertake to give children problems to think about and work on. They show the children scientific criteria for judging. Is science an art form? Why do we have certain kinds of research and not others?

Museums: Who operates museums? What do they do? What areas of life do they study? How are exhibits prepared? Who comes to the museums? Preparation of an exhibit with the children . . . one which they work on. Suggestions for alternatives to museum structures. How do museums present non-white cultures? Why? Are there ways to change museums? How are plundering, collecting and exhibiting related to museums?

Art, Music and Design: What do artists do? Where do they work? How is their work involved in the community? How is the art market presently organized? Are there alternative ways? Working with artists in their workshops through the Corcoran Gallery, Juilliard String Quartet, rock bands, etc. Encouragement of creative designs of buildings and free forms.

The Defense Establishment: Why do we have armed forces? Why do we have nuclear weapons? How much do we spend on military purposes? What people benefit from the armed forces? Who serves? Are there other ways of protecting American society? What are they? Are the armed forces another form of play? What happens in war to people? Study within the Department of Defense and discussion by leading Defense experts. Playing of war games and then of a peace game to settle disputes.

Health Seminar and Health Knowledge: How do hospitals and clinics operate? What signs do doctors and dentists look for which show health or disease? What is the human body like? How does it function? What different ways could hospitals, clinics, etc. operate to ensure a healthy society? What systems of medical care do other countries have? Who operates the drug companies? How are they monitored? (Discussion of insurance, neighborhood centers, etc.)

Architecture and Planning: What are the different schools of architecture? Who runs the architecture business? Why do certain buildings get built and not others? Are there new ways of considering what should be built? Who should design streets, houses and buildings? How are models built? Students should make their own models. How should plans for the future of a city be drawn? Who should draw them?

Television and Radio: How do television and radio work technically? Who controls television and radio? Why are there commercials? Why are there networks? Children learn in a television studio how television operates from an engineering and presentation point of view. Are there other forms of telecasting where there can be real participation? Children learn to operate television and radio stations; present themselves on television and radio.

Newspapers: How do newspapers work? Printing, collecting information, advertising. What gets reported? Why? What is news? What are the different ways a newspaper could operate? High school students come forward to show their newspapers. Put out school newspapers.

Courts, Police, and Jails: Why do we think we need police? What are the causes of crime? Do we need jails? What other disputes get solved in the courts? What are protections which citizens need in the courts? Which groups of people benefit most from the police? Who do the police protect most, or do they protect everyone? Are there other ways to operate a police force besides the way cities presently do? Are there new kinds of courts which can be developed for neighborhood disputes?

Bureaucracy—The Study of Public Welfare: What was its original purpose? How did it get started? How much does it cost? Who operate as welfare and social workers? Are there other groups in the society that receive welfare but don't think about it that way? Should there be welfare? Should there be standards for people in order to get welfare? How could welfare be organized differently?

Perhaps universities might undertake specific programs of graduate study to begin such schools along similar lines. Graduate students would be encouraged to work as a group to start such schools. For them there would be three major activities: (1) planning the operation of the mini-school program; (2) teaching in it; and (3) doing a critical evaluation of one's own work and of the program, setting out other models for schools either in theory or practice.

Students of education themselves would be opened up to a subject matter of education which would be both exciting and human. They would be involved in bringing a new kind of teacher into being—the *teacher of the community.* He would be studying and causing the institutions to change their own directions in reconstructive, non-hierarchic ways just through the commitments and activities which they would undertake to open such institutions.

We may note two other organizational methods which would have the effect of changing the basis of the school. In the last several years Joseph Turner, Jencks and I have attempted to work through a variety of models building on the present public school to a lesser or greater degree:

Model I is the straight organizing of a school by parents receiving money from the federal government and foundations, operating according to basic rules such as non-discrimination because of race. In this case, the school would receive 20-year charter grants and would be organized by parents and teachers. The only other requirement to obtain funds would be a certain number of students—say, fifty.

Model II is a model school system where various projects are tried, which has independent power and controls its own destiny, hiring and firing policy. It has been tried in Washington, D.C., with partial success.

Model III is a university school system in the ghettos with professors, graduate students and others teaching in this system. The university would contract with the city school board and now be responsible and accountable for what goes on in the local schools to a new local board of parents and citizens of the immediate area. This administrative method has been tried with success in Washington, D.C. in the Adams-Morgan residential area with Antioch College and the Morgan elementary school. In the first year, the problems were the narrow base of community involvement, mistaken emphasis on needing "experienced" teachers, and inadequate discussion with the local school board on what was to be taught. The principal believed himself to be responsible to the community. Consequently, Antioch College thought of itself in an advisory or consultant capacity rather than as the major moving force in the school. By the second year, however, the college had changed its relationship formally, and the local community organized, controlled and staffed the school. The local board included teachers from the school, teenagers, parents, and citizens of the neighborhood elected by the local community.

In my view, however, Models I, II and III assume the answer to two primary questions: They assume that children learn best in school, abstractly, and they assume that teachers are those who teach in school. These innovations —and here I am taking ones which I have been intimately involved with and have formulated with others—accepted constraints and assumptions which defeated their own objectives. We assume the wretched notion that children and adolescents have to be in school and that middle-class children should be in school for twenty of their first twenty-five years of life. By this assumption we strengthened the hierarchic and the custodial sense of relationship against the child and the adolescent. They are denied the chance of making their own personal space or associative space with others in terms of what is useful to them either as individuals or in a group. Indeed, in the middle classes the activities that the young are supposed to perform are limited to consuming goods and spending. That is the *immediate* expectation from the Dream and Plantation Colonies of what they are supposed to do in the world outside of the school.

In a society involved in decolonizing and reconstructing, continuing, drop-in and drop-out education from formal schools becomes an important way of acting and finding oneself. The society itself turns on to education as a central basis of citizenly and human activity. John Dewey hoped that the individual could educate himself through his work. His views were distorted in practice and the plantation economy distorted his views to mean educating for a job. Now the distinctions between work and education are no longer sharp and educating by necessity becomes a continuous activity consonant with a person's whole life. This change is a renunciation of habits endemic to most cultures. Historically, one believed that the purpose of education was to show how to initiate the maturing individual into the life and culture of the group. Where the group itself sees its culture packed away in museums or spread in atomic bombs there is no reason for the young to want to join, or for us to insist that they should. Further, the idea of initiation through a mechanism such as "school" assumes a society that is static and unchanging. (Note p. 345.) In such a society values are well-defined and relevant to problems that beset those being trained or initiated with the older members of the group knowing what should be known and what should be taught. This is not true of American society. While it is hierarchic it is non-traditional, just because the rhetoric of democracy and technology forces rebellion in practice at the traditional.

The sad fact is that technology and massive change have resulted in people of all ages not knowing or understanding what a few may know, or understanding how what is known changes the lives of the many. It would seem that this crisis in American society can only be dealt with through two means. One is continuous education for understanding and political control over technology. The other is wholesale destruction of machines. The second tactic, while more romantic and immediate, will most likely not be considered as serious except in a nuclear war where the technologist and technology will have exhausted themselves and nature as well. They will have willed destruction through technology, saving for themselves the right of destruction. The first possibility asserts the uncomfortable fact that technology will not be given up. And consequently all members of the body politic are forced to ask Aristotelian questions of themselves and the technologists: "Now that you (we) know that you can build it why should we?"

Perhaps technological ignorance and its liberating mechanisms may force children and adults to regain the basis of understanding with each other. As Aries has suggested, children prior to the seventeenth century lived much the same lives as adults.[1] With the sense of self-controlled time which adults may acquire, and the idea that education could go on in the adult work world with children finding some part in it—as in the Israeli kibbutz—in an immediate and gratifying way to both children and adults, it is possible that in American society the bifurcation between work and play, adult and children's world will become less sharp than it appears to be. This view results in certain conclusions about children's education. The schools are to be reconstructed by giving up the idea of the self-contained classroom and the building structure as the dictator of educational content. The child then leaves the particular classroom and inquires into the entire community as his classroom, with the understanding that the immediate neighborhood place that he lives is his base first to become aware of and, if he chooses, to join. The second conclusion is that education is no longer limited to a time of a person's life which we accept for extrinsic and non-educational reasons. This means that the terrorization, subtle or blatant, of children into assuming that they are to learn at the rate which is set by an administrative structure which has interests that are not theirs is to be eschewed. Children and adolescents will not be expected to go to school in lockstep. Instead, they would be encouraged (as they are already, but now it would be viewed positively) to drop out, say, in the fifth, or eighth or eleventh grades to return a few years later. They would learn at their speed and work at problems which they encounter and things which they create.

Cognitive and experiential education would become interchangeable. The problem and self as part of the problem in pragmatist ways would become the formal method of inquiry. Diplomas as they are presently known and grades would not be the measure of time spent in school. Indeed, the system of education would be so integrated into work and self-controlled time that fake ways of knowing whether or not a person knew would be given up. *In such a system of educating, parents would take back the right of education from the state.* No doubt they would build their own schools or kibbutzim for the children establishing places for children to be away from parents but in the immediate community near them. In some cases economic enterprises and places of work would begin schools for children so they could be near their parents and be aware of the work they do.

Once we accepted the idea of greater flexibility about when to go to school it would be possible to see that people can learn at their own speed. This has been tested in various ways by programmed learning groups. What we are to note from such studies is not that there are a set number of things to be known and that they must be taught in an authoritarian way. The important conclusion is that people can learn at their own rate at any age without fooling themselves into thinking they have learned something if they have not. When we act on the idea that education is not limited to any particular time in a person's life, we are then relieved of worrying about such questions as "he's a drop-out." He may be, but if the institutions of the society are so structured as to encourage him to come back to find the sorts of work and education he needs at whatever age without the corresponding opprobrium of not being in work or school at a certain time in his life a great personal problem for him passes. It should be noted, and I do not mean this facetiously, that an entire generation of Americans will have to return to school or be retrained. Here I refer to those in the armed forces, the CIA, the advanced technologist and others who will have to be retrained to other professions before we can relatively peacefully reconstruct our body politic. This practical problem of how education is needed for this class suggests again that education is not received, nor is it limited to one stage. Education becomes educating, and the laws of society are so written as to reflect this purpose.

When educating becomes part of rebuilding the society and we assert that it goes on throughout a person's life, certain immediate policy implications are derived. A national educational credit system would need to evolve which guaranteed funds to individuals throughout their lives to educate themselves. Each person at birth would receive a trust account for education (and other needs such as health) allowing him to act on his needs and purposes to an amount equal to that spent for obtaining a Ph.D.

The University as Body Politic

The university is not only a place of inquiry which concerns itself with the great theoretical-practical questions and extends mythically as the Source of Reason. It is a community of place with passions, interests and functions to be performed. The university is the modern body politic which now begins to show us what the political structure of other corporate and community bodies should be like.

As a body politic the university is not only an association of equals-toward—that is, a community of scholars in search of truth—it is also an association of equals-in. Operationally this means that whereas functions are performed or are raised which touch all the people in their magnitude and consequence, we are thrown onto the democratic rather than the hierarchic principle of authority. Thus, for example, the janitor, cook, professor, and student must participate in the decision process of the university regarding aspects of life which are clearly concerned with the economic, political and social rights within the university community.

There is an irony to members of the progressive labor groups and SDS on a university campus, who are usually children of the upper middle class, attempting to find the working class by leaving the campus. Instead they should see the working class in their own body politic: the janitors, laboratory assistants and cafeteria workers who are in the same situation, the same body politic as the students. I have suggested elsewhere that the basis of political organizing between the students and the working class may vary from place to place. But experience in that direction and attempts at legitimating relationships within a body politic—especially one so central to the basis of America—is that the university must go on within the university. The needs are not hard to define, nor are the demands.* Students in private universities could hold on to parts of their tuitions and pay the workers directly.

For a young person, such rights would relate to him as a full member of a political community in which he has rights to privacy, against self-incrimination, freedom of speech and action, as well as sexual freedom. The university community would give new meaning to a document like the federal Bill of Rights, and undertake to set a community to fulfill those rights. The Bill of Rights would no

---

* The problem of talking about demands is that the word itself sets up an authority relationship. That is to say, one becomes the giver and the other the taker. The better formulation must start with the idea that space exists either to do, or to take. As the saying goes, "If you ask the rabbi, nothing is kosher."

longer be a merely formal political matter between the state and the individual, since people have their rights abrogated by corporate power. To be sure, people may have the power of free speech, but not in the corporate unit in which they live their lives. Thus, students may have rights to privacy, but not against an oppressive dormitory system or dormitories planned by administrations. Obviously, formal rights are necessary for creating the spaces to obtain reconstruction.

The reconstructed intent of a charter from the state for a university is to free it from the external controls of the state. But such freedom can only be predicated on such institutions operating democratically. (Note the Plantation Colony where the same argument applies to the operation of the economic corporation.) Thus, universities would undertake to operate according to rules of community which are written by all members who work and study within the community. University charters would be re-written or re-examined to guarantee that there were democratic controls, a definition of rights within the community, and incorporation of rights generally recognized in law such as the Bill of Rights. Where groups within the university could not get on within the charter of the university, they would receive a new charter for themselves. The right of exodus—without penalty—would be protected or the right of organizing within the university as a group would also be encouraged.

To reinforce excitement in learning and knowledge, and to act politically in order to maintain peace in the university body politic, the universities will find themselves legislating a system of hiring in which students will have the power to hire a number of faculty whom they want on campus without control from either the faculty or administration. They will receive an amount from their tuitions to bring to the campus people whom they want to learn from and whom they have the power of the purse

over. The types of knowledges which will emerge from
this group of teachers will be different from the kind
which would ordinarily come from the academic profession. Faculties themselves will continue to hire people
for their departments (from their specialization or guild)
with the likelihood that those hired by them will be more
tradition minded and see knowledge as their personal
property. In this uneasy compromise the university
president—especially if he has the electoral sanction of
the university community—rather than the trustees will
also undertake to hire professors as people who he believes should be at the university. This political stand-off
between the groups could also result in the saving of the
university as a place of inquiry. Without this direction
it is likely that the university will be a place of action and
experiment to show us how to live graciously and with
privilege going to the forum or mall for talk. Whether it
will be a serious place for inquiry is open to question.
As Whitehead has pointed out, the university's role in
this regard switches from time to time so that the most
serious work is performed outside of the university in one
historical period and inside it at other times. What is
clear is that the university could be an action community
governing itself.

If, as I suggest, the reason for the state no longer fastens
upon us intellectually or emotionally, the practical effect
is that authority must rest somewhere. We may assume
that authority rests in the human association among people rather than in abstract conceptions of obedience. In
the university, where there is a possibility of building a
community through association and common purpose, we
may begin to understand why it may become necessary to
exercise historic relationships which exclude the power
of the state and thus force the confrontation of the reconstructed university community with state power. It can
accomplish this end if the university sees itself as a com-

munity which is chartered to act outside of the needs of the state—but in the needs of the community. The university, by what is taught and researched by its teachers, should find itself in conflict with state power—that is the purposes of the Violence Colony. The long-term values of the university are reason and passion. The values of the violence colony are control and destruction. While reason and passion can lead to control and destruction, it is more likely that there will be conflict between the purveyors of these different values.

Legitimating Authority and the University's Values

For a body politic to be acceptable to those living within it, authority has to be shared in a way that is acceptable to the citizens of the body politic. Take a symbolic example: Why should a president of a university be chosen by a board of trustees? The choice of the president of a university is something which involves the entire membership of the university community. Through a system of voting and participation, it would be possible for students, faculty, workers, researchers and administrators to participate in choosing a president. This procedure would help in changing the perception of the student as having no part in the governing of the institution in which he will live.

In the thirteenth century we find an intriguing situation. The chancellor at Oxford was at first appointed by the Church of England, but very quickly he became the university's representative, and the university faculty chose who the chancellor was going to be. They could not be overruled. The chancellor's jurisdiction was enormous, extending to all criminal cases (by 1290) which would include a student (scholar) of the university even if it involved someone from outside the university. "In 1290, of all cases in which either party would be a scholar, only such as involved a charge of mayhem or homicide were left outside his jurisdiction."[2] The authority of the university judicially was, according to Davis, at its greatest in 1450, when the university was allowed to assume jurisdiction over all people involved with the university who might be charged with a felony. They were to be tried by a jury composed in equal parts "of privileged persons and townsmen, before a steward, who should be appointed by the chancellor but approved by the Lord High Chancellor."[3] By this time, the chancellor already had power to assume jurisdiction in matters of debt, rent and contracts relating to personal property which involved townsmen and scholars. The chancellor also had the power to impose punishment for disturbing the peace, taxing rights in the area of the university domain, and sanitary controls over the streets.

The outlines of the past become our political instrument for reconstruction. It is likely that students, workers and faculty will seek a more active role in choosing the university president. There would be no need for trustees, who are an appendage of the state, to watch over the college (or are they representatives of the college to the outside world?). In any case once the university is a body politic only those within—or elected from the outside—have a voice. Imagine now a university community, acting as a body politic, electing officers of the university, including the president, for a term of years. His task as leader of a political community is to extend the authority of the university against the state. First, under newly-drawn charters, he would undertake to protect the members of the university and extend their numbers. The protection of the members becomes a worthy thing because the president and his faculty know that they speak with the authority of the community, not only for the trustees. They know that the activities of the people in the university involve the highest aspects of the inquiry of man. Because the members of the university community see humane purpose to what they do, they now are ready to stand against the state for those purposes because in so doing they are aware that they are speaking for the greater human community.

But symbolic changes without changes in day-to-day operating structure or objectives are not enough. There needs to be a humane purpose for the university beyond that of the few who from time to time speak from the university. Purposes are proved in the subject matter studied. Once that judgment is made, then the universities must say good-bye to war research and all the other researches which end up serving as manipulating tools of humanity. Debates and disruptions around what should be studied and why, as well as confrontations, will no doubt continue in attempts to build the university into a democratic and humane institution. One purpose of these disruptions is to clarify the kinds of subject matter that are learned and taught. With this confidence, the university community would demand immunity for itself as a separate governing entity from state incursions. The people within it and the alumni of the institution would see themselves joined in a relationship in which they would recognize that the university has its own rights and powers when it ceases to do the bidding of the state.

The university would then acquire its own political purpose, which would be tied to the purpose of human inquiry and the solution of human problems. The political purpose could include its own judicial system. For example, a court having to do with disturbances of the peace might be made up of people from the city and students, if for no other reason than that defendants should have the benefit of being tried before their peers. The university might undertake a specific taxing system which would help in the support of inquiry. (The task of a national legislature would then be the granting of endowment amounts to universities with the requirement that they be invested in rebuilding cities.) The university body politic would set the terms of how it intended to live within the society at large. Since by the year 2000 in the United States it is expected that 65 percent of the population will be in college or will have gone, we may expect that the political power of the university groupings will be enormous and will command the greatest share of the dollar as against the Violence Colony and the military. What started out as a symbiotic relationship with the pyramidal national security state will end in a confrontation. Both will be struggling over the same "objects"—material resources, money and young people.

The political influence of the university and education is related to its power to invest and its geographic expansion. Further, the university will educate virtually one hundred percent of all officers of the economic corporation, the military and the church and the state. Servicers have the habit of ending up as owners.

Since 1940 the number of people who attend a category called higher education has grown from 1,708,000 to 7,181,000. The book assets and operating costs of universities have increased from $5,194,000,000 to $50,500,000,000, and the number of people who are involved full or part time has increased from 2,077,000 to 8,058,000. Higher education is the secular religion, having the influence and importance of religion during the early Middle Ages. For example, in the ten largest states in the United States, universities—when viewed as an economic corporation— rank as the largest single employer in their states. Although it is true that the individual liberal arts college, the free-standing college, finds that its role is now usurped by the university, it is in no danger of dying because of its political potency. In many congressional districts there are usually two or three colleges which in economic terms represent an important employment and prestige source. Congressmen will be quick to protect the over six hundred colleges which fall into this category.

Given the ideology of education as the instrument to make a man whole, the economic need which the society has for its perpetuation, its use as a technological server to the authority structure, and the need to *fill time* of the young, we may expect "education" to grow in importance and to become the paramount institutional structure which organizes the lives of the largest numbers of people. This will especially be true as the machines which are made reflect the need for specialized training in some university setting. Specialists will be forced to use the university to continue to qualify as specialists. And specialization may be reversed to come to mean concern with the interplay of phenomena and forces rather than its present one-dimensionality.

Because the ideology of education supports the purpose of wholeness and personal liberation, there is a basic contradiction in the schools. Those who are responsible in the university for the maintenance of the hierarchic structure by the historical nature of the university are forced to maintain a personal stance of freedom within their hierarchic structure far beyond the freedom which is allowed for in other hierarchies, such as the military or the economic corporation. That contradiction is the basis for extraordinary change, since the ideology of freedom (as distinct from the reality) within the university setting is much more similar to the more classic definition of citizenship, that is, equality of association toward. Its form cannot remain hierarchic and continue without reverting to internal repressive measures. But universities are not prisons.

The awakening consciousness of the young is not a passing fashion. They appear to have moral and political leadership. The engaged professors who are radical in thought and action while remaining bourgeois, are involved with the young in changing the nature of the university. As the university structure does not readily change, there will be other strategies that no doubt will be considered. Perhaps a national students' union will begin to formulate a national program for education and students' rights. Students might begin new colleges in which the student organization would pay the faculty members, bargain for tuition rates with established universities, protect draft resisters and constitutionalize the university.

To effect these purposes, students will find that they will have to act as organizers of student unions and as intellectual-social entrepreneurs in setting up new colleges. In defining their purpose, they will find that there will be many professors, artists and other creative people prepared to teach as part of a national student union rather than in the present university system.

In the reconstructed model the university becomes a community which is open to all who want to learn, and the assumption is that the people who are connected to it choose to be connected. The only requirement placed upon them is that they are expected to participate in the political control of the community, and that as student and professor or administrator they are expected to learn, experiment and work toward the development of a scientific and humanistic method for resolving problems. They would be expected to carry on moral inquiry beyond the particular speciality in which they were involved. The organization of the university would be cooperative and non-hierarchic. By the nature of inquiry and discourse, what is to be known is questioned and what is to be questioned is to be known. Each proposition is neither self-evident nor is it to be based on the authority of magic and violence. As a place of community it cannot have a billion in the bank while its workers are making $1.50 an hour.

Such a university finds new and continuous relationships outside of a particular place joining to it people who want to teach and learn. The classroom now is a more informal place and relationships to the university extend to others that are adjunct to it.

Take the case of a new city college in Washington. The question is the standard one raised by overcrowded schools and physical structures: "Do we take in everyone and flunk out those whom we don't want after a short period of time," says the administration and faculty, "or do we require high standards to get into the college because of limited resources?" The question would better be formulated if there were those who wanted to teach and those who wanted to learn and the university administration acted as a broker to bring these groups together. The college might have a pool of adjunct professors who teach in their respective living rooms or bars. Such teachers would take on tutorial relationships with three students. In this frame of reference, the tutorial relationship would mean that the student and the tutor are part of a college without physically being part of a series of buildings. To this extent, the college is relieved of worrying about the problem of space as a controlling factor in concern about the let-in philosophy as against the flunk-out philosophy of higher education.

In the major cities of the United States there are people not connected with the universities who are qualitatively equal or better than those who teach in them. They would be prepared to be part of a university program of education. Once we see educating as a continuing process not bound by the walls of a place called university, we are liberated to think again about standards intrinsic to learning rather than colonizing needs. Students should be encouraged to go where they want to for education, without feeling self-conscious about being peripatetic. Many excellent colleges since the end of the second world war have farmed their students out to learn in effect on their own. The colleges realize that their own resources for teaching and research are limited. This realization gives greater meaning to the university as a freeing institution.

Independent and tutorial study will encourage the student to develop greater insight and problem-solving ability.[4] The process of independent and group study is directly related to the need by the university to prepare institutions and facilities for teaching functions so that the student does not feel totally thrown. By the student's and the professor's being part of an extended university, but setting themselves experimental problems which require cognitive knowledge (that is, abstract and indirect knowledge out of the situation), we will find students using a real problem which requires their cognitive and sensory skills to resolve. I am not referring here to the seminars in upper class colleges that tour the slums. They use the slum or poverty as their instruments of learning much in the way the grade school class might visit the museum to see how the Eskimos live. Rather, the educational experience which is required is in the nature of the existential. The project and social invention of the student is addressed to a problem of the self and the other which demands his moral and intellectual strength and commitment. In this way, the problem becomes the student's in human terms. It then has experiential meaning. (I have referred to the beginnings of this method in Chapter Nine.)

Techniques and Lines of Inquiry in Rational Reconstruction

There is a bias among the educated that those institutions which are based on reason (a large assumption) have very special responsibilities to bring about an end to the war system, world poverty and the colonized status of man. This Faustian conceit is one which gives the university its special status and which requires radical change in the curriculum of the university. In any such change, its work will relate to the highly-theoretical and new modes of the experimental practical. In the social sciences, universities dealing with the hope of education are jeopardized because their students and professors will be forced to deal with real problems that are life, not a preparation for it. Students will then find themselves confronting a colonized system with an appreciation of risk and with an appreciation of social invention in a project which they would undertake. The way the social world is organized becomes a problem of education since where the society is collapsing, the educator's task is to change the social organization of the society in such a way that it does not repeat the mistakes that led to the collapse.

Sit-ins at universities are the basis for two new directions. One of the directions is political, the other epistemological. I do not mean to deny that they are unrelated. The political change is, of course, in the legitimation and assertion of groups who now want to be part of the body politic of the university. The question of epistemology is the profoundly more complicated one because the questions which are being asked by the actions taken demand facts which are about old institutional relationships and the requirements of building new institutions. As I have said elsewhere such questions develop a set of facts and values that are not oriented to organizational methods laid out in a vertical hierarchy.

When the young occupy a building, say, for example, a radiation laboratory at Stanford University, they are attempting to say something about the relation of ethical value to knowledge. It is obvious that this question can no longer be avoided, and the university will be forced to opt out of the idea that it is supporting value-free research which in reality buttresses the basis of the imperial and colonizing structure. Social knowledge in this view would not reinforce the colonized systems but rather challenge them. A particular methodology would follow. The teacher, whether professor or theologian, helps the student with projects which stem from his dissonant and human feelings. They begin by testing the idea that the young, by doing, will gather new facts that are humanly important and will transform those doing the study.

In a policy study which Jencks and I carried out with members of the Bureau of the Budget, we learned this transformational technique almost by accident. In the study, the working group was asked to consider the changing nature of work and to consider encouraging fundamental change in the society by a system of sabbaticals for everyone in the work force, paid for through the social security system. We asked social planners to consider as serious the idea that people in the society should have one year out of seven to loaf, change jobs, travel, go back to school. At first, there was much amusement at such a notion, because it could not be considered as a potential project which they could get "them" to accept. The argument of the group as a group was that such an idea would not be politically acceptable. We argued, however, that the question of political acceptability was beside the point. We asked them to participate outside the framework of the hierarchic other and inside the framework of a suspension of political disbelief. Was the idea a good one? What was the consequence of their idea? What were its historical parallels and antecedents? Would such an idea cause reconstructive turbulence in the pyramid and build on the idea that man could come to himself given a political structure which allowed this to happen?

Then we began to see a most extraordinary situation

develop. While reluctant at first to think about the sabbaticals, under the leadership of William Cannon, now Vice-President of the University of Chicago, and then an Assistant Director of the Bureau of the Budget, this group of elite civil servants prepared a proposal. They agreed to "staff it out" *as if* it were a serious potential elitist plan for the American society. When they began working on this idea, they came forward, at first individually, and then as a group, to talk about their ideas which they had been ashamed to talk about with their colleagues for fear of being laughed at and for fear that such ideas would somehow jeopardize their status within the bureaucracy. We found ourselves legitimating their right to think about ideas which did not have to relate to their view of what their roles demanded. The basic result of this method may be not only the social inventions and programs which are created, but also intellectual and emotional liberation which is allowed when people think outside of the system of the hierarchic other.

Perhaps the students should dare the professors to come up with knowledge, facts and values that build alternative institutions. If the professors could be shaken out of their tendencies to see knowledge as property to be husbanded and sold one piece at a time, but instead to be opened to the play of inquiry and its importance, the system of rational reconstruction might begin to operate.

Rational reconstruction will work best with those who view themselves as thinking that their real property is not things, money or real estate, but rather intelligence. They will be the most likely candidates for this method. Consequently, a bureaucracy which is comprised of people who view as their work and stock-in-trade schemes and proposals are the most likely candidates to appeal on a rational, reconstructive level if they are young enough or clever enough to believe that their fate is not merely determined by the economic and social structure. Several years ago the British conservative philosopher Karl Popper suggested that the utilitarian standard of the greatest good for the greatest number was far too ambitious for a government to undertake. Promoting happiness was too much. He argued that the promotion of happiness was an individual concern best left to individuals. On the other hand, the politicians in the body politic had a very important *positive* task. It was to promote the greatest amount of lack of suffering. Social inventions and public policy in Popper's view are to be built on knowledge which does not lead to greater suffering. Now the question remains whether we are talking about a qualitative or quantitative suffering. That is, are we talking about millions suffering little or a few suffering much (usually is it the other way)? This question can begin to be answered when we devise a matrix which explains the likely effect of various activities.

Obviously, certain actions by insurgent groups will cause greater suffering where there is no willingness to give up power by entrenched groups. In this sense the revolutionary and the reconstructivist may appear in the short term to be causing greater immediate suffering than the colonizer who espouses order and stability. This view through the prism gives a terribly distorted picture of reality which can be corrected by the questions that are asked about particular actions and institutions which exist or are proposed. The questions which we might ask are now crude, of course, awaiting the refinement of those who care to improve the procedures and ways of thinking about doing and action. What is clear is the present need for a procedure which judges actions by those undertaking them and those who study them.

A methodology for judging our practical actions cannot wait for profound change to occur first in the society.

Indeed, integral to any profound change must be a method of judging which is simultaneously developed through the projects and social inventions put forward. Such a methodology is not neutral. For example, there is nothing neutral about surgical procedure, which is now internalized in our system of action and thought. Surgical procedure is predicated on the value of saving the patient's life. There is an entire *prior* value system which assumes that value over others.

The procedure which I suggest as a tentative way of organizing analysis of an action or recommendation of change in public policy turns out to be profoundly political in that, by the questions which are asked, changes in the value structures of the society are required which assert that value be defined outside of the modern pyramidal state. That is to say, values no longer remain a word to be studied or scorned, but instead become a reflexion of a profound set of purposes and judgments which stem from emphasis on the protection of human life, or, as Popper has suggested, not arranging or structuring greater pain. In this sense, the theoretical problem is to find and ask those questions which result in comprehensive, comprehensible and unambiguous values. A social contract's purpose is to protect the living and to develop social inventions and knowledges which secure particular broad objectives. *Empirical research becomes the basis of finding answers to those questions which celebrate humanist values.*

Such humanist research then supplies the ground for debating questions of power and interest. The type of inquiry becomes the procedure which is as habitual as surgical procedures are prior to operation. They are the prior prerequisites for judging. It should be noted that the questions to be asked are *not* questions based on class. Instead, they are environmental and ecological

questions which discern responsibility as being beyond
the immediate particular economic, political and social
interests of those who have or want power.

Such questions are not limited to judging new projects
and social inventions. They become a primary tool in
analyzing the effect and nature of the pyramidal state
which by its nature takes on repressive functions and
in its operation is destructive of human values. My
argument is that any public policy should be mediated
through a series of questions which for whole categories
are the same. Thus, the question under analysis could
be a 2000-mph airplane, the establishment of a new
town, the making of 10 million automobiles, the building
of a highway, the development of a chemical and biological warfare program. Obviously, the level of certainty that can be known will be different in each case and
dependent upon the subject matter, it may be necessary
to have different standards of certainty regarding conclusions. However, this point does not vitiate the idea
of preparing procedural questions which become the
basic questions to be asked prior to undertaking a particular action, doing or program. The problem in the
context of the pyramidal state is that it is dubious that
such questions will be decisive indeed, even instrumental
in dismantling the pyramidal structure. The reason, in
part, is the ideology of waste, accumulation and expansion which has created the system of illusion and
reality. This operates in practice as if the body politic
can only survive in a framework wherein people's liveli-
hoods are to a great extent dependent on death-oriented
structures. This ideology has now worked out its own
mode, program-budgeting and systems-analysis which
accepts the values, assumptions, and purposes as given.
The analysis which is used turns out for the most part
to be an economic one in terms of cost benefit according

to the assigned mission of the particular institutional structure. What is interesting is that the mode of analysis which is provided in this case stems from work done at the RAND Corporation and at General Motors; that is, in the defense area and in cars, two of America's major industries. Perhaps a series of questions can now be asked upon which an accurate judgment of a particular project or social invention can be made which rejects this ideology. These questions should relate to a matrix the values of which are constantly re-examined. These questions to be asked can serve as a primary basis for rational discourse about change:

(1) What is the effect on the people who are living in the immediate area of a particular activity if it is undertaken? For example, uprooting people for a highway which would probably result in the early death of older people, concentration camp fences in the cities to keep children away from the inner city highway, probable destruction of the social fabric of those who live in the area. What are the probable benefits to certain groups? Highway contractors and more profits, greater employment in the local area, greater access for traffic and continued existence of the automobile industry.

(2) What is the effect on men? Will different classes of men be affected differently?

(3) What is the effect on children? How will they be affected by the action? Which children? Hosts as against users?

(4) How will women be affected by the action? Will they be helped or hindered? Which women? Hosts against users?

(5) How many people are affected by the action undertaken? For example, if a modern power plant is built, should those not apparently aware of its effects

be protected through government or should they have a direct voice in deciding whether it is to be built?

(6) How does the action affect the natural habitat of the area? In the foreseeable future; in the next several generations?

(7) How does the action affect the level of noise and, once it is built, the assault on the eye of the individual? (Are such questions now more than matters of taste?)

(8) How are animals affected by the action undertaken?

(9) How does the action taken fit with apparently unrelated other actions in the immediate area, regionally, nationally, internationally?

(10) What is the effect of the action on a) water, b) land, c) air?

(11) What is the cumulative effect? Are there long-term effects which differ from short-term effects that compensate for disruption for children, women, men, air, land, water? Are there long-term effects which have bad results for land, water, sea, air, men, women, children so that the apparent action is in fact illusory?

(12) Does the action cause better distribution of services?

(13) Does the action result in democratization of power?

(14) What are the points of intervention of the wrong judgment is made?

Such questions would be debated locally in worker-community assemblies, legislatures, Congress and in the Cabinet over all issues. In effect, such questions would become a procedure for governments and assemblies which would have to be answered prior to the action undertaken whether the action was constructing a building, destroying another nation, or building a highway. This procedure should become as accurate and habitual as surgical procedures prior to an operation.

The facts which such inquiry yielded could result in a new value structure which emphasized the humanistic and artistic vision just because of its practicality.

Through confrontation, rational reconstruction takes the more existential form of personal risk which tests the limits of colonized reality. In the testing, the individual or the group consciously undertakes to change the facts and values of the colonized relationships. The method of confrontation reconstruction remains non-violent, but the non-violence does not indicate lack of risk or pain. It indicates the basic notion that by what is done daily, through the methods used, the ends are defined and the decolonized reconstructive reality can be built. For example, the blacks undertake to follow through the work of Martin Luther King, Jr., and his Poor People's March. The people march and sit in. But while they march and sit in, they now undertake to *show* through their actions two new possibilities, what they want and the way it should be gotten and built—so that the nature of the society changes. They undertake to organize the white and black community to rebuild a street, perhaps along the lines that Dolci and Fox might do it in Sicily and New York. They propose and undertake its contradiction by building a sium in front of the White House in the manner that Frank Smith did in 1966. They sit in at electronics labs risking jail and presenting alternative inquiries for scientific talent to work on. They develop, in short, a method of inductive thought and action through the creation of situations that cause self and other to respond in human and reconstructive ways.

16

From
Dream Colony to
Active Communicating

The technologically-revolutionary nature of TV and radio assures the possibility of the formation of groups to address themselves to the use of them in new ways. Groups of people who are anxious to uplift others, present wild opinions or package new programs, keep the Dream Colony in a state of instability. The chance for accidental contradiction to the colonized reality is greater in the broadcasting media than in the other colonies. Part of this accidental possibility relates to a measure of control outside of the Dream Colony which rests in the law. Under its statute, the Federal Communications Commission has the responsibility of regulating the radio and television industry. However, because the regulators do not enforce the law, its right of regulation may rest in the people where the regulator no longer is willing or able to act. In a recent case, the *United Churches of Christ v. The Federal Communications Commission,* the US Court of Appeals has intimated that the public may have the right to enforce its own will when the FCC no longer acts in the public interest. That is to say, the public has legal standing. "Since the concept of standing is a practical and functional one designed to insure that only those with a genuine and legitimate interest can participate in a proceeding, we can see no reason to exclude those with such an obvious and acute concern as the listening audience."[1]

The Supreme Court has now extended this view by holding that the broadcaster is a trustee for the public who is responsible to it. The broadcaster is to be kept to strict account in order to ensure that access is maximal for the public(s) to use the media as its instrument of communication. This legal framework is a backdrop to the growing consciousness among the black poor and the young white upper middle class that the media are public property. The result of this consciousness is the likelihood of a series of confrontations in the broadcast industry between an entrenched ownership system on the one hand, whose profits are quite extraordinary and who are constantly attempting to extend their political and economic power to other media, as against community groups which are attempting to find legitimate means of communication between themselves and others. This latter group may now be joined by performers (directors, cameramen, writers and actors) who see their allegiance changing from that of servants to network owners and managers to that of communications professionals who respect their craft and see themselves needing involvement with communities and publics to deepen their understanding of their work. The result of such groups with skill joining together with community groups would be to revivify communications and communication on principles wholly different from those which presently operate in the Dream Colony.

It is true that the legal framework and the consciousness of new groups who have become aware of the importance of media communications (once they are reported on by the media as *problems* and objects) are now in conflict with the practice of the Federal Communications Commission, which has favored settled ownership control over the airwaves. While licenses are granted by the FCC on the basis that radio and television stations must serve the public interest, and they will be reviewed with this principle in mind, this provision of the act has been reduced to a matter of form because there are few challenges to licensees and because this area has been viewed as already settled since it is regulated and requires enormous technical expertise. The result of this view, which has emerged since the second world war, is that the FCC has transformed its function under the communications law to one of protecting those who obtain licenses: a gift, as it is said in the broadcasting trade, as valuable as obtaining a license from the government to print money. The FCC has viewed its institutional role as protecting stability in the communications industry. It shrinks from attacking corporate entities which have invested considerable sums in equipment, people and resources to use and huckster the public. These corporate entities have, of course, their own power among various Congressmen, knowing that they are able to help or hurt the candidacies of members of Congress. (In many cases, politicians have real economic interests in broadcasting stations or have helped their friends obtain such stations in exchange for political support.) The politician, of course, may not be re-elected or he may die, but the station remains. Its management and owners find themselves with continuous political power.

The outlines of the transforming process in the television/radio media are fairly clear. We may begin with the fact of interest on the part of the listener in what is presented to him through the media. The listener comes to learn that he need no longer act as an isolate from fellow listeners. He will learn as much when he sees that those *publics* which are politically inclined undertake to enforce present law and protect the property of the public. One of the publics most capable of taking such action is found in and around the university. Such commitment is present among those in the colleges and the universities who see themselves as involved in communications, or who intend to become professionals in television and other media. It is not unlikely that such groups would organize sit-ins at networks because of narrow and poor broadcasting. Once the issue of poor broadcasting is raised in this way, it is likely that other *publics* will begin to complain that they are not part of the process of decision which determines what appears on television. (For example, black groups, working-class groups, hippies.)* In some cases the complainants will have prepared their own programs which they want to show on television. Since historical and legal precedents in this field are invariably couched in the language of public interest, it is clear that if vocal, action-oriented groups emerge to see the television media as a *public* function, the courts will be constrained from supporting the view that the communications industry is an enterprise for the purpose of allowing advertisers and broadcasters to reap profits from the sale of public airwaves. Presently the commercial method of broadcasting is similar to a situation in which I sell you the right to use the Brooklyn Bridge—public property—and then argue that the right to sell you the bridge gives

---

* Note that such activities have already begun in New York and Los Angeles.

me a vested interest in that bridge. I do not believe that this view would be sustained even in an unreconstructed authority structure.

Political action on the part of the public would have the effect of taking back rights already established by law. It would enable the FCC (because it now had a constituency) to begin to change the electronic communications industry. Three activities would mingle and support each other: First, groups would seek licenses which are now held by commercial stations on the grounds that present arrangements in the communications industry reflect private control over public property; second, the use of various peaceful demonstrative community techniques, such as picketing and sit-ins, would be appropriate to underscore the fact that the media has arrogated to itself rights and property which are publicly shared and which cannot be unilaterally held by corporate power but must be democratically controlled; and third, the technologist and artist would develop new means of communications and networks that would result in participation response and in creativity with audiences and groups with which he needs to relate. Through invention, new programming and political legislation, they would help the audience become an active participant rather than a passive bystander.

A politically-reconstructed communications network could be operated and controlled publicly through a combination of election and appointment of workers within the media and the listening community. The Populists in nineteenth-century America explored such ideas for control as they would relate to other economic and political situations. Beyond the system of participation, which would control television, television itself becomes the instrument for participation. People sitting in their homes or in community assemblies would be able to communicate with each other through the media of television and radio, with people joined together in continuous discussion and response. A new communications network would help in bringing about a new political contract between the individual and his representative. There could be thousands of television networks which operated to bring participation of now isolated people into the workings of government. Modern technology could become an important auxiliary method for participation and consultation of people with political representatives in the United States and elsewhere. While a new politics is served through technology, the relationship between the artist and the audience could become more creative and interdependent.

In Plato's *Ion,* Socrates describes the myth of connection between the audience and the artist as a series of iron rings held together magnetically. Each person who participates in the artistic process of communication is inspired. The chains of communication can now have their own immediate feedback in which the audience differentiates itself into groups and individuals who themselves are actively inspired. This is the wonderment of a modern technology. However, the likelihood of communications (television) becoming a central basis for communication to reconstruct the participatory political community or develop a new humanist aesthetic rests on practical changes in control. For example, patents for communications need to be held by the public and not by the great corporations.

Present reformist plans do not speak to such political and aesthetic developments which stem from the present legal framework and the consciousness of new groups. The reformist has accepted the cession of the media to private control and hopes instead to find spaces for specialized audiences. Public broadcasting becomes a nook in the corner of broadcasting already ceded to the great corporations. During the period from 1965 to 1967 various television proposals were put forward by the Carnegie Corporation and the Ford Foundation. The more reformist of the two was that of the Ford Foundation. It called for a new television network which would be similar in content to Great Britain's Third Programme and paid for by taxing the carriers of commercial television. The structure itself followed the audience/performer dichotomy in which the audience maintains itself as an isolated, undifferentiated mass. Its board of directors would be made up of public-spirited, virtuous citizens of the kind who operate as colonizing managers in schools, universities, corporations and the national security aspects of the pyramidal state.

The Carnegie Corporation's proposal was less reformist in that it did not attempt to get AT&T, NBC, or other members of the Satellite Corporation to tax themselves for another network. It was able, as a result, to advance its cause more successfully than the Ford Foundation. Some of the suggestions which the Carnegie Corporation put forward were embodied in the Public Broadcasting Act of 1967. The Act provided for the construction of educational television and radio broadcast facilities with public funds, the establishment of a non-profit educational broadcasting corporation which would not be a network and the authorization of a study on educational broadcasting and instruction.

The authorization of this bill in Congress, specifically with the idea of putting money into buying television and radio equipment, is useful, even though the amount of money authorized for this venture was to be no more than $12.5 million a year.* However, the basic facts are not changed by such legislation. The average cost of running an educational television station is $260,000 a year, which is the approximate cost of buying one hour

---

*It should be noted that this program was not funded because of congressional insistence on cutting "unnecessary" frills during wartime.

of time on commercial network television. It should be noted that Japan, one of America's protectorates, spends $250 million per year on its non-commercial television system, in a country which has half the population of the United States and a much smaller geographical area, according to the chairman of the Carnegie Corporation, James Killian.

By beginning from the fact that the airwaves are public property, we may be less intimidated with the idea that private enterprise funds the initial resources for capital equipment in broadcasting. The strategic question remains: How are the public(s) to be able to recover the broadcasting media for themselves? If the FCC were more oriented to the idea of public(s) control, it would be possible to argue that the matter is for that regulatory commission, since it holds by reference the mantle of the people's authority. The reality, of course, is that the regulatory commission is hobbled and will remain so without organized public(s) action.*

The political activity that has to emerge in the communications and broadcasting field will appear to lead to disruption. The likely programmatic and political result will be more locally controlled stations by widely differing community or neighborhood groups who will program to their constituencies in terms of the needs of the particular area. As local groups, including cities and towns, become more aware of the potentiality of such possibilities, we will see that they will attempt to receive from the federal government either the license-granting power or license-operating power of stations, or both. Community governments, civil rights groups, the student

---

* A word is in order as to why I refer to public(s). The Federal Communications Act is aimed at the protection of diversified programming, locally controlled and conceived. In practice this has not worked, since the networks control the airwaves in their prime time and local towns and cities neither allocate the station bands nor, as a general rule, do they own any stations themselves.

movement, church groups and right-wing groups will
undertake to challenge the licenses of network-owned
stations and other stations that do not meet the criteria
of public interest in their broadcasting. During this period
of turbulence in broadcasting, new definitions of public(s)
interest will be arrived at. Part of this will come from
new artistic forms and from political techniques such as
non-violent sit-ins and guerrilla theater, which no doubt
will attempt to change the operations of the media by
parroting them in the places of media business themselves. This has already happened to one educational
TV station in New York, where a group disrupted the
regularly scheduled program to put forward its views.

In any discussion of what should be presented on television, the inevitable question of censorship and whose
taste shall govern are raised in defense of the present
system of broadcasting. This question has usually had
the effect of stopping any serious discussion of how the
First Amendment could be related in a positive way to
stimulate new impulses in programming. So long as the
issue is viewed only in legal terms and not in economic
terms, the questions seem to founder on the edifice of
opinion which holds that one man's judgment is as good
as another. And, since the corporations are so powerful,
their opinion and judgment are even a little better. The
broadcast corporations and advertisers have been eter-
nally vigilant in defending the free speech amendment
of the Constitution as it related to their control over
programming. Of course, the way the owners exercise
their vigilance in defense of the First Amendment is in
their affiliation contracts with networks, where the networks set the terms of what should or should not be on
their affiliated station in prime time. Programming and
free speech become a commodity to be bartered for a
price through the sanctity of high profit.

Once we remain in the economic realm with the First

Amendment, certain interesting formulations can be discovered. It is well within the purview of the FCC and the present Communications Act to stipulate certain points and require others. While the FCC could state that it does not intend to supplant its judgment of programming for the bureaucratic judgment of the broadcaster and networks, it could require that the First Amendment be observed through reserving time on stations to put on programs which would be paid for from profits of the station. Each year a prescribed amount from profits would be set aside for programming, experimentation and training of individuals and community groups which presented programs. Station owners in this formulation are viewed as trustees.[2] Consequently, the only argument which remains is what returns should the public pay the trustee for his services, and what are the ground rules as laid out by the local community and the FCC for him to operate within.

The fact that television stations are a communications system which is public property will strengthen the arguments of those who will undertake non-violent activity in such public buildings—especially as they will come to reflect a legitimate need to reassert the media as an instrument of the public. Once the process of change in the broadcasting industry begins, systems will have to be found to again legitimize authority in them. No doubt such ideas as the election by the public on the local, state and national level of national television networks will be put forward. Similarly, one could envisage a plan in which different interests were reflected in the operating of networks as well as local stations: (1) those who work as artists in a technical or unskilled capacity; (2) those who would be elected by the public to a board of directors and who have no financial interest in the operation of the network; and (3) those who are connected in an administrative way with the operation of the network. This

same method of public and worker participation could
be emulated by all stations that had more than a thousand-
watt power. Furthermore, the basic idea of protecting
local communities and giving the local community control
over setting limits on corporate authority could have the
effect of more open programming, while assuring that
surplus or profits of the media would be invested through
the community/professional, worker boards in social
activities immediately relevant to the particular area.

The paradox is that advertising on television usually
is related to those goods or services which may have a
negative effect on people. The most obvious recent example is cigarettes. Advertising for cigarettes has been
banned from the air. The problem which faces television
station owners is that reform groups might prevent certain
advertisers from appearing on television because of the
negative consequences which their products have. Obviously, such a situation would not become a general rule
in the foreseeable future but it is of enough concern to
even lay the basis in the minds of broadcasters for a new
way of funding a television communications system.

One method is through a focus of tax support in which
an individual taxpayer allots a portion of his tax to a
variety of different networks or television stations. Some,
including Commissioner Cox, have raised the specter of
governmental control over television if television were
publicly supported. Surely the answer depends on the
method of public support. If a variety of television stations
and networks were developed with avowedly different
purposes in fact reflecting different tastes and values
in American life and if there was actual participation in
the governance of the stations which one felt himself a
part of, the idea of governmental control over television
would not happen. Direct involvement by the people is
neither governmental control nor merely public support.

A word about newspapers is necessary. The facts of

commercial integration between television, radio and
newspapers as part of empires of families or groups are
too well known to be discussed here. But a new phenomenon should be noted. Over the last several years we have
seen the emergence of underground newspapers which
appeal to younger people and which set the tone of news
that is of interest and concern to them. These newspapers
should be encouraged and expanded to the point that
they become direct and obvious competition to the commercial newspapers. (Professors and leading journalists
should write for them.) It should be noted that the underground papers are supportive of whole communities and
teach young people how to pass on economic and moral
aid to people who find themselves floundering.

The commercial newspapers, which pride themselves
on press freedom, are, of course, directly tied to news
sources and the pyramidal authority's way of looking at
the world. This will be contradicted as journalists will
reject the views of the corporate or official sources they
had thought they depended on. I would suggest one
change in the media which would have a powerful democratizing effect. As a new class of educated develops (educated in the sense that its members can read and write)
the commercial newspapers will be challenged to print
pages of articles that are unsolicited, under the theory
that freedom of the press does not exclude freedom from
expressing one's view. In this sense, the broadcasting
media, by their inclusion of different people on the media,
will force the newspaper media to print unsolicited articles where now they reluctantly print letters. It is not
a leap in political imagination to predict a situation where
in each *New York Times* ten pages were given over to
people who wrote on subjects of general and specific
interest to different publics without having to be a re-
porter for *The New York Times* (e.g., doctors, workers
on the line, bureaucrats, etc.). And so with other news-

papers. The result would be a profound change in the quality of news reporting and new seriousness that is not now present because long-term continuous issues could be engaged.

Newspapers would be obliged to print such articles in the public(s) interest. The Federal Communications Act might be amended for this purpose. Under this suggested direction, newspapers would be required by law to print a daily amount of unsolicited material. The amount of material might be determined according to the size of the newspaper's audience. The larger the audience, the more material it would have to print. This direction would revivify the free press conception as laid down in the Bill of Rights.

Roots of the Reconstructive Tradition

Many have believed that the Communist Party or Marxist thought or both bring the potentiality of a new political and economic future. The revolutions in the societies of China, the Soviet Union, North Vietnam and Cuba, suggest that something new is happening. And yet I think that one would be mistaken if he believed that there is a change in fundamental authority relationships in those societies. For whatever reason—lack of a material base, encirclement by enemy nations, personal power drives of individuals and groups who repeat the pyramidal relationship because it is the only way they know to keep power—there seems to be little more than throwing a new elite group to the historical surface which intends to operate as the colonizer. So let us accept in a fit of disbelief and skepticism, that there are other models

besides the practice of the communists to point to for
clues. When I speak of "us," I mean those people who
by feeling, training, and experience are thrust into a
midwife role of bringing into being the next stage of
history through their ideas and action examples. Needless
to say, there will be conflict between such people who
will hawk their analysis and solution. (Who will *live*
them?) Dream-selling is not the sole province of the
colonizer. It is also the degenerative activity of those
who stand for the "future" in negation of the present.

To be aware of the danger of such activity as midwives
for a future, it is well to reflect on models from other
times which are important in defining the role of the
reconstructivist. Less self-conscious ages can afford to
study past traditions as movements unto themselves.
However, times of turbulence and insecurity breed an
historical egocentrism which starts from the assumption
and pretense that what others have done in the past is
irrelevant to them except as instruments about which to
speculate, study with condescension or use. In the America of the Now we stand naked and trembling, trying to
find models to emulate or people with whom to relate.
It is not enough to perform acts. We require a tradition
for understanding what we are doing.

To read history and reconsider human experience
is to open oneself to the crush of the Now. In that now
we undertake liberation with its attendant gain and risk,
to develop a systematized structure of freedom. While
we reinterpret the past in light of the now, the past that
we seek to recover informs us of our personal and humanly collective now. There is a history and we seek to
find it *outside* of the colonized role that historians record
as history. But we are trapped, for when we seek human
models we are presented with men who are seen in the
context of roles.

There are several traditions which have their relevance

to us and which we begin to see as models to study for our utility and benefit. They are the prophetic, cynic, sophistic and philosophe traditions which serve as the basis for the reconstructive tradition in our period. It would be easy to show how a new class of intellectuals has roots with what has gone on at other times by those whose commitment and concern were never less than our own.

With the caveat that no biography is identical to another, no period is the same as another, we can learn in the mythic sense what we *like* to think a historical movement was, so that our own practice is founded in some sense of tradition. We all have and want a history. But for our own projects, one task is to find the right human models who also confronted and experimented with their lives at a time of tumultuous transformation. While we must emphasize the project in the sense that the living have the ability to create their own traditions, our identity with others demands that we reject the view that we are devoid of the past or that man stands outside of Nature as his trainer.* We have an obligation to create those

---

* The sense of tradition which was felt by the American Indian is one that we should envy because it stems from their idea of wholeness with the universe. In Western civilization, tradition came to be the basis of dividing an individual from his sense of wholeness. The project has been his attempt to find it. The reconstructivists now attempt to reach for this wholeness through their actions. The Indian view was far more lofty . . . and less egocentric. At the occasion of a meeting between the governor of the Territory of Washington, and the Indian Chief Seattle, Seattle spelled out clearly the Indian's sense of wholeness:

There was a time when our people covered the whole land as the waves of a wind-ruffled sea covers its shell-paved floor, but that time has long since passed away with the greatness of tribes now almost forgotten. I will not dwell on nor mourn over our untimely decay, nor reproach my pale-face brothers with hastening it, for we, too, may have been somewhat to blame . . .

We are two distinct races, and must ever remain so, with separate destinies. There is little in common between us.

To us the ashes of our ancestors are sacred and their final resting place is hallowed ground, while you wander far from the graves of your ancestors and, seemingly, without regret . . .

Our dead never forget this beautiful world that gave them being. They

projects which find the tradition of wholeness. Is that a contradiction? Perhaps. But there are intellectual and life traditions which have tried to capture this elixir. They give us standards to judge ourselves.

In each of the models I have chosen, the agents of transformation attempted to start new projects. The traditions they created emerged from great social conflict and uncertainty. Their periods were marked by shifts in power relationships in the body politic such as changes in the idea of personal responsibility as against community responsibility and hierarchy, profound political dissatisfaction, and a growing economic gap between groups and classes within those respective societies.

The Prophets

From Amos, Hosea, Micah and Isaiah in the eighth and seventh centuries B.C. to the time of Jesus the prophet's unique role was that of attacking social injustice, living in his own life the word of God and presenting to God what man was. Needless to say, the prophetic role was one which struck fear and respect in the hearts of people. But one wonders whether the prophets inspired love and empathy. They were too sure, too correct; they saw too much. When we think of the Old Testament prophet, the image which invariably comes to mind is that of an

---

still love its winding rivers, its great mountains, and its sequestered valleys . . .

Every part of this country is sacred to my people. Every hillside, every valley, every plain and grove has been hallowed by some fond memory or some sad experience of my tribe. Even the rocks, which seem to lie dumb as they swelter in the sun along the silent seashore in solemn grandeur, thrill with memories of past events connected with the lives of my people.

The very dust under your feet responds more lovingly to our footsteps than to yours, because it is the ashes of our ancestors, and our bare feet are conscious of the sympathetic touch, for the soil is rich with the life of our kindred.[1]

unsettler. I mean this in two senses. He unsettled others, their routines and ways by what he did. And he moved about rejecting the standards of life which might have been developed in his immediate community. To others, he might have appeared as a know-it-all, especially since he said that he carried God's message. Further, the prophet did little work as defined by the communities he wandered to while living in such a way as to cast doubt on the lives of others. Erich Kahler has written that the prophets refused "to cut their hair, to drink wine, and to become inebriate with anything less than the sober and intrinsic ecstasy provided by the spirit of God. They wandered through Palestine in their old Bedouin garb."[2] But aside from their poor clothes and their lives which showed Divine and human forgiveness—as in the case of Hosea at a time of great political sorrow and turmoil— the prophets persisted in telling unpleasant truths which people did not want to hear. Indeed, according to modern theologians, the mark of the true prophet was his willingness to tell unfavorable prophecies. His being in the world depended on his belief in God and the powerful idea that he was a vessel through whom God spoke. He did not speak for self, only for God.

Ezekiel was God's watchman *for* the people of Israel to God. His task was to emphasize the personal responsibility of man to God, but God made clear that the prophet was to give warning. And if he failed it would be upon the responsibility of Ezekiel. (How could such a responsibility be carried?) Yet, although he spoke only for God, he was a man who expected and was accorded respect on the basis of his humanity. At least, in the case of Micah, man and God approached each other in a unique relationship in which both were bound by one unconditional law. This duality (speaking for God to man and viewing God as bound as man was by a solemn covenant) required that the prophet elevate himself above the counterpoint of arguments and discourses.

In his social existence the prophet lived the problems of his time. He assumed that by the way he lived, God's will was expressed. The prophet lived for God to man and for man to God. Indeed, Martin Buber avers that even by the way the prophet speaks, he is the true mediator. In his speech "the hearing of the utterance is itself a 'sight' of the intention."[3] By living the problems of his time and commenting upon them, he is able to use language which struck like thunderbolts against those classes and groups who offended the will of God—or, I might add, the will of the just man. Paul Tillich pointed out in *The Shaking of the Foundations,* that Isaiah exhibits profound insight when he identifies himself with his unclean people in the very moment that he is made worthy of his exceptional vision. He chooses the prophetic rather than the mystical. For even in the greatest ecstasy a prophet does not forget the social group to which he belongs, and the common contaminations which even he himself cannot lose. He identifies with the colonized.[4]

Unlike the mystical ecstasy, the prophetic ecstasy is never an end in itself; it is both social and political. Perhaps this can best be seen in the social welfare laws at the beginning of the seventh century B.C. as expressed in Deuteronomy, which make clear the responsibility of the rich for the poor, the prohibition of economic oppression, the stricture against delay or deduction in payment of wages, the taxing of the landed gentry for the poor and the cancellation of debts every seven years. Discharged slaves were to be given their own economic means so they could get their own start. "Thou shalt furnish him liberally out of thy flock, and out of thy floor and out of thy winepress." (Deut. 15: 14) When the prophet spoke, he attempted to give his language material expression. His actions were a sign of what was necessary, of what had to be. He jumped from what we might term his "internal knowing" to "doing."

In our time we have come to believe that there is no event in and of itself which is not a sign for something else, some other moment or catastrophe. Because of this sense of internally knowing we have come to believe that there are people in themselves who reflect a future. They are the ones who, blessed or damned, take on the signifying meaning which indeed tells the story of a time. The prophet is such a person. As a result he is forced by the contradiction to what is in the external world and what he feels internally to act politically. It is not that his feelings are different than others—it is that he jumps to action. The result is that he "causes" conflict and turbulence. In that process, he induces and fulfills the terms of his prophecy. When a man is told by Jahweh, "Go, prophesy against my people Israel," he is forced to become a politician-teacher and indeed finds himself in direct confrontation with the authority of the time.

Imagine Jesus in the city of Jerusalem. He must have found himself surrounded by the misery of the wretched, terrorized by the Roman Administration and liberal mediationists, the Pharisees. Jesus was thrown into becoming the prophet-politician-teacher who by the questions he raised protected the poor and spoke to their condition. He questioned the law of the Pharisees and its relevance to the wretched. If Jesus did not come to Jerusalem as an iconoclastic prophet, he did come to fulfill a prophetic mission.

There is an important irony. Given the situation in Jerusalem, sacrifice was dictated by the dialectic not between those who stood totally opposite to each other, but rather to those who seemingly stood closest to each other in understanding and analysis. The prophetic role taxed the "best" people of the society most. The

prophet's language caused new structures to come into
being after challenging the most decent of society's elements. The prophet cannot stop himself from confronting
liberal reformists when he finds that they serve as the
ornaments and ideologists for institutions staying the
same. The prophet, Martin Luther King, Jr., understood
in the Birmingham jail that the "good people" were
telling the movement and him to go slow. He knew that
it was they who would always have to be confronted. He
so stated this in his letter to his fellow ministers, a rabbi
and some bishops. The ministers told him to go slow, and
while Martin King showed his humanity to them and
patiently laid out the foolishness of their position, he
could not escape from making clear to them their own
dubious role. "Shallow understanding from people of
good will is more frustrating than absolute misunder-
standing from people of ill will. Lukewarm acceptance
is much more bewildering than outright rejection."[5]

The modern prophet may indeed decide to speak and
act against that group of people who view as their spe-
cialty the problem of another or the reinforcement of
colonization, whose livelihood is directly related to
studying and using the other, but not changing one's own
group. When placed in a situation in which those who
are challenged are no longer the traditional enemies
(the foolish or uneducated), but rather are the university-
educated—the people just like those who themselves
might undertake the prophetic condition in a modern
time—one is both uncomfortable and indeed in danger.
But what is the substantive basis of the confrontation
and the prophetic message?

In a seminar at MIT, Harvey Cox stated that "perhaps
what we need now is a new understanding and a new type
of prophecy." To him that meant the discernment "of
the signs of the times, the clarification of the moral options
presented to human beings, and the summoning of man

to accountability in the light of the moral traditions."[6]
He realizes, and I agree, that there are two very important
conditions: first, that the enemy is the megalife and the
megamachine; a condition in which a process attempts
to make the decision for another, and second, that a
prophet is no substitute for a movement, since the single
prophet, no matter how daring and persuasive, can be
distinguished from the babel of voices and actions which
invariably mock any original prophetic impulse.

In the first case, the megalife is predicated on the pharaohistic view of man in which one's humble life is dictated by the success of the pharaoh's life, "his prosperity,
its prosperity, his health, its health. The community lived
and flourished vicariously through the king. . . ."[7] As
Mumford has noted, the pharaoh undertook massive
projects which were to protect him, but which the slaves
allowed because they had accepted the flim-flam of the
pharaohs who endowed themselves with power, terror,
authority, command and special "knowledge."[8] Of course,
it was the prophet who began to break down this power
through his demands for individual justice and actions,
which reduced the power of kings to that of ordinary men
in the face of God. The present insurgent role of the religious is not that different from the old prophetic role.
If we accept the formulation I have suggested, that a few
are spending the treasure and lives of the many on the
basis of their manipulation of the old symbols of power,
authority, flim-flam and "specialized knowledge," it is
no wonder that we tremble when the prophetic role is
taken on by modern churchmen such as the Berrigans.
They demand by their actions that each of us re-examine
the question of how one renders meaning and loyalties to
others, the community, the future community, to tradition
and to himself in the midst of terror and the pyramidal
state. They create discomfort and anguish. This is an old
question in the religious realm.

In *Treatise on Christian Liberty,* we are able to find
some insights on this question and on how Martin Luther's
meaning, basically within the religious realm, affects
man's being in the political world. There is not a dichotomy which allows man to perform one way for man and
another way for God. The inductive method of practice
and experiment shows us that there is no dichotomy.
"No political state or hierarchy can impose itself on
conscience. One thing and one thing only is necessary
for Christian life, righteousness and liberty." What Luther
deduced from this was that "neither pope nor bishop
nor any other man has the right to impose a single syllable
of law upon a Christian man without his consent; and if
he does, it is done in the spirit of tyranny."* But now
that statement has to be reinterpreted as to the exact
ways that modern men spend their lives, beguiled and
put down through methods which sound scientific, authoritative and correct. It must be reinterpreted so that
we can begin to understand when obligations cease and
how new meanings of freedom come into being. In the
second case, the prophet is drowned out by a system
which knows how to package back, through fashion, style
and media 1000 voices who seem to be saying what the
prophet says. The colonizers have false prophets. When
Martin Luther King, Jr., was killed, the colonizers attempted to keep order in the cities by flashing pictures
of King on television with the mellifluous voice of the
announcer or the Mayor or the President using King's
life as the instrument to keep order and the pyramid

---

*There is much evidence to suggest that Luther was the architect of keeping
oneself in a particular role as laid out by temporal authority. Indeed, his own
support of the princes over the peasants suggested a very clear view of the importance of pyramidal authority. Franz Neumann, in *Behemoth,* holds Luther's
thought responsible for the dichotomy between self and conscience on the one
hand and role that one plays out in the world on the other. Consequently, perhaps I am involved in not doing justice—or perhaps doing too much justice—to
Luther's phrase.

in tact. Most of those engaged in order-keeping were the members of the middle class who are those most in need of prophetic *action* which cuts through the language of everyone that now becomes a babel of sameness.

When a movement is strong, it can expose by its actions the difference between the manipulation of a prophet's words by the established forces of the State and bring to fruition aspects of the prophet's mission. When I say that at this stage in American history the prophet and the movement must confront their own class, it means a number of related ideas and actions. No doubt it means that there is no running away from the poor and those who are most obviously in a custodial situation: the lame, mad, the young. It is among them that political support exists for a prophetic voice—and where the suffering is most immediate. Yet, where support is does not define where the struggle is. To a greater extent the prophetic struggle is against the seemingly rational, the seemingly cool, and the seemingly wise. The prophetic task is most needed in the middle classes, who in their objective search not to be misled, invariably end up being the easiest to fool. They are the ones who say that very little can be different just because of the nature of man. Avoidance of extremes and moderation in all things is their political and intellectual advice. Fearing false prophecy, they shore up that tradition in the universities and in the churches.

Perhaps there is no other choice but to risk false prophecy. Most of what we learn about false prophecy is that it is optimistic, that it promises something other than what is. As Reinhold Niebuhr said, we mistake our own dreams for the word of God. Yet there is that nagging doubt which Bonhoeffer shows us. "Houses and fields, and vineyards shall yet again be brought in this land," cries Jeremiah, just as the Holy City is about to be destroyed, a striking contrast to his previous prophecies of woe. "It is a divine sign and pledge of better things to come, just when all seems blackest. . . . It is not easy to be brave and hold out, but it is imperative."

The optimistic mood should not be discounted as false prophecy because it is a source of inspiration and hope. It is the human condition. Although the prophetic voice speaks to us from God, such a voice does not require that we give up hope, or refuse to listen to the calls within us that dissonance creates. What easier course is there than to say that human activity in the world is perennially unjust or continuously sinful? It is easier to accept these words than to live in the world where all must take their chances and through their projects create new facts and values. It is easy to say that the people have a death instinct, that it does not matter that they are powerless, since if they had power the same choices would be made. When people say this, they are telling us that there is no change that is of any use. And when that is said, they shrink, "and in sheer resignation or pious escapism, they surrender all responsibility for the preservation of life and for the generation yet unborn. Tomorrow may be the day of judgment. If it is, we shall gladly give up working for a better future but not before."[9] Just as the prophets of old had no choice but to act in the world, the new prophets will be pressed to make harsh judgments on corruptions which could lead to reconstruction of the political structures.

The Cynics

Alongside the prophetic tradition, there is now waiting for its own rebirth another form of practice and thought which is highly political but which attempts to go beyond political structure and the cause-effect view of reality upon which political action has been predicated. This group, in part similar to the cynics, are philosophers who teach by query and personal example. The cynics were called dog philosophers, and self-consciously they identified themselves with the "lowest" parts of the social order. They were poor, had long hair, treated everyone alike (it is generally thought that Socrates inspired the cynics in terms of life style), told jokes, and attempted to find truth through the renunciation of worldly pleasures and goods. Since they did not accept the notion of class, authority and status symbols, they could emphasize the building of new communities which would not be governed in the old ways. Their task, so we are told, was as complex and important as the cleaning of the Augean stables. They intended that there be a way to deflate emphasis on power, pleasure and wealth. As I have suggested, once one leaves the old authority symbols as the frame of reference for either giving or suspending judgment, new relationships and new ideas of social knowledge develop. When the ideas of the cynics galloped through the Roman Empire, they apparently gave rise to the mood of weariness in the Roman Empire, just as they had done in the Athenian Empire. In both places, concern developed for world citizenship and the privatization of authority. It was hard to follow orders of those who were primarily sanctified through their ability to coerce and characterize others.

In our own time, we begin again to see the same signs which are expanding by geometric proportions. In the American empire the young find no modern world space, so they begin to live in primitive ways. They are trying to show us by example the necessity of returning to a much more unadorned existence.

These groups of the young who do not accept the vertical authority structure are the basis for creating a new philosophy which will also have profound effect. The ancient cynic slogan, "recast the coin," is the basis of the practical and theoretical work of those who appear un-

washed and outside of the arm of authority or the colonized reality. The spaces which they create by living in
the ways they choose imperil the traditional authority
system because the liberal parents who may be bound to
it secretly believe in the need to recast the coin, but find
they do not know how to work toward a different community. In Washington this pehnomenon reaches to the
children of Cabinet officials who participate in new experiments in cooperative living and communality qualitatively different from the usual bohemian year abroad
for the bourgeois. (One is reminded of nineteenth-century
Russia, where the children of the ruling classes interested
themselves in anarchist and utopian social experiments
which ended up undermining the basis of their class
position.) Bands of young people now travel together
attempting to find community in the way they live and
practical knowledge which makes them less dependent
on the pyramids. They build their own communities
around newspapers and houses, creating new spaces
which, by their being, compete and appear more obvious
for people to accept and live within. Older people should
strengthen these groups, help them, and be open enough
to respect the traditions which are now being brought
forward. Metaphorically speaking, we should supply the
young with bricks—the spaces necessary to recast, and
the seeds for the flowers of our children.

Perhaps it is somewhat cruel to say that the last generation of middle-class adults have had no traditions. They
were too busy attempting to find opportunities. But the
children of that group are different. Those who have
become hippies, the modern cynics, seem to be attempting
the rediscovery of the deepest humane traditions which
could have the likely result that nature, including man,
could survive on this planet. As I have suggested elsewhere, the old will continue to learn from this cynical

and "flowered" tradition by seeking from the young the ways to act on the deepest needs of humanness.

The Sophists

During the period of Pericles the sophists (the intellectuals, as they are called by Calhoun) came to Athens. They were by all accounts an extraordinary group. In our time, of course, they have received a rather unkind shuffle just because they charged their students fees to learn rhetoric and discourse and doubted the authority structures which the Platonists desperately attempted to resurrect. Of course, when you charge fees for what one knows, the incentive may mean that one ends up talking only to the highest bidder. That was a serious problem with the sophists. In fifth-century Athens, they invariably ended up talking to the newly rich. But yet they served the unique function of changing the currency of what was useful or important in Athenian society. They brought persuasion and education to replace privilege and tradition as the means of judging right from wrong and prescriptions of what to do. During the Periclean period, while family status was always central, it became less important as the landowning aristocracy lost some of its power to the merchant and trading class. As invariably happens after great wars, new elites are thrown (or throw themselves) to the surface to share in the fruits of victory or defeat. The landowners had suffered badly in their victory over the Persians in 478 B.C. since they had to pay the costs of the navy. The Greek navy's victory opened up new trade routes that coincidentally, made way for a new trading class in Athens which then cut down the power of the Athenian landowners.

The Sophists came to Athens just at the time when they

could show how to use argument and discussion—their method of education—in the popular assembly when it was split between the traders and the landowners. Apparently, prior to the time the Sophists taught their form of rhetoric, differences were settled on the basis of authority and status of one's family. By fifth-century Athens, education was the new mode of communicating in the body politic. There was a central belief in education and the power of knowledge in making men wise in thought and good in human character. And the Sophists were no exception to this belief. According to Werner Jaeger, the Sophists attempted to educate the people's leaders. They addressed "themselves to a select audience, and to it alone. Their pupils were the men who wished to become politicians and eventual leaders of their states." The Athenian naïveté and expectations of the benefits of education were no greater than our own. Although we see now how brutalized knowledge becomes when it is in the service of power, we still hold out instinctively for it as man's instrument for progress and perfectibility.

In certain ways, many of the clergy and engagé professors are modern-day sophists with several emendations to the older sophistic tradition. They address themselves to students who supposedly will be "tomorrow's leaders." Excellence is not judged only by persuasion or technique but through experiment and action. The sophist finds that his pedagogical role is a political one. It is to counteract foolishness, mis-education, desperation and misery, passivity and profilism to create self-governing units in which the wretched and colonized end that condition and exercise control and self-judgment. Yet, while the modern sophist reaches through the society to change, teach and build new models of association, he must be aware that the present organizational structure of the society forces the need to educate those already in power who have been chosen by others or who have arrogated to themselves the power to destroy everything. They are to be challenged and confronted in that power by the modern sophist when those with power function not in terms of a promulgation of a series of *goods* in a particular situations, but merely to attempt to retain or extend their colonial power without attention to consequences. It is also the task of the modern sophist to analyze the types of knowledges which the university creates, what their purpose and utility are, whom they serve, and whether they solve or reflect problems.

From what definitions and operative principles can such a challenge be made? Werner Jaeger in *Paideia* refers to an essay by Antiphon, a leading sophist, in which Antiphon says,

> In every respect we have all the same nature, Greeks and barbarians alike. This can be seen from the natural needs of all men. They can all satisfy needs of all men. They can all satisfy them in the same way, and in all these matters there is no distinction between barbarians and Greeks. We all breathe the same air through mouth and nose, and all eat with our hands. We honor and respect men from noble families, but those from ignoble families we do not honor and respect. In that way we are like citizens in different nations.[10]

If we return to this basic yearning of people and view that yearning as the starting point (it may be called Jeffersonianism, Christianity, Marxism, or reconstructivism), we begin to see the necessity of attempting new projects through knowledge and action and working out types of knowledge which reflect that system of values which are meant to be direct and small but which carry within them the seeds of profound change if they "fit" human subjective needs. The method or the project may be wrong in the particular since it develops from the situation in which a person finds himself engaged and formalized into an existential-experimental situation. His perception may be wrong (that is, he may think he sees one reality but later we learn after unpeeling it that it is something richer than he saw), which itself will create a new reality. What he does may be wrong. That is, it may not fit for others beyond himself and his relationship in small groups. But no matter. What he does when he becomes conscious of what he is doing, and when others join in, is that he creates a mode of handling problems according to the basic intuition and experience which he feels. His method is correct since it stems from the obvious, the naive and the sense of relatedness. This subjective view is, I take it, what Protagoras means (should have meant?) when he said that man is the measure and that it is better to study and act accordingly to the world of man than to contemplate the world in which God resides. "Concerning the gods we shall not hear inquiry because of the difficulty of the subject and the shortness of life." The Sophists made strong headway into the Athenian scene because they showed that knowledges were relative and that certain insights and knowledges were just as, or more important than, those which sprang from authority per se. They noted that perhaps to know how to make a shoe well was as important as commanding an army. That view, needless to say, had its critics. It was argued that that view was clearly wrong since the shoemaker's view did not attach to prestige or authority. The shoemaker had to be inferior. But once the question was raised, the idea which encouraged people to believe that one sort of knowledge and one sort of virtue was as good as another, it was possible for experimentalism in politics and science to take hold. It was not until the Renaissance and more fully in the Age of Enlightenment, when the ability to make things or set new commercial relationships in motion forced the redistribution of political power and the redrawing of the social contract, that the powerful insight of the Sophists emerged in the center stage of the history of Western thought and action. Correlatively, the project method sets in motion new relationships which require the redrafting of the social contract. The facts and values developed in these projects become the basic datum for the redrafting of the social contract. This was true in the Age of Enlightenment and it is true again.

The Philosophes

It is unnecessary to retell the history of the importance of the philosophes to the coming of the French Revolution. Ideas which were developed by Diderot, Rousseau, and to some extent Voltaire and D'Alembert, affected the style and the strivings of revolution. However, it would be foolish to view the philosophes as a group which brought about the revolution or was primarily responsible for it. Indeed, a more persuasive interpretation of the work and action of the philosophes would be that their purpose was to discover natural laws of governing similar to those which had currency in the natural sciences. Those laws were Newtonian and stemmed from an ordered, not a disordered universe. After all, Turgot the philosophe entered the service of the king to show how the ordered laws of the sciences could be applied to the political economy. He wanted to make the kingly system work. However, Turgot was dismissed summarily within eighteen months. The point is that the philosophes attempted to put the process of challenging authority and ruling of kingly authority on the road of reason. They hoped to get the challengers and the kings to accept the ordered laws of man and the universe.

The higher dialectic of reason came about because of a change in the technology of the time, and consequently, the economics. The philosophe became politically important with the emergence of a public which could buy books, pamphlets and drawings. Once he could receive support, praise and objective correlation from the bourgeois, the intellectual was no longer economically dependent on the king or the aristocracy. No doubt the one who best understood how to appeal to the emerging common sensibility of the bourgeois class, while personally keeping a foot in the boudoirs of European royalty, was Voltaire. He was an independent entrepreneurial type, a typical intellectual with schemes and proposals, who found ways in his personal life to escape from the private patronage system and to reach out to a larger audience for acclaim, wealth, and protection. By so doing, his former patrons took him even more seriously (almost as a political power) because he had an audience and spoke for it. The fact that the philosophes found new audiences beyond patrons does not mean that they did not incur personal risks for their intellectual and political achievements.

We have a clue to the existential nature of the philosophes in the life and work of Rousseau. He attempted to objectify his own conflicts. As he suggests in his *Confessions,* Rousseau could not understand why a man of primarily good instincts and intentions should be made a knave and fool by the structure of society. Because of that perception he saw the inside of French jails throughout his life. His question is the same question of experience and feeling which we ask today. What is the dissonance which I presently feel because my humanity cries out beyond the yoke of the colonized reality? As in the case of Rousseau, our feelings must be rediscovered and treated as natural. Our reason must stem from those feelings and give us the method necessary to transform the colonized reality. It is not useful here to take up the view that, at least in the case of Rousseau, his stance caused a frightening sort of narrowness. There is ample evidence to show that his break with the philosophes meant that he ended up seeing only the state and only the individual; that there was no other relationship which man could have. He fled to the country to rediscover nature, broken by the style of the salon life and the continuous contradictions between the poor and the rich, the wretched and the frivolous. No doubt the same plaguing sense grips those of us who have attempted to remain autonomous. We think we have staked out for ourselves a place which allows us the role and the humanness of relating to the powerful and the powerless—and in the bargain to be economically protected. History will tell us whether this is an inherently unstable stance which is quite untenable, especially as it is clear that the emergent structures that are built by the reconstructivist compete and confront the structure of the powerful. There is a schizophrenic quality to such a situation for the reconstructivist. To be praised, courted or imprisoned is the usual result of a self-conscious group which attempts to relate to the powerless and powerful, while appearing all-knowing and irreverent. The social history of the philosophes was exactly in that tradition. While the philosophes did not seek political power in an ordinary sense, they did view themselves as detached, who sought only truth. Theirs was a philosophy of thought which attempted to illumine events, forces and objectives in the foreseeable and immediate future. They were not shy or retiring fellows seeking immortality by eschewing the battles, the praise and blame of their world. Instead they saw themselves as attempting to bring about change in their time. Diderot, the leading Encyclopedist, said,

> Our philosopher does not count himself an exile in the world; he does not suppose himself in the enemy's country, he would fain find pleasure with others, and to find it he

must give it; he is a worthy man who wishes to please and to make himself useful. The ordinary philosophers who meditate too much, or rather who meditate to wrong purpose, are as surly and arrogant to all the world as great people are to those whom they do not think their equals; they flee men and men avoid them. But our philosopher who knows how to divide himself between retreat and the commerce of men is full of humanity. Civil society is, so to say, a divinity for him on the earth; he honors it by his probity, by an exact attention to his duties, and by a sincere desire not to be useless or an embarrassing member of it. The sage has the order of leaven and rule; he is full of ideas connected with the good of civil society. What experience shows us every day is that the more reason and light people have, the better fitted they are and the more to be relied for the common intercourse of life.[11]

We may begin to see certain emerging conclusions about the modern sophist or intellectual, social philosopher or prophet. He is not tied to one class. Where the situation is without risk or *pro forma,* his human condition is that of a nibbler and pest. In some cases societies provide for his upkeep and use him to totalize the system while offering it harmless comic relief. For example, the professional dissenter licensed by the state as in England in the seventeenth century, means little to the basic relationships between groups and individuals and merely reinforces the court-fool aspect of the mouth person who himself may suffer from feeling that he can do little except nibble and prod, which he does in the way that he knows it is the way he earns his daily bread. The other relationship in which professors do battle with each other through their pens and pencils may be personally amusing but hardly interesting as a means of advancing knowledge or the reconstruction of society. Such arid academism is not the way to show how to reconstruct a society or indeed to develop knowledges and personal stances which give clarity, direction and criticality to others. They are empty of risk, especially in a technological age which deprecates technology and things and instead emphasizes communication through the written and spoken word. Rhetoric replaces actions. And actions are reduced to symbols for the communications' mill which is used by the intellectuals for their own power. Whole bureaucracies are predicated on the written word, advisors mediate, those with the higher education man the bureaucracies and stay within the confines of the given system waiting out their lives for a moment of freedom. Intellectuals who would have once been part of a salon set now continue their own salon or palace court (the university) while being feted and needed by the colonizer.

In recent years, very powerful events have forced knowledge and action to be very strongly related. Nuclear weapons and imperial wars, where they can be seen and shared, force intellectuals to stand with those who are the objects of such treachery: where they are themselves the objects. The salon is given up except as a place to organize others away from the colonized reality financially, morally and intellectually.

The Reconstructivist

We may begin to draw some conclusions about the place of the critical proposer analyst in the American society with a view to comprehending his tasks. There is not very much one can say about the prophet. When one appears, he is heard and joined by the reconstructivists, even though his chances for personal survival are not very great. Some may say that the reconstructivist may have an easier time, even though he has consciously chosen to eschew the violent power of the State or the actions of the street revolutionary. The intellectual celebration

of the Rough Rider mentality in the clothes of Che Gue-
vara may have its coffeehouse charm, but that view in
the American context calls upon a form of totalitarianism
which destroys the sense of feeling and empathy upon
which a new politics can be based.

  While his task is less romantic than that of the revolutionary guerrilla, the task of the reconstructivist is more
human, at least as it may relate to the conditions and
potentialities for fundamental change in America. The
reconstructivist accepts the toughness and suffering of
Martin Luther King, Jr., who in his challenge to the colonizer refuses to break the possibility of community by
viewing the victims of evils (those who do it) outside of the
human community. It is an approach that seeks honesty
and acts publicly. It is different from the revolutionary
mood. "The revolutionary guerrilla force is clandestine. It
is born and develops secretly. The fighters themselves use
pseudonyms. At the beginning, they keep out of sight,
and when they allow themselves to be seen, at a time and
place chosen by their chief."[12] No doubt this is the political
and military stance of the hunter and the hunted. It is
also in its phenomenological structure the perpetuation
of the colonized relationship in which the hierarchic
other chooses for the individual or the group. Debray's
view does not reflect either a change in human behavior,
nor does it necessarily mean that once there is revolution, peaceful or violent, there is necessarily a change
in human relationships. The individual may still find
himself in lockstep. But I do not want to be misunder-
stood. In the third world and among American blacks,
the revolutionary stance may be the only way to get
fundamental changes against the violence of the state,
especially as oligarchs do not willingly give up power.
Suffering demands either exodus or that power be
wrested. There is ample reason for the wretched and
dispossessed to adopt the revolutionary stance. The

problem is that revolution may continue to trap, since it appears that the individual and the group give up part of their power of decision. Another question remains to be raised, and it has been stated by Martin Buber. In *The Prophetic Faith,* Buber says that Ezekiel in his Messianic prophecy sees Israel as a community, but in his vision and reproof of the present, he sees it as a multitude of individuals, each one of whom is responsible before God himself and alone. Such personal responsibility is full and entire. "No one has to bear an inherited sin; no one shares in accumulating new guilt; no one has to answer for his fellow, but each one has to answer fully for himself. This is the special character of the time of the great transition—[that] every man—has a covenant relationship with God."[13]

Buber's view contemplates personal and group responsibility for self with others. The system of revolution contemplated by the Guevaraites, Maoists or Stalinists denies the potentiality expressed by Buber. No doubt there are situations where the terror of authority is central, and the idea of man's being limited by authority of the hierarchic other is important in certain situations— but not in politics or in the definition of self with others. Here the governing principles are space and freedom. This is an old argument not limited to class but revolving around the potentiality of man in his immediate situation. While Mills might have maintained that men must obey others like Charlemagne and Akbar until they understand persuasion and freedom, I would agree with the judgment of Macaulay who said that "many politicians of our time are in the habit of laying it down as a self-evident proposition that no people are to be free till they are fit to use their freedom. The maxim is worthy of the fool in the old story, who resolved not to go into the water till he had learned to swim. If men are to wait for liberty till they become wise and good, they may indeed wait forever."[14] This judgment not only is one which can be made on the colonizer who holds down the colonized; it can be made in our generation against the revolutionary who insists on a style of life and action, of discipline and denial which ends up being worthy only of the trapped and enslaved. The revolutionary is trapped by the delayed payoff view of the middle class and the sacrificial view of the religious mystic who assumes that he ceases to exist except in the case where a leader or a group insists that he does exist. Brunet, the communist in Sartre's *Age of Reason,* while he is free of ambiguity is also free of freedom. His nothingness is in the doing, which is dictated by the hierarchic other. That one can be free and still proceed unambiguously is the task of reconstruction.

It may not be given to the revolutionary to allow for that openness of feeling. Consequently the tragic result of his rhetoric and his action is to lead to reforms and repression chaining people even more to the colonized reality of pyramidalism in the likely event of repression/ reform or the unlikely event of the revolutionary's victory in revolution. Thus, we are set back upon our reason and our bodies as the basis for changing the colonized reality. Sit-ins, marches, jails, so be it. But the violence of the hierarchic other is not reconstruction or the transformation of human relationships even if it is undertaken by those who speak against colonization. For the violence of a moment is the basis upon which a further "justice" will be built: one which people will again revere publicly but hate in their hearts.

Is there an intellectual organizational structure for carrying on the theory and practice of reconstruction? The universities in the area of social science and social knowledge are timid about developing and relating knowledge and action which transform the colonized structures of society. This timidity has grown into grave differences between older and younger faculty, students and administrators. (It is not invariably the case that the colonizer is the administrator. In many situations, it is a faculty and professional guild that views its knowledge as pieces of property to be savored and held only by them.) The continuous disruptions and confrontations at the universities since 1964 are signs that the universities, as I have said, are the new bodies politic. But in the process serious inquiry will become secondary while the various groups at the universities adjust their political relationship to each other. The process of *modern* research in the social sciences is not at the university.

Many people find that they are unable or unwilling to work within the university on areas they think important. Thus, even research as an end in itself is now under grave attack because the mores of a university department structure, which continues to define problems in terms of particular disciplines, are outmoded. The colonizers themselves have realized from their perspective and purposes the flaw in this situation. Since 1946, research institutes such as RAND emerged, separate from the university, to "solve" problems specifically for the colonizer-client and from his assumptions.

In the period from 1970 to 1975, more professors and students will be thrown out of universities. Their recourse in some cases will be to start or work in institutes developing an analysis which will attempt to make Marxist and pragmatist thought relevant for programmatic purposes. Perhaps there is a tragic parallel. During the Weimar Republic institutes flourished as the German University, surviving at the sufferance of the State and seeing culture as a Thing. They could not find us values from which to know their corporate identity in order to confront and survive.

The most important institute in the social sciences, the Institute for Social Research, where Adorno, Marcuse, Fromm and Horkheimer worked, flourished for a short time. Its flourish was short-lived as the space of the German society closed, as the intellectuals found themselves separated from rational practice and as internal pressures stopped people from publishing under the guise of excellence. Critical thought could not find its way into the social and political life of Germany except in the most perverse forms. The authoritarian form dominated all aspects of political action in Germany, and the left was not excluded from this domination.

In the United States, the attempts at consciousness and liberation which have occurred in art and politics are not authoritarian either in their form or content. And the colonization which exists on American man is just because the impulse of man in America is beyond his role or beyond the profile of the beside-himself which the man wears. In practical terms there is hope for ourselves. Bonhoeffer's humanistic optimism would not be misplaced in America as we develop a theory and practice of reconstruction. It is this faith which guides a group of us at the Institute for Policy Studies.

In Washington the Institute grew from two basic conditions. Some of us could not live comfortably in an intellectual, political and moral sense within the government. On the other hand, statecraft, the relation of self to others and institutional structures, was our work. If we could not state clearly and in action, reason and project alternatives within the government which stemmed from the obvious needs of people, then perhaps it was possible to do so outside of the government, reaching out to individuals within that structure as well as other institutions which by their presence and operation were oppressive. The university reflected many of the same problems of the government; indeed, its role was as handmaiden and friendly partner in the pyramid. The research which passed for knowledge and serious inquiry appeared to us to be a new form of mandarin rhetoric used by people to justify the irrational with "rational" arguments.

The second condition was that action *qua* action was not enough. Action needed to be informed with reason and purpose. Action as politics does not allow the distance necessary for judgment or the fact that politics itself remains one facet of man's *ought* life. Thus, activity which was not informed by thought and practice was not viewed as sufficient. If choice in action is not informed by reason and judgment the action itself will be unique and recalled only in some kind of collective unconscious. Nothing will be learned.

In European thought the idea of philosophers being involved in the world was viewed as contradictory to their role. Yet in America the supreme arrogance continues in which action and thought are not separate and that each needs the other. The informed action and practice become the way of judging critically. And thought which relates the action to other actions becomes the way of tapping those impulses of man's history which are basic and humane. Such notions meant that those involved in reconstruction were not to get caught in the modes and fashions of the moment; and yet would be open, and where necessary, would organize and lead in the practice of reconstruction: the "continual interrogation and correction"—and dismantling—of colonizing institutions.

Fortunately, there was a critical mass in Washington who saw these matters in similar ways, viz., Barnet, Waskow, Jencks, Michael, Kotler, Burlage, Alperovitz, Goodman, Bazelon and myself. And there has been the extraordinary financial support of a group of gifted people. IPS in Washington has now grown to fifty people and has spawned the Cambridge Institute in Cambridge, Massachusetts, where Alperovitz and Jencks have now gone. New institutes are emerging in Atlanta organized by Sue Thrasher and Howard Romaine, and in San Francisco organized by Barry Weisberg and Franz Schurmann.

While the Institute Fellows are beset by political controversy, fund-raising, lecturing, writing and emotional drain because of the competitive natures of people who grew in one social frame of reference and who attempt to build another, a basic condition obtains which applies in the whole society. Since greater numbers of people cannot live within institutional structures such as the university or the government or the media and do honest and liberating work which they might have believed was the purpose of such institutions, a new kind of hybrid institute for scholarship and action will form in contradistinction to the university, drawing on and criticizing such institutions which have as their purpose the development of a new society.

Each of the institutes works with other scholars and activists on the problems of reconstruction and trains young people and those within institutions to organize a basis for the reconstruction of American life. The methods used are the project, social invention, rational persuasion and confrontation. Each institute becomes the engine for profound change because it takes seriously the cries of anguish and dissonance which people now express. Its task is not to educate servants of the colonies. Its task is to help servants question and study the State. The institutes are required to help people build new projects which are to be studied, changed and experimented. They are the alternatives to the struggle of colonization.

Simultaneously, a new definition of leadership is pursued. It is unnecessary to belabor the destructive and precarious nature of leadership in the pyramidal society. In a society reconstructing itself, however, leadership takes on quite different qualities from those ordinarily ascribed to it. In pyramidal hierarchic organizations the leader is to command respect, keep his distance, be somewhat paranoid, manipulate others, make decisions, and feign interest. He is to accept the notion that he holds collective responsibility, and consequently, he must be prepared to be sacrificed. In this sense he is invariably preparing himself to be cannibalized by the organization he is leading and those who want to be leader. This type of leadership is dominant in all major forms of life, the military, the competitive economic system, productivity, as well as tasks defined through politics, education and commerce.

In a society undertaking to decolonize and reconstruct itself, new meanings of leadership become obvious. Some types of them appear unsatisfactory because they do not inspire, that is, give breath to those who have none. For example, the McCarthy campaign was an interesting case of private man seeing himself as a leader in a non-authoritarian way. But his self-centeredness denied reaching out to those who were prepared to listen and join. In the early nineteen-sixties I had a friend by the name of Bob Moses, a leader of SNCC, a prophet. He led by being. He would say little but his presence was a source of strength. It was to say to people that they would have to stand up, that he was scared too, but that he had confidence and trust in other people. He assumed that others were adequate, that they were competent and capable to work and be heroic. Leadership meant the creation of spaces with the understanding that respect begets respect, trust begets trust and openness begets openness. This is the primary way to develop selfness with others and to develop a movement (and then a society) of shared values.

Transformation in the meaning of analysis and political leadership holds important clues for future rela-

tionships among the reconstructivists. We imagine a
group of institutes federated together in the purpose
of reconstruction with common intellectual purposes
and agendas, where in each place the huddling effect
would probably occur. Where individuals "huddled"
for intellectual sustenance as well as political and economic protection in a period of political turbulence,
they would protect themselves from being crushed under
the bricks of the crumbling colonized structure. The
space provided at such institutes for the beginning of
horizontal structures which develop through decolonized
knowledge, persuasion and the project becomes the
container and the model for the development of alternative institutions. Each of such institutes organizes itself for teaching and creating the bravery and wisdom for
decolonization and reconstruction.

Epilogue

It is often said that totalitarianism grows out of the mindless romanticism of "underground" people. The underground man, to use the phrase of Hazel Barnes and Dostoyevski, is the anti-hero whose life may be wretched in his own eyes and harmful to others. However, he maintains the choice of persona-assertion, which is foisted against others. He is like Jacob Bronowski's anti-heroes: ". . . pícaros, coneycatchers, pirates and bohemians [who] are figures of protest against social conventions, who express our longing for the saturnalia."[1] Serious critics believe they see such aspects of romanticism among the young in America today. They argue that Germany and its youth movement gave rise to Hitler. This analysis cannot be viewed as a reasoned one.

The basis of Hitler's power was not caused by the romantics. It came from the serious people in Germany who believed in authoritarian, pyramidal structures and accepted characterization of themselves. Where they looked for romanticism it was the romanticism of totalitarianism finding its ground in the structure of organized social life Kafka describes. For example, the influence of the German poet-leader Stefan George fell very neatly into the hero-worship of pyramidal structure. George himself believed in the purity of hero-worship in an attempt to find a type of Platonic purity. His movement was hardly that of the free-wheeling romantic spirit.

> Trained to worship the hero as such, the youth of the country [Germany] could no longer distinguish between true greatness and only brilliant criminality.[2]

The Germans (almost regardless of political persuasion) believed in the military, in rigid class distinctions, in monopoly profits or cartelization, in a violent soul that would be expressed and contained in the actions of the State as manifested finally in the decisions of a hero-leader. And beyond these attitudes they believed in the racist and imperialist mission, for reasons of class opportunity and racial purity. Such beliefs were welded into a totalitarian ideology which descended beneath man. The Nazi and fascist ideologies vested and rationalized bestial criminality into the function and roles of the pyramidal structure. The "romantic" superman image was the cover for a society in which people accepted the principle that the process of genocide was the way for people to live and earn their daily bread.

The irony in American society has been that the youth now seem to be asking for true greatness while attempting to expose the brilliant criminality which the institutions, including our universities and technical corporations, have created. In this sense, we really can do little other than stand with the young in doubting the colonies which yield hero-worship and picaresque madness. Thus, one can only disagree with the brilliant psychoanalyst, Bruno Bettelheim, who, caught in the space capsule on earth of the University of Chicago,* sees the youth rebellion in America as symptomatic of German youth and its disdain for universities and learning. But the point is quite different. Most of the youth want to learn but not be cremated in the process. They do not want to learn at the economic expense of the poor or learn and create knowledges which by their method and purpose are destructive of man and nature. These are laudable purposes, hardly picaresque in scope.

* An interesting administrative story could be told of how that university took on the making of parts of the atomic bomb for the purpose of building a "first-rate" physics department.

In People's Park there was an attempt to recapture a sense of wholeness and simple, obvious life activities on the part of the street people and students. The picaresque attached to the brute weight of a state whose military and propertied class, through technical organization can only think of ways to devour the young.

The problem with Bronowski's analysis of anti-heroes and to some extent Bettelheim's view, is that it gives too much away to the pyramidal structure. That is to say, it assumes that rational self-interest (the Kantian hypothetical imperative) or predictability is the basis of what a society, by its structure, has to be, and that the manner of social conventions that are adopted are the ones which, by the nature of man, have to be adopted. Further, it is assumed, as for example scientists have assumed, that these conventions are "rational." If this were true then the sense of tragedy which Reinhold Niebuhr speaks of would be correct for it would mean that "reason" had already won, that what is has to be, and whatever emerged from the pyramidal structure had to emerge. Such a view leaves too little to man. In part it is the pícaro adventurers masquerading as reasonable men in the pyramids who are presented through their roles as reasonable and who have their freedom with us. Can anyone from the position of reason defend the 2500 troops on the campus of the University of California with their weapons against students and ex-students who started a park on an empty lot? The picaros are those who have drawn their breath, power and reason against the simple, the human, and the obvious.

In so doing, they have given up the life instinct and cannot begin to find it in themselves (that spark of the Hasids) or their roles. Michael Maccoby, in his important psychoanalytic study of the American population, has pointed out how finely balanced in a distributive way the death/life instinct is in America. Needless to say, the institutions themselves have given the balance over-

whelmingly to the side of necrophilia. Seven years ago
this balance could be seen in the National Security Council. In 1968, R. F. Kennedy pointed out that six of the
fourteen who participated as members of the executive
committee of the NSC were prepared to and did vote for a
course of action which would have meant nuclear destruction for hundreds of millions of people. Each of the members of that august committee was in suit and tie. Each was
a "rational" man, progressive, seemingly not totally in-
decent, graduates of our prestige schools who were able
to add, subtract and skim in a flash. Yet, each of those
men was a pícaro, daring the fates, God and the conventions of living. Each was in the service of death.

Those like Dostoyevski who attacked such "rational"
progressives in the nineteenth century were correct. They
feared that the programmed world of reason with its loga-
rithms and formulas would be the death of man's freedom
and will. They saw that anyone's state or "plan" would
use self-interest reason to destroy man in his reason and
freedom. They saw that revolt was necessary. The result is
that revolt, acts of injection through the project, become
ways of testing and laying out the basis of a future with
space to try and work through definitions of personal
and group life. The pícaros who help sustain colonized
and characterized reality need to be confronted with such
projects. Who are the adventurers, the Berrigans or
Charles Hitch? Perhaps the Hitches will come to see that
their activities, which seem rational and useful, are in
fact debilitating and quite mad. Perhaps they will come to
see this irremediable reality. And if they do not?

I am reminded by the *Washington Free Press* of Eldridge Cleaver's comment, "When the sane people don't
do it, when all the good middle class people don't do it,
then the madmen have to do it, and the madmen say that
we're going to have freedom or we're going to have chaos;

we're going to be part of the total destruction of America or we're going to be part of the liberation of America."[3]

What, then, is possible for man? I would hold that he is so pasted onto the envelope of colonization and characterization into the beside-himself that it is hard to know whether he has a different nature. What we are able to see is that in his pyramid he is pyramidal. And when he is momentarily liberated, as when he reaches for a new political form, or makes love, or understands and creates the elegance of mathematics and music, he is free. Because of such momentary glimpses where we see man in freedom, it is possible to speak of reconstructions as within man's reach. Such proposals as I have suggested are aimed at giving greater space to the individual and the groups which he forms and feels a part of. They are not aimed, God knows, at happiness, although in some cases that condition might even obtain. If men cannot build on such moments and they enslave themselves again once they break the old pyramid, at least we will see that that choice was cooperative rather than one made by those who happened to have been pyramidal rulers for the moment.

We are unable to say with the certitude of a new ruling class what is the only correct direction. But in a sensate way we can achieve more than any ruling class can get for itself. We can begin to recover humanness. What is right in a shared-authority and non-hierarchic society is not known because it is only in the Now, the immediate, that we are beginning to test and draw together the rejected notions of the past which can build the facts and values of a quite different society. We are just beginning to transform ourselves to comprehend the facts and values that could emerge. Yet our task is also a negative one. What we can begin to know is the practice of what we are doing and the knowledge of man which teaches us internally useful standards that simultaneously limit and extend us. Such practical knowledge does not start from the assumption that man can make himself into a god or a bird, but precisely because he cannot and should not. Such a knowledge of insight and practice teaches us that it is not one moment too late to reject the collective pyramidal consciousness of thinking which encourages a ground for children in schools to win science prizes by crossing monkeys and birds, to reward the pícaro who comes forward with the splashiest way to destroy nature and society like nuclear tests on the moon, or the colonizing act which results in another social control mechanism, or the economic colonizers who find ways of dominating more people through the medium of goods and profits. We know enough to reject those roles as they appear in a movement which itself may, out of fear, terror and hopelessness, borrow from that framework. We begin from the negative prescription and seek through the practice of existential pragmatism the integration of human reason and passion in the project of reconstruction.

Notes

INTRODUCTION

1. C. Wright Mills, *Power, Politics and People,* Irving Horowitz, ed. (London: Oxford University Press, 1967).
2. Simone Weil, *Selected Essays 1934–1943* (London: Oxford University Press, 1962), p. 156.
3. *Ibid.*
4. John Dewey, *Problems of Men,* introduction (New York: Philosophical Library, 1946).
5. The evasion often took the tone of self-congratulation: ". . . America has proved Karl Marx wrong in theory and in prophecy, and wrong everlastingly. In one form or another, this article of faith is accepted by men of all religions, races, creeds, functions, classes, incomes, statuses, I.Q.'s and ideologies."—William A. Williams, *The Great Evasion* (Chicago: Quadrangle Books, 1964), p. 24.
6. Wolfgang Köhler, *Dynamics in Psychology* (New York: Liveright Publishing Co., 1940), p. 108.
7. John Dewey, *Art as Experience* (New York: Minton, Balch and Co., 1934), pp. 35–37, 326–49.

CHAPTER ONE

1. R. D. Laing, *The Politics of Experience* (New York: Pantheon Books, 1967).
2. David Riesman, with Nathan Glazer and R. Denney, *The Lonely Crowd* (New Haven: Yale University Press, 1950), p. 7.
3. David Riesman, *Individualism Reconsidered* (Glencoe: The Free Press, 1954), p. 231.
4. McGeorge Bundy, *Strength of Government* (Cambridge: Harvard University Press, 1968), p. 59.

5n. Carl Jung, *Memories, Dreams and Reflections* (New York: Pantheon Books, 1967), p. 226.

6. Sigmund Freud, *The Ego and the Id* (New York: W. W. Norton & Co., Inc., 1961), p. 35.

7. Frantz Fanon, *The Wretched of the Earth* (New York: Grove Press, 1963).

8. Laing, *op. cit.,* p. 35.

9. Elias Canetti, *Crowds and Power* (London: Gollancz, 1962).

10. Clark C. Abt and Ithiel de Sola Pool, "The Constraint of Public Attitudes," in Klaus Knorr and Thornton Read, eds., *Limited Strategic War* (New York: Praeger, 1962), pp. 199, 240.

11. Jacob Bronowski, *The Face of Violence* (New York: Meridian, The World Publishing Co., 1967), p. 64.

12n. Adrienne Koch and William Peden, eds., *The Life and Selected Writings of Thomas Jefferson* (New York: The Modern Library, 1944), pp. 700–01.

13. Susanne Langer, "The Process of Feeling," *Philosophical Studies* (Baltimore: Johns Hopkins Press, 1962), p. 11.

14. Koch and Peden, *op. cit.*

15. Martin Buber, *I and Thou* (New York: Charles Scribner's Sons, 1958), p. 11.

16. Hazel E. Barnes, *An Existentialist Ethics* (New York: Alfred A. Knopf, Inc., 1967), p. 129.

17. Jean-Paul Sartre, *Being and Nothingness: An Essay on Phenomenological Ontology* (New York: Philosophical Library, 1956), p. 524.

18. *Ibid.,* p. 433.

CHAPTER TWO

1. Mikhail Bakunin, *The Political Philosophy of Bakunin,* G. P. Maximoff, ed. (Glencoe: The Free Press, 1953), p. 136.

2. Conversation with Mr. Cohen by author.

3n. Weil, *op. cit.,* p. 110.

4. J. W. Gough, *The Social Contract* (Oxford: Clarendon Press, 1936), pp. 215–20.

5. Charles Beard, *The Rise of American Civilization* (New York: The Macmillan Co., 1927), note especially p. 311.

6. Alexander Hamilton, *The Federalist Papers,* No. 24 (New York: New American Library, 1961), pp. 160–61.
7. *Ibid.,* No. 25, p. 166.
8. *Ibid.,* No. 28, p. 182.
9. Leopolde von Ranke, *History of England, Ferment of the Modern World,* vol. 3 (Oxford: Clarendon Press, 1875), pp. 3–22.
10. Hamilton, *op. cit.,* No. 36, p. 223.
11. Georges Bernanos, *Tradition of Freedom* (London: Dennis Dobson, 1950), p. 161.
12. Hearings before the Committee on Armed Services, House of Representatives, for fiscal year 1969, to authorize procurement of aircraft, missiles, etc., p. 9663.
13. Marcus Raskin, "Nuclear Reality and Political Anxiety," *American Journal of Psychiatry,* 1964, p. 831.
14. Ernst Cassirer, *Myth of the State* (New Haven: Yale University Press, 1946), p. 175.
15. Senate Resolution 45, December 12, 1927. 69th Congress, 477, part 1.
16. John Locke, *Civil Government* (Everyman), p. 228.
17. *Ibid.*
18. *Ibid.*

CHAPTER THREE

1. Richard P. McKeon, ed., *The Basic Works of Aristotle* (New York: Random House, Inc., 1941), p. 1139.
2. Friedrich Engels, *The Origin of the Family, Private Property and the State* (New York: International Publishers, 1942), p. 101.
3. Bertrand Russell, *Roads to Freedom* (New York: Barnes and Noble, 1965).
4. Max Lerner, *America as a Civilization* (New York: Simon and Schuster, 1957), p. 284.
5. Beardsley Ruml, "The Profit Motive," in Adrian Klaasen, ed., *The Invisible Hand* (Chicago: Henry Regnery Co., 1965), p. 158.
6. Adolph A. Berle, *The Modern Corporation and Private Property,* preface to 1932 edition (rev. ed.; New York: Harcourt, Brace & World, 1967), pp. xli–xlii.

7. Samuel R. Reid, *Mergers, Managers and the Economy* (New York: McGraw-Hill, 1968), pp. 73, 128.

8. Dartmouth v. Woodward, 4 Wheaton 518 (1819), and Taylor v. Terrett, Dist. Col., 31 US 43.

9. John Dewey, *Intelligence in the Modern World*, Joseph Ratner, ed. (New York: Modern Library, 1939), p. 422.

10. Selig Perlman, *A Theory of the Labor Movement* (reprinted from 1928; New York: The Macmillan Co., 1966), p. 190.

11. *Ibid*, p. 198.

12. Alfred P. Sloan, Jr., *My Years with General Motors* (New York: Doubleday and Company, Inc., 1964), p. 408.

13. Robert Theobald, *Dialogue on Poverty* (Indianapolis: Bobbs-Merrill, 1967), p. 108. See also Robert Theobald, *The Challenge of Abundance* (New York: Charles Potter, Inc., 1961), pp. 96–101.

CHAPTER FOUR

1. John K. Dickinson, *German and Jew* (Chicago: Quadrangle Press, 1967), p. 194.

2. John Holt, *How Children Fail* (New York: Delta Books, 1964).

3n. Carl Kaysen, "Data Banks and Dossiers," *The Public Interest*, No. 7, Spring, 1967, pp. 52–61.

4. Mario Savio in the introduction to *Berkeley: The New Student Revolt*, by Hal Draper (New York: Grove Press, 1965), p. 6.

5. Marcus Raskin, "Decision Theory in Statecraft," *Scientific American*, August, 1964.

6. James B. Conant, Dept. of State 1963: A Report to the Citizen, Dept. of State Publication 7530, General Foreign Policy Series 187, May, 1963. Quoted in Neal D. Houghton, ed., foreword to *Struggle against History* (New York: Washington Square Press, 1968), p. xxi.

7. Erich Kahler, *Man the Measure* (New York: George Braziller, 1965), p. 438.

8. Köhler, *op. cit.*, p. 7.

CHAPTER FIVE

1. House Report No. 572, 90th Congress, p. 11.
2. "Broadcasters in America and the FCC's License Renewal Process: An Oklahoma Case Study." A statement by Commissioners Kenneth A. Cox and Nicholas Johnson, June, 1968.
3*n*. Marshall McLuhan and Quentin Fiore, *The Medium is the Massage* (New York: Random House, Inc., 1967), p. 131.

CHAPTER SIX

1. Martin Heidegger, *Discourse on Thinking* (New York: Harper & Row, 1959), p. 51.

CHAPTER SEVEN

1. Woodrow Wilson, *The New Freedom* (New York: Doubleday, Page, and Co., 1913), pp. 1–30.
2. Randolph Bourne, "Twilight of Idols," in *War and the Intellectuals* (New York: Harper & Row, 1964), p. 59.
3. John Dewey, *op. cit.*, pp. 421–22.
4. Elinor Graham, "The Politics of Poverty," in Marvin Gettleman and David Mermelstein, eds., *The Great Society Reader* (New York: Random House, Inc., 1967), p. 223.

CHAPTER EIGHT

1. Quincy Wright, *Study of War* (Chicago: University of Chicago Press, 1943), vol. 2, p. 1110.
2*n*. Weil, *op. cit.*, pp. 161–62.
3. Nicholas Berdyaev, *Slavery and Freedom* (New York: Charles Scribner's Sons, 1944), p. 17.

CHAPTER NINE

1. Milovan Djilas, *The Unperfect Society* (New York: Harcourt, Brace & World, Inc., 1969), p. 16.

2. Albert Rabil, Jr., *Merleau-Ponty* (New York: Columbia University Press, 1967), p. 124.

3. Bertrand Russell, *Human Knowledge* (New York: Simon and Schuster, 1948), pp. 403–04.

4. Buber, *I and Thou,* pp. 1–34.

5. Buber, *Eclipse of God* (New York: Harper and Brothers, 1952), p. 166.

6. And yet this is the way man begins to feel his freedom. "But the world of Thou is not closed. He who goes out to it with concentrated being and rises (?) power to enter into relation becomes aware of freedom. And to be freed from belief that there is no freedom is indeed to be free."—Buber, *I and Thöu,* p. 58.

7. Johan Huizinga, *Homo Ludens* (London: Routledge and Kegan Paul, 1949). Also, Huizinga, *Men and Ideas in the Middle Ages and the Renaissance* (New York: Meridian, 1959).

8. Dewey, *op. cit.,* pp. 288, 299.

9. Henri-Charles Puech, *Valentinian Theodotus,* in *The Mystic Vision,* Bollingen series, vol. 6 (Princeton: Princeton University Press).

10. Köhler, *Dynamics in Psychology,* pp. 1–8. Also, Köhler, *Gestalt Psychology* (New York: Liveright Publishing Co., 1947).

11. Arthur I. Waskow, "Looking Forward," in Robert Jungk and Johan Galtung, eds., *Mankind 2000* (London: Allen and Unwin, 1969), pp. 78–99.

12. William Barrett, *Irrational Man* (New York: Doubleday, Anchor, 1967).

13. John Dewey, *The Public and Its Problems* (Chicago: Gateway Books, 1946), pp. 202–03.

14. *Ibid.,* p. 208.

CHAPTER TEN

1. George Herbert Mead, *Mind, Self and Society* (Chicago: University of Chicago, 1934), p. 155.

2. *Ibid.*

3. *Ibid.*, p. 158.

4. Anatol Rapoport, "The Question of Relevance," *Etc.*, vol. XXVI, No. 1, 1969, pp. 17–30.

CHAPTER ELEVEN

1. Dietrich Bonhoeffer, "Who Stands Fast?" *Letters and Papers from Prison* (3rd ed.; Chatham: W. and J. McKay and Co., Ltd., 1967), p. 26.

2. John Dewey, "Individuality and Experience," *Journal of the Barnes Foundation*, Jan., 1926, vol. II, no. 1, pp. 1–6. Also, "Why I Am Not a Communist" in *The Meaning of Marx, a Symposium*, by Bertrand Russell and John Dewey (New York: Farrar and Rinehart, 1934).

3. C. Vann Woodward, *Reunion and Reaction* (Boston: Little, Brown and Co., 1951), p. 15.

4. Waskow, "Looking Forward," *Mankind 2000, op. cit.*

5. Milton Kotler, *Neighborhood Government* (Bobbs-Merrill: New York, 1969).

6. Discussion of Kotler's IPS Memoranda on Neighborhood Government, 76 Yale Law Journal, 1247–1260 (1967).

CHAPTER TWELVE

1. Gabriel Kolko, *The Roots of American Foreign Policy* (New York: Beacon, 1969), pp. 11–12.

2. Marcus Raskin, Review of Christopher Lasch's *The Agony of the American Left, The Washington Monthly*, vol. I, No 4, May, 1969.

3. Marcus Raskin, "What is to Be Done?" *The New Republic*, Sept. 28, 1968.

4. David Friedman, "The Prospects for American Radicalism," *New Politics*, vol. VII, No. 2.

5. Jean Jaurès, "Historie Socialiste," Georges Sorel, ed., *On Violence*, tr. by T. E. Hulme (New York: Peter Smith Publishers, 1941), pp. 193–95.

CHAPTER THIRTEEN

1. John Dewey, *Reconstruction in Philosophy* (New York: Beacon Press, 1948), p. xxvii.
2. Peter Kropotkin, *The Conquest of Bread* (New York and London: Benjamin Blom, 1913, reissued 1968), pp. 16–31.
3. Kahler, *op. cit.*, p. 446.
4. Georges Lefebvre, *The Coming of the French Revolution* (New York: Vintage, 1947), p. 155.
5. Hannah Arendt, *On Revolution* (New York: Viking Press, 1963).
6. *Ibid.*, p. 252.
7. John Dewey, *op. cit.*, pp. 488–90.

CHAPTER FOURTEEN

1. Marsh v. Alabama, 326 US 501 (1940).
2. Tinker v. Des Moines School District, 393 US 503 (1969).
3. Peter Drucker, *The Age of Discontinuity* (London: Heinemann, 1969).
4. British Political and Economic Planning Organization, *World Population and Resources* (London, Allen & Unwin, Dist., 1955), p. 53.
5. *Ibid.*, pp. 53 ff.
6. René Dubos, *So Human an Animal* (New York: Charles Scribner's Sons, 1968), p. 220.
7. "Restoring the Quality of our Environment," Report of the Environmental Pollution Panel, President's Science Advisory Committee (The White House, November, 1965).
8. Alfred P. Sloan, Jr., *op. cit.*, p. 442.
9. "Restoring the Quality of Our Environment," p. 87.
10. *Ibid.*, p. 68.
11. *Ibid.*, p. 66.
12n. Berle, *The Modern Corporation and Private Property*, preface to 1932 edition (rev. ed., New York: Harcourt, Brace & World, 1967), pp. xxii–xxiii.

CHAPTER FIFTEEN

1. Philippe Aries, *Centuries of Childhood* (New York: Vintage, 1965).
2. J. P. Davis, *Corporations* (New York: Putnam Publishing Company, 1961), p. 279.
3. *Ibid.*
4. Samuel Baskin, *Higher Education* (New York: McGraw-Hill, 1965), p. 68.

CHAPTER SIXTEEN

1. United Churches of Christ v. the FCC, 395 F 2d, US Court of Appeals, Dist. Col., March 25, 1966, p. 1101.
2. Red Lion Broadcasting Co., Inc. v. the FCC, 37 U.S.L.W. 4509, 4516 (June 10, 1969), in *TV Today: The End of Communication and the Death of Community*, IPS, Washington, D.C., 1969.

CHAPTER SEVENTEEN

1n. Quoted in John M. Rich, "Chief Seattle's Unanswered Challenge" (Seattle: John M. Rich, 1932), pp. 33–36, 40. Reprinted in Dubos, *So Human an Animal, op. cit.*, pp. 137–38.
2. Kahler, *op. cit.*, p. 135.
3. Martin Buber, *The Prophetic Faith* (New York: The Macmillan Co., 1949), p. 57.
4. Paul Tillich, *The Shaking of the Foundations* (New York: Charles Scribner's Sons, 1948).
5. Letter by Martin Luther King, Jr., in Staughton Lynd, *Non-Violence in America* (Indianapolis: Bobbs-Merrill, 1966), p. 470.
6. Discussion at the Center for the Study of Democratic Institutions, 1967.
7. Lewis Mumford, *Myth of the Machine* (New York: Harcourt, Brace & World, 1966), p. 171.
8. *Ibid.*
9. Bonhoeffer, *op. cit.*

10. Werner Jaeger, *Paideia: The Ideals of Greek Culture* (Oxford: Basil Blackwell, 1945), vol. I, pp. 320–28, and vol. III, p. 73.

11. Diderot note for discussion of Philosophes' attitudes: Kenneth Unwin, A Century for Freedom (London: Watts & Co., 1946) and P. A. Wadia, *The Philosophers and the French Revolution* (London: Swan Sonnenschein & Co., 1904).

12. Régis Debray, *Revolution in the Revolution* (New York: Monthly Review Press, 1967), p. 41.

13. Buber, *The Prophetic Faith,* pp. 186–87.

14. Thomas Babington Macaulay quoted in "The Moral Element in Free Enterprise," F. A. Hayek, *The Invisible Hand,* Adrian Klaasen, ed. (Chicago: H. Regnery Co.. 1965), p. 71.

EPILOGUE

1. Bronowki, *op. cit.,* pp. 1–83.
2. Kahler, *op. cit.,* p. 587.
3. *Washington Free Press,* Spring, 1969.

Index

About the Author

MARCUS G. RASKIN was born in Milwaukee, Wisconsin, in 1934. He graduated from the College and the Law School of the University of Chicago. He is co-director of the Institute for Policy Studies in Washington, D.C., and is a trustee of Antioch College. He was a member of the Special Staff of the National Security Council under President Kennedy, a member of the U.S. Disarmament Delegation to the eighteen-nation Geneva Conference in 1962, and was on the President's Panel on Educational Research from 1963 to 1965. Among his books are *After 20 Years: The Decline of NATO and the Search for a New Policy in Europe* (co-authored with Richard J. Barnet) and *The Viet-Nam Reader* (co-edited with Bernard B. Fall). He has written articles on foreign policy, political philosophy and education in the *New York Review, Ramparts, Scientific American* and other magazines. He has lectured at many universities, and he presented the Campbell Lectures on Christian Faith and Morality to the American Chaplains and Campus Ministry in 1967.

Marcus Raskin is one of America's leading political scientists and political philosophers. He was a member, along with Coffin, Ferber, Goodman and Spock, of the Boston Five draft conspiracy case, and is a leader in the antiwar resistance and the new politics.

P 402

DATE DUE

APR 20 '88		
GAYLORD		PRINTED IN U.S.A.